G000060334

A MAN WITH A MISSION

A MAN WITH A MISSION

To Myrtle
with love & best wishes

John *2009*

Canon John Taylor OBE

Book Guild Publishing
Sussex, England

First published in Great Britain in 2009 by
The Book Guild Ltd
Pavilion View
19 New Road
Brighton, BN1 1UF

Typesetting in Times by
Keyboard Services, Luton, Bedfordshire

Printed and bound in Great Britain by
CPI Antony Rowe

A catalogue record for this book is available from
The British Library

ISBN 978 1 84624 360 8

This book is dedicated to Rose

Contents

Back in the UK

East Africa

CONTENTS

Thailand

ix

Foreword

We are all 'one-offs' – all unique. But it must be said that John Taylor is most certainly one of the most one-off 'one-offs' I know! The story of his life as he has laid it before us, in what I hope is simply his first book, testifies to one who has lived life to the full, not only or even primarily because he has seen the world and met interesting people, but because he has lived his life for others.

Christians know that fullness of life is found in loving God and loving your neighbour. This is the pearl of great price that John Taylor has discovered. It is a costly life, and requires sacrifice and large heartedness. It has perseverance and trust and joy as the spiritual gifts to be prayed for and worked at, as the person responds to the ambiguities and opportunities life presents to him or her.

I have known John Taylor for nigh on twenty years and have been his bishop for fifteen. So my testimony is to his faithfulness and fruitful life in the years of ministry in England yet to be written about. I know him to be a priest who changes lives and people's circumstances for good. He has made it easier for people to believe in a living and loving God.

Though he has travelled the world, the 'place' that has made it all possible is his prayer desk, the constant amidst the changes and chances, the losses and the gains, the fulfilments and the disappointments.

The book is fascinating! Read and enjoy.

The Rt Revd Lindsay Urwin OGS
Bishop of Horsham

Acknowledgements

A cardinal sin for any priest when giving thanks to those who have helped him make a project possible is to omit, even if by oversight, the name of a single person who has been involved.

Although this book has been written during the computer age, when I started writing it, I was largely ignorant of the intricacies – and potential – of modern information technology. It soon became obvious, however, that without the aid of a computer, it would never get off the ground. What is more, without the help of willing parishioners and friends who patiently initiated me into its use and who continue to help sort out my problems, or who have given sound advice, proofread or corrected my drafts, the book would still be unfinished. My deepest and heartfelt thanks go to them all – as well as to members of my family who have been very supportive throughout. To avoid incurring the cardinal sin of omitting anyone by name, therefore, I ask them all to accept this general thank you. In any case, they will know from the scriptures that what they do in secret will be recognised and rewarded in heaven!

Introduction

One of the bonuses of writing an autobiography is that, to do so, you are forced to go back to the beginning; to where it all began. Usually, that is when you were born. But as this book is all about my vocation to the ministry, it begins with my calling from God. How did that first manifest itself? From a very early age, long before I even understood what was really happening to me, I felt a deep desire to experience God's love and protection. I so wanted to be near him. As will unfold, I had a very unhappy relationship with my father, and I sometimes wonder now whether I looked to God to provide what was missing in my father. As I grew older the logical way to achieve that closeness seemed to be by becoming an active member of the church. But because of the negative influence of my atheistic father, that was not allowed to happen. My father did everything possible to stop it; long walks on a Sunday morning, during which he would berate the church and the existence of God. My father had what is commonly known as 'the gift of the gab', which he used to devastating effect. One of his favourite sayings, in autumn as the leaves fell from the trees, was, 'That's exactly what happens to us when we die. We fall to the ground and just rot away.' Luckily for us it was my father who faded from the scene as he was sent on an overseas army posting shortly after the beginning of the war.

My desire to grow closer to God coincided with the realization that, before anything else, I needed to learn more about the Christian faith. This came to pass. During my national service I became confirmed. I studied and qualified as a lay reader. Later on I achieved the necessary qualifications to enter theological college, where I passed G.O.E. (General Ordination Examination) and was made a Deacon. Finally I passed the priest's exams and was ordained. But at the end of it I realized that learning had not of itself helped my growth in spirituality (although it had given me a clearer idea of what it meant).

For some, spirituality means meeting God in quiet contemplation; for others it was more about getting involved in the messiness of life - and finding that God is there too! Some are inspired by the insights and writings of the great divines; others learn best from ordinary Christians they meet in the here and now. The common denominator for all is of course prayer and meditation, which, combined with all other aspects of His grace, brings us to a closer walk with God.

Having been priested I then had to decide which path would lead me towards the deeper spirituality I still earnestly craved. More learning (whether to study for an external degree?) or just getting on with the job for which I had been trained? I decided I was better suited to be a worker-priest, so that was the path I followed.

So how far have I progressed? I now know that any success requires all the help and grace that you can get. Growth in spirituality requires total commitment to the Christian life, using every channel of God's grace. What I can say is that through my ministry with seamen and other ordinary people, whether that be in prisons, hospitals, school assemblies, and of course through the church, I have been helped along the way.

The Missions to Seafarers, which is that part of the Church of England that cares for the material, social and spiritual needs of all seafarers irrespective of nationality, colour or creed, provided the perfect backdrop for what I was striving to achieve. Clubs are provided (some with accommodation) wherein the seafarer can satisfy his 'daily needs' whether by means of food and drink, a shop and a library, social activities, or a chapel. But above all there is a chaplain to provide for his spiritual needs. So was created the ideal setting to enrich my ministry. I will always be grateful to that society for the opportunities it gave me to draw ever closer to Almighty God, and experience in the messiness of life, his love. Originally called the Missions to Seamen, the organization's name was changed in 2000 to acknowledge the increasing number of women now at sea.

My parish work since has taken me further along the path that brings ever nearer that great and wonderful day when the kingdom of God will cover the earth, as the waters cover the sea.

INTRODUCTION

My life, and therefore the account of it so far, divides itself into convenient periods: my early life, then working as a lay reader with The Missions to Seamen in the UK and Hong Kong, this being followed by ordination, leading to curacies in the Rhondda Valley, then Missions to Seamen chaplaincies in Dar-es-Salaam and Thailand. Because my ministry up to the time of leaving Thailand was, I consider, a joint venture with my wife, Rose, it seems the perfect place to stop. Whether I continue with a second volume, remains to be seen.

Because almost every word in this book is written from memory, and not, like similar writings, taken from a diary, I am aware that its chronological order may not in every case be totally correct. This does not worry me however, because it in many ways reflects my life. People always come before things. This tends to lead to disjointed activities or, to put it in another way, 'The best laid plans of mice and men go astray'.

MY EARLY LIFE

Chapter 1

To Be, or Not to Be?

Depending on where I cast my eyes, either firmly fixed to the front (a phase I vividly remember from my national service days), or turned back to view what lay behind, so the scenario changed, and with it thoughts about my future.

For, by gazing back down into the valley from which I had earlier that morning climbed, I could see the building site from whence I had begun my journey. It was, as usual, bursting with activity. Bulldozers, diggers and all the other machinery that dominate such a site, frantically engaged in their given tasks. Viewed from my vantage point, sitting literally astride the peak of a mountain overlooking the Rhondda Valley, it became startlingly clear that those machines also dominated the workmen who serviced them. Like busy ants they scurried from one giant machine to another, responding to their every need. What was more, it suddenly became crystal clear to me from my vantage point that I too (site engineer or not!) was subject to those same disciplines.

If, however, I cast my eyes ahead I was treated to a magnificent panorama of unparalleled beauty. Rolling hills topped by wispy clouds that meandered gently and serenely on their way, caressing only the highest peaks as they passed by. Their movement amid an otherwise static scene compelled my eyes to lock on to them. As they did, I was enabled to throw off the shackles of time and space, and so become totally absorbed in my thoughts and prayers. Thus was created the perfect setting and with it a sense of purpose to complete the mission to which, at the tender age of twenty-one years, I had set myself on that warm spring day in the nineteen hundred and fiftieth year of Our Lord.

That mission? To determine the course of the rest of my life. Whether to continue in my present career as a civil engineer, or respond to a calling, which appeared to be urging me increasingly and relentlessly towards a vocation within the church. A vocation (if I dared to fully comprehend the consequences) leading eventually to the priesthood. The venue could not have been more appropriate, for I knew that it was from mountain peaks that Jesus was wont to retire from the world, to pray and seek his Father's will.

As I knelt and prayed on that lovely spring morning I began to comprehend more clearly why Christ often chose such a venue. The panorama constantly changing in colour and texture as the moving clouds repainted the canvas; the spring sun suddenly breaking through the clouded sky, highlighting a field of yellow corn or a magnificent cluster of trees resplendent in their fresh green foliage; it all evoked a sense of awe and wonder at God's creation and purpose. Not only that, but smaller things such as a tiny butterfly, reluctantly yielding to the influence of the morning breeze, made me acutely aware of God's presence and love for all creatures both great and small. And that included me. Although God ruled from his heavenly throne, through the presence of the Holy Spirit He was present whenever a soul, however faltering or inadequately, tried to communicate with His creator. This deeper awareness of God's omnipresence gave me a new confidence, and with it a much needed boost to my sense of maturity, which I knew to be essential to counteract the optimism and exuberance of youth. So I prayed that God would guide me into making the right decision: whether to continue in my present career as a civil engineer, or explore further this growing conviction of being called to the priesthood.

As I pondered on these things a passage from Mark's gospel came to my mind. Jesus was walking along the shore of the Sea of Galilee when He saw two fishermen, Simon and his brother Andrew, mending their nets. 'Leave your nets and follow me, and I will make you fishers of men,' said Christ. Was Jesus, I dared to ask myself, really saying the same thing to me?

As if in obedience to a hidden command, my eyes turned downwards to the valley below. There I saw a typical Welsh mining village with its tiny terraced houses (one of which immediately reminded me of my baby sister's dolls' house) huddled together as if in mutual defence against the mountain that towered above. There was little sign of activity at that time of the morning. The men, I surmised, had already gone to the pits. The women no doubt were already engaged in their housework, for which Welsh women are so proudly known. Indeed, the only sign of movement

4

was the rippling waters of a small stream, which meandered through the centre of the village, appearing to cut it almost in half. There were, however, signs of life further down the valley. Reflecting the sunlight as it turned, the pithead wheel rotated slowly but relentlessly above the entrance to the mine, as if emphasizing the exacting price to be paid for the hard-won coal being mined so far below. But what dominated the whole scene and brought my eyes back to the village itself was the church steeple, which rose majestically from the centre of the village, with its weather vane seemingly pointing straight at me, urgently demanding my attention. My eyes, as if following the script of a play, moved down from the spire's proud summit to the porch door at its base, which was invitingly open. The difference between the two views that I could embrace by simply turning my head could not have been more contrasting. Nor, with a sudden start, I realized, would be my life, depending on whether I retraced my steps back to that busy, hustling building site (where actually I was absent without leave) or blazed a new trail down to that church in the centre of the village below. For it would be from that church, I decided, that I would (if that was to be the path I would tread) dedicate my life to God.

Which way did I go? I will tell you, but before I do, let me share with you something else. The sight of those massive diggers, reduced by distance to the stature of mere dinky toys, and miners' cottages likewise reduced to dolls' houses took me right back to my childhood. As I reflected on it, I came to see that (although I couldn't possibly have realized it at the time) there were pointers all along the way that had led me to this moment of truth. So before I tell you which way I did go, I invite you to come back with me into the past.

With no fanfare of trumpets I came into the world on 22nd February 1929. As I was born only sixteen months after my eldest brother, and was within fourteen months succeeded by my younger brother, I enjoyed the limelight for only a very limited time! My first memory was of coming out of hospital (I believe I was about three at the time) with a very sore throat, and being fed with ice cream, which made the discomfort almost worthwhile! I remember going to a party very shortly afterwards but, presumably because I was not yet fully recovered, being barred from joining in the more robust party games. One of the games I was allowed to participate in however was 'guessing the name of a chocolate doll'.

I was somewhat bemused when one of the grown-ups (no doubt feeling sorry for me) suggested a possible name for the doll and was not too surprised when the name was announced to find that it was indeed the correct one! So at a very early age I learnt one of life's most important lessons, every cloud has a silver lining!

I also have an early memory of school, but this taught me an entirely different lesson! The whole class took part in a play and, although I cannot recall the plot, I do remember I was asked to bring one of my mother's aprons from home, which was to be the foundation of my costume. Months passed, which meant that the year was now drawing to a close. As usual at the end of term my teacher had a cupboard clear-out and came across my apron, which she gave me to take home.

Christmas was by now approaching and with it the problem of buying Christmas presents. As we received very little pocket money this was always a worry. Suddenly I had a brilliant idea. I would give my mother the apron! The teacher had obviously forgotten all about it, I had forgotten all about it, and so, I reasoned fiendishly, would she! One Christmas present problem solved! Needless to say she recognized it immediately, and so I learnt my second lesson. Deceit doesn't pay!

From then on memories flowed thick and fast, although I cannot be sure of their chronological order. These included those concerning the beginning of the Second World War. I can vividly remember Neville Chamberlain's speech on the radio, and him saying, 'as a consequence we are at war'. We were at the time on holiday at Hayling Island. My father was not with us but Mother told us that he would be coming down that night to take us home, which he did. In pitch darkness we set off for London, but hadn't even got off the Island before my Father informed us that the car was almost out of petrol. All the petrol stations were of course closed. It was then that I first learnt of the power of money. We stopped at a bus depot, and after a lot of heated discussion and some passing of cash, petrol was siphoned from a bus and we were once again on our way.

I remember the first bombs being dropped and, early the next morning, going out with my father to view the damage. A stick of bombs had strafed the railway lines near our home. Just as we arrived, and to our great excitement, an unexploded bomb suddenly went off, shooting debris high into the sky. I also remember being out on the streets when the first dogfight took place over Croydon. An enemy plane was shot down and as it came closer to the ground bullets from it were cascading all around. (I always presumed that the pilot was killed with his fingers jammed onto the firing button.) There was, I recall, no sense of fear, so I was somewhat taken aback when a stranger picked me up, rushed me into his house, and unceremoniously dumped me, together with other members of his family, into a cupboard under the stairs!

Although it took some time to understand what was happening, we children eventually came to realize that there was another war going on, and that was in our own home. Just as the initial excitement of the early war days was replaced by a growing realization of its horror, so we began to comprehend that unhappiness and fear, and indeed physical pain too, were part and parcel of that conflict in our own family. Although I did not know the name for it at the time, I know now that my father was a sadist, and that, even more hurtful than the physical punishment we endured, was the mental cruelty inflicted on us.

I am not going to dwell or elaborate on this period, indeed I have only mentioned it at all because of the bearing it had on my development and future life. For it seemed to me even then that in a way that I couldn't even begin to comprehend, all that happened was part of a divine plan. It appears that my mother thought so too, because I heard her say to a very dear friend some sixty years later, 'good came out of evil after all'.

In the book of Jeremiah it says, 'Then the word of the Lord came unto me, saying "Before I formed thee in the belly I knew thee; and before thou came forth out of the womb, I sanctified thee, and I ordained thee a prophet unto the nations".' I eventually came to believe that those words applied also to me, for I found my vocation despite the fact that there was no history of ministry on either side of the family; that as children we had no church upbringing whatsoever; that my father was an avowed atheist, and was vitriolic in his attacks on the church; and, as I only found out many years later, that he forbade my mother, under threat of serious physical harm, to have any of us christened.

I vividly remember on one occasion my father shouting at my mother in the hallway of our house. At seven or eight years of age I had the temerity to interfere! I do not remember my exact words except that they were vaguely of biblical origin (although where I got them from I have no idea). My father was incensed and hit me with such force that I sailed across the hallway, coming to rest in a heap after crashing into the door under the stairs. I remember staggering to my feet and crying, 'I'm going to dial 999,' advancing towards the telephone that was (unfortunately for me) on the hallway windowsill, right behind where he stood. I was hit again, and this time did not get up. Apart from anything else I was completely winded, which at least had the effect of frightening my father to the extent that the shouting and beating stopped. Even as I lay there I remember offering up a sort of prayer of thanksgiving that the immediate problem was now over and that my mother and I were all right.

There are other unhappy memories about the hallway of our house. Like many households, getting three children ready for school was a hectic time. More often than not it was a last minute rush to be ready in time to meet the school deadline. In our house it was different. With what was to be a foretaste of my national service days, before we were allowed to leave we had to pass Father's inspection! It was far stricter than any I experienced in later life, with dire consequences. If, for example, one's shoes didn't pass muster one had to start all over again. Cleaning the offending shoe inevitably meant that you were now yourself unclean. Hence another (cold!) shower. Getting dressed inevitably took up more time. Furthermore, if one failed we all had to wait so that we left for school together. This meant that we were all late, which in those days automatically led to corporal punishment.

By far the worst, however, was the mental cruelty, some examples of which I just cannot bring myself to record in this book. They are just too painful.

One I can share however was in connection with my health. For the first ten years of my life I was constantly affected by bronchitis, and in fact missed a lot of schooling as a result. My father couldn't stand my coughing, which, being beyond my control, led to conflict. One day (when I was about six or seven) he told me, 'In your chest are lots of bubbles. Every time you cough you break one. Once they are all burst, you will die!' I believed him of course, but despite my utmost efforts couldn't stop. I was convinced therefore that every time I coughed I was hastening my death, which, apart from causing immediate stress, gave me nightmares as well.

Peter, John and Paul (having passed inspection) off to school

That's enough about this unhappy period in my life, except to say that my father remained an atheist and a sadist (as far as I am aware) until the day he died. From his deathbed he specifically stated that he did not want me to visit him in his final days nor attend his funeral, which request I honoured. I have been told that in his last days he did appear to question whether there was a God, and for this I am extremely grateful. But this however happened too late to change my earthly relationship with him and, as a consequence I carry scars of his rejection to this day.

By comparison my mother was loving, kind and sacrificial in bringing us up and teaching us the importance of Christian virtues. Above all she was a brave soul to whom we, her children, owe a debt beyond repayment.

As I recalled these and other incidents of my childhood on that mountain peak I came to see that through these experiences I have shared (and of course there were many more) God had already taught me many truths. The failings of human nature ... that discipleship was no easy thing and that Jesus meant it when he said, 'If you wish to be my disciple then you must take up your cross and follow me'. I also came to realize that my father's rejection was in some way (that I couldn't fully comprehend) compensated for by the love of Christ.

As far as the negative influence of my father's presence on our lives was concerned, the Second World War proved to be our salvation. His war work necessitated a move to Cardiff, and soon after he enlisted in the army, he was posted abroad and, apart from brief leaves, did not return until after the war was over. Even then he only remained in the UK for a short while before accepting a position in Japan, which to our great relief he accepted. Despite the rationing and other shortages, this period proved to be an extremely happy time for us all. We made many good friends, particularly, as far as I was concerned, with a neighbouring family (no doubt in the first instance because the daughter and I were of the same age and she stole my heart!). The friendship soon extended to the whole family and within a short time I looked upon their house as my second home. They were devout Roman Catholics so it was not surprising that I started going to early mass with them, but not without incident. As was the custom in those days, everyone fasted, and so (although of course I was not receiving communion) did I. As a consequence the first time I attended church I fainted! The second time, I was allowed a cup of tea before leaving, so didn't! Safely reaching the pew (and being determined not to cause any more disturbances) I knelt down, closed my eyes, and began to pray, only to be dug sharply in the ribs by my sweetheart, Frances. 'Wake up,' she hissed.

'I was not asleep,' I indignantly replied, 'just shutting my eyes and saying my prayers.'

'You don't shut your eyes to pray in our church,' she retorted scornfully, 'you gaze at the statue of the Blessed Virgin Mary.'

As I approached my teens, thought was given to my future. Actually it was decided over the garden fence! Mrs Harris (a formidable, worldly-wise lady as well as being our next-door neighbour) informed my mother that civil engineering was the up and coming profession to be in. Mother was impressed, so shortly afterwards I was enrolled at Cardiff Technical College and studied civil engineering, which I very much enjoyed.

Around this time the interdenominational youth group to which I belonged started to go to church on Sunday evenings. The club had an interesting history. It used to be the youth group of the local Methodist church, meeting in its hall. The minister severely limited the club's activities, causing much frustration, which finally led to rebellion. The minister made the mistake of going to the toilet and was immediately locked in by one of the teenagers! That was the end of the relationship between church and the group. Undeterred, they moved to a local council hall, and the club grew and flourished. For my sins I became the sports secretary. Not surprisingly (seeing their earlier connection) on Sunday evenings members would go to the church of their choice, then meet together afterwards for fellowship. I teamed up with a Church of England group, and so came about my introduction to Anglican services. My mother had started attending church at the Missions to Seamen in Cardiff docks, and on occasions I went with her. I immediately felt at home in their form of services and worship. After one such service I was surprised to hear the Mission Padre say to me, 'You ought to join the church. We need people like you.' I remember looking around to see who he was talking to but there was no one else! I didn't take him seriously at the time, although I was to remember his words when, about six months later, the new Chaplain who had replaced him, said almost exactly the same thing.

Chapter 2

National Service

In 1946 I received my national service calling-up papers (which proved to be one of the best training grounds possible for anyone considering a vocation to the ministry). At that time one had the option of finishing one's education, or of being called up upon reaching the age of eighteen. I decided on the latter course on the grounds that, if I managed to be selected for a regular commission in the Royal Engineers, I would be sent at Government expense to Cambridge to finish my civil engineering education. Unfortunately I was not selected for a regular, but only for a short-term commission (that is for the duration of my national service). In the end even that was not to be, but that's jumping the gun!

My calling-up papers informed me that I had to report, in one month's time, to Maindy Barracks in Cardiff, which was at that time the HQ of the Welsh Guards. It was with a great sense of apprehension, but also of awe, that I passed through those imposing gates on a cold Friday morning in November 1947. We were quickly kitted out with uniforms and issued with a rifle, which took us to lunchtime. I admit to being pleasantly surprised by the meal (despite what we had heard beforehand). After about ten minutes a young duty officer appeared and inquired if everything was all right. There was a general murmur of agreement, after which the officer started moving away. But before he was out of earshot one of those at our table said, 'I have a complaint to make'. The duty officer stopped, turned and returned with what I judged to be a very purposeful step. 'What's your complaint, soldier?' he asked in an icy voice.

'There's not enough salt in the potatoes,' came the confident reply.

'You mean potatoes, SIR,' the officer replied.

'Sir,' came the reply, but this time in a far less confident tone.

'Sergeant!' screamed the officer, and within a few seconds a sergeant appeared by his side. 'Sir,' he replied in a voice that could be heard all over the mess.

The duty officer pointed accusingly at the luckless soldier and said, 'Put this man on a charge for making an unnecessary complaint. There are salt cellars on the table!' Lesson number one very quickly learnt – don't complain!

Lesson number two came shortly afterwards. Immediately after lunch we found ourselves on parade for the first time. Suddenly there appeared a figure that put fear into the heart of every man except one (more about him in a minute). There before our very own eyes was the infamous Regimental Sergeant Major. Included in the instructions we received regarding our call up, was the order to have a 'severe haircut' before reporting for duty. This I had faithfully done, but I still felt the remaining hairs on the back of my neck rise as the RSM began his inspection. The comments he passed on to almost every soldier were masterpieces of the English language. To make it worse he advanced not in front of us but behind. The moment of truth came as he stood, I judged, right behind me. In a voice brimming with distaste he asked, 'Am I hurting you?' I was frantically contemplating my answer when Snowy (as we had already nicknamed him because of his shock of dyed blond unruly hair, and who claimed to fear no man), who was standing next to me, replied, 'No, mate.' Snowy came from the notorious Tiger Bay area in Cardiff Docks, and had no respect for any type of authority or, as it transpired, for anything else! We assumed that he was in what we would now call the local Mafia.

'Well, I bloody well should be,' the RSM screamed in his ear, 'because I am treading on your hair.' There followed a pregnant pause, finally broken by the now already familiar voice of the RSM. 'Sergeant. Put this man on a charge, for insubordination and not obeying an order to have his hair cut.' As Snowy was marched away at the double he was heard protesting in a loud voice, 'but I did have a haircut before I came!' The order was quickly and efficiently obeyed. Within about twenty minutes he was back, looking almost completely bald. The only comment came from the RSM: 'That's a bit better.'

Before being dismissed from the parade ground we were informed that we could go home for the weekend to dispose of our civilian clothes but had to be back on duty by 8 am on Monday morning.

This did not apply to Snowy, who had been confined to barracks for seven days. We wasted no time in getting our belongings together and preparing to depart. I was surprised to see that Snowy also seemed to be packing up his civilian clothes. Why became obvious when he informed anyone who cared to listen, 'Cardiff City are playing at home tomorrow and I'm not missing the game for any bloody RSM. I'm off.' Sure enough, off he went, as did everyone else.

Eight am on Monday found us back in barracks and on parade, under the watchful eyes of our platoon corporal. We hadn't been there for more than a few moments when who should appear, breathing fire and brimstone, but the RSM.

'Corporal,' he bellowed in a voice that could be heard all over the parade ground, 'is everyone present and correct?'

'No, Sir,' he replied, 'one man is absent without leave.' Needless to say it was Snowy. The RSM nearly had convulsions. The corporal, who knew him well, confessed to us afterwards that he had never seen him in such a state.

'Let me know the second he arrives,' he exclaimed through clenched teeth.

At about 10.30 am we were back on the parade ground under the watchful eye of the Drill Sergeant, who had great pleasure in telling us that, even without Snowy, we were the worst bunch of recruits he had ever had the misfortune to set eyes on. Then it happened. Sauntering past us in a nonchalant manner came Snowy. He was smoking a cigarette, which he waved airily at us as he went past. The Drill Sergeant noticed the distraction, saw Snowy and abandoning us completely, charged over and arrested him in a most forceful manner. When questioned he said, 'Well I wasn't going to miss Cardiff playing at home for you or anyone else. And once home I saw no point in hurrying back, so I didn't!' All I can say is that Snowy didn't see Cardiff play the following week nor indeed for a very long time. It was also the last we saw of him, for I believe that after serving time in Colchester (the Army glass house, as the prison was universally known) he was dishonourably discharged.

The next day I was interviewed by the Company Adjutant, who told me I was being considered for a commission and would shortly be sent to a selection conference. I decided to tell no one about this, but the secret soon became general knowledge when the duty

NCO appeared in our barrack room, when we should have been enjoying a break. 'Stand by your beds!' he screeched. We did. 'I am looking for four men, who are musically gifted' he intoned in a silky voice. Four hands were quickly raised. They were equally quickly dispatched under the care of our corporal to a destination unknown. The NCO continued, 'I understand that one of you is hoping to become an officer in the Royal Engineers.'

Rather sheepishly I raised my arm. 'Oh, it's you is it?' he observed rather dryly. 'OK, come with me.' As I followed behind I admit to feeling rather surprised that action was being taken so quickly! The action turned out to be of a different nature. We turned into a building, and then on into a room. In it were paintbrushes and paints and nothing else.

'It's all yours, Sir,' he muttered sarcastically. 'You've got just four days to finish this building before going off to your selection conference.' With that he left. Upon returning to the barrack room I found four indignant musical colleagues. All that was wanted, they said, was a piano moved! Lesson three: never volunteer for anything. Lesson four: never admit to anything either!

The four days flew and before I knew it I was on my way to an OCTU (Officer Cadet Training Unit) selection conference. I was immediately struck by the luxury of the centre after the rigours of the barrack room. For a start we had sheets and a proper mattress, a very nice mess hall and superior food. Instead of NCOs there were lots of officers, including a Brigadier who everyone treated as if he were God! But they were all very pleasant, and I really appreciated the whole experience. The conference was very challenging and included written tests, interviews and group activities. One such I shall never forget. We were taken to the side of a river. On the ground were bits and pieces of poles, etc, and we were told we had to use them to get across the river. Having forgotten never to volunteer for anything, I was rash enough to offer to be the person at the end of the poles as we attempted to get across. We rigged up a contraption that looked rather like something from a *Punch* cartoon, and I then climbed onto the end of it. Slowly it was swivelled round, and in no time all dry land was behind me, and I was perched gingerly over the water. The swivelling finally stopped, with me precariously perched on the end of it, but still, alas, some twenty feet from the far shore! I had a rope around my waist. Not to protect me, I hasten to add, but so that I could pull things over the water once I was on the other side. Unhelpful advice came from those who had wheeled me out, and none of it proved of any value at all. I decided there was nothing else for it but to let go, which I did. The water was icy, and the current fast, but I scrambled on, up the bank, and onto dry ground on the other side. A few half-hearted cheers wafted across the stream that separated us, but I was more interested in the slightly amused face of the officer who was monitoring our every move. To this day I do not know whether my efforts determined that I would not be offered a regular, but only a short-time commission, or none at all!

But the joy and sense of relief at being accepted for a commission overcame everything else, and I returned home a very happy man. OCTU itself was a wonderful experience and, although I did not in the end become commissioned, I would not have missed it for anything. The course consisted of two halves. The first was basic training, during which time one was assessed, not only for suitability

368 Officer Cadet Course   No. 1 Training Battalion, R.A.S.C.

Photograph by Mays, Aldershot

Back Row: Amis, P.S., Beaman, J., Bell, C.J., Berkley, H.J.N., Brotherton, L.J., Brown, E.H., Burrell, J.J., Chisman, P.T., Chrisp, G.W., Crisp, G.G.A., Haigh, D.
Centre Row: Halliday, J., Heaton, W.M., Isherwood, G.A., Jackson, J.H., Jones, R.P.S., Kellit, M.J., Mort, J.W., McDougall, D., Mackintosh, M., McMurray, A.J., Marshall, R.P., Martin, D.F.
Front Row: Montagu, H.E., Nutbeem, R.W., Ross, H.L., Scott, B.D.K., Taylor, J.R., Thompson, A.P., Trueman, T.G., Warnford-Davis, D.M., Warnford-Davis, J.D., Witham, B.D., Wrintmore, E.G., Harland, R.B.

16

for commissioning, but also regarding which regiment or corps one would most usefully be posted to. I passed (I was surprisingly informed) with flying colours. On reflection I believe that it was my enthusiasm rather than my abilities that got me through! I was then informed that, provided I successfully completed the second half of the course, I would be commissioned into the Royal Artillery. This would take place at Aldershot, famous, apart from anything else, because its RSM was the most well known and respected in the British Army, none other than Sergeant Major Britain.

I well remember boarding the train that was to take me to Aldershot, and not being surprised that nearly all the other occupants in the carriage were fellow cadets. Having successfully completed basic training there was confidence in the air, especially between two of them who were boasting in very loud voices that they weren't going to be intimidated by one Sergeant Major Britain. I felt embarrassed and said nothing. Which was just as well because the next day whilst on parade, on came the formidable, indeed awe-inspiring RSM Britain. As soon as I saw him I knew it wasn't for the first time. So did the two cadets who had been boasting in the carriage. He had been a fellow passenger in our carriage and had heard every word! Elephants and Sergeant Majors never forget a face, as the two cadets soon found out. The RSM literally wiped the floor with them, and from that day onwards his every order, without question, was obeyed.

OCTU proved to be a very demanding and challenging time; nevertheless, at the back of my mind, I retained an awareness of being called to the church. Indeed it was at Aldershot that God found yet another way to sow a seed in my heart. It was during the Padre's half-hour (which was welcomed by us all as it provided an opportunity to relax from the hard rigours of training). 'You chaps,' the Padre said, 'once commissioned, will need all the help that you can get. If you haven't been confirmed already then you jolly well ought to be.' I had not, so I now attended confirmation classes and was duly confirmed by the Bishop of Guildford. Church attendance now became increasingly important to me as I ached for a deeper relationship with God. In the meantime the course continued and the time for commissioning grew ever nearer. Cadets were from time to time given various posts of responsibility. It was considered a good sign if you were given one during the last fortnight, as it indicated that you would be there until the end to

17

complete it. I was made OC of all the barracks, which meant apart from anything else that I was responsible for discipline in the barrack rooms. A cardinal rule was that no one was allowed to plug in any electrical instruments in the barrack rooms, but had to use the areas provided, such as in the ironing room. One evening I was getting ready to go down to Aldershot to have my final fitting for my Sam Brown uniform. No cadet would dream of going out without pressing his trousers, so I duly went down to the ironing room only to discover that for some reason there was no power. I returned to the barrack room, plugged the iron in to a socket (strictly against the rules of course) finished the task and was just going to unplug when a fellow cadet who had also returned unsuccessfully from the ironing room, said, 'Please leave it in, John, so I can press my trousers too'. I did and went off to finish my ablutions.

When I returned I could see that I was in serious trouble. The Commanding Officer, together with the RSM, had called in to have a friendly chat with us, only to find a cadet doing the unthinkable, 'ironing in the barrack room'. When asked why, he replied, 'I found it plugged in, Sir, so I used it'. The next question was literally barked by the RSM. 'Who plugged it in?' sealed my fate. I was doubly charged for not only breaking the rules, but breaking the rules I was supposed to be enforcing! Because I was so near to being commissioned and had (up to this moment) satisfactorily completed the course there was an inquiry as to whether or not I should be RTU (returned to unit). As a consequence, instead of (as was the usual practice) being sent away the next day, I remained there for four more days and actually witnessed my fellow cadets receiving their commissions. It was a very demoralizing experience. On reflection, however, even that setback seemed to be part of God's plan for me, because my new posting led me to even more committed church attendance, and through it a deepening sense of vocation.

I remember vividly my first Sunday in Stanley camp, just outside Coventry, which is where I was posted after leaving OCTU. I had made inquiries about the nearest church, and was told that it was in a village about three miles away. I set my alarm, which duly awoke me at the appointed hour. I dressed quickly (of necessity as it was freezing cold), and ventured out into the breaking dawn. It had snowed quite heavily during the night, so I blazed a virgin trail through the snow, singing loudly as I went 'Good King Wenceslas' and other carols. It seemed to take an age to get there, and as there was about three inches of snow it was pretty hard going too. Eventually the village came into sight, and shortly afterwards the church itself. It was still not fully daylight, but a dim light above the porch of the church seemed to radiate a wonderfully warming and inviting glow. There were not many people present, but I was deeply moved by the service. To my great delight the Vicar invited me back to his house for breakfast. I will never forget the warmth of that kitchen and of his family too. That breakfast of eggs and bacon, tomatoes and mushrooms, washed down with a large mug of steaming hot tea, was one of the most enjoyable meals I had partaken of for a very long time. I left with a wonderful sense of truly belonging to the body of Christ, and a growing desire to become more and more involved in it.

Not unsurprisingly I had little enthusiasm for the rest of my time in the army, so I was very relieved when 'demob' drew near, and with it an opportunity to attend a course of one's choice in preparation for return to 'civilian life'. I chose a civil engineering refresher course, only to discover that my heart was no longer in it. Actually demob was delayed for another six months, but this gave me an opportunity to attend another course of my own choosing. This time I opted for musical appreciation, which opened up a new world for me, especially the joys of church music.

Chapter 3

Back to 'Civvy' Life

My old firm, DI Williams, which had been taken over by Wimpey's, had nevertheless kept my job open. But from the first day back I was unsettled, and it wasn't very long before I knew I had to make a decision about my future. That is why some two months later I found myself on that mountain peak overlooking the Rhondda Valley, aware that before the day was over I would know in which direction my future lay.

The end of my national service coincided with my father's return from Japan. Any hopes that family conflicts were now behind us were dashed almost from day one. The omens were not good, for I remember opening the door to him, not having seen him or he me, for about three years.

'Hello, Peter,' (the name of my eldest brother) he said to me.

'I am not Peter,' I replied, 'I am John!' Because of my age there was no more violence but the mental abuse continued. He tried to deter me from attending church services and mixing with Christian friends. Two years later he even tried to stop me marrying my future wife by visiting her parents and telling them that, as a priest, I would never be able to support her. He repeatedly told me I would be wasting my life by entering the church (for by now I had shared with my parents my growing sense of vocation to the ministry). He made it abundantly clear that if I did he would have nothing more to do with me, and that I could not count on him for any help whatsoever; furthermore, that he would cut me off from any inheritance (which in fact he did).

I have many times since joked about making the decision of whether or not I should enter the church. 'I was not,' I tell those prepared to listen, 'a very good engineer, nor very civil either, so I thought I'd better do something else!' But it was no laughing matter on that spring day back in 1950, as I earnestly sought God's will about my future. This brings me back to that moment of truth on that mountain peak overlooking the Rhondda Valley. I did decide to leave civil engineering and enter the church. I did scramble down to the valley below, enter through that open church door, and on my knees commit my life to God. For I now felt certain that, like Jeremiah, I had been called from my mother's womb, and at the age of twenty-one years was accepting that call. How, you might wonder, did my father take the news? I arrived back at our house just before the evening meal. As it happened only my mother and father were at home so I decided to convey my decision to them during dinner. I waited until what I prayed was an appropriate moment then said, 'I've got something to tell you'. My mother looked rather anxiously across at me, but my father appeared not to have even heard. Taking a deep breath I continued, 'I'm going to enter the church'. There was a long silence before my father eventually spoke. Not in a raised voice as I rather dreaded, nor even with a show of anger. Rather as if trying to placate a mentally ill patient. 'Wynn,' he said to my mother, 'make him a hot cup of milk, give him an aspirin, draw the curtains, put him to bed, and he will be all right in the morning.'

The next morning I resigned my job, and applied to The Missions to Seamen at Cardiff for the post of lay assistant. I was duly appointed on the condition that I qualified as a lay reader within six months. I informed the Warden of Ordinands of the Church in Wales of the steps I had taken. He wanted me (subject to interviews and Bishop's acceptance) to enter St Michael's Theological College in Llandaff straightaway. I declined, being convinced (in view of my non-religious upbringing) of the need to test my vocation as a layman first.

But not only that. I had come to understand that a vocation to the church need not necessarily be to the priesthood. I felt sure that, by working with The Missions to Seamen in a lay capacity, I would eventually be able to determine exactly to what I was being called. So at the age of twenty-one I began a new life within the church. Because of my non-religious background I had no doubt that I had a huge mountain to climb, but was in no way over-awed. Rather, I experienced a great sense of exhilaration at being able to celebrate my coming of age in such a wonderful way.

Chapter 4

Coming of Age

I was not left long in doubt about how much there was to learn, nor indeed how much I needed to mature. No sooner had my appointment been confirmed than my new boss, Padre Freddie Laight (the Cardiff Chaplain) announced that he was shortly going off on holiday. 'Don't worry though,' he assured me, 'nothing will happen whilst I am away'. How wrong can you be! But before I relate some of the things that did, let me tell you about my first day at the Mission. Before my appointment I had become a regular voluntary helper at the Mission, so had naturally 'sussed' everything out! I not only knew the routine, but also what was wrong with it. Even more importantly, how I was going to put it right. So I planned my first day something like this. We would, I presumed, start with prayers. And in this I was proved correct (so far, so good.) Then, over a cup of coffee, I would lay out my excellent plans to the Padre, who, I felt positive, would be grateful for my suggestions, endorse them immediately, and then leave me to implement them. These were: I would spend the morning visiting the ships in port, inviting the seamen to the Mission dance we were holding that evening (which, needless to say, I was going to MC.) I rather fancied myself as a dancer, so was as much looking forward to the evening for my own enjoyment, as for the pleasure it would give the visiting seamen. After lunch I intended to visit sick seamen in hospital. Again, I must admit to mixed motives, as I was rather sweet on a nurse who worked in the ward! The evening I would devote to running the dance.

What actually happened was, well, rather different. After prayers, instead of making for his office, he took me to a part of the building I didn't even know existed. It was in the basement. He opened a door, which revealed darkness, a damp horrible smell, and nothing else. 'Watch your step, John,' he said. As my eyes

22

gradually become adjusted to the dark, I made out his dim figure disappearing before me down a long flight of stairs into the depths below. There was nothing for it but to follow, so I did. A faint click from somewhere ahead produced a dim light, just enough to illuminate a long corridor, with various rooms leading off from it. Padre had by now produced a large bunch of keys, with which he attacked one of the doors. After many attempts it grudgingly creaked open to admit him, reluctantly followed by me. As I entered, an even damper, more horrible smell assailed my nostrils. With a grunt of satisfaction Padre found the light switch, which revealed rows and rows of books, musty, dusty, and old. 'This,' said Padre with what sounded like a trace of pride in his voice, 'is the library'. Quick thinking prompted me to say something like 'I'm not very keen on reading old books, thank you,' but my words were drowned out by a fit of coughing brought about by a cloud of dust that had engulfed Padre as he picked up the nearest volume. 'This place obviously needs a good clean,' he remarked unnecessarily, fixing his steely eyes on me. 'See you later then, John,' he muttered after which (I thought with rather indecent haste) he disappeared from view.

Strangely enough, after I had got over the shock of the change in plans and wasted a little more time wondering if there were trade unions to protect the rights of lay assistants, I set to work. After about three hours of blood, sweat and tears I felt really pleased with the result, and half hoped that Padre would return to congratulate me on my work. He didn't. By now hunger and thirst were crying out for attention, so, with a last satisfied look around the room, I locked the door and headed for civilization. As I reached the top of the stairs the Padre's wife met me. 'What on earth have you been up to?' she cried. 'I hope you don't think you're going to sit down to lunch with us in that filthy condition!' And with that she swept majestically past in the direction of the dining room. I retreated to the washrooms, looked in the mirror and saw what she meant! Some ten minutes later I reappeared, only to find that the Padre and his wife had almost finished their meal, having put mine in the oven. I was slightly miffed at this, and was wondering how best to make my feelings known, when Padre spoke again. 'John,' he said in that steely voice that I had discovered for only the first time that morning, 'we've got a problem.'

'We?' I exclaimed weakly, but before I could continue Padre was off again in an unstoppable flow.

'Yes, we've got a problem. Today, Mrs Jones, the church cleaner, normally comes to work. Unfortunately she's rung to say she's sick so she won't be coming in,' I could hardly believe my ears as he continued, 'but don't worry because I know where all the cleaning materials are.' He then added helpfully, 'and if there is anything missing, there's a useful little shop just around the corner that sells almost everything you might need.'

There followed a pregnant silence, which was finally broken by Mrs Padre. 'I don't want to rush you, John,' she said, 'only I've got a hair appointment in twenty minutes, and Padre is running me up to town!' Gulping down the remainder of my food, I reluctantly accompanied Padre to a cupboard, situated on the top floor of the building, just outside the church. 'I'm sure you'll find all you want in here,' he said cheerfully, whilst I marvelled at how quickly he could change the tone of his voice to suit one mood or another.

Defiantly I refused to move until the retreating sound of his footsteps could be heard no more. Then, grudgingly, I opened the cupboard door, vaguely wondering as I did, what was in another similar adjacent cupboard, although I was in no mood to explore. In any case there was enough in the one I opened to occupy my attention. One thing I know for sure I will never enjoy the smell of polish again. Brooms and buckets, cloths and rags, mops and bottles of cleaning liquids, and polish galore assailed my eyes and nostrils as I delved into the mysterious interior of that store. If the truth were known, just as with the library, once I did get started I found some satisfaction in what I was doing. Nevertheless, a church is a very large area to clean, and even larger to polish. But as the afternoon wore on, and with more and more of the finished task behind me, I gained my second wind, and within another hour the job was almost finished. I have a favourite prayer that says in part 'as the shadows lengthen and the evening comes'. Well, I suddenly realized the shadows were lengthening and the evening was coming, and with it the dance, which was, I reminded myself, going to be the highlight of my first full day at the Mission. This cheered me up no end, although it was not until I heard the band warming up in the hall below that I was finally able to put all the equipment away. Feeling rather pleased with myself and in an air of finality,

I shut the cupboard door. Before making my way downstairs I remember vaguely wondering once more what was in that adjacent cupboard. The sound of the band, which had broken into the first dance, overcame my curiosity, however, so with a light, indeed springy step I descended the stairs to enjoy the delights that awaited me below.

I didn't get there! I had almost reached the bottom when I found further progress blocked by the Padre.

'Oh there you are,' he said in that, by now too familiar, tone of voice that sent warning vibes racing through my veins.

'How's it gone?'

'Great,' I cautiously muttered.

'Let's have a look,' was his rejoinder. He pushed past me without further ado and bounded up the stairs. I followed in a more leisurely manner, so by the time I rejoined him the church was bathed in bright lights, which I was delighted to see made everything shine brightly. By now he was halfway down the church, hands and eyes everywhere, and a seemingly disappointed look on his face, as inspection refused to reveal a single smut of dust or dirt. With increasing confidence I watched him nearing the end of his inspection. He left the pews and advanced towards the altar. My confidence soared, because I knew I had done a good job there. But, alas, it was at the altar of God that he finally got me.

'But John,' he said with what I swear was a cry of triumph, 'you haven't cleaned the brasses'. I knew it would be a waste of time to say, 'But you didn't ask me to!' In any case he had already turned on his heel, and without as much as a backward glance at my despairing face headed towards, yes you've guessed it, that second cupboard. Adopting once more his breezy and helpful voice, he said, 'You'll find all you need in here'. And then, as if to rub salt into the wound, he said. 'Oh and whilst you're at it, apart from the brasses on the altar, and the plaques on the wall, you might as well clean up the brasses in here as well.' He cast a critical eye over some of the contents of the cupboard, 'they obviously need some attention,' he unhelpfully remarked. 'See you later,' was his parting shot.

As he disappeared downstairs in the direction of the dance floor, I felt stranded and alone, completely disillusioned, and extremely angry. This final straw convinced me that my first day in the church was also going to be my last! I toyed with the idea of leaving there and then, but pride prevailed, and I decided I would at least finish the job before departing for good. The brasses on the altar were not too bad, neither were the plaques on the wall, as they were obviously cleaned on a regular basis. But when I saw the brasses in the cupboard I despaired, as they obviously hadn't seen the light of day, yet alone any Brasso, since before it was invented! With extremely bad grace, and increasing anger, I persevered at my task, until finally there was only one item left. It was a huge tray, black with age, ungainly looking, which obviously hadn't been out of the cupboard for a very long time. To make matters worse, what sounded like the 'last waltz' drifted up from the floor below. All my pent-up anger and frustration I took out on that offending object. I literally smothered the plate with Brasso, selected a new rag, and then attacked it with all the venom I could muster. It took ages and ages but finally patches of gold appeared where before there was only black. With them came a startling revelation. I discovered that there were words around its perimeter. What on earth could they be? I wondered. Because of its size I had attacked different parts of the plate at a time, rather like working on different parts of a jigsaw puzzle. Just as one gains great satisfaction as the various pieces suddenly start to come together, so did I as the words around the rim started to form a sentence. 'THE LORD' I could now plainly see, and a little further on the single letter 'A'. Then at the other end I came to see the word 'GIVER'. With increasing curiosity I hastened to finish off the remaining areas, so that I could complete the sentence, and with it my work. At last it was finished, and this is what I read: 'THE LORD LOVETH A CHEERFUL GIVER'. What I had been cleaning was obviously a collection plate.

What I also realized so forcibly was that during my first day at the Mission the last thing I had been was 'a cheerful giver'. Like a skunk in the dead of the night I slunk back into the church, dropped on my knees, confessed, and rededicated my life to God. But this time with the promise that, come what may, I would try to be 'a cheerful giver'. As I arose to my feet, so the band began the national anthem. The dance was over, my first day as a lay assistant was over, and although it hadn't worked out at all as I had planned, I had learnt some very valuable lessons. I also realized that the Padre, far from being an ogre, was in fact a very wise man, who saw I needed to be pulled down a peg or two to get my priorities right. The lesson had been learnt. As a consequence no one stood more rigidly to attention, or sang the words of the national anthem with more feeling, or indeed stood taller than I did, in that Mission Chapel at the end of my very first day as a lay assistant in the church.

Chapter 5

The Honeymoon is Over

One of the most valuable lessons learnt on my first day as a lay assistant was the danger of pontificating, especially to a Mission to Seamen chaplain. The beginning of my second day reflected that newfound wisdom; after prayers I decided to let the Padre have the first word. He did. 'John, I want to see you in my office.' What an earth is he going to throw at me now, I wondered? Are there other parts of the building as yet unknown to me, with fresh horrors to reveal? The news he gave me was even more unsettling. He began with praise, of a sort. 'On the whole, John,' he said, 'You didn't do too badly yesterday [instantly recognizing his technique the alarm bells started ringing]. I have therefore decided that I can safely bring my holiday forward.'

'Forward?' I interjected with a growing sense of panic, especially as I noticed that steely look in his eyes that once again defied contradiction. 'Forward,' I repeated, but this time in barely a whisper...

'Yes, John,' he said, 'we're off at the crack of dawn the day after tomorrow. But don't worry, that gives me plenty of time to brief you on all that needs to be done.' Noticing the look of apprehension etched on my face he added, in what I am sure was meant to be a reassuring tone, 'don't worry, because nothing will go wrong'. He began to enumerate a huge list of tasks to be carried out, which left me feeling certain that nothing could possibly go right. To use a popular phrase I then entered into a steep learning curve, which made the next two days absolutely fly.

I was introduced to the petty cash system (sadly, more about that shortly); the communication system between Missions worldwide; how and when to pay the staff; order food for the canteen; cope with awkward customers; open and close the Mission. He gave me the names of committee members, and which one to contact

28

depending on the problem that arose. I felt like saying at that point, 'But you said that nothing would go wrong,' but before I could even open my mouth, he was off again giving me details about the Sunday Services, and how to prepare the church for them. On top of this he pointed out that I would have to prepare sermons for the two Sundays he would be away. One point I did (forcibly) make was that, in keeping with my newfound importance and responsibilities, I would need my own office from which to operate. He had already informed me that he would be locking his up for the duration of his holiday. He was silent for about 15 seconds. He then enthused, 'I have just the place for you, come and see.'

Are we off to the cellar again? I wondered, but no, we went off in a different direction, and along yet another corridor that I didn't even know existed. We stopped outside a closed door and as he prepared to open it so into my mind came a picture of a magnificent room (almost as magisterial as his office) rightfully reflecting my new station in life. He partially opened the door and said before disappearing (as he was wont to do in such circumstances) and with what I considered an indecent haste, 'See you later'. I fully opened the door and excitedly moved forward, only to be brought to a sudden halt. Why? Because I could go no further: there was nowhere further to go! My office proved to be no more than a glorified cupboard that boasted nothing in it but an old kitchen sink. Experience to date had taught me that complaining would not only be useless but a complete waste of time, so I didn't. Two hours later, with the sink covered with two sides of an old box that had transformed it into my desk; a small bookshelf alongside another wall and a rickety chair rescued from another store, I took a critical look at the transformation. As I reviewed my first ever office I had to grudgingly admit to myself that I did so with something approaching pride, even if it wasn't big enough to have another person as well as myself in it at the same time! Any interviews, I reluctantly decided, would have to be conducted elsewhere.

Before I knew it, the rest of the day had passed, Padre had said goodbye and gone. As I locked up the Mission and set off home I couldn't make up my mind whether I was looking forward to the morning with apprehension or exhilaration. In almost his last words to me before he went away the Padre had warned me that the word would soon get around that he was away on leave, and

29

Robed as Lay Reader in Cardiff 1950

that there was a new young assistant at the Mission. 'They may try it on so be careful,' he said.

'Don't worry, Padre,' I confidently replied, 'they won't get the better of me!' Sadly, and as usual, the Padre was right!

'Morning Padre,' was his opening gambit. Modesty made me confess that I wasn't the Padre, but his assistant.

'Oh good,' he replied, and then, in a silky tone that should have set the alarm bells ringing, but didn't, 'that means that you will be kind, understanding and helpful'. Suitably flattered, I listened to his story. Today I could drive a bus through its weaknesses and inconsistencies but on that first day in charge my eyes were too full of tears, and my soul incensed against the cruel world for being so unsympathetic towards a fellow human being's needs, that I would have believed anything. The long and short of it was that if I didn't lend him the outstanding rent payments, and give him money to buy some food, his wife and young family would be left starving, to say nothing of being thrown out into the street.

The amount asked for, I realized with a shock, was the equivalent of about two months of my wages. Not only that but it would use up over half of the petty cash that the Padre had left me to run the Mission during his absence. As I struggled to digest this fact (and I believe my facial expressions told all) his voice cut across my thoughts. 'Padre,' he said, 'please forgive me but I must get back to my dear wife who will be frantic with worry, buy some food for the kids on the way, and as promised will pay you back at the end of the month when my money comes through!' After that there was only one thing to do, which I did. I gave him the money.

Needless to say, I never ever saw him again. Instead of receiving sympathy when Padre returned, he told me that I should not have given it, and therefore would have to repay the petty cash from my wages. This meant that I worked for the first two months without any remuneration whatsoever! No sooner had he gone than another suffering soul arrived. This time the story was very different, but the end result the same. I gave away a little more money. The petty cash was at that time kept in a tin in the general office, which is where I conducted the interviews. I took it out, gave him the money, and put the tin back in the drawer. He thanked me profusely and departed, whilst I, feeling like a combination between Father Christmas and the Archangel Gabriel, treated myself to a well-earned cup of coffee. The rest of the day passed without undue incident and so it was a very satisfied young man who later that evening locked up the Mission and went home.

I arrived back the following morning to a scene of great excitement. There had been a break-in during the night, and amongst other missing items was the petty cash tin, complete with its contents. I consoled myself with the thought that if it had been stolen the day before there would have been a lot more money missing! The police came and were pleased to find what they thought were some encouraging fingerprints. They said they would inform me of any developments and left. I got on with the rest of the day and indeed the week, which seemed to pass in a flash.

I must be careful not to paint a picture of all the activities of the Mission taking place in the building. From day one Padre had emphasized that one of the most important of my duties was ship visiting to inform the men of any activities going on at the club and to inquire if there was any way in which one could be of help, especially if they had any special needs or problems. Also to deliver magazines and libraries to ship's crews; to minister to any spiritual needs, or just to be friendly and, in a nutshell, to offer the services of the church and above all to be an ambassador for Christ. All this for a young, inexperienced lay assistant was an awful lot to take in, and presented a challenge far beyond what I knew to be my capabilities. I had already learnt, however, that it is always easier to undertake a task if one has a special reason for doing it. Despite then having a good excuse for ship visiting (I could tell the men that there was a dance taking place that night) my courage failed me when I approached my first ship's gangway. It was a small, grimy and dirty collier, but what really put me off was a shirtless, huge, pot-bellied giant of a man (probably the bosun) who looked even more threatening than the guards at Buckingham Palace! Like a dog turning on his back in the presence of a larger and stronger challenger, I chickened out, sneaked past the gangway, and moved on. Completely demoralized I returned to base with mission failed.

Over a cup of tea I relived the experience and despair overwhelmed me. If I couldn't fulfil this most basic of tasks, how could I ever become a disciple going out to proclaim the gospel? I could see no other option than to resign. As fate would have it one of the Mission superintendents (as they were called in those days) was visiting Cardiff, so it was to him that the following morning I offered my resignation.

The Reverend Tom Kerfoot, for that was his name, turned out to be one of the wisest priests I have ever known. He listened to me in silence, but with a gentle smile of tolerance on his face. There was a pregnant pause before he spoke; no rebuke, no acceptance of my resignation, just, 'God bless you for your honesty, John'. He went on to explain that mine was a common experience amongst newcomers to the Society. Then he said 'When you visit the ships tomorrow morning (with a strong emphasis on the word *tomorrow*), as you approach the ship start saying a prayer for the crew, and keep praying until you reach the top of the gangway and meet the first crew member.'

I did go ship visiting the next morning. I did as he suggested, and it worked. I continue that practice still today, but have now expanded it to hospital and gaol visiting as well. It has never, ever let me down.

If I thought the first week had been eventful by the end of the second week I knew that it was really only par for the course. That second week truly became an initiation of fire. I had just finished the morning's opening duties when a telegram arrived, addressed to the Chaplain. It was pretty stark considering its contents, although it did say that there was a letter following giving more details. It stated that a young cadet had been killed in an accident on board his ship in a South American port, and would I inform his next of kin. I knew from the address where he lived so, after a short visit to the chapel praying for guidance and help, I set forth to his parents' house to break the news.

A lady, whom I assumed to be his mother, answered the door. I introduced myself as 'the man from the Mission' and was immediately invited in. She showed me into the living room, which I noticed was afloat with photographs of her son in his cadet's uniform. Before I could even begin my mission, she, noticing my interest in the photos, began to tell me how well he was doing and what a wonderful son he was. I asked if her husband was in. She said yes and called for him to 'come and meet the nice young man from the Mission'. Once introductions were over I said I had some sad news to give them. Possibly because of my young age they didn't seem to grasp the seriousness of what I was trying to say, so making my task even more difficult. Inevitably, however, I came to the moment when I told them that their son had been killed in an accident on board ship. This news was at first greeted by silence. Then, as the news hit home, came one of the most agonizing screams I have ever heard before or since. His mother rose from her chair and ran screaming out of the room, out through the front door and disappeared down the road crying, 'My son is dead'. Her husband at first seemed too shocked to move, but after a few moments he too rose from his chair and went running after her, leaving me alone in the house.

After what seemed an age they both returned and the father started asking me what had happened. Having no more than the bare details contained in the telegram I was unable to give them the answers they craved. I promised I would obtain them as soon as possible and let them know. It was a very much shaken and deeply traumatized lay assistant who returned to the Mission to make those inquiries.

I was mortified that I had caused such distress, although on reflection came to the conclusion that, given the circumstances, there was not a great deal more that I could have done. I determined that if a similar situation rose again, I would make sure that I had all the necessary facts at my disposal, before venturing forth.

Unbelievably another did, and only two days later! This telegram did provide more details than the previous cable, but not enough to enable me to venture out with the confidence I needed. So I rang the Chaplain who had sent the telegram direct. My first ever overseas call incidentally! The news he gave me was not over helpful. The man concerned was an able seaman of about fifty years of age. He was a very heavy drinker and this had proved his downfall. He had been out drinking, staggered back to his ship, missed his footing on the gangway, fell into the dock and drowned. The name given as his next of kin was not the same as his own, which should have set the alarm bells ringing in my ears, but due to my inexperience didn't. The address I also noticed was not in a nice suburban area like the previous one, but right in the heart of the roughest part of the infamous Tiger Bay. I gleaned a few more details, none of which helped me very much. I offered up a quick prayer for help, took, as it were, a deep breath, then set off on my mission into the heart of Tiger Bay.

Without too much effort I found the address, which was in a tenement block, and rang the bell. After what seemed an age a dim light came on, and shortly afterwards the door opened to expose (and I use the word advisedly!) a lady of doubtful age and even more doubtful occupation. I was immediately petrified and acutely embarrassed by her attire (or rather lack of it) so didn't know what to say, or how to begin. She had no such problem. 'Yes, Dearie,' she said to me in a seductive sort of voice, 'how can I help you?' I had by now turned beetroot so was immensely thankful that the light was as dim as it was. All I could think of in reply was to stammer, 'Can I come in?'

'Of course,' she replied, and then, sensing my embarrassment, said, while giving my arm a gentle squeeze, 'don't be nervous, darling, everything will be all right'. She turned on her heels (very high heels I might add!) and preceded me up a long flight of stairs that seemed to go on forever. It was not the length of the stairs that riveted my attention, however, but the remarkable way in which she preceded me. At first I assumed that it was her high heels that were making her sway from side to side and gyrate her bottom in such an acrobatic manner. I was transfixed by all this, but at the same time became very much aware that I was entering into new, uncharted and very dangerous territory. Things couldn't get worse, I tried to reassure myself, and then immediately regretted having even thought it, because they did.

We reached the top of the stairs, whereupon she turned and gave me what I took to be a seductive smile before disappearing through an open door. I took a deep breath and followed her in. The sight that met my eyes I will never, ever forget. In the centre of the room, looking rather like an operating table was a, well, sort of bed with leather straps hanging down on either side. With increasing panic I averted my eyes elsewhere, but what I saw frightened me even more! On the wall were more leather straps unmistakably situated to affix to the neck, arms and legs of a human being. The walls were decorated with what I can only describe as instruments of torture including vicious-looking whips. To complete the decor were pictures that had to be seen to be believed. The only items in the room that didn't petrify me were two chairs, so I immediately made for one of them and sat on it. Partly because I felt if I didn't I would fall down, but also because the chairs seemed about the only unthreatening objects in the room. I remember blurting out, 'Please sit down,' and half hearing her reply, which was something like, 'Anything you want, love, is OK by me.'

This breathing space gave me the chance to collect my thoughts, and to decide how best I was going to extract myself from this nightmare. I said, 'I'm afraid I've got some bad news for you.' Her sweet-natured voice immediately became hard and icy. She jumped to her feet and advanced in a threatening manner, until she was leaning right over me. 'Don't say you haven't brought any money with you,' she grated out.

'Oh no, it's not that,' I stammered and immediately regretted my choice of words, for just as quickly as it had disappeared the sweet innocent smile and voice returned and she replied something to the effect that anything I wanted was possible! Propriety decrees that I draw a veil over the next few minutes, which I can best describe as rearguard action.

I take up the story again at the point when I managed to arrive at the moment of truth. I told her the real reason for my visit. Her husband had sadly been drowned in a South African port.

Remembering the dramatic impact of similar words to the parents of the young cadet earlier in the week, I broke the news as gently and as compassionately as I possibly could. My weak knees became even weaker as, with increasing dread, I awaited her response. For what seemed an eternity there was silence that I knew couldn't last.

'What did you say his name was?' she asked incredulously. I repeated it with trembling lips. She jumped up from her chair and advanced towards me. 'He's not my husband,' she exploded, 'he only sleeps with me when he comes to Cardiff. And what's more,' she continued in an increasingly indignant voice, 'the bastard left owing me money.' By now and like a colossus she towered over me. 'The bastard left owing me £45,' she repeated. 'I trust you've brought the money with you.'

The events of the next few minutes are still little more than a blur. What I can remember is never having been more relieved to leave a building than when I descended those stairs with obscenities ringing in my ears, as I fled into the darkness beyond. Never have I been more relieved to close a door behind me and make my way back to the comparative normality of everyday life. Before returning to the Mission however, I stopped off at the nearest pub and ordered myself a stiff drink!

Shortly before I joined the Mission staff a new night-watchman had been taken on. When I met him for the first time my immediate reaction was that he was not the normal sort of employee found in such a position. In the first place he was very much younger than usual for such a position. Secondly he was extremely intelligent so (in my opinion) wasted in such a job. He was also very religious. There was an Anglo-Catholic Church just down the road that celebrated early-morning mass, which he used to attend regularly. Shortly before Padre left on his holiday he confided to me that he had recently been released from prison, after serving five years for forgery and theft. Padre had taken him on to help in his rehabilitation. His competence and ability were immediately obvious and within a very short time he was promoted to 'manager'. Padre came to rely upon him more and more, and within a short space of time entrusted most of the finances of the Mission to him. For some reason I just couldn't take to him, suffering pangs of conscience as a result. It was the first time that I had ever worked with an ex-prisoner. Was this affecting my judgment? I agonized. During

Padre's absence I had taken on certain administrative tasks, such as counting up and banking the takings from the canteen. The canteen assistant who had worked at the mission for years, who was loved and respected by everyone, told me that her stocks didn't balance, and furthermore that the takings didn't balance the sales. My suspicions about the honesty of the manager grew, but I didn't know what to do. Padre was away, so I couldn't turn to him. I had no proof so couldn't go to anyone else.

Further observation of his activities convinced me that something was seriously wrong. The canteen assistant told me that there appeared to be missing cartons of cigarettes. So, when I saw him put two in his car I determined to act. As he drove away I followed on my bike. If he had gone far I would have lost him, but luckily he didn't. He pulled up outside a tobacconist shop next door to the church he attended, and went in with arms full. He came out with arms empty. Padre's holiday was due to end in two days time, so I decided to do nothing until he returned. In the meantime I thought of the break-in when the petty cash tin was taken, and not unnaturally wondered whether the manager had been responsible for that too.

Never was I more pleased to welcome back anyone than Padre on his return. As soon as possible I told him of my suspicions, including the saga of the cigarettes being left in the shop down the road. Never was anyone less pleased than Padre to hear my news. I felt sickened to the stomach when he asked me if I wasn't being uncharitable, and prefabricating some of the facts because of what I knew of his past. For the second time in my short career as a lay assistant at the Cardiff Mission I almost resigned on the spot. Luckily for me I didn't also mention about the possible connection between the manager and the break-in, because it turned out that was none of his doing. Indeed the day after his return we had a visit from the police who told us that they had arrested the young man I had helped a fortnight ago. He confessed that he saw where I put the petty cash so decided to return that night and take the rest of it. He was a well-known petty criminal and his fingerprints matched those they had found at the scene of the crime.

Padre's first question to the police was, 'Did you recover the money?' I immediately sensed a change in Padre's attitude, which I felt was going to affect me adversely. I was not mistaken.

'No,' we were told, 'but we have recovered what he spent it

on.' With that was produced (wait for it!) a bright green suit and a pair of yellow shoes. I was just thinking I wouldn't be seen dead in either of them when the Padre fixed me with one of his steely looks and said, 'You know, John, I think they might just fit you!' He then added insult to injury by adding, 'We know how much they cost, so by you buying them we can recover some of the cash.' Without even pausing for breath he continued in a cheerful voice, 'That means you will have less to pay back to make up the balance.'

'But...' I attempted to say before even that one word was lost in his continuing dialogue, 'Putting the tin back in his presence, and leaving it in such an accessible place was asking for trouble.'

My misery was completed when he told me that I should never have been taken in by the other hard-luck story either, so I would have to pay that money back as well. So I ended up with a bright green suit, a pair of yellow shoes, and a debt that took me months to repay. It was a hard lesson, but I must say that it was a lesson well learnt, which has stood me in good stead down through the years. The only light on the horizon came when Padre told the police of my suspicions regarding the manager; they proved to be true, so just as quickly as he came, he went. Unfortunately for me a disillusioned Padre decided not to take on another manager, so I ended up with a lot of extra responsibility. One good thing I discovered very quickly in my new profession was that one didn't have much time to grieve over what had gone before, because there was always something exciting waiting to take its place.

Like any young man, I had heard of alcoholism but had no concept of what it really meant or of its devastating consequences, not only for the drinker but also for the immediate family. There were a lot of retired seamen who lived around the Mission and used it as their club. It was from them that I learnt to play draughts, and came to marvel how, even if they had had a few too many, they could always beat me with ease. We also had a lot of drop-outs who used to come to the Mission for shelter, including alcoholics of the worst kind. Once they started on a bender there was no limit to their drinking, and if they couldn't find a normal drink, they would consume anything that came to hand including methylated spirits. The sad thing was that once over their binge they in the main turned out to be very friendly people. I became quite attached to one such alcoholic, who would often turn up late in the evening very much the worse for drink, and almost incapable of standing. The stench was awful. Padre had set up a couple of rooms for such people down in the basement (past the infamous library that I discovered on my first day at the Mission).

As they came in, whoever was on duty took them in tow, and down to one of these rooms to let them sleep it off. One night when I was on duty 'my friend' came in in a paralytic state. I took him by the arm and led him to the basement door. I opened it, unfortunately loosening my grip on him as I did. He slipped and fell down the stairs. There were at least fifteen of these concrete steps and as he landed in a heap at the bottom I felt sure that he was dead. But he wasn't. He struggled to his feet, shook himself and then, apparently little the worse for his fall, stumbled off to his room. On another occasion it was me, and not he, who got hurt. He came in to the Mission very much the worse for drink, refused to go down to the basement, made an awful nuisance of himself, and then became most objectionable. I attempted to remove him forcibly, whereupon he produced a knife from his jacket and lunged out at me. Luckily because of his condition I was able to partly parry the blow, but was nevertheless stabbed. That scar I carry to this day. Another lesson learnt, to be very wary indeed when dealing with alcoholics.

Needless to say life was not all bad and there were some wonderful moments too. One of them was to have (although I didn't know it at the time) a huge impact on my future life. The Missions to Seamen had clubs in many of the ports in the UK, and indeed throughout the world. The nearest to us was the Newport Mission, some twelve miles away. Padre told me that a party of volunteers from Newport would be coming to visit us shortly, and a programme of events was arranged, including a church service that I was to take. The day arrived and I duly robed in my cassock, surplice and newly acquired lay reader's badge, which I wore proudly for the first time. Included in the group were some Mission hostesses. These were girls from the local churches who used to come and help entertain the seamen at dances and other social occasions. One of them was called Rose, who (although no sparks were to fly during the visit) was to become my future wife, but more of that later. In the meantime the months rolled on and I grew in confidence and experience. So much so that Head Office in London decided that the time had come for me to move on. I was not so sure, but Head Office had the last word. As a consequence some nine months after I started at Cardiff, I was posted to our Mission at the Victoria Docks, London, but not before Cardiff had two more experiences to impart.

Just as in Newport, we too had some local girls who had been recruited from local churches to assist us in entertaining seamen. They were very carefully chaperoned whilst at the Mission and not allowed to go home unaccompanied. Some of the girls lived locally, and once the dance was over it became my lot to escort them home. This was not an entirely unpleasant task, especially as I had a soft spot for one of them called Barbara. I usually ended up at her house last, actually a building belonging to the Seamen's Union, where Barbara's father was caretaker. I duly met her parents, who were very kind to me and usually offered me a cup of tea before I left. It transpired that Barbara's father was very keen on chess, and when I confessed to being able to play soon found myself sitting opposite him with a chessboard in between. Not exactly what I had planned for the end of my evening but then life very rarely does turn out as planned! The only problem was that for me it was at the end of a very long day, but for him, being a night watchman it was just the beginning! The second problem was that he didn't like to lose, so if I won he immediately demanded a return match. As a consequence it became later and later before I left to go home. One night we had two games and then he begged me to stay on and play a third. But as it was by now well past midnight and I knew I had a long and busy day ahead, I insisted on leaving. All the rest of the family had gone to bed, so I left him alone and departed.

At about 5 am the following morning I received a frantic phone call from his wife asking me to come around as soon as possible. 'Something's dreadfully wrong,' she cried. Within a very short time I was met by her at the door. She rushed me along a corridor, to a small cloakroom, which was also used to make tea, etc. It had a glass mottled door through which I could see a body lying on the floor. The door was locked so I smashed the glass and went in. The body was her husband. As I entered the room I smelt gas. I found the stove was in fact fully turned on but unlit. I turned it off, and dragged him out. We immediately called the emergency services who, despite their best efforts, were unable to revive him. So I experienced my first suicide in very unpleasant circumstances. Needless to say I suffered huge pangs of conscience. Would it have happened, could it have been avoided it if I had stayed? Why hadn't I sensed how desperate he must have been? Was there something lacking in my nature so that he hadn't felt able to unload his problems to me? It taught me yet another lesson about life. Things are very rarely what they seem on the surface.

As the time for my departure drew ever nearer I felt very strongly that I would like to leave something behind as a memorial to my time there. I was too inexperienced to realize that it is the person's personality and character that is remembered rather than anything he has, or has not, particularly done. Understandably I had grown much attached to the Mission and particularly the Church, so I decided to paint it before I left. Padre immediately began to put objections into my path. In the first place it was far too big a task for me to undertake. Secondly I wouldn't have time to finish it. Thirdly we didn't have the equipment, scaffolding, ladders, paintbrushes and all the other necessary equipment to do the job, and in any case there was no money available to finance the project.

My background knowledge of the building trade and civil engineering overcame his argument that it was too big a task for me to undertake or that I hadn't enough time to complete it. My pre-Mission contacts took care of the loan of ladders; the brushes I assured him were no problem, for I had made many friends on the ships that visited the ports, including the quartermasters. From the same source I assured him would come the paint. In the whole of my time at Cardiff it was the only argument I ever won! I might have won the battle but did I win the war?

After prayers one Monday morning I began. The church, I would remind you, was on the second floor. It was an old Victorian building so the ceilings were very high. The church had a typical pitched roof, so to get to the highest part of the walls meant stretching the ladders even with extensions to the very limit. When I think of the safety regulations today I shudder! But then I had no fear and worked away on my own, at times perched at the very top of an extended ladder, arms sometimes stretched to the limit, striving to reach the highest point. Slowly but surely the work progressed. I started on the west wall, which was the easiest as it had no windows. The side walls presented more problems as they contained stained glass windows, but they weren't too large or high up so eventually they were completed too. Three down and one to go!

41

But it was the east wall that presented a huge challenge. The top centre of the wall extended up to the highest point of the church. Furthermore it was above a huge stained glass window, which made the safe positioning of the ladder very difficult. The ladder plus extension was tantalizingly short of where I needed to be. Nothing daunted I ascended, reached the very top rung and stretched to the limit of my height and covered the area with precious paint.

Then disaster struck. The ladder started to slide down the wall. I slid with it. Down it came, reached the stained glass window and continued downwards. About two-thirds of the way down the window and (to my horror) the glass broke. Hanging on for grim death I suddenly found myself no longer in the Mission but outside. Outside it and about eighty feet above the ground! The breaking glass drew the attention of people in the street below. They looked up and saw not one of the angels depicted on the window but me. After what seemed an eternity, but in fact could only have been a few seconds someone called out 'hold on' and started running towards the Mission doors. Needless to say I did just that. Within a very short time the church, was full of people, headed by Padre. Every one was offering different advice. Possibly because I knew his voice more than the others I heard Padre pleading, 'Please, John, be very careful'. Many eager hands were holding the base of the ladder and luckily the section that had gone through the window was resting on the stonework at the bottom of the window, so was stabilized. Very slowly and gingerly I started to descend the ladder. I could sense, if not actually hear, the huge sighs of relief as I reappeared inside the church. As my feet began to near the ground, I began to dread with increasing apprehension what the Padre was going to say.

I had already worked out that I would have to work for the rest of my life to pay for the window, but what else was going to befall me I daren't even begin to contemplate. My feet finally touched terra firma and to my great surprise clapping broke out. I turned from the ladder to face the Padre, and watched spellbound as he began to speak. 'Thank God you are safe, John,' was all he said. He took me in his arms and embraced me.

'I'm so sorry,' I stammered in reply, but had no chance to say anything else because he continued, 'All that matters is that you are safe'.

Everything had happened so quickly, and in any case it was almost as if it was someone else and not me who had been hanging out of the window, that I hadn't had a chance to be afraid. But, after a few minutes on the ground, reaction did set in, and I started shaking uncontrollably. Never did a warm cup of tea taste better; never had a chair felt as comfortable as the one they sat me in. Later on, as I engaged in my evening prayers never did a more earnest prayer of thanksgiving come out of anyone's lips than out of mine. As a consequence of that fateful day I was for a long time remembered, not for what I had said or done, but for being the only person who had viewed the church from the outside of a stained glass window 80 feet from the ground! Shortly afterwards the Mission became destined for demolition to make way for massive developments in the port area, so the window never was repaired. As for me I became fully involved with preparing and packing up my few belongings and saying goodbyes prior to taking up my new appointment in the port of London.

I think of this chapter in my life as 'truly coming of age'. Most of the events that I have described have been of a practical nature. Nevertheless they can only be truly understood in terms of the unfolding of my vocation. Wherever one works with the Missions to Seamen the pattern is the same. The day begins and ends with prayer in the Chapel and the day ahead is offered to God. The results at the end of it are likewise commended to Him. Of all the experiences I have described, the most exciting and thrilling were connected with taking part in the church services. Leading worship is an enthralling business, but very humbling too. One can usually sense whether the sermon has gone down well or not! On the rare occasions when one feels that it has, it is humbling beyond measure to have to stand at the back of the church as the congregation departs. On the other hand on the many more occasions when one doesn't get it right, it is even more agonizing to make one's way to the back of the church, at the end of the service. But of all the experiences to date, including my time at Cardiff, one stands out above all others, and even now, some fifty years later, I still get a thrill when it comes to mind. I was serving at an early morning communion service. The Padre had just finished the prayer of consecration, and was making his own communion. I knew that in a few moments I would be receiving mine. I was kneeling at the side of the altar, when suddenly and overwhelmingly I was filled with God's powerful presence and love. The ecstasy of the moment overcame everything else, and I just never wanted it to end. It did of course but its impact remained and indeed seemed to cap all that had gone before. As I prepared to leave for London I was confident that I had now truly 'come of age'.

Chapter 6

Life in London

My arrival at the Mission in the port of London brought back vivid memories of moving to my second school. The first was a typical nursery unit, small, unthreatening and very friendly. The oldest children in the senior class were not much bigger than me, but in any case it seemed no time at all before I had progressed through the forms, so becoming a member of the top class. Came the time to move on to my next school and everything changed. Frighteningly I found myself the youngest in a vast complex of seemingly 'giant' boys and girls! The teachers were far more awesome; even more so when they wielded canes in their hands. School was no longer fun, but a hard and demanding workplace.

I felt exactly the same when I moved from Cardiff to the Missions to Seamen in London. The building was vast. Instead of just the Padre and me, the spiritual staff varied from six to eight at any one time. An army of employees worked in the building: bedroom cleaners; kitchen workers and porters; administrative and management heads of departments; booking office clerks; maintenance and vehicle mechanics; canteen workers – to say nothing of the seamen themselves. There were about 160 beds, as well as staff quarters for about twenty permanent staff. One of the first things I had to learn (and very quickly too) was the 'batting order' of all involved. I was pleased to discover that the 'spiritual staff came first, but being the latest and junior member I nevertheless found myself surrounded by superiors who delighted in telling me what to do!

What an assorted bunch they were. Two or three were chaplains, and these posed no problem. The lay readers were all right too, but some of the others were unbelievable! There were those seeking to find for themselves a place in God's order of things. One was an ex-nun who had only recently renounced her vows and left her convent. She saw the Mission as a sort of halfway house. I don't

45

The Missions to Seamen, Port of London

know why she renounced her vows but I do know she wasn't cut out to work with seamen! Another was a shadowy figure, who, rumour had it, was a defrocked priest. He was an oddball indeed, and I knew him no better after nine months than on the day I arrived. Then there were failed students. Some had been to theological college but hadn't made the grade. Others had been before church selection boards only to be told that they needed more experience before entering Holy Orders. They had (just like me) come to the Mission to gain that experience. Then there were theological students who felt that they had a particular vocation to seamen's work, so came during holiday times to test it.

Then there were others who quite frankly shouldn't have been there at all. One such person was Philip Johns. He was extremely well educated, had a very good voice and used to sing German operatic songs. That apart, he was an arrogant prig. He would only read scripture lessons that he chose (mainly from Proverbs). They were always very long because he loved the sound of his own voice. I remember nervously preparing for my first sermon there, only to be told by him, 'Don't worry about it. Just regard your congregation as so many heads of cabbage!' I was not surprised to learn a few years later that not only had he been sacked, he was barred from all Mission stations, having fallen foul of the law. I came to see that there were just as many people within the church who were 'seeking' as those outside it. If there has to be a place for them to sort themselves out, then I suppose the Missions to Seamen was as good a place as any, but not at the expense of seamen whom the Mission was there to serve.

At the Mission in Cardiff one mainly dealt with visiting seamen from the ships in port. Ships using Cardiff docks were in the main only small, including many UK colliers as well as others from the continent. These men were the 'salt of the earth', and as they were on the whole on short runs, their lives were not all that different from those working ashore; but not so in the Port of London. In the first place, because they were staying in the Mission one got to know the seamen better. Many of them returned time and time again so became regulars, especially those from Stornoway. They seemed like giants to me but, as I found out after working with them, if handled properly, were quite manageable! Not so the stewards from the Union Castle ships and similar passenger lines. Until I arrived at London I had little or no idea about homosexuality, and had certainly never seen it in operation. At Victoria Dock Road that innocence was lost forever.

Although the spiritual staff obviously had its own specific function in the Mission plan, we were roped in to help out or fill in other spheres too, such as relieving in the booking office or the canteens, driving the minibuses to pick up men, or deliver ship's libraries and other relevant items. We also took turns in being what was rather grandly called 'the duty officer'. In all these ways one gained huge insight to every aspect of life, from the inspiring and holy to the seedy and pathetic. It was as duty officer, above all else, that one came face to face with life in the raw. There was a constant stream of down and outs who came begging for a meal or a bed for the night or for a handout or the price of a train ticket to get home. They had an uncanny way of finding out when there was a very young, junior and 'wet behind the ears' duty officer, as I soon found out to my cost. Their skill at rendering a heart-breaking story, of appealing to your better nature, or of completely conning you into giving them what they wanted would have swept the board in any Oscar award competition! With the Cardiff experience behind me, however, I was able to cope quite well. But it came as a huge relief when, after about three weeks, a new, younger and junior member of the spiritual staff came to join us, which meant attention mercifully turned to him!

There were very strict rules at the Mission, and it was the duty officer's responsibility to enforce them. One was that no drink was allowed in the building. Try telling that to the marines! At about 10.30 pm, after the pubs had closed, the men (and particularly the Stornoways) would return in a very happy and noisy state and, like the gathering of the clans, in great numbers. There wasn't a rule saying no visitors were allowed in your room, but as they were fairly small, common sense was supposed to prevail. There was a very strict rule that there was to be no noise, such as radios or loud talk, after 11.15 pm. Reality was very different. At about 11.30 a complaint would come down from one of the floors that there was a deafening racket going on down the corridor, and would someone come up and put a stop to it. Up would go the night porter, and down again he would come without achieving anything. There was only one thing to do, and that was to send for the duty officer. At twenty-two years of age (and without the benefit of a dog collar) one approached the offending culprits with fear and trepidation. There was no problem in finding them because the noise could be heard not only on the floor, but all over the building. Drunken singing has never appealed to me since! Plucking up courage, one attempted to make an impressive entrance, but that was rarely possible. Often it was impossible to even get a foot inside the door for bodies everywhere (I once encountered 19 in a single room). On other occasions one got in only to trip over a crate (or crates) of beer. I never did discover how the men brought them in past the watchful eye of the duty porter whose specific job was to see that they didn't!

One of the helpful perks was that the seamen called any member of the spiritual staff 'Padre'. 'Hello Padre,' was the usual opening slurred remark, followed immediately by someone saying, 'get the Padre a drink.' To accept one was of course fatal. To reason that others were trying to sleep didn't work either. 'Tell them to come and join us' was the stock response! In the end one just had to raise oneself to maximum height, engage in eyeball contact and say 'OUT!' Amazingly it worked and the party dispersed. Confiscating the remaining drink was not always as easy, but I never actually failed, and I was never physically attacked either.

Other situations were much more difficult to cope with. The duty officer was encouraged to spend time in the main entrance during the latter part of the evening, because if trouble loomed, it was far better to deal with it outside the Mission than within. In those days there were very few women at sea, and another strict rule was that no females were allowed into the Mission after 9.30 pm. That is not to say that the system was foolproof! Men, who could conceal crates of beer, could no doubt conceal other illegal goods too. During my early days I made some ghastly mistakes. I have already referred to some of the stewards of the passenger ships being homosexuals, and of my ignorance of the complications that could create. On only my second night as duty officer I was standing as advised in the foyer of the Mission when two couples approached with the obvious intention of entering the Mission. The girls looked really lovely, and very well dressed, so didn't look at all like (as they were known in those days) 'ladies of the night'. But rules were rules and my job was to enforce them. Plucking up courage, I approached the offending couples. The men, I recognized immediately, were regulars at the Mission so this gave me the opening I needed. 'You know the rules, lads. No ladies allowed after 9.30 at night.' The men said nothing but one of the ladies spoke up and said in a rather gruff voice 'But we live here too!' Only then did I realize that they weren't women at all but men dressed up as them!

The very next day I was asked to visit the room of one of the 'ladies'. I found her sobbing uncontrollably. The wardrobe was open and on the shelves was the most amazing collection of scents, sprays, and powders to say nothing of ladies underwear – I had ever seen! I was already learning that people are more important than things so I turned my attention to the distressed occupant of the room. 'She' eventually stopped her crying enough to tell me that her boyfriend had just jilted her. This brought on a fresh outbreak of tears, which left me feeling completely useless and out of control. I was extremely relieved that there were senior and more experienced chaplains on the staff who were better able not only to sort 'her' out, but also me.

Up to this moment I have deliberately omitted to mention another very important strand in the Mission fabric, and that was the 'lady warden'. In batting order they came immediately below the spiritual staff, which on occasions proved too close for comfort. Lady wardens were usually middle-aged, rather refined individuals, whose purpose was to supply that 'woman's touch' in the Missions. Depending on the personality of the individual, they operated either like hospital matrons, of whom everyone was petrified, or as kindly motherly figures whom everyone loved. Whatever their personality they all believed that 'cleanliness was next to Godliness', which meant that they had influence in almost every sphere of Mission activity.

Whatever one thought of one's current lady warden, there was no denying that she contributed immensely to the happy atmosphere in the Mission and to the comfort of the seamen. Because I was one of the elite 'spiritual team', lady warden Marjorie Guthrie (for that was her name) couldn't (in theory) tell me what to do. Nevertheless there were occasions when she did! Like, for example, when one was filling in on canteen duty. With uncanny timing she would appear and inspect the washing up! Or on occasions little notes would appear in one's cubby hole in the booking office, suggesting that the staff lounge had become rather untidy since I had use of it, or that the cleaner had remarked on the untidy state of my room. But these were only petty annoyances, and tolerable, especially as I had to admit (if only to myself) that there was justification in her remarks. This set me thinking of ways to overcome this problem. I found an answer all right but not to everyone's satisfaction!

Let me explain. Our senior chaplain had very good relationships with the local churches. They enjoyed having a Mission nearby and offered to help in any way possible. At one of our staff meetings we discussed possible ways of attracting the seamen to Church. Someone came up with the brilliant idea of having girls in the Mission before the service began. They would mix with the men and, when the church bells began to ring, say they were going

50

off to church, and would invite the person they were talking too to join them! It worked a treat – until I had an even better idea.

I warmly greeted the young ladies when they arrived and then spun a tale of woe. 'My cruel Padre works me so hard that I don't have time to clean my room properly. My washing and ironing is all piled up. I have shirts, which sadly have more buttonholes than buttons. My socks are full of holes. My cupboards need a good clean out. I have no cakes or goodies to offer visitors when they arrive. My windows are so dirty that I can't even see out of them any more.' I ended rather lamely, 'what I really need is that magical woman's touch!' I got it! Sympathetic hands on my shoulder, and words of comfort in my ears abounded as I led the girls to my room. Once inside it became a hive of activity. So much so, I had a job to find somewhere to sit whilst my room, my cupboards, my windows my clothes, my shirts and anything that moved were transformed in the shortest of time into Persil-white brightness. Tidiness replaced chaos; in fact when I returned to my room after church was over I thought I had entered the wrong room! Sadly there is not a happy ending to my story. Padre did a tour about twenty minutes before the service was due to start to see how the girls were getting on, and how many potential seamen they had in tow. To his consternation he couldn't find any of them, indeed panic set in as he imagined the worst! One of the staff then told him that he had seen them (rather like the children following the pied piper) heading in the direction of the lay reader's quarters.

As he approached, the sound of laughter coming from my room identified the culprit! But by now the transformation was completed. My room was once again spick and span, my washing and ironing dealt with, my windows clean, and my spirits sky high. We didn't have as many seamen as usual in church that evening, but I consoled myself with the thought that Philip Johns was preaching so they didn't miss too much after all. The Padre went to great lengths to explain to me why the girls were there, which wasn't for my benefit. He didn't want a repeat performance, to which I had to agree.

As I settled down for the night in my spick and span room, serious thoughts were raised in my mind about the advantages of having a lady-love in one's life. I little dreamt then that within a year that would come to pass! I had been in London for just a month when we were told that a theological student named Stephen

Roberts would be joining us for the duration of the summer holiday. He was Irish, very near to the date of his ordination, and was very keen on the work of the Missions to Seamen, so would eventually become a chaplain. He duly arrived, and we took to each other immediately. We teamed up and worked well together in ship visiting and other duties. He had only been with us for a fortnight, however, he was told by the senior chaplain that he would be relieving the chaplain in Newport, South Wales, who was going off on leave. Sure enough, only two days later he was gone. I missed him terribly, so was delighted to receive a letter from him a few days later giving me all his news. The main thing he wanted to tell me was that he had met one of the girl volunteers at the Mission, a beautiful Welsh girl called Rose, and was very much taken with her. Subsequent letters updated me on the romance and, although she was not completely won over he obviously was becoming more and more smitten with her.

I had also become very interested in a volunteer at the Port of London, a lovely cheerful and bubbly girl called Rhona; I therefore didn't pay too much attention to ravings about Rose. My eyebrows lifted somewhat when he told me that she was seriously considering joining the Missions to Seamen as a trainee lady warden. 'I am doing my very best to put her off,' he told me. I should mention that Rhona was the secretary of Tom Kerfoot, the Assistant General's Secretary at head office, so was a mine of information on staff movements. It was through her that I learnt that Rose had been interviewed and accepted for training as a lady warden. But it was through a distressed Steph that I learnt that she was to be posted to, of all places, the Port of London! His letter was full of nothing else, but just before he ended he wrote in very large capital letters, 'Keep your bloody hands off.'

Because my heart was increasingly warming to Rhona, his instructions presented no immediate problem. The fact was, however, that Rhona's responses to me were about as warm as Rose's to Steph, so there were occasions when I idly wondered whether she was the 'beauty' that Steph claimed she was. I was soon to find out. The senior chaplain sent for me.

'John,' he said, 'you're Welsh, aren't you?'

'No, Padre,' I replied, 'my family moved down to Wales at the beginning of the war because of my father's work, and, although he then joined the Army and went abroad, we stayed there.'

'That's good enough for me,' he said. 'I've got a job for you. There's a young Welsh girl called Rose Weight who's coming to join the staff as a trainee lady warden. I want you to look after her and see she doesn't get homesick.'

That's all I need, I told myself, to become a nursemaid at twenty-two! To be honest, I forgot that she was arriving the next day, because my mind was centred on Rhona, who I knew was going to be on duty in the canteen that evening. It was, in fact, when I went to the canteen to see Rhona that I noticed there was a new and very beautiful girl assisting her. Rhona introduced us, and from that moment onwards, things were never the same again. The chore of being a nursemaid disappeared in a flash. As Rose poured me out my first cup of tea she mentioned that she knew a good friend of mine called Steph Roberts. Even as the words left her lips, an image of his letter to me flew into my mind: 'Keep your bloody hands off'.

That night I struggled long and hard with my conscience. Steph was my best friend. Padre Ford, on the other hand, had ordered me to look after Rose, and make her feel at home. What was more, I realized that I wanted to. As I mused on my dilemma the expression 'All's fair in love and war' suddenly burst into my mind, and from that moment on Steph was (as far as I was concerned) a goner! Next morning, after ascertaining that we were both free that afternoon, I offered to take her to the local shopping area. She agreed. I then casually threw in the fact that there was a good film on at the local cinema, and that we would just have time to take it in before returning for evening duty. Again she agreed.

The afternoon couldn't come quick enough for me, nor could the first (shopping) part of it. However, by about 3.30 there we were in the cinema (no expense spared, for I purchased the most expensive seats in the house), the lights were dimmed and the film began. Instead of the titles that flashed onto the screen, into my mind came Steph's words, 'Keep your bloody hands off'. But by a determined act of willpower I managed to get the words replaced by, 'All's fair in love and war'. After about ten minutes and in the most casual manner possible I slid my arm around the back of her seat. I braced myself for a possible rebuttal, but none came. Ever so slowly I moved my hand until it was lightly touching her shoulder. I held my breath but again no objection, so I exercised just the slightest pressure, which again brought no rejection. I sat there hardly daring to breathe, so as not to break the spell of sheer exhilaration that engulfed me. A few minutes elapsed and then came a turning point in my life. Rose seemed to relax her body, moved almost imperceptibly towards me, and then rested her head on my shoulder. I slowly reached down to her face, put my hand on her chin, and tilted her face towards me. Then, in that cinema, in the middle of the afternoon, I kissed her for the first time. As I did I knew that the experiment of having young instead of middle-aged lady wardens was doomed. That Steph Roberts was banished into exile and that I was in love with the person with whom I wanted to spend the rest of my life. I've long forgotten what the film was about, but I will never ever forget that first kiss with Rose.

Chapter 7

Romance at the Mission

Courting is rarely smooth going, but believe me it can be horribly compounded when living in a Christian community! In the first place, there are community rules that have to be obeyed. In our case some of them (because we were in different departments) were different for her than for me. In the second place, she came under the authority of the lady warden, whereas I didn't. Living in a community inevitably results in a lack of privacy. Most rooms are communal, apart from one's bedroom, but that was strictly out of bounds to anyone other than oneself. This meant that there was nowhere private where we could meet. Gossip (which can so easily lead to scandal) had to be guarded against, and if there is ever a place where gossip (good, bad, and indifferent) abounds, it is within a Christian community! Courting requires space for both parties, as well as time together. In the Port of London Mission, both were in very short supply. This meant that most of our early courting took place out of doors and away from the building. But London too was a very public place, with little or no privacy. It was also very expensive, so even a trip to the cinema became a rare treat. We did, however, discover that public transport, especially the buses, were comparatively cheap, and that you could jump on and travel a very long way for a very small amount of money.

The number 45 bus, for example, could be boarded near the Mission and take us up to Hyde Park Corner. We loved going to Speaker's Corner and listening to the various orators. We were particularly thrilled whenever Lord Soper (as he later became) was preaching; I used to marvel at his ability, especially as I knew I would never be able to match the skills he possessed. Window shopping was another cheap way of passing time. Sometimes we would push the boat out and go to Lyons Corner House for a snack, but usually it was to a cheap working man's café back near

55

Father Christmas (with the aid of Rose and Rhona) giving out presents

the Mission, away from West End prices, where for a modest sum
one could enjoy steak, eggs and chips. At this time I hardly drank
at all, but Rose enjoyed a beer. A beer and lemonade would be
ordered, with the beer inevitably put before me, and the lemonade
in front of her. As soon as the waiter had moved away we swapped
glasses! Rose also enjoyed a cigarette, whereas I never smoked at
all. But in every other aspect our courtship was as normal as could
be, except that we found it very frustrating to be unable to find
the time and privacy that every courting couple needs.

Working in a Mission meant lots of evening as well as daytime
duties. But because we came under separate jurisdictions, we were
often working at different shifts. Inevitably, and especially as the
winter months drew in, we were forced to spend more and more
of our time together in the building. The stress at having little or
no privacy began to take its toll, so I realized that something had
to be done.

One of Rose's tasks as a trainee lady warden was to issue clean
sheets and towels to the bedroom cleaners. With such a large
number of bedrooms there was quite a large linen room. Within a
very short time Rose proved to be so efficient at the job that she
was made OC of it, and entrusted with its key. Not the most
romantic of places, especially as the dirty sheets were also deposited
there before being taken to the laundry, but as any seaman will

tell you, 'any port in a storm'. It gave us a haven during the day, but evenings still presented a huge problem.

One of the facts about Missions in those days was that there was no such thing as a romantic atmosphere! We had a staff common room, which was lit more like a barrack room than a lounge. So under 'any other business' at our weekly staff meeting I suggested that we should make the room more comfortable and attractive. No one else seemed very interested, or wanted to get involved, but I persisted with my request. Perseverance brought its reward, for I was given a limited budget and told to get on with it. I did so with great enthusiasm, ably supported by Rose. The result was quite a transformation, with softer lighting and a more homely and relaxing atmosphere. Rose and I loved it and frequented it as often as possible. So much so that it soon became known as 'John's and Rose's den'. Encouraged by this development I suggested that it would create a finishing touch to have a fish tank in the lounge. On the assurance that I would look after it, this request was also granted and before long there it was. Nothing looks more attractive than an illuminated fish tank at night with all the other lights turned off. Thereafter Rose and I spent an inordinate amount of time tending to the needs of the fish, and then sitting down on the settee admiring our handiwork. Our love for each other flourished, so much so that six months later we became engaged. Despite being engaged we were still not allowed in each other's rooms. However, we were left more and more alone in the lounge and before long it became the unwritten rule that it was our retreat.

Not everyone honoured this arrangement, however, and as there was also a constant turnover of staff, plus visitors, we were often disturbed. I soon found the answer. If we heard footsteps advancing along the corridor I would grab Rose, engage her in a passionate embrace and remain in it until the embarrassed intruder moved away. All went well until one evening a visiting Archbishop from an overseas country walked towards our sanctuary. On hearing footsteps (and not knowing who it was) we immediately moved into our 'passionate clinch routine' and that was how he found us when he walked into the room. We were not surprised to learn through the grapevine that a senior management meeting had been hastily convened for the following morning. By midday we were informed that as we were engaged and were to be married shortly,

I could now escort Rose to her room, provided I agreed to the strict conditions laid down – which I did.

A public address system operated from the booking office at the entrance to the Mission, which had the effect of making that office the hub of activities. As the spiritual staff also had to relieve the booking clerks at meal times etc, we all became familiar with the system. If I had a penny for every time I heard the message, 'Will John Taylor please report to the booking office' I would be a rich man! Usually one groaned on hearing 'the summons' as it usually signified a problem looming, or an unpleasant task to be undertaken. It was not long, however, before Rose and I learned to use it to our own advantage. It always gave me a thrill to hear her voice calling for me, and I like to think it was the same when I called her. We masterminded our own secret code, which meant we could send messages of endearment to each other without anyone else being the wiser. I always knew it was something special if she asked me to go the linen room – likewise if I asked her to come to the duty office.

They say that true love never runs smoothly; we certainly had our ups and downs. One of our first tiffs was conducted in (almost) total silence. A daytime retreat was organized for the spiritual staff. It began with Holy Communion in the Chapel, followed by breakfast in silence as there was to be no talking throughout the day. The trouble was that not everyone managed to observe this rule! Within a few minutes of sitting down for breakfast there were one or two whispered conservations breaking the golden rule of silence. Others soon fell by the wayside. This was my first ever retreat, however, and I was determined to keep up the no speaking rule. All went well until the ladies started serving us with breakfast. Rose's task was providing a choice of cereals, and trouble started with the very first person she approached. 'Good morning, Rose,' he exclaimed in his penetrating gruff voice. She gave him a charming smile, which was cut short by a glare from the retreat conductor, who uttered one word: 'Silence'. The guilty party either didn't hear or thought silence meant speaking quietly, for he continued, 'let's see what you've got for us'. At this the retreat conductor realised that he had lost control, and retreated into his porridge. He still had one faithful adherent however – me! Rose approached and gave me a beautiful smile, and said, 'good morning, darling'. I pretended not to hear, and I saw the smile disintegrate into a scowl. 'Good morning, John,' she repeated icily. I raised my eyebrows and finger pointed to my mouth. Her response was, 'the others are talking to me, so why can't you?' I tried to look angelic but this infuriated her even more, and without further ado she poured a version of cereal that she knew was not my favourite into my bowl and moved on.

Proposals for marriage are supposed to be very romantic occasions. Ours wasn't, neither in the place, nor in the manner of proposing. It was actually tied up with the question of money. Rose had an insurance policy from which she discovered it was possible to borrow up to £40. This was the amount we had worked out would enable us to get married, have a honeymoon (bed and breakfast only at a boarding house in Seaford) and return with about 15 shillings (75p today) to see us through to the end of the month. The letter from the Insurance Company agreeing to the request duly arrived. A coded message asking me to report to the linen room came across the tannoy. Once I arrived the letter was opened and, on reading that our request had been granted, we jumped for joy. Without further ado, I suggested a date for the wedding, and she agreed.

After our engagement it wasn't only the strict conditions that we still had to abide with, but also the advice from well meaning folk, who bombarded us with dire warnings, including prophecies of gloom. When my father learnt of our engagement he visited Rose's parents and told them that I would not be a worthy son-in-law; that I was in no position financially to take on a wife, and that they should dissuade Rose from marrying me. I don't know what they made of my father, but at no time did her parents make any attempt to make her change her mind. In the meantime, preparations went ahead for the wedding, which was to be held in a local church, and The Reverend Tom Kerfoot kindly agreed to conduct the ceremony. The reception was to take place in the Mission, which proved a real blessing as so many wanted to be involved, to say nothing of the reductions in the cost. Courtesy of the local Vicar there were no charges for the service either!

There was still a great deal to be sorted out. For a start there was the question of my good friend Steph. Despite his command that I should 'keep my bloody hands off', the adage 'All's fair in love and war' had proved a more powerful argument, but he was still my friend. Steph is a wonderful, laid back Irishman, and obviously did not hold my treachery against me – we have remained firm friends down the years and are godfathers to each other's sons. There was also the question of Rhona, of whom I was still very fond, as indeed was Rose, for they had by now become close friends. We had already decided in the interests of economy not to have a white wedding, but spend the money on a suit for me and a going-away outfit for Rose. This meant that Rose would not have bridesmaids but a maid of honour. I needed a best man. Rhona and Steph became the obvious choices, and we were delighted when they agreed to our requests.

Steph had by now been ordained and was serving his first curacy in Belfast. By one of those strange coincidences, I was asked to go to Belfast and relieve the Padre there, who was going on leave. I duly arrived in Belfast, made contact with Steph, and agreed to meet him a few days later, actually on his first day off. We duly met with me under some apprehension, as I was not sure how he was going to react to my actions over Rose. I thought I would get off to a good start by saying how much the dog collar suited him. To my surprise he said, 'The first thing I want to do is get it off'. We went to the nearest public convenience and Steph disappeared into a cubicle to take it off and replace it with a tie. Off came the dog collar and on went the tie. The trouble was there was no mirror in the cubicle to help him in putting on his tie, so he came out to avail himself of one outside. Whilst he was doing so someone came in and entered the very same cubicle that contained his dog collar. We had to wait for ages but eventually the gentleman emerged holding the offending article, which an embarrassed Steph retrieved.

Steph had met Rhona during the short time we were together in the Port of London, and seemed quite pleased to learn that she was to be the maid of honour. He arranged to have a week off before the wedding and come over to London, staying in the Mission so that he could get to know her better, as well as be available for rehearsals, etc.

Before all that came to pass, however, the padre sent for me yet again. He explained that the chaplain in Glasgow was due to go on leave and, because I had satisfactorily carried out the relief in Belfast he was now sending me up to Scotland. I didn't know whether to be pleased that I had passed muster or sad because it would mean separation from Rose. I didn't have much time to dwell on it, however, because two days later I was on the train to

Glasgow. The padre there met me at the station, and took me immediately to the Mission. He explained various workings, and gave me notes on procedure as well as the duties of the various members of staff. Then it was off to my digs. Somewhat to my surprise we drew up outside the YWCA. He noticed the bemused look on my face and asked me what was wrong. I told him. 'Surely we should be outside the YMCA not the YWCA?' I volunteered.

'Och aye,' he said, 'there is no problem. The YW is cheaper than the YM!' – end of story. With that he whipped me off to his house for supper. I met his wife and five children, who made me feel very welcome. We then sat down for the meal. 'Hope you like roast beef,' he offered. I replied in the affirmative but with some apprehension, as there was only a very small joint on the table. What are the others going to eat? I wondered to myself. The answer – roast beef! I watched in amazement as he managed to carve the thinnest slices possible, with such success that there was indeed beef on every plate. No sooner was supper over than he explained that they were away to an early start in the morning so, after a hasty goodbye to his family, we were off to the YWCA. He dropped me outside the building and I was on my own.

Once in my room I decided to study the notes he had given me about Mission procedures and staff. Then I realized that I had left my briefcase at the Mission. By now it was almost 10 pm but as I didn't feel the least bit tired I decided to go down to the dock area and collect it. The padre had given me instructions on how to get there, and I followed them without any problem. It was about 10.30 when I arrived and, as I knew the mission shut at 10 pm, I expected to find it closed and in darkness. Imagine my surprise, therefore, when I turned into the street where it was to see a light coming from the open front door. Just before I reached the entrance myself I was surprised to see a couple slip into the Mission. I went to follow them in but was stopped by the person whom I assumed was the night watchman. Stopped, that is, until I introduced myself. An embarrassing quarter of an hour followed when I first of all got rid of the 'lady of the night' plus her client, closely followed by the night watchman. He admitted that after the Mission closed and all the staff had left he earned some extra money by letting prostitutes come in with their clients. I had no alternative but to dismiss him on the spot.

After he had gone I made myself a cup of tea and settled down to read the notes. I had already realized that I couldn't leave the Mission unattended so would have to spend my first night in Glasgow not tucked up in my little warm bed in the YWCA but in the Mission acting as night watchman. I consoled myself with the knowledge that the first job in the morning was to ring up the employment exchange to obtain a replacement. Comforted by this thought I returned to the notes. I nearly died as I read on! The first thing I discovered was that one of the jobs of the watchman was to stoke the boilers that heated the building. Apart from the central heating there was a swimming pool in the basement of the building, and there were very precise instructions about how, when, and to what extent the heating had to be controlled for the pool. It was hot hard and tiring work and, as I had never wanted to be a night watchman come handyman, I didn't enjoy it one little bit. Worse was to follow! I then discovered the night watchman was also the cleaner! It was a large building, with many rooms and, as I quickly discovered when I started to clean, the previous occupant of the job hadn't been very efficient at his job. Memories of cleaning the church in Cardiff came to mind, but it wasn't only the church that needed cleaning, but many other rooms as well. I finally finished just as the first members of staff arrived. They were most surprised to find me there, dirty, unshaven and very tired. One of them quickly rustled me up a cup of coffee, which lifted my spirits and my optimism. Thus heartened, I made a quick call to the labour exchange requesting a new night watchman, convincing myself that thereafter it would be business as usual, except of course for what transpired after 10 pm once the Mission was closed.

Alas, the best laid plans of mice and men go awry. The labour exchange had no one on their books they could send along at the moment. How long before they had? I asked.

'Can't tell you,' they replied, but they would send someone along as soon as they could. That turned out to be five long days and nights, by the end of which the lay reader in charge, acting night watchman, acting cleaner and boiler stoker, was exhausted, disillusioned, very miserable, missing Rose like mad, and longing to return to London. Needless to say, the phone line between Glasgow and London Missions became red hot. I remember the first. 'Hello, darling,' she said, 'how's it all going?'

I told her.

'You must be very busy,' was her immediate response.

'Busy,' I replied, 'I'm so busy I haven't even had time to go to the toilet!' Apart from the manual tasks, the real work of the Mission had to go on; hospital and ship visiting, taking services, and running activities in the club.

There were, of course, some highlights. One was visiting a ship in port that I had visited a fortnight earlier in London. 'Hi, padre, what are you doing up here?' said one seaman. Another chipped in, 'How could you possibly leave your lovely Rose and come up to Scotland?' I had the opportunity to visit Loch Lomond, as I had to travel to that area to give a talk on the work of the Mission. I also made some very good friends amongst the staff and volunteer workers. One advantage of being so busy is that it makes the time pass quickly. After the first week a new night watchman was taken on, so things eased somewhat. The days ticked by until it was time to return, which was the greatest highlight of all! Rose met me from the train, and the warmth of her greeting made the whole experience worthwhile. And, yes, separation does make the heart grow fonder. My abiding memory of Glasgow remained as a city of trams, pubs and hospitals. My first impression of meanness (brought about by that small joint of beef, and being billeted in the YWCA because it was cheaper) was replaced by the kindness and generosity of the staff and friends I met.

This was not the only time that we were separated during our courtship. Apart from the Missions at Victoria Docks and Gravesend, the Society also boasted a 'Floating Mission' on the River Thames. This was a converted vessel renamed the *John Ashley*. Historians will know that The Reverend John Ashley, a Church of England clergyman back in 1835, took his young son for a walk on Penarth cliffs (where he was on holiday) to show him the ships at anchor waiting to come into the port. The little boy gazed at them for a long time, then turned to his father and asked, 'Who looks after the men when they come into port, Daddy?' John Ashley thought for a moment, then said, 'No one'. He was profoundly affected by his answer and determined to do something about it. Being a man of independent means he immediately resigned his parish, and moved down to South Wales. He hired a rowing boat and rather hesitantly set out to visit his first ship. He was amazed and gratified by the warmth of the reception he received. Thus encouraged, he continued visiting ships and soon realized that there was a real ministry waiting to be developed. He also came to see that what the men wanted was to have somewhere safe to go when they came ashore. They were used to being met, not by friendly faces, but by those who were after their money! It has often been said that seamen have more to fear from the sharks on the shore than of the sea! Especially in those early days, when men were paid off with cash, there were many waiting to fleece them as they stepped ashore.

John Ashley purchased an old wreck lying on the beach, and had it renovated sufficiently to enable it to be used as a basic mission. In it he set up a writing room and library, as well as a small hall which doubled as a chapel. From these humble beginnings The Missions to Seamen has grown to a society that has well over 150 stations all over the world, serviced by chaplains and their staffs. Never in my wildest dreams did I ever envisage that one day I would be such a chaplain, serving in London, Hong Kong, Dar-es-Salaam, Bangkok and Rotterdam.

The current *John Ashley*, plied the River Thames, visiting the ships moored up on the buoys, either waiting for a berth, or unloading onto lighters. In due time I was detailed off for a week's tour of duty. The *John Ashley* was at that time operated by Padre Freddie Laight (who, being the first priest I served under in Cardiff, guaranteed me a very warm welcome). The accommodation was sparse, the food very basic, and the work taxing. One took one's turn in being sailor, cook, movie operator, librarian and cleaner, working all hours, sometimes in very bad weather. We would pull alongside a ship berthed on the river, clamber on board and introduce ourselves. In time the *John Ashley* became very well known, and visits were eagerly looked forward to, but in the very early days we could never be sure of our reception. However, just as with the first John Ashley, our visits were usually extremely well received. The men used to love to come on board, exchange books in our library, sometimes attend a short service in the tiny chapel, or just talk. Some of their most precious possessions were photos of their families, which they proudly produced and expanded upon. Apart from the chapel, canteen and library, the main hold was where we showed movies. I quickly became an expert at this, and at first enjoyed watching the films (although I must admit that after seeing the same film six times running, the novelty wore off). We also had the usual games, chess, packs of cards, dominoes, etc. One thing I did become expert at was playing draughts. A skill I have retained to this day ... the trouble is no one will now play with me! I found the whole experience most rewarding. However, I missed Rose a great deal, so it was not with too heavy a heart that we eventually pulled up alongside a jetty and, like any sailor going off on leave, I was up and away back to Victoria Docks, and Rose.

The weeks flew by, and the wedding was suddenly only just over a week away. We used to hold weekly dances at the Mission, at which I used to be MC. About thirty girls (mainly nurses from the local hospital) used to attend the dances. Unbeknown to us, they had made a collection to buy us a wedding present. Marjorie Guthrie warned us that during the evening whilst we were dancing there would be a roll of drums, the music would stop and that we were to remain where we were. Sure enough, came a roll on the drums, people all around us melted away and we were left alone in the centre of the floor. The roll of drums continued and a side door was opened, obviously to allow someone to make an entrance. Instead there was an almighty crash, followed by an agonizing silence. Then, after what seemed an eternity, Marjorie Guthrie appeared through the open door, carrying a huge tray, that had on it a couple of plates, two cups and a broken sugar bowl! The rest of the pieces lay in hundreds of broken shapes on the floor. On a more positive note, the chef on a Union Castle ship in port had made us an incredibly beautifully decorated wedding cake, which was not dropped, but duly presented, greatly admired, and devoured at the wedding.

Chapter 8

Our Wedding

I had for quite a while been suffering with toothache and was determined to have everything in apple pie order before the great day. I had booked an appointment with the dentist, who took one look in my mouth and said, 'right, two teeth are coming out'. Out they came and I left, not feeling too bright, but glad that the ordeal was over. That night I woke up in a pool of blood, my gums heavily bleeding and I was rushed by ambulance to the local hospital and immediately admitted. They had a difficult task stopping the bleeding which necessitated me being detained for four days. This meant that the last-minute arrangements, including buying the wedding ring (the insurance money only came three days before the event) still had to be purchased. Guess who went with Rose to buy it – Steph. Rose giggled when the shop assistant, assuming Steph to be the bridegroom, said, 'I presume you will be in mufti on the day, Sir?' In the end I was still in hospital on the day of the wedding, and had to sign myself out against the hospital's wishes, so that I could be present. Steph fetched me a chair to sit on during the ceremony, as well as fortifying me with a glass of brandy (my first ever!) just before it began. They say it is usually the bride who has all the fuss made of her but on our wedding day it was me!

That apart, it was a truly wonderful day and everyone did us proud. The decorations, the food and the happiness flowed, and when later we boarded the train (in a first-class department, another first) I was the happiest person in the world. The journey down to Seaford didn't take very long, but long enough for us to open up lots of envelopes that had been pressed into one hand or another during the day, all of them containing gifts of money. This ensured that we had no financial problems over the honeymoon period and could even splash out on a few occasions as well. The honeymoon

Our wedding day, 13th September 1952

was magical, despite the fact that we were only in a bed and breakfast hotel, so had to be out all day. Luckily the weather was perfect and we enjoyed long walks over the cliffs and downs. We returned one week later, and on the train back counted out what we had left. Thirteen shillings and sixpence, I remember, enough to last us until the next payday.

We returned to a tiny little flat that had been prepared for us (a palace as far as we were concerned) with its own front door, privacy, and all we needed for our first home. There was only one drawback: because the whole building was centrally heated we had no fireplace. In those days there was no television so one needed a piece of furniture as a focal point. So on our very first payday we ventured forth and brought an electric fire (our first ever hire purchase!). Over the years we purchased many more items of furniture and fittings, but nothing ever replaced the thrill of that first purchase as man and wife.

Our marriage brought about an immediate change in our fortunes. In those days a husband and wife were not both allowed to be employed by the Mission. The reason: they expected the wife to be an unpaid curate! History shows that's exactly what Rose became. Without any shadow of doubt she became 'the power behind the throne'. But our dual role as a team only began once I was ordained. In London, however, we just could not afford to live on a lay reader's salary, so Rose had to look for another job. It was soon forthcoming in, of all places, the central office of the Missions to Seamen. What about the non-working Mission wife rule, you might well ask? The problem was solved because she worked for a clergyman who had an office there but was not strictly speaking employed by the Mission. In fact, Rose was a highly trained and very efficient secretary, and as a result her salary increased considerably. For the first four years of our life together (one in London, and three in Hong Kong), during which time she worked as a secretary, she earned far more than I did! Needless to say the extra money was a great help. There was another advantage. Being at head office she became a mine of information, and often knew about a forthcoming event or item of news before I did.

She came home from work one day and told me that the padre stationed at Hong Kong was coming home on leave during which time he was going to select a lay reader to go out and work with him on a three year contract. Shortly afterwards I was agreeably surprised to be told to present myself at head office on a particular day for an interview – not so pleased when I arrived to find there were other Mission lay readers also present. As I was the newest and the youngest I didn't expect to be chosen, and indeed as the weeks went by and I heard nothing I put the whole matter out of my mind. Until one day, about a month later, Rose said over our evening meal, 'What are you doing on (and named a date about six weeks away)?'

'Nothing special as far as I know,' I replied.

'What about taking me on a slow boat to China?' were her next words! She then told me that I had been selected to be chaplain's assistant in Hong Kong. Two current songs at that time were *I'd like to get you on a slow boat to China* and *They tried to tell us we're too young* (which was the advice so many gave when we decided to get married). They became our favourite songs, and indeed remained so for the next twenty-eight years.

The news of my appointment was not universally welcomed. Rose's parents, who up to this point had been very supportive, now turned against me. She was the baby of her family, and very much loved. 'How dare you take her to the other side of the world?' they demanded. I don't think they ever really forgave me. My father's reaction was the opposite. 'The further away he goes,' he volunteered, 'the better!' Other comments hinted at unfair influence (because Rose was working at head office). Rose, however, was strongly supportive, especially over the opposition from her parents, but in any case before we knew it we were on our way.

HONG KONG

Chapter 9

On 'A Slow Boat to China'

We set sail on a Ben Line 11,000-ton tramp called the *Bennatow*. It was manned by British officers and Chinese crew and had accommodation for eleven passengers, most of whom were young tea planters going to Singapore. Having only been married for a few months, it became an extended honeymoon for us. I like to think that Rose only had eyes for me, but as she was stunningly beautiful, and the only woman on board, the same could not be said about anyone else! In 1953 wives of crew members were not allowed to sail with the ship, although in later years, senior officers and then other crew members were allowed to bring their wives.

Thinking about it now, it must have been difficult for some of the married men to see us together, although nothing was ever said. They knew I was going out to work with the Missions to Seamen in Hong Kong and, without exception, thought a great deal of the Society's work, and admired the chaplains, and their assistants. Not so the tea planters however! More than one of them told Rose that if she wasn't happy with me, she only had to come down to Singapore, and they would look after her!

Our first port of call was Gibraltar. I will never forget the thrill of sailing through the Straits and shortly afterwards seeing the 'Rock' come into view as the early morning mist lost its battle to the rising sun. Going ashore for the first time on foreign soil (even if it was on British territory) was an unforgettable experience. We were there for about 48 hours, which was long enough for us to explore and meet the famous apes on the rock, have a ride in a horse-drawn vehicle, and have our photos taken standing by a British bobby!

The next thrill was going through the Suez Canal. There were lots of British troops on the banks but being only a tramp steamer they took very little notice of us. Not so the next time we went

'On a slow boat to China',
1953

through on a passenger ship. They lined the banks as we went past and called out to the passengers, 'Get your knees brown' – but that's another story!

We knew we were really on our way when we arrived at Aden. No sooner had we dropped anchor than we were surrounded by what they called 'Bum' boats. These were small boats crammed with everything imaginable to buy: leather goods of every description, clothes, pictures, toys, you name it and they had it. Goods came up to you in buckets; you inspected, bargained, and then either retained the article, or sent the money agreed back down in the bucket. Aden was a duty-free port, which not only meant that things seemed incredibly cheap, but that there were a multitude of items not available in the UK: toys, cameras, binoculars, watches and anything you wanted. No sooner had you stepped ashore than wristwatches were on your wrists, binoculars around your neck, and leather belts around your waist; handbags on ladies' arms, and pornographic literature (although compared to today's copies pretty mild stuff) openly displayed. Without exception, however, the most sought-after goods were binoculars and mechanical toys from Japan. Again compared with today's toys unremarkable, but for us, post-war with nothing comparable in the UK, they were sensational.

An element to us that was entirely new was the concept of bargaining. Unheard of in the UK, in Aden it was the way of life. Crew members, and those who had been there before, would say only offer half the asking price to start. One would return to ship thrilled to bits with goods purchased, convinced that you were the best bargainer who had ever stepped ashore in Aden, only to find that someone else had bought the same item for 25 per cent less! Aden really was a paradise for those passing through, but the most abiding memory was not about buying anything but being offered money for something I possessed.

I have already told you that Rose was stunningly beautiful with jet-black hair, classical features, radiant skin and a perfect figure. It wasn't only on the ship that she turned heads! We were returning after yet another run ashore when a local Arab sidled up to me and said, 'How much do you want for your wife?' I was too shocked to reply, but he took my silence as a bargaining technique and said, 'I could get her into one of the best Harems, so I'll give you £5 for her.' Never has Rose clung more firmly and closely to my arm than she did then and all the way back to the safety of the ship. I have often joked that on the return journey three years later I looked in vain for that Arab, prepared to bargain, but alas I never saw him again.

We set sail for fresh waters amid growing excitement, as the Queen's Coronation was coming up, and a special dinner was planned to honour the occasion. The day duly arrived and we sat down in a beautifully decorated mess to enjoy a fabulous Chinese meal prepared by the crew. Exotic dishes followed one after the other, and the wine flowed. Some time later the Captain asked the chief steward if he knew why we were celebrating. 'Yes, Captain,' he replied. 'Today Queen Catchee clown top side!'

The journey so far had been full of excitement, new experiences and, as a consequence, provided much to ponder; the thrill of embarking on a ship for the first time and waking up to the vibration of the ship's engines; looking out of the cabin's porthole and seeing nothing but sea; going up on deck and seeing flying fish racing in the wake of the vessel; the wonder of suddenly seeing the Rock of Gibraltar rising majestically out of the mist; and above all experiencing the sheer thrill of being on such a journey with a new beautiful wife on 'a slow boat to China'. Together we journeyed through the Suez Canal, with awareness that geography learnt at school was actually coming to life before our eyes, followed by the unbelievable sense of adventure in going ashore in a foreign port. I was off to exotic Hong Kong as a servant of the church, knowing that the next three years would determine whether, or not, I did have a vocation to the ministry and that in three years' time I would either be returning to take up where I had left off in civil engineering, or entering theological college and training to be a priest.

There was also, I recall, a huge feeling of responsibility, because I was not going alone, but with a young beautiful wife at my side; someone who was prepared to sail into uncharted waters, leaving behind family and friends, partly in fulfilling her own vocation but, overridingly, to be with me. Such a level of excitement couldn't last, with one emotion following another in such quick order, and luckily it didn't. After leaving Aden we set sail across the Indian Ocean, not to see land for many days. So a routine settled around us, which allowed our feet to touch ground, and reality to take hold. Also, it must be admitted, a few doubts emerged. How would we settle in? We had been warned that some expatriates found it very difficult, if not impossible, to settle into such a very different way of life. How would I get on with my padre, and would I be able to fulfil the expectations that had resulted in my appointment? Would we be able to manage on my salary, or would Rose have to get a job? What sort of accommodation would we have? Many of these questions (with hindsight) should have been asked before we left, but lack of experience decreed that none of these queries had, up to this moment, even crossed our minds. There was, on the other hand, a total trust in God (although experience over the years proved that you can't leave everything to him!). Mission field or not, we learnt that God helps those who help themselves. The enthusiasm and optimism of youth won the day, however, as we sailed on into balmy days and beautiful sunsets, enjoying wonderful food, and new experiences, our happiness was complete. It proved to be the perfect honeymoon that augured well for the future.

Our next port of call was Kosichang in Thailand. We anchored in the bay and waited with great excitement for the agent's launch to come alongside. We were disappointed to learn that we were not going alongside, but that our cargo would be discharged and loaded from lighters. We would discharge in three days, and then take a week to load up with rice. Sadly no one gave us the opportunity to go ashore, and we were too ignorant of the procedures to ask. In later years we found that Bangkok, the capital of Thailand was only about 35 miles away. If the truth were known we had no money anyway. As we lay at anchor, we had no idea that twenty years later we would be living in Bangkok. As it was, we swung around the hook for the best part of a fortnight before finally setting sail for our final destination – Hong Kong.

There was just one more port of call before we reached Hong Kong and that was Singapore. This was where some of our fellow passengers were leaving the ship, which meant of course that they had many contacts and friends there. Some of them came down to greet and invite them to a party that evening, to which we were also thrilled to be included. We were taken to a fantastic house (the owners, we were told, were millionaires) where the party was to take place. We were amazed therefore that when it came to the meal, it was provided in part by a street vendor, who appeared on a glorified sort of tricycle, complete with oven, on which the food was cooked. It was our first taste of noodles, which were delicious. It was also the first time we had encountered chopsticks and as there were no other eating utensils, we very quickly learnt how to use them. Not only were we invited to that party, but during the week that the ship was in port we were taken out on no less than three other evenings, so we experienced the delights of Singapore.

They included the incredible and world famous Bugis Street. The whole area was full of fantastic restaurants, food stalls and vendors selling everything under the sun. Chicken kebabs were mouth-watering and moreish: we sat at a table overlooking the sea, helped ourselves to as many as we desired, and then placed the sticks in a pile. After which the vendor counted up the number in front of you, and charged you accordingly. But what had to be seen to be believed were the transvestites, plying their wares; it was impossible to tell that they weren't women, of incredible beauty, and possessed of fantastic figures. Understandably the atmosphere was electric, almost surreal.

The Chinese food, which could be eaten either in the restaurants or on tables outside, was out of this world. No matter what dishes one chose, the sweet was always the same. Durian, described as nutty and sweet, smelt terrible, but once you had acquired the taste, divine.

The botanical gardens were beautiful and a 'must' for tourists.

A transvestite from the famous Bugis Street, Singapore

At first we were thrilled to see the monkeys that lived in the park, but actually they became a nuisance, as they would steal food out of your hands. There were also two famous entertainment complexes known as 'the Old and New Worlds'. Singapore then was a wonderful combination of Chinese, Malayan and expatriate communities, harmoniously entwined. One part typically 'China town', another (particularly around the cathedral and the British Cricket Club) as English as you could get. The famous Raffles Hotel summed it all up, and justified Singapore being known as the gateway to the East. As far as Rose and I were concerned it just heightened our excitement and anticipation for Hong Kong, in which we were not disappointed.

Chapter 10

Life in Hong Kong

We entered Hong Kong by night, which, even in those early days of colourful advertising, was a magical experience. The lights of Hong Kong are surely one of the wonders of the world. Not only were we greeted by a blaze of colour, but also the neon lights in Chinese letters and signs. Apart from the signs there were also the lights of the buildings and houses on the peak. I was reminded of the biblical verse, 'Lift up your eyes unto the hills from whence cometh your hope'. If we didn't know it before, we knew it now – we had arrived in the mysterious, exotic Far East. We tied up alongside the famous Kowloon wharf, already occupied by about five liners. The agent brought us a message from the Mission, saying that due to the lateness of the hour, they would not pick us up until the following morning. So in great excitement and with no little apprehension we spent our last night on board.

The Mission launch, *The Dayspring* (so named from *Luke 1. 78*, '*The dayspring from on high has visited us*'), came about 9.30 am, by which time we had been ready for about three hours, and said our thank yous and goodbyes. In no time at all we had disembarked, climbed on board the launch, and sped across the harbour to Wanchai on Victoria Island, which is where the Mission was. It took some getting used to seeing the padre dressed not in a suit but in shorts and an open-necked shirt. There was a crew of four on the launch, the captain, the engineer and two sailors. Padre was very keen on things being shipshape and, as we landed at the pier opposite the Mission, it was done in the style of a Royal Navy VIP barge, with boat hooks at the ready. There was a reception group awaiting us made up from the staff at the Mission, as well as some of the local committee, which was overwhelming for both of us. After introductions we were escorted to our accommodation in the Mission, which turned out to be a lounge with a small bedroom off it. We were left on our own for a few minutes before Jimmy (who was to be our servant) appeared with a lovely grin on his face, and a pot of tea. After drinking it Rose asked the first very pertinent question, 'Where's the loo?' No matter how hard we looked we couldn't find it, for the simple reason there wasn't one.

My first question then to padre, who had retired to his office, was 'where is it?' Padre, I might add, was a bachelor, and seemed rather taken aback by the question. 'Oh, it's just along the corridor from your flat,' he answered rather nonchalantly.

'Yes I've found that myself,' I replied, 'but that is marked up as the men's toilet.'

'I know,' he replied, 'you will just have to stand guard outside whilst Rose is in there!' Not a very good beginning to our first half hour in our new home. I didn't like his answer one little bit, but that was nothing compared to the reaction by Rose. The honeymoon was now definitely over! So was my honeymoon period with my new padre.

In some trepidation I returned to his office and told him very forcibly that such a situation was not satisfactory, and that something would very soon have to be done about it. It was not easy to stand eyeball to eyeball with one's boss within an hour of arriving on the other side of the world. I felt very vulnerable, but tried not to show it. They say that faint heart never wins a fair lady, so I stuck to my guns, and won the day. Within a month, there was a small bathroom installed off our bedroom and my days of standing guard outside the men's toilet were over. The second unpleasant fact to rear its head was the small amount of the pay I was to receive. It would barely be enough to support Rose and myself. The crowning indignity, however, was when it was conveyed to us very forcefully that we were not to have children during the tour. There was neither the accommodation nor the wherewithal for us to have them. All this goes to show you just how naive we were back in 1953. There was no studying the small print – why? Because there was none to study!

Luckily Rose was immediately offered a very good job as personal secretary to the company secretary of Jardine Matheson, the most prestigious and famous firm in Hong Kong, its beginnings apparently shrouded in drug smuggling.

Apart from the Mission on the island, there was a Merchant

The Missions to Seamen, Hong Kong

Navy Sports Club on the mainland, and it was here that most of the sporting activities including football matches were played, the arranging of which was one of my major responsibilities. Within a short time I was appointed as manager, and the extra income ensured, together with Rose's salary (which nevertheless far exceeded mine) that we were able to live comfortably if not lavishly during our three years in the colony.

The main Mission was a wonderful building. It contained accommodation for about fifty men. This was used mainly by officers studying for their certificates, and for the changeover of ships' crews. It was also home for many Chinese seamen, when they left their ship for leave. It boasted a very fine church; officers' and other ranks' lounges; a large hall with stage that was used for many events, including dances, which were very popular; a restaurant and snack bar; games rooms; curio and other shops including a hairdresser, and a photograph shop. This meant that we were able to supply most of the seafarers' needs. The Mission was built around an open courtyard with balconies on every floor that looked down on it. This made a natural arena, which was used by both the Merchant and Royal Navy personnel for boxing matches, which were eagerly anticipated and greatly enjoyed.

The Mission had an interesting background. During the Second

The Mission Launch *Dayspring 11*

World War it was used as a brothel for Japanese officers, and there existed a strange echo of this to my day. As I started to familiarize myself with the workings of the Mission I was surprised to find that no matter how busy or slack we were, certain bedrooms were always booked. They were at the back of the Mission, which meant they were separated only by a very narrow lane from the houses on the other side of the road. This surprisingly was the attraction – why? Because the building opposite housed a brothel. In the hot weather windows and curtains were kept open, and at such times those facing rooms were very popular indeed!

The staff of the Mission numbered about fifty. There was a European manager called Joe Hawkins, but all the rest were Hong Kong Chinese. I played no part in the actual administration of the Mission, but got to know them all very well over the three years we were there, and was much richer in human relationships as a consequence. Joe was a particularly interesting character. He had lived in Hong Kong for most of his life, was married to a Chinese lady, which meant his background created the perfect base for dealing with Chinese staff. He was particularly helpful to me as my sense of vocation developed and, as I later notified the Warden of Ordinands back in South Wales, he examined my background and soon picked up that I needed better academic qualifications than I had at present before I could be accepted on a theological course. So I embarked through correspondence courses on a matriculation course, which required about two hours' study per day. Finding the time was one thing, finding somewhere to study was another. Joe came to my rescue by secretly giving me one of the rooms, where I could retreat without anyone even knowing where I was. That I passed was in large part because of his thoughtfulness and help.

There was also a retired Nonconformist minister called Ian who used to help out at holidays and other times. Like all retired clergy he was also called upon from time to time to officiate, particularly at funerals. Sadly, he was crippled, with the result that one leg was much shorter than the other, and he wore a very thick and heavy boot on the affected leg. This tended to make him rather slow and ponderous in movement, but not (being a typical Nonconformist) in oratory! Soon after we arrived a local ship's captain died and, as Ian had known him for many years, he was asked to officiate at his cremation. A brand new crematorium had recently been built in the colony, so, partly out of respect for the captain, but also because we wanted to see this magnificent new building, we all went along. The coffin was placed on a platform, which on cue descended down through the floor, creating a grave-like atmosphere. There was a little contraption that the minister held in his hand, which, at the appropriate moment (by pressing the button), activated the descent of the coffin. Anglicans tend to use a set liturgy on such occasions, whereas Nonconformists are happier with extempore prayers, which, with due respect, could go on for a bit! Ian was so involved in the full flight of prayer that he forgot where he was standing. At the appropriate moment he pressed the button and the coffin started to go down. Unfortunately for Ian, he started going down with it! At first, being so wrapped up in prayer, he didn't notice that he was on the move. But I did, and as he started disappearing further and further from sight I decided it was time to act. 'Ian,' I called out rather desperately, 'you're going down with the coffin.' My cry brought Ian out of his prayer but not onto safe ground, as he continued on a downward path. He then realized what was happening and his cries for help could I am sure have been heard all around the colony! Being a cripple didn't help matters, as he could do nothing to help himself. Willing hands, however, rushed forward and grabbed his arms, which were by now all that was left in view. The dead weight as he dangled helplessly nearly proved too much (I know I was in danger of joining him) but others joined in the rescue, and slowly but surely he was pulled to the surface. That proved to be the first and last service at which Ian officiated at the Crematorium.

I quickly settled into my new routine. My main tasks were not to rescue ministers but to visit the ships as soon as possible after they arrived; to enquire if all was well, and if there was anything we could do for them; to organize events, and display posters on the activities that were already arranged. There were at any one time about forty ships in the port, ranging from huge liners most of which took up the shore berths, to small tramps, which plied the Chinese coast and anchored in the inner and outer harbours. There was also a permanent force of Royal Fleet Auxiliary ships, which meant we got to know the crew members very well. There was also the Royal Navy base 'Tamar', with a constant influx of Royal Navy ships. They had their own chaplains of course; nevertheless there was a lot of interaction between the RN and the Merchant Navy. The RN had their own club, The China Fleet Club, which was situated next door to the Mission.

My duties also included arranging for libraries to be delivered to the ships, and exchanging them with the library already on board. Books were provided by The Seafarers Education Service, which had bases all over the world, including Hong Kong. They also arranged education courses for seamen, and we acted as agents by helping men who wished to avail themselves of this service.

A very time-consuming part of my work was arranging football matches for visiting ships. In those days nearly every ship of any size had its own team and gear, and there was even a ships' football league, which was keenly contested. We also arranged rugby and cricket matches from time to time. Sometimes a ship would be one or two short of a full team, which meant finding players from other ships, as well as making up the numbers myself. As a consequence I became extremely fit, and on many occasions refereed a football match, played in the next, then finished off the afternoon by refereeing the third.

The crew apart, the Mission launch could accommodate fifteen men so was invaluable for ship visiting, picking up men from their ships and taking them either to shore, the Mission or the sports ground. Another popular event was launch picnics, including surfboard riding. We would draw alongside a ship and welcome the invited party on board. There were some wonderful islands off Hong Kong with exotic beaches, perfect for picnics. The temperature of the water was ideal for swimming and surfboard riding, and as a consequence these events were always quickly booked up and very much appreciated, especially riding the surfboard. After everyone who wanted to had a try we moved closer to the beach and dropped anchor. Most seamen could swim, especially those who came on these outings, but that did not mean that they were all good at it. We had to be continually on the alert for men who were tiring, or who had swum too far out to sea. This meant that the person in charge had to be a competent swimmer himself. All too often that meant me, and as I wasn't a very good swimmer when I arrived, I knew that I had to do something about it.

The Royal Navy was continually running life-saving classes, so I duly enrolled in one. The course was very challenging, especially as every test was done not in a pool, but in the sea. The day for the life-saving exam arrived and it was a very nervous candidate who lined up with the others. I knew I was the weakest in the group, and to this day am convinced that it was only because I was one of a mutually supportive class that I passed. I don't remember all the tests, but apart from what one had to do, there were time limits for doing them. I found myself at the tail end of nearly every exercise, but by a huge mental and physical act of willpower I managed to stay up with the others. In the end there was a 100 per cent pass rate. The PE instructor was very pleased with us, but no one was more relieved than me, or more proud to have my life-saving badge sewn on my costume. The mere fact that I had it gave me a lot of confidence, which was just as well as very shortly afterwards I had to put all my newly won skills to the test.

Older residents told us that before the Second World War there were no sharks around the islands, but that during the Japanese occupation they started to appear. This followed when the Japanese killed Hong Kong residents and threw the bodies into the sea. As a consequence there were now lookout posts in some of the popular surfboard areas. To ride a surfboard one had to swim out to the surfboard, which was attached to a rope about 30 yards long. The rider lay on the board, the launch started up and, once the rope was taut, he climbed onto the board, stood up and then sped through the water, manoeuvring it according to his ability. The trouble was at the end you had to fall off, at which point the launch turned round to pick you up. On one such occasion a seaman who was next in line to have a go jumped into the water and swam out to the board but took much longer than was usual. It became obvious to me that he was not a strong swimmer. However, he reached the board and off we went, but no sooner had he stood up than the lookout sounded the shark-warning siren, which meant that everyone had to leave the water.

He of course had only one option and that was to fall off, which he did. It immediately became very obvious that he was in trouble. There was nothing for it but for me to dive in and get him out. By the time I reached him he was in serious trouble, panicked and grabbed me, pulling us both under the water – and all this with sharks in the vicinity! My training enabled me to break the hold, turn him on his back, calm him down and wait until willing hands pulled him on board, and then me. There was no more surf-riding that day, and indeed after that incident we changed the rules, allowing only those who were competent swimmers to have a go. As a consequence there were some who were not allowed to surf-ride, but they had their enjoyment when we moved into shallow water, dropped anchor and went ashore for the picnic.

Amongst every group there was usually at least one character who proved to be a pain in the neck! I soon devised a way to deal with these! As we neared the beach of the island where we were going to drop anchor, I sidled up to him and said in a whisper. 'If I tell you something, promise me you won't tell anyone else.'

'Cross my heart, padre,' was the usual reply.

'Well,' I would continue in a confidential undertone, 'on the other side of the island there is a nudist colony, and if you climb up the hill to that point, you overlook it and enjoy a marvellous view!' Invariably of course he would tell his mate and as soon as we landed they would disappear from view. No sooner had they gone than I told everyone else what I had done. Hong Kong was very hot in the midday sun, so climbing up a steep hill through thick undergrowth was very tiring indeed. About half an hour later

The wife of the Governor of Hong Kong visits the Mission

they would reappear in the clearing I had indicated, looking in vain for the colony that wasn't there. We would all shout from the beach where we had been enjoying an ice-cold beer, and they would realize they had been conned. I very rarely had any more trouble with that individual for the rest of the day.

The work was not of course only caring for the material and social needs of the seafarers, but for their spiritual wellbeing as well. I must say, however, that being very new to the work and the workings of the church, this aspect of the seafarers' wellbeing I left very much to the padre. One event in which I was actively involved, however, was in inviting all cadets in port over the weekend to come to the Sunday evening church service at the Mission, to be followed by dinner with the padre in his flat. One of the highlights I remember was making the cadets eat their sweets (including jelly!) with chopsticks. This always caused a laugh!

Apart from our Mission duties and contacts, we also made friends with other expatriates who worked and lived in Hong Kong. There was one particular friend who (for reasons that will become clear) shall be nameless. He was, we believed, a hardened bachelor, who had a very fine flat, a very efficient servant, and entertained us and many others royally on many occasions. The time came for him to go on leave, and after fond farewells he left, promising to send us the usual postcard whilst in the UK. What duly arrived was not a postcard but a long letter telling us that he had met and fallen in love with a wonderful girl, had proposed and been accepted, and would be returning shortly to arrange the wedding. It was a transformed friend who returned, had the flat completely redecorated, and enthusiastically made all the necessary arrangements for the great day. He decided that, as Hong Kong would be new to her, they would not go away on their honeymoon, but use their flat as a base from which to explore the delights of the Island and the mainland in Kowloon.

She arrived the day before the wedding and we gave her accommodation for the night, as our friend was determined to carry her over the threshold for the first time on the great day. Everything went perfectly. The bride was beautiful, the service perfect, the reception fabulous. As was inevitable the time came for the bride and groom to say their goodbyes and leave, which they did. We didn't expect to hear from either of them for a long time, so I was amazed to receive a tearful phone call the very next morning, with the plea for me to please come round immediately and try and sort something out. On arrival an embarrassed husband and a weeping wife met me. The problem was quickly revealed. She loved the wedding, the flat, and everything that followed, and fell asleep in a state of bliss. The trouble came about half past seven the following morning. She was awakened by the servant shaking her into life, smacking her on her bottom and saying in a well-rehearsed voice, 'Come on, Missie, it's time to go home!' I remember preaching shortly afterwards on the theme 'Be sure your sins will find you out'!

Most of the seamen we worked with were birds of passage, so it was not so easy to make close friends, but some would come and stay for a longer period. One such person was an officer called Alan Jerkins, who was at that time fourth engineer on a ship with an Asian crew. Towards the end of his watch (as was normal practice) he toured the engine room to see all was in order, and stumbled over a dead body lying on the floor. To his horror he saw that he had had his throat cut. Standing near him was an Asian crewman who admitted knifing him because he had been insulted. Alan quickly summoned assistance. The man was apprehended and the ship made for the nearest port, which proved to be Kobe in Japan. A Royal Navy frigate duly arrived and took the prisoner away.

Because it was a British registered ship, the murder trial had to take place in a British colony, the nearest being Hong Kong. Alan was required to be present as a witness, so was paid off his ship and sent to us at the Mission. I befriended him as best I could, although I never realized the state of his distress, or that he was having continual nightmares as he relived the moment he found the body with the head almost completely severed. Alan was a very keen sportsman so I was able to fit him into many ships football teams, and table tennis matches. I used to take him ship visiting, and included him in as many launch picnics as possible, and Rose and I also tried to involve him in our social life. We learned that he was engaged to be married, was missing his fiancée terribly and longing to get home. In all I think he was with us for about four months, so I got to know him very well and we became firm friends. Nevertheless, I did no more for him than any of the other seamen I met in the course of my work. With new and exciting things happening all the time, if I am honest, once he left, he became just one of literally hundreds, even thousands, of seamen who passed through our hands.

I was delighted, therefore, when some years later I received a letter from him, updating me on all that had happened since he left Hong Kong, and saying that he would love to meet me again. The opportunity arose for me to have a little break so I duly went up to Peterlee, just outside Newcastle, and met him and his wife. I had a wonderful few days with them, much of it spent on the golf course, as we were both very keen players. I was simply amazed and somewhat overcome when he recounted the time he spent in the Hong Kong Mission. Probably because of the trauma he was going through at that time he had a photographic mind of the tiniest details that had completely slipped my memory. He had mementos, photos, papers, and stories galore to recount, most of which I had completely forgotten. But what amazed me most of all referred, not to his time in Hong Kong, but some time later. He decided to leave the sea and take up teaching; his wife Maureen already being in the profession, supported him 100 per cent. He trained and duly qualified before going on his first job interview. He was shaken, however, when he found about eight others who were also applying for the post. Each of them was asked to write a short essay on the person who had most influenced him in his life. The person Alan wrote about (so his wife informed me) was me. As already stated, although I did all I could for him at a very difficult time, I really did no more for him than for any other seaman – it was not specifically what I did for Alan Jenkins that impresses, as much as the work of the Missions to Seamen in general.

Hong Kong was not only our first posting abroad, it was also of course our introduction to the expatriate way of life. Many expatriates find it very difficult to cope with a different culture, and our experiences echoed that fact. We were still young of course and that helped a lot. I was very lucky in that I made a good friend of a Hong Kong Chinese called Chui Kwok Hung, who was of similar age and interests to me, one of which was table tennis. He was in a different class to me, and indeed if he had taken it up professionally without doubt would have reached world-class status. In fact, the standard between the expatriate level of table tennis and the Chinese was so great, that even those of county standard couldn't compete. It was for this purpose that I set up a European table tennis league that became well established and very popular.

But back to Chui and our friendship. We played a great deal of

The winners of the European Table Tennis Championships

91

table tennis together, which no doubt brought my game on a huge amount. After a session we often would go out to a local Chinese restaurant for a meal. A typical Hong Kong restaurant was very much 'spit and sawdust', and anyone who has experienced 'the call of the east' will know what I mean. Under each table there was a large spittoon. The noise of 'the call of the east' (as it was universally known) was a constant backdrop to every conversation and meal. The Chinese had the habit of clearing their throats and then, with expert precision depositing the saliva into the spittoon. They say that one gets used to anything in time, but it is also true to say that some things are easier to get used to than others! On one occasion, and after I had got to know Chui very well, 'the call of the east' was particularly vibrant in the restaurant where we were eating. In some exasperation I turned to Chui and said, 'I find that pretty revolting'.

Chui looked at me for a long time and then replied, 'not as revolting as something you do!'

'What's that?' I indignantly replied.

Chui said, 'Well, if I can bring myself to mention it, you take out a handkerchief, blow your nose, and then put the filthy thing back in your pocket!'

There was, however, a far deeper cultural gap between us, which was in the difference of our religion. I often went to his house and always found, in a very prominent place, a Chinese altar to the gods with joss sticks burning, giving off their unmistakable sweet aroma. After about two years, by which time we were very firm friends and I knew I wouldn't offend him; I raised the subject of religion. Chui was an extremely intelligent person, well educated, and very bright. He loved to discuss serious matters so was very willing to talk about his faith once the subject was raised. I said to him, 'Chui, I don't understand how a person of your intelligence and learning, including some knowledge of Christianity, can gain satisfaction in worshipping joss sticks.'

What he told me affected me deeply, and made me even more ecumenically minded than I was before. Chui worked as a civilian clerk for the British Army stationed in the colony. At one stage in his employment he was appointed to the chaplain's office. His nature being as it was, it was not surprising that he became interested in Christianity and one day asked the chaplain if it were possible for him to attend some form of instruction. The British forces supply chaplains for Anglicans, Roman Catholics, and Nonconformists, as well as Jews. Depending on the size of the garrison, so the number of chaplains. At this time Hong Kong only had one. It matters not, from the point of this story, of which persuasion he was, sufficient to say that he agreed to give Chui instruction, which he did. As was inevitable, he came to the end of his tour of duty and was duly posted elsewhere.

His replacement was of a different persuasion, however, and although he agreed to continue instructing Chui, he caused much confusion by conflicting teaching. Nevertheless, Chui persisted in his learning and after a while came to terms with the different emphases being conveyed. Then disaster struck. The new chaplain was taken ill and sent back to the UK. The third chaplain appointed was of a different persuasion altogether, and told Chui in no uncertain terms that a lot of what he had been taught was wrong, and the only true Christian faith was the one to which he belonged. By now Chui was so confused and disillusioned that, as he put it, 'I went back to my joss sticks'.

We were privileged to attend some wonderful parties and functions in houses and hotels during our time in Hong Kong, but what I found far more satisfying was helping people from the opposite end of the spectrum. I came to hear of a very poor family, consisting of a Chinese husband and an English wife, with many children. They lived in a tenement block facing the harbour, not very far from the Mission. I determined to visit them and see if there was any way in which I could help, but was not prepared for what I found. The whole family lived, ate and slept in one large room. The baby's cot was hanging up on the wall! Apart from the baby there were three young girls, with the oldest about eight years of age. The mother only had one child's dress however, which meant that the family could never all go out at the same time! Despite their poverty and the lack of space the room was spotlessly clean, and the mother retained a quiet dignity that could not fail to impress. I was able to help out with some clothes, etc.

There were also many orphans on the island with little hope of a worthwhile future. So 'Stanley Seafarers Training School' was set up, where children were not only cared for but also taught the elements of seamanship, so that on reaching the right age we could find employment for them at sea. Rose was a highly efficient secretary, so worked on a voluntary basis as secretary to the school.

That orphanage is still going strong today and I sometimes marvel how many young people's lives have been transformed because of Rose and others' caring and selfless work.

Other attempts at changing lives were not as successful. Throughout the Orient begging in its various forms is a way of life. Outside Jardine Matheson offices right in the centre of Victoria was a prime spot for beggars and for many weeks a Chinese lady and her nude baby occupied it. During the cold season Hong Kong can be distinctly chilly, so the sight of a mother with her entirely unclothed infant touched many heartstrings, including Rose's. She was taken aback, however, after leaving work on the Friday (being payday) and giving rather generously from her wages, only to find on the following Monday that the same lady was back in place, holding the same unclothed baby! Nothing deterred, both of us decided to put a stop to this once and for all. We took mother and baby to one of the many stores in the city, and clothed her from top to toe with new clothes. Mother profound in her thanks, Rose and I pleased with our ingenious plan, left her with no mean sense of achievement. Twelve hours later Rose returned to work to find the same mother complete with nude baby, begging from the same spot!

Another ruse was, when boarding a sampan (a water taxi) at Stanley to get to the world famous fishing restaurants in the harbour, to be greeted by the lady of the boat and her small child. No sooner had the sampan pulled away from the jetty than the little child would advance with hand outstretched and say in perfect English, 'Hello, Daddy!'

Before leaving this little section on the poor, it should already be obvious that 'all that glisters is not gold.' This can work both ways. Take, for instance, the time when we were invited to a reception at the cathedral. I have forgotten what the occasion was, but I do remember that all the cathedral clergy were there, including the latest arrival and junior member of staff. He was sitting in a chair knitting a woollen carpet'. I remember turning to Rose and saying, 'The poor chap, he can't even afford to buy a carpet.' Doing the rounds we were introduced to him only to find out that he was Lord Beaumont, probably not only the richest clergyman but also possibly (at that time) one of the richest men in the world!

I cannot close this section without referring to Bishop Hall of Hong Kong, who shortly after the end of the Second World War became famous for ordaining the first ever woman to the priesthood. When the Japanese overran the Island all the chaplains were interned (including Cyril Brown, the Missions to Seamen Chaplain of Hong Kong at that time, who later became the General Secretary of the Society and actually appointed me to my post). As soon as the war was over those interned were repatriated, so for quite a long time there was a desperate shortage of clergy. The headmistress of one of the schools on the island, who was also a highly regarded deaconess, was ordained by Bishop Hall in an effort to overcome the shortage. When the news of his action reached Canterbury there was a huge outcry of protest. Bishop Hall was very gracious and withdrew her license to officiate, although her title was renewed many years later when, by an Act of Synod, women were ordained into the priesthood. I went to see him at his palace shortly after my arrival on the island. The first thing he did was to lead me into his private chapel to bless me. I was most impressed with his holiness and obvious concern for all. I had cause to visit him towards the end of my tour so made my way to the palace, which, to my surprise, I found was occupied by refugees from mainland China. I would find the bishop, I was told, at the rear of the palace. Sure enough that's where he was – in a ramshackle sort of tin outhouse built on to the side of his palace. It, like his previous office, was curtained off down the middle. As I entered he arose from his desk, led me through the curtain into the makeshift chapel on the other side, and again blessed me before we returned to his office for my interview. I will never forget him and believe him to be one of the few saints I have had the privilege to meet.

By contrast the opulence in the colony (especially coming from the UK so soon after the end of the war) was mind-boggling; not only for the very rich Chinese but also for the leading trading firms such as Jardine Matheson, which gave lavish parties on special anniversaries or other occasions. Because Rose worked for the company secretary we were invited to a very special anniversary party that went on for twenty-four hours! Each period of the day or night was enacted within the background of a different culture, complete with food and fantastic decorations. At twelve noon a group went off to West Point where the company's famous noonday gun was situated. Rose and I took the opportunity to sneak off and go home!

Paper-made house and car at Chinese funeral

The Chinese way of celebrating was different in that instead of firing the gun they let off extremely powerful and incredibly loud crackers. This was partly to scare away the evil spirits, hence the emphasis on noise. Another notable difference was their belief in the afterlife, which was reflected in their funerals. Cleverly made out of paper were all the things that the deceased liked most, whether they be cars, buildings, money or food. As part of the funeral service these images were burnt, so ensuring that when the deceased arrived on the other side, all that he needed was there waiting for him.

The funeral processions were very colourful and impressive, including bands loud in drums and cymbals. The more important (and rich) the deceased, the greater number of bands. We were watching one such occasion shortly after arriving in the colony, when a Chinese gentleman came up and said proudly, 'There are more bands in the procession today than were at the Queen's coronation!'

Sickness and death are hard enough to cope with when surrounded by families and loved ones. To be sick or dying thousands of miles from home denies those concerned even the small blessings and comfort. It is for this reason that I have always taken particular care to ensure that seamen in hospital were not left alone, and if possible visited on a daily basis. Every hospital in the colony had my telephone number with the request to contact me immediately should a seaman be admitted to one of their wards. Strangely enough, the main Seamen's Hospital was right at the top of the peak, and as I didn't have a car this meant using the famous peak tram. On one particular occasion I received a call from the hospital to say that a seaman had been taken off a ship passing by the colony and was in intensive care. It was, I remember, a beautiful day so I enjoyed the views from the tram as we climbed to the peak. The man I was visiting, however, could see none of this as he was unconscious, and actually remained so until he died some five hours later. I rang the Mission to say that I would be remaining with him until the end, which is what I did. As I sat holding his hand, my heart went out to those who would mourn his passing, even sadder because they couldn't have been with him at the end. I like to think that when they learnt that someone had been with him at his death, some comfort would be the result. Five hours can normally seem a long time, but on this occasion it passed in a flash.

With the end of the Second World War the British Government commandeered what remained of the German Merchant Navy, to replace the decimated British Merchant Fleet. Sadly it was a move that backfired as the Germans were forced to build new and improved ships containing the latest in technology. This meant that within a few years the British ships became competitively obsolete, which hastened the end of the British Merchant Navy as one of the largest in the world. We noticed this particularly in Hong Kong because whenever a new German ship came into port it drew either admiration or jealousy from the shipping fraternity.

Great excitement awaited the arrival of the *Schwabenstein* on her maiden voyage but excitement turned into dismay as she was ignominiously towed into port, because her main propeller shaft had broken. It transpired that a new shaft would have to be made in Germany and then brought out to the colony. This meant the ship and crew would be with us for about six months, giving us an excellent opportunity to get to know the crew and offer them help in every way possible. Their football team played about three times a week, and soon became excellent and far too strong for most of the other ships' teams. They were regular guests on our launch picnics, and great users of the facilities and activities we offered them at the Mission. Although by the very nature of the work a great deal of our activity was devoted to the material needs of the seamen, we were of course always there in case spiritual ministry was also required.

The following two examples show what I mean. By means of an introduction let me say that, when one visited a ship, there were four very important people with whom it was essential to establish good relationships. The first was obviously the Captain, but as he was always feted by his agents in port, most of the time it was no more than a courtesy call. The second was the Chief Engineer, being second to the captain, as well as in charge of all the engine crew, he also merited a courtesy call. (A few years ago the shipping association carried out a cost saving exercise to see how they could cut down the running expenses. The answer: 'The two people that were the least necessary were the Captain and the Chief Engineer'.)

The Chief Officer, on the other hand, not only ran the ship but was also the person who could give the crew time off for leisure activities, so was obviously a great man to have on your side. The fourth and almost equally important was the Chief Steward. Not only was he in charge of the catering staff but of the food as well. 'Would you like to stop on board for lunch?' were words of music to the ears after a busy morning of visiting up to a dozen ships, to say nothing of the glass of cold beer that came with it (wine wasn't as popular or common in those days). I was talking to the Chief Steward of the *Schwabenstein* one morning when he told me he was very worried about one of his men. He had been married shortly before the ship sailed for Hong Kong, and was obviously disappointed that the enforced wait due to the breakdown would delay his return to his young bride. But even more upsetting was the fact that she was writing him tearful letters that, as time passed, were becoming increasingly angry, complaining that he wasn't writing to her. The Chief Steward asked me if I would go and sort him out.

I cornered him in his cabin and started to read the riot act.

'But padre,' (I soon gave up trying to explain to the men that I wasn't a padre but only a lay reader) he said, fighting to keep the tears out of his eyes, 'I do write to her every day, I tell her how much I am missing and loving her and I can't understand why she says she isn't hearing from me.'

'Right,' I said, 'you sit down and write to her right now and then we will go ashore together to post it.' So I sat and waited whilst he duly wrote, signed and sealed the letter, and off we set towards the Post Office. We didn't however get that far before the mystery was solved. We left the dock area and proceeded alongside a large brick wall towards the shopping centre. About a hundred yards from the dock gates he stopped, took out his letter, kissed it and attempted to put it through an opening in the wall.

'What on earth are you doing,' I exclaimed in alarm. 'I'm posting my letter in the letterbox,' he replied.

'That doesn't say letterbox,' I exploded, 'it says litter box!'

Not quite the end of the story, because up to a few years ago I still heard from him – a happily married man with lots of children. As for the ship itself, delays continued and it became obvious that the crew would be with us over Christmas. Remembering that this was a German ship, that it was still shortly after the war, and that not many of the crew spoke English, I was surprised when the Captain asked me if I would take a service on board for them on Christmas morning. I readily agreed but I must say that it was with no little apprehension that I stood before the assembled crew to lead them in their worship. I needn't have worried. Amongst the carols we sang was 'Silent Night', which had its origins in their country. It was sung as sweetly as I have ever heard it. My address was mercifully short, but had a rapt congregation nevertheless, and as for the Lord's Prayer, to hear it in German for the first time was an extremely moving moment. I will treasure the memory of that service for as long as I live. In fact, I think the Mission's ministry to that stranded ship in Hong Kong shortly after the war epitomizes what the Missions to Seamen stands for – the material, social and spiritual welfare of all seafarers irrespective of nationality, colour or creed.

In Hong Kong there were, as in most colonial places, the very rich and the very poor. During our time there we had the opportunity to witness life in both spheres, and the difference was colossal. The rich lived in great opulence, in magnificent houses, with many

99

A typical junk in Hong Kong harbour

servants. The higher one's status the further one lived up the peak. One reason for this, in the early days before air conditioning was of course that the higher one went up the peak, the cooler it became. The peak tram and the Kowloon ferries always were, and always will be, institutions in the colony. There is an unwritten law that if anyone tries to commit suicide by jumping off the ferry and is rescued by a fellow passenger, then that person becomes responsible for his life thereafter. There was a time when suicide attempts were fairly common from the ferry, but thankfully this practice has become less popular in recent times.

In those days some of the most senior of British shipping companies, such as P & O, Blue Funnel and British India lines, ran cadet ships which had regular officers, with the engine and deck crews made up of cadets. We always made a special effort to do as much as possible for them, which was greatly appreciated. The cadets were of a very high calibre, but that does not mean that they didn't get into trouble from time to time, and had to be both literally and metaphorically 'bailed out'. On one occasion two cadets went to a local cinema where a film they particularly wanted to see was being shown. They arrived only to be told that the

100

cinema was full. They had to be back on duty later on that day, so they couldn't wait for the next performance. Not to be outdone, they marched in, evicted two indigenous citizens from their seats and settled down to enjoy the film. Not for long, however. The outraged citizens informed the local police who promptly came along and arrested them. In those days most of the junior police officers were British and through fairly constant contact I got to know them quite well. About 5 pm that afternoon I received a phone call from the duty Inspector.

'You'd better come down to the police station as soon as possible,' he said, 'I've got a couple of your cadets in the cage.' This was a steel-grilled area, where all prisoners were herded together before being dealt with on an individual basis. When I arrived the 'cage' was full of heaving bodies, and almost lost in the middle of it were the two cadets looking and feeling very sorry for themselves. Apart from being arrested they knew they were in serious trouble on the ship. In the first place, they would be missing when their shift started, which was considered a very serious offence. In the second place they seemed destined to spend a night in the cells, which meant being absent without leave. Finally, to have a criminal record meant automatic expulsion from the Merchant Navy, and an end to their careers.

All this I explained to the duty officer. At first he didn't want to know, but gradually he softened his stance and, to my great relief, agreed to let them out on bail which solved two problems. They could return in time to catch their shift, and would not be absent without leave. I thanked him profusely, but my words became stuck in my mouth when he told me the amount of the bail. It was beyond my means and a quick word with the cadets revealed that it was beyond their means too. Cap in hand, I went back to the Inspector. After offering up a silent prayer, I explained that we couldn't possibly raise the bail, so would he please lend us the difference. He was not amused but eventually turned out his wallet and offered what he had. Alas it still wasn't enough, so hardly daring to believe what I was saying I asked him if he could please reduce the bail. Presumably mesmerized by my cheek he agreed to an amount that was covered by his, mine, and the two cadets' available cash.

I took them back to their ship and arranged for them to be released from work the following morning. They duly appeared before the magistrate, who tore strips off them to such an extent that I believe they thought they would never see the UK again. What they didn't know was that I had been able to speak to him earlier and he agreed that a conviction (which would mean a criminal record, and therefore the end of their naval careers) was in the circumstances not the right penalty. He let them off with a very severe warning, and as a result two very relieved cadets, with, I'm sure, a lesson well learnt, were returned without any stigma to their ship.

My efforts on their behalf gave me a good name amongst the crews, so I was mortified one day when visiting another cadet ship to be approached by the Chief Officer, who told me in no uncertain terms to 'get off my ship before being thrown off'! I insisted on knowing why, and he proceeded in no uncertain terms to give me the answer: 'Because you are a paedophile' (although they were not the actual words he used).

I insisted on seeing the Captain, who said, 'Hello, John, what can we do for you?'

'Did you say "John", sir?' the Chief Officer asked the Captain. Being assured that he had, the Chief Officer turned to me and with profound apologies explained that he had accused the wrong man. Being 'the man from the mission', he had mistaken me for someone else. Another incident a few weeks later when a Royal Naval seaman who had been a guest for the night at the Mission complained to me of being sexually abused by a member of the chaplaincy staff, forced me to the conclusion that I had to do something drastic. Because the person concerned was one of the most well known and liked chaplains in the Society, whereas I was only a young and unknown lay reader, it took a tremendous amount of courage to report him. However I did and, despite his denials, he was within a very short while sent home.

There was, for us, a happy sequel to the story. The priest who came out to relieve him before a permanent chaplain was appointed, was wonderfully kind, and allowed us the use of one of his bathrooms whenever we wanted it. As we had only enjoyed showers for over two years this was a godsend.

Whilst in Hong Kong I was given a very fine camera, and enthusiastically took up photography. The harbour, with its junks, often coming out of the mist; the Chinese people, especially the elderly with their wonderfully lined faces; the brightly coloured neon signs; to say nothing of the magic of the shops' contents themselves, was a photographer's paradise. Slides were the 'in thing' at that time, and I loved to show them to anyone who wanted to see them. The new padre was an obvious victim, so one evening we retired to his flat, and I projected them onto a wall. The problem was that I was short-sighted so had to go close to the wall to see if they were in focus. Padre noticed this, and insisted that I had my eyes tested, which resulted in me wearing glasses from then on. I have already mentioned that upon our arrival in Hong Kong we were told that because our accommodation wasn't suitable we couldn't have any children. By pure coincidence we were not so blessed during our time in Hong Kong, yet on board ship during our return journey Rose conceived. Padre Lawler (for that was his name) insisted on taking credit for this because he claimed that it was because I was wearing glasses that Rose became pregnant!

Before we knew it, it was time for us to take our leave of the colony and return home. During our three years we had not only been blessed with some wonderful experiences, but I had become convinced that I wanted to be ordained. An interview with the Archbishop of Wales had been arranged for me shortly after our arrival in the UK and providing all went well I was to start training at Llandaff Theological College in the autumn. Our sadness at leaving the friends we had made was compensated for by the thought of what lay ahead.

The last few weeks were taken up with farewell parties, packing up the items we had collected, and saying our goodbyes. We also received an embarrassing amount of farewell presents, many of them to do with my passion for photography which almost led to disaster, as I shall reveal shortly. We had entered Hong Kong by night and departed early in the morning. Instead of the bright lights there was a mist over the waters, which hid the peak and most of the city of Victoria, including the Mission that had been our home for the last three years. So we slipped silently away, but left much behind; wonderful memories of the last three years; a sense of achievement, and of being truly blessed. Above all, the inner glow that confirmed my vocation to the ministry, and a sense of gratitude for everyone and everything that had made me certain that I now wanted to be a priest.

The path that had taken me from a vague feeling of being called to the church to the moment of truth, when I knew I wanted nothing else, was in large part due to the guidance and help I had received along the way. I was delighted therefore that shortly before we left Hong Kong we had an opportunity to return the favour for someone else. A Chinese lay reader, also called Chui, who had been helping us in the Mission felt called to become more involved, leading eventually to a desire to devote his life's work to Chinese Seamen. There were a huge number of them passing through the Port of London, so Head Office decided to set up a Chinese Mission with Chui as its first lay chaplain. He and his wife had never been outside the Colony, so it fell to us to enlighten them as to what they might expect. It was in our flat that they used a knife and a fork for the first time and experienced their first English dinner. We saw a great deal of them before they left for the UK shortly before we did. We promised to visit them on arrival in London, so I went to see him the day after we arrived; I was met by his wife, who was thrilled to see me. He was out ship visiting, she told me, but expected him back shortly. I waited impatiently for his return, and indeed after about an hour he arrived. I was very much taken aback when, as soon as he saw me he broke down in tears, indeed he was totally distraught.

'What on earth is the matter?' I asked him. It took him quite a while to compose himself, but eventually it all came out. We had already learnt from our time in Hong Kong how the Chinese hate to lose face. One of the biggest insults (and indeed not only for the Chinese but for anyone) was to be spat upon. Chui had been talking to a group of men about Christian baptism, when one of them made some derogatory remarks about Christianity, and said, 'This is what I think about water for baptism'. He then spat in Chui's face. Recounting the incident brought on more tears, and it was obvious just how deeply he had been affected by what had happened. I did what I could to try and uplift him, but knew it would take him a long time to get over it. The next two years passed very quickly for me, so the next time I saw him was after I was ordained. I went up to London for an interview with the Missions to Seamen head office, and then went down to the Port of London to see Chui. Just as before, he was out ship visiting when I arrived so (remembering the last time I was with him) I awaited with no little apprehension for his return. The transformation couldn't have been more complete. His face was radiant, and his

104

smile a mile wide. This time he needed no encouragement from me to give me his news. He had just baptized that same seaman who two years earlier had spat in his face.

Footnote. My table tennis friend, Chui, and I kept in touch by regular correspondence down through the years. When I finally retired in 2007 the parish arranged a wonderful service and party for me. My children wrote and told Chui what was happening and, unbeknown to me, he decided to leave the colony for the first time in his life to be with me on that occasion. My children put on a sort of 'This is your life', which ended by them telling me that Chui was among the congregation of some 350 souls. A remarkable and very moving reunion.

Chapter 11

The Lull Before the Storm

It's hard to imagine a greater contrast than the hurly-burly of our hectic last few weeks in Hong Kong with the first two weeks on our ship going home. Nothing to do but eat, drink and be merry! The only timetable to be met was to respond to the gong that signalled meal times. The sea was beautifully calm, and we enjoyed each other's company anew. We were very much aware that, whereas many people have to pay to go on a cruise, we were enjoying it for nothing. 'Everything,' as they say, 'in the garden was rosy.' The first few weeks passed without seemingly a care in the world, one glorious day idyllically following another.

I have already mentioned that shortly before leaving Hong Kong, and at the insistence of the new padre, I purchased my first pair of spectacles. But those same lenses also put other facts into focus, and as a consequence clouds started to appear on the horizon. Some of which would not go away. So we were forced to sit down and consider our present state, and how best to plan for the future. As we did, it became painfully obvious that the calm waters would soon become choppy, and that the entrance to the port of our ambition (my eventual ordination) was fraught with problems; that there were dangerous passages to be navigated before we would reach the haven where we wanted to be. Writing this some fifty years later, I am amazed that after contemplating all that lay ahead we embarked on such a path at all! I am sure that the optimism of youth took us a long way down the road, plus the fact that I have always strived to look on the positive side of things. So I reasoned: 'If God be for us, who can be against us?' because I was utterly convinced that I was being called to the priesthood. I was positive He would open the doors, and provide the wherewithal for it to happen. But, as I say, when we sat down to think it all through, we realized that there was indeed an awful

106

lot to be overcome before we could hope to arrive at our eventual destination.

In the first place, whereas I was by now certain of my vocation, would others be also? My entering Theological College depended not upon me but on the hierarchy of the Church in Wales. I was due to meet with the Archbishop soon after arrival in the UK, the Warden of the College, the Warden of Ordinands, and goodness knows whoever else. Any one of them could put serious stumbling blocks in my path. I might add that I had at one time contemplated seeking ordination in Hong Kong. The Bishop of Hong Kong had the right to ordain me, just as he had ordained the first ever woman into the priesthood a few years earlier. He was aware of my desire to be ordained and, although the subject had not been broached officially, I was given to understand that he would not be unsympathetic were I to approach him. There is an expression 'being ordained through the back door'. Sometimes, when the normal channels to ordination are blocked, it is possible to find other means to reach that destination. There are, for instance, candidates who have been rejected by one diocese, only to be ordained in another. I was positive in my own mind, however, that I wanted to become ordained only through the most stringent of channels, and that nothing less would suffice. Nevertheless, as we approached the UK I couldn't help but wonder whether I should have been less fussy and approached the Bishop of Hong Kong first in my quest for the priesthood.

We also came to see that, whether I was accepted for training or not, there were other obstacles to be overcome. On the negative side, if I was not accepted, what then? I had immensely enjoyed my time as a lay reader but one of the reasons I wanted to be ordained was because I was very conscious of the limits of that ministry. That included not being able to celebrate the sacraments, or take weddings and baptisms, or give absolutions and blessings. Furthermore, because of these limitations there was realistically no chance for a reader ever to be appointed as Head of a Mission, vicar of a parish, or to a chaplaincy post. There was another worry. During my time as a Lay Reader I had met colleagues whose desire for ordination had for one reason or another been denied. In many cases it left them depressed, bitter and even twisted. I don't know whether it was the memory of being 'returned to unit' during my national service when I was within one week of being commissioned, but the thought of being rejected seemed unbearable. But if this were to come to pass then should I continue as a reader, or return to the profession for which I had originally been trained, that of civil engineering?

On the other hand, assuming I was accepted, how on earth were we going to manage financially? My small remuneration during my time in Hong Kong meant that we had been able to save hardly anything for the future. We had no home of our own and no furniture. I understood that the college tuition would be free but there were no grants for married men. Nor was there married accommodation, which meant not only that we would be separated but also that I needed a home for Rose, and of course for me during vacations from College. I would be required to reside at the College for three years, which was the normal time allocated to a nongraduate for qualifying and passing the General Ordination Examination (the mandatory qualification for ordination). Students didn't qualify for the dole, so how on earth were we going to live during that time? The small amount of our savings would definitely be exhausted long before the three years were up.

To further complicate matters, Rose informed me that she believed she was pregnant, which meant finding work would be extremely difficult if not impossible. Her pregnancy was indeed confirmed shortly after arrival back in the UK and although we were delighted with the news it all added to the obstacles that beset us. After weighing all these things up we came to the conclusion that without 'divine intervention' it just wouldn't be possible, but if it really was His will that I should become a priest then that divine intervention would indeed be forthcoming. So there and then we stopped worrying and prayed instead. 'Thy will be done.'

Indeed we went further. We hadn't seen our parents for three years so decided that, before we started on the long and no doubt financially difficult journey and despite what lay ahead, we would take them out and give them the night of their lives – no expense spared! My mother was at this time looking after her father in Harrow on the Hill. Rose's parents were coming up from Newport in South Wales for a few days to be there when we docked in London, which meant that including us there would be a very full household.

I was certainly apprehensive about how I would get on with my in-laws. Whereas it is not true to say that I took Rose to Hong

108

Kong to get as far as possible away from them, it is true to say that I was told before we embarked that they would never forgive me for taking 'their baby' away. I always felt that this was rather unfair, as Rose decided without any influence from me to leave home and join the Missions to Seamen as a trainee lady warden in London, which was, of course, where we met. So, I reasoned, taking them out for a special night couldn't do any harm, and could possibly help to oil future progress. Whilst still out of the country I had enlisted the help of my brother to make all the necessary arrangements, which he did. We warned our parents to be ready to go out on the first Saturday evening after we arrived, as we were taking them out for a meal. What they didn't know was the full extent of what was planned.

They say 'the best planned efforts of mice and men go astray'. This nearly proved to be the case, indeed when I think about it all these years later it still sends shivers down my spine. As the time came nearer for us to leave Hong Kong, we were 'feted' beyond our wildest dreams. Friends, staff, Rose's firm and seamen all combined to give us a truly wonderful send-off. 'Losing face' is something the Chinese dread above all else. Many of them were guests at one of the earlier receptions before hosting their own. It followed therefore that the party they gave had to be bigger and better and therefore more grandiose than any that had gone before! Inevitably the meals were Chinese, and as one followed another so the number of exotic dishes grew. So did the number of presents. Some who knew of my new love of photography gave me additional equipment, including a slide projector, special lenses, a camera tripod and other photographic paraphernalia. Hong Kong was at that time one of the main 'duty-free' ports in the world. People came from near and far to shop there, and although there were marvellous goods to be purchased, there was also a drawback, in that you were only allowed to bring in a certain amount of 'duty free' into your country of origin.

The exception was if you had purchased and used the items for six months, which was usually the case for expatriates working in the colony; the items were then classified as second-hand, thus escaping duty. We had of course made many purchases during our three years, so had no trouble with these items, but the many farewell gifts I had been given didn't come under that category. The Chinese shopkeepers, however, had an answer for everything, including the customs regulations! Almost automatically when purchasing an item one was given a seven month or longer backdated receipt. The presents therefore came complete with receipts. It was common knowledge that Customs officials were looking not so much for people purchasing goods for themselves as those who were taking advantage of duty-free prices to sell on and make a large profit. I knew of course that the receipts were falsified but in the knowledge that they were presents given for my use, and not for resale, I squashed any conscience that I might have had, and duly listed my presents with receipts alongside all the others we had acquired during the last three years, ready to present to the Customs on arrival at the UK.

The excitement at seeing the white cliffs of Dover, the thought of seeing loved ones again, and all that lay ahead, was exhilarating. Drawing alongside the quay as the ropes secured us to dry land, and seeing the welcome parties lining the docks, took everything else out of our minds. Needless to say everything was packed and ready to go. We were told to wait in our cabins for one of the Customs officers, so immediately retired to our cabin to prepare for him. There came a knock on the door which revealed a bright-looking young man. Warning bells should have struck when I saw the newness of the gold braid on his sleeves! He produced the standard piece of card with the Customs regulations on it and asked me to study them. This I did as nonchalantly as possible, and handed it back.

'Have you anything to declare?' he asked. I shook my head and then handed over my purchases list complete with receipts. He studied them for a while, and then rather ominously went and shut the cabin door.

'I see you're interested in photography,' was his opening gambit. This time I nodded in the affirmative.

'Tell me,' he continued in a tone of voice that I sensed had definitely hardened, 'why did you buy the extra lenses before the camera? The same with the tripod. Surely you would buy the camera first then the other items later?' There followed a deafening silence during which pictures flashed through my mind of me being led off in handcuffs to the nearest police station, going to gaol instead of the Archbishop's Palace, and wearing arrows on my shirt instead of a dog collar! There was only one thing to do and that was to come clean, which I did. As my tale unfolded I thought of all my Chinese friends who above all else hated to lose face. This was exactly what was happening to me now! He listened in silence, after which he took out a notebook and proceeded to list many items plus the amount of duty that was to be paid. My heart sank to my boots as the list lengthened and the total grew until it reached a figure that was completely beyond my meagre means. He started totalling the amount up. Then he stopped, gave me a fixed glare and said, 'Do you think we are not aware of what's going on in Hong Kong? We've known about backdated receipts for years. I see you're a lay reader with the Missions to Seamen,' he continued.

'Yes,' I replied and added rather lamely, 'and was hoping to have gone on to be ordained.'

'Um,' he muttered as he rechecked his figures.

He then thrust the total under my nose, before asking me how I was going to pay.

Once again there was nothing to do but tell him the truth. 'I don't know,' I stuttered, 'I haven't got that much!' Then followed what seemed an eternity, during which flashed through my mind even more horrific pictures of disaster and ruin, including rotting in a debtor's prison.

The Customs officer spoke for the last time: 'Don't ever try to fool us again,' he said, and with that he tore up his list, said 'Good bye and good luck,' and disappeared through the cabin door. I can't number the times I have preached since on the text, 'Be sure your sins will find you out'.

Shortly afterwards we disembarked, to be warmly greeted by our parents. Then, complete with our many purchases plus a huge sense of relief, we sped away to my mother's house and all that lay before.

The next two days were busily spent making sure all arrangements were in order, both with regard to interviews with the Church in Wales, and our special evening out on the Saturday. Grandad rather impatiently inquired where were we going, and how were we going to get there? This was because he prided himself on knowing the numbers and routes of all the local buses. He was completely taken aback when I informed him that we had hired a chauffeur-driven limousine for the evening. A few minutes later, complete with chauffeur's peaked cap, the driver arrived and off we went.

'What a waste of money,' grumbled Grandad, who was being chauffeur-driven for the first time in his life! 'Why couldn't we go by bus?' was his next contribution to the conversation.

'Because it's too far,' was my answer. As the journey continued towards the West End his murmurings grew quieter and finally stopped altogether.

I had reserved a table at one of the best and most famous restaurants in London. We were greeted with charm, escorted us to our table, and then served with a truly sumptuous meal. At least, Rose and I thought so! Rose's mother nearly choked on hers at one stage in the evening, and Grandad started complaining again about how expensive it all was. 'A complete waste of money!' he muttered between mouthfuls of succulent steak. I noticed, however, that it didn't seem to affect his appetite! Nor did it mine. Nothing deterred, we continued with the meal, including being serenaded by some musicians around the table as we ate.

So the meal ended, but not the rest of the night. Out we went to find the chauffeur complete with limousine parked outside. Next stop, the dress circle of the London Palladium for the evening show. The star was Harry Secombe, who proved to be in scintillating form. As he sang 'When you come home again to Wales', the audience went into raptures and we dissolved into tears. I remember squeezing Rose's hand and we both saw it as a positive sign that all would be well when we went down to Cardiff for interviews in two days' time. After the show we retired to a very nice coffee bar where we enjoyed nightcaps before finally returning home.

Before retiring to bed Rose and I reflected that, when we decided to get married four years earlier, we borrowed £40 to be able to do so. That night in London also cost £40 but we felt it was worth every penny. Some thought that we were wrong to 'blow' such an amount in our precarious financial position, but we saw it as a wonderful opportunity to give our parents a night to remember and, in a funny sort of way, to reinforce our trust in God.

The sermon at church the following morning touched on a raw nerve. The preacher was referring to the moment of truth, and that when it came we needed to face up to it. It brought home the realization to me that shortly, in the Archbishop of Wales' palace, I too would be facing that moment of truth. My mind flashed back to an incident during my national service, when I was waiting in a side room before seeing the CO, who was to tell me whether or not I was to be sent to OCTU. On a sudden impulse I knelt down on the hard floor and prayed that what I was to hear would be good news. As I knelt on that cold floor, so the sun came out and shone through the window and bathed me in a warm light. It was a wonderfully reassuring moment, and there and then I offered myself to God. That interview turned out to be rather like the curate's egg: 'good in parts'. I had been accepted only for a short-term commission, for the duration of my national service. It has often struck me since that, if I had been accepted for a long-term commission, I would have had to serve for at least ten years, and as a consequence would almost certainly never have been ordained. At the time I had no inkling that my future was to be tied up in the church, so it was with mixed reactions that I heard the decision. But having just offered myself to God in that outer room I felt strangely at peace. In exactly the same way, as I attended church on that Sunday morning and listened to that sermon I felt equally at peace, and from that moment began to look forward to rather than dread the days that lay ahead.

Later on in the day I started to think of mundane things such as what was I going to wear when meeting the Archbishop. As I did it struck me that the one thing I didn't have was a suitable suit. Those made in Hong Kong were far too thin and definitely non-clerical. So first thing on Monday morning I went out and blew an increasing hole in my pocket by purchasing a dark suit. Not long after, the four of us – mother, Grandad, Rose and I – set off for South Wales. The journey was fairly uneventful, except that Grandad continued to moan about the cost of the Saturday night outing, and my mother kept offering rather unhelpful advice on what to say to the Archbishop. Rose was naturally rather pensive, but without any doubt I was the calmest of them all.

I must admit, however, that a certain amount of tension crept in as we drew up outside the Palace, which wasn't helped one little bit when Mother suddenly exclaimed. 'John, you can't possibly see the Archbishop with those brown shoes on.' I looked down at the offending articles and had to admit that Mother was probably right. In the first place, they clashed horribly with my new austere suit, and secondly (to be politically correct) they should be black. A glance at the watch showed there was no time to go off and buy replacements, but the same glance also took in the fact that Grandad had on a pair of black shoes. Problem solved, well almost, as they looked about two sizes bigger than mine! Despite Grandad's loud protestations I relieved him of his footwear and tried them on. They were indeed too large, but after a few minutes of practising shuffling rather than walking I said my goodbyes and, to the background of cries of 'Good luck', disappeared into the Palace.

To be honest, I don't remember a great deal of what went on, nor of the length of time I was there. But I gradually sensed that the Archbishop was talking in a very positive manner, so that without actually saying it I knew I had been accepted. Other interviews followed but, knowing I now had the Archbishop's backing, I grew in confidence and as a consequence found them no problem at all. The last interview with the Warden of the College was concerned only with domestic matters and the rules of the College. My family came to pick me up about three hours later, and they knew immediately by the huge grin on my face that all had gone well and that I was now an ordinand of the Church in Wales.

As we sped away in high spirits, during which time I gave Grandad his shoes back (appeasing him by saying I was sure that it was his shoes that had done the trick), I realized that, although the major obstacle had been overcome, there were many more yet to be navigated. Where were we going to live? How was I going to finance the next three years? What was going to be the Missions to Seamen reaction to me leaving their employment? I was at present still on paid leave, which was a great blessing. Rose was almost certainly pregnant, which, even in those days was an expensive exercise, and would tax our meagre savings to the limit.

We had planned to spend a little time staying with both parents, so from Llandaff we went to Newport, where Rose's parents lived. Mother and Grandad said their farewells and departed, leaving us alone. The news that I had been accepted was greeted rather half-heartedly, and it wasn't long before searching questions started being asked. They were understandably exactly those to which I too was seeking answers. There was however an added edge to them because so many of them centred on Rose. The fact that I had taken her away from them to the other side of the world was bad enough, but now, especially as she was pregnant (and this news was also greeted even less than half-heartedly), what sort of man was I to go off to college and leave her to fend for herself? Rose immediately sprang to my defence, which actually didn't help matters at all, although it did bring about a temporary truce.

My meeting at the Missions to Seamen head office, on the other hand, couldn't have been more positive and helpful. In the first place they were delighted that I had been accepted for ordination. They said some very nice things about my work as a lay reader and then, using a popular saying on the media at that time, concluded, 'we will be keeping our beady eye on you. Once you are ordained we expect you to come back and join us as a Chaplain!' Furthermore they put their money where their mouth was. 'We need help at the Newport Missions to Seamen,' they told me, so during college holidays, etc. they agreed to employ me as a lay reader. This was wonderful news, and lifted a great load off my mind.

It didn't occur to me at the time that I would be expected to continue my studies during vacations, which in actual fact was the case. This put a great deal of extra strain on me as I strived to combine study with what amounted to a full-time job, once I had left the college precincts. As the money situation grew even more desperate I also worked at the weekends. Looking back at it all now, I am convinced that it was only by the grace of God, indeed by divine intervention, that I was enabled to finish the course and become ordained.

The remaining weeks to the start of term fled by, especially as I was already working at the Newport Mission. I referred earlier to the truce that existed in the Weight household. Because I was out working all day and often in the evenings as well, it wasn't too bad for me, but I could see that Rose was getting more and more stressed and unhappy. Probably the hardest thing of all for Rose to bear was that any talk about her expected baby was taboo. Even knitting things for the baby was frowned upon, and had to be carried out in the privacy of her bedroom. On the other hand her parents had agreed that she could live with them whilst I was in College, which was a huge relief, and for which I was extremely grateful. But it grieved my heart to see Rose becoming increasingly unhappy, and I couldn't help but wonder where it would all end.

The day for the start of term arrived, so after fond farewells and no few tears I left her and went to St Michael's Theological College, Llandaff, which I expected to be my base for the next three years. My emotions were confused: thrilled that I was actually starting theological training, but sad that I was leaving Rose in such unhappy circumstances. On that first day, however, I could see no option, but did not despair because I was convinced that God was in command so somehow everything would be all right in the end.

115

BACK IN THE UK

Chapter 12

Life at St Michael's 1958–60

I soon had many other matters to occupy my mind, particularly getting used to the College routine. Most of my fellow students were part of what was then known as the 'theological sausage machine': private, grammar or high school followed by university and now theological college. The majority were three or four years younger than me and single. I, however, had been out in the big wide world for five years, was a married man and expecting to be a father before long. As with most students, college was a time for vigorous debate, exploring all sorts of doctrines, but I also had acute personal problems to cope with, including an unhappy wife whom I was missing terribly. College was a time of concentrated study, because I had in the main been used to practical work for the last five years, I found it extremely difficult to get down to prolonged study. University graduates were

St Michael's Theological College

expected to pass GOE in eighteen months, whereas non-graduates were given three years to complete the course.

Overshadowing all else was my desire to be ordained and get back into what I saw at that time as the true work of the church. Only in later life did I come to see the value of being resident at such an institution, where, as well as being taught the Queen of Sciences, one was schooled in a disciplined spiritual life. The regular pattern of early meditation, followed by Matins and then Holy Communion in the morning, Evensong and Compline at night, set a pattern of worship that was impossible to better. Although for various reasons it has not been possible for me to maintain it over the years it nevertheless set a benchmark, to which I have always aspired. Although I enjoyed college routine, I was distressed to see that Rose became increasingly unhappy in her parents' house. So much so that I was forced to the conclusion that it couldn't continue, and that I had to do something about it. Two wonderful and amazing things then happened. Coming back to Cardiff meant that I could renew old friendships, which I did, including Frances, my first ever sweetheart. It was because of her that I started going to church. Frances possessed a deep and meaningful faith. I had no idea at that time of course that I would one day develop a similar deep faith, but within the Church of England. As we grew older, although we both retained a deep affection for each other, our relationship became more like that of a brother and sister.

Frances and her husband Ken lived very close to the college, so it was easy for me to see them quite often. As one does with old friends I shared with them my concern about Rose, but never dreamt what the possible outcome might be. Ken and Frances then told me they had been thinking a great deal about Rose's unhappiness and had decided to offer her the hospitality of their home until I finished college. I was completely overwhelmed by this, which still rates as one of the kindest acts I have ever known. It was totally unexpected, totally sincere, and overwhelmingly generous. But even as I sat reeling from their incredible offer, I knew that I just couldn't accept such a huge sacrifice on their part. I saw it, however, as one of those mysterious ways that God works for those who love and trust him. So even as I turned down their offer I just knew that something else would come up, and sure enough it did.

Another friend, who also lived near the college told me of a neighbour who had been recently widowed. He lived in a chalet bungalow, and was wondering whether he could find someone who would keep his house clean and prepare him a cooked meal for when he came home from work in the evening, in return for the living accommodation in the upstairs rooms of the chalet. I immediately went to see him, explained our situation, including the fact that my wife was pregnant, which didn't seem to worry him in the slightest. I took Rose to meet him the next evening, we all got on very well, and in no time at all it was agreed that we could move in as soon as we liked, in fact the sooner the better! We left in a daze, scarcely able to believe our good fortune. Rose would now be only a short distance from the college, compared with Newport which was about twelve miles away so too far and expensive for me to go during any time off. He confirmed that we could stay there without paying rent in return for cleaning the house and providing him with a daily meal. From the word go everything went perfectly. For six days of the week he went off to work, came home in the early evening, had his meal, and then went out again to visit friends. He had hardly any visitors, so most of the time it was as if we were living in our own house. He was no bother at all, in fact we hardly ever saw him. He was very pleased with the way that Rose kept the house spotless, and more than happy with the meal she prepared and put ready for him every day. Our financial problems were eased, and the tension surrounding the house in Newport was gone. What is more we were able to use the excuse of the obvious benefit of Rose being close to the college as an argument for her leaving home, so avoiding any bitterness or bad feelings. Not for the first time in our lives we learnt that if the good Lord doesn't give, he sends! We understood anew that if God were for us, no one could be against us. Our hearts were truly thankful, but not only that, we were left with the certain conviction that what was happening was all part of God's plan. So we praised him secure in the knowledge that all was indeed in accordance with his will.

This is not to say that there were no problems left! Money, despite all our good fortune, was still incredibly tight. Rose like any mother wanted the best for her baby. As all parents expecting their first child do, we made a list of our needs. There were, we discovered, charities that help ordinands and curates, and thanks largely to them we soon had all the baby clothes we needed. What we still didn't have was a pram, but again we needn't have worried.

My brothers and sister had also thought of this, so they clubbed together and bought us one. I happened to be there when it was delivered and the joy on Rose's face as she used it for the first time I will never forget. The Additional Curates Society also proved to be a godsend for the rest of my time at college as well as for the first few years of my ministry. Not only did they provide clothing, but it was of the highest quality, especially the ladies' dresses which were often designer-made. On many occasions I took pride in the fact that Rose was the best-dressed lady in the room.

I had brought my photographic equipment to college, but unfortunately couldn't afford to use it. Like all similar institutions, there were from time to time official photo sessions. With tongue in cheek I offered my services, and to my delight was accepted as college photographer. I took many official photos, made a small profit on them, which allowed me to take those precious family shots especially of my son, who was born during my time at St Michael's.

We named him Michael, which pleased the college no end, although in fact that was always going to be his name, chosen whilst we were on the way home from Hong Kong.

Through my photography I also won first prize at a college competition. We had to present a poster on a mission theme. This coincided with the building of the new College chapel. So I set up my camera on myself posing beside the half-built church. The caption on the poster read 'Whom shall I send? Here am I, send me.' (Isaiah 6.8) The College prize was £20, which proved a real godsend. I later took photos of members of the staff, some of which turned out better than others. The one I took of the warden was actually the best, and when shortly afterwards he was appointed as a bishop, he used it for his press releases.

The election of the college warden as a bishop inevitably caused a change in the staff. John Poole Hughes was appointed as the new chaplain, and I hit it off with him from the word 'go'. I think possibly because he and I were the only two who had served with the church overseas. For domestic reasons he had just returned to the UK from Tanganyika. His mother was very ill, and in fact died a short time later.

I referred earlier to the fact that most of the ordinands were products of the so-called 'theological sausage machine'. As a result many of them were very naïve about life. Furthermore, just as

My first effort (as official photographer) of the group photo

many children are baptized and confirmed through the influence of their parents, I came to the conclusion that some of my fellow students were becoming ordained following family wishes. I wondered with some apprehension how they would get on in their parishes. For example, a small group of them used to spend an inordinate amount of time practising kneeling down in such a way that their cassocks completely covered their shoes. There were also long debates on which sort of clerical gear suited them best. As I got to know them better, I softened my stance, and in time learned to praise the Lord that within His church He had space and purpose for the different gifts that they had to offer.

Part of our training was in pastoral care, including baptism. By now the birth of our first child was imminent so every time children's work or baptism arose I was immediately nominated as the volunteer and left holding the baby! Because of the impending birth I found it very difficult to concentrate on college study. My heart was with Rose, especially when the time came for the birth. I was given permission to go and visit her the second I received the news that she was in hospital. As the days passed I grew more and more apprehensive, so when three telegrams were delivered to me at the college I opened them with trembling fingers. However, they were all from fellow ordinands, and I have to admit very witty! Michael was born during the height of the cricket season; in fact there was a test match on the day he was born. One telegram read. 'Four out so far, the last one was a duck!'

The expected call finally came, so to the cries of 'best of luck and love to Rose' I sped from the lecture room to the hospital. By the time I arrived my mother-in-law was already there, and it was she who informed me that I had a son. I was thrilled with the news but saddened that I hadn't been there at the birth, and that I wasn't the first to know. To make things worse when I was allowed to see Rose her mother came too! There and then I promised myself that the next time would be entirely different, and it was. Despite the circumstances, I can think of nothing more exhilarating than the joy of seeing one's wife and baby for the first time. I must admit however that (especially with mother-in-law present) I didn't handle it very well. When I came to pick him up for the very first time I made matters worse by saying, 'He isn't very handsome is he?' In fact he was thin and scrawny, so what I said was perfectly true, but definitely not the right way to describe our newborn son to my darling wife who had just brought him into the world.

Sheer necessity forced me to get back into college routine as quickly as possible because exams were imminent. We were examined in thirteen subjects; graduates took them in two batches, non-graduates in three. Because I was working full-time every weekend for the Missions to Seamen, I had to burn the candle severely at both ends. Because of my short nights, the first session after lunch especially found me feeling very sleepy. I became fully awake, however, when the lecturer announced, 'Today we are going to examine the hearing of confessions'. Up to this moment I thought that they were confined to the Roman Catholic Church. I was flabbergasted to learn that it was very much part of the Anglican ritual too. He said regarding confessions, 'None must, all may, some should'. The thought of making confession to another human being was at first beyond my comprehension. It was hard enough to say sorry to God! After the lectures and debates I began to see that for some people there was indeed much mileage in going down that route. But what made me decide to pursue it further was when we were told, 'Once you've been in orders for five years, if a person asks you to hear their confession, you have no alternative but to do so.' If you haven't made a confession yourself, how can you possibly comprehend what an effort it must be for the confessor? I thought about my own reaction and had to agree that he was right. So I made my first confession. The effort was indeed immense, but so was the reward. It was as if layers of grime had been washed away through the blood of the lamb. Although I presume that my life up to then had been no better or worse than the average young person of my age, the sense of relief, of light and of joy, raised me to new heights of peace and serenity that I hadn't before believed possible. I still find making my confession difficult, but so worthwhile. Hearing confessions, I rate among the highlights of my ministry.

Another new experience was attending retreats. I mentioned earlier that I attended a so-called morning retreat at the Missions to Seamen in London, when we were supposed to be in silence, but in fact it didn't even last through breakfast! Retreats at St Michael's were entirely different. They usually lasted about four days, and were conducted in complete silence. At mealtimes one of the staff read from a spiritual book or the scriptures. We attended (apart from the usual routine of services) three or four addresses during the day, which were followed by periods of meditation. The first twenty-four hours were incredibly hard to get used to, especially, as far as I was concerned, the silence. But as the retreat moved on into the second and third day so the silence became increasingly precious, and a huge help in focusing on what was to follow. Indeed, when normal speaking was finally restored it seemed as if others were invading one's own space, and it was a job not to resent the intrusion. For me retreats are one of the most effective ways to progress in the spiritual life, and although I was not able to maintain the frequency experienced in college, I did succeed, certainly in the mission field, of attending an annual retreat. Whenever possible I also went on a lone retreat whenever I had to make a major decision regarding my work or future.

Our preordination retreat was conducted by a saintly priest, who told us that the future effectiveness of our ministry would depend almost certainly on attending at the very least, one annual retreat. I was amazed therefore to find on finally returning to the UK after later years overseas that, whereas in the mission field we moved heaven and earth to attend retreats, back in the UK there was no such urgency. Whether or not my ministry has been blessed is not for me to say, but of one thing I am certain: without the influence that retreats have had on my life my ministry would not have been as rewarding, nor would I have made the progress I have in my spiritual life. It is on retreats that one is able to come face to face with Almighty God. In such a situation there is nowhere to hide. One sees God in all His omniscience, and oneself in all one's weaknesses. In such circumstances there is only one conclusion, 'Jesus is the way, the truth, and the life'.

College was not of course all work and no play. I have always been a very keen sportsman, including tennis and, as there were courts in the grounds, I played whenever possible. The college chaplain, John Poole Hughes, was also a keen player and rivalry was intense between us, especially when a doubles knock-out competition was arranged. John teamed up with another member of staff and I partnered a fellow student. Somewhat to my surprise we reached the final, as did John and his partner. A final between staff and students was an obvious attraction, and almost everyone turned up to witness it. The number of students naturally outnumbered the members of staff, which proved a tremendous advantage to us. Every winning shot was greeted with cheers, and every one lost by groans of dismay. Christian college or not, the heckling had the desired effect; the staff got decidedly rattled, and we moved from strength to strength, eventually emerging as winners. We were often reminded of the importance of sportsmanship, but for once both the staff and students failed to live up to the very high standards demanded by such an august body of men!

Rivalry between staff and students however paled into significance compared with that between the local Baptist Theological College and us. The annual football match was, put quite simply, undiluted war! Fouls, which would do justice to any FA Cup Final, were nothing compared to what went on at that game! To be honest I wasn't sure whether I was pleased or terrified when I saw that I had been picked for the team. Luckily for us we had more students to pick from than they did, which is probably why we eventually won. I learnt more about differences between the Nonconformist churches and the Church of England on that pitch than in one year in the lecture halls at St Michael's. Especially when it emerged that three of their players weren't students at all but players from the local league!

It was not long after that infamous football match that the date for exams arrived. There were thirteen subjects to be taken. Graduates took them in groups of seven and six. Non-graduates took them in two groups of four and a five. I opted for five, and was agreeably surprised to find that I achieved good results in them all. Needless to say this was a great relief, and encouraged me to study even harder for the remaining eight. All agreed that the hardest subjects were Latin and Hebrew. Unlike many of the graduates I had never studied Hebrew at all, and found it depressingly difficult to make progress. I was then offered a lifeline: that because of my age I could opt to take another specialist subject instead. I chose the first Epistle of St Peter, and the chaplain was delegated the task of coaching me in it.

However, it wasn't passing the subjects that worried me as much as that our funds were shrinking alarmingly, especially since the birth of Michael. I still had almost two years to go, and after even the most optimistic of assessments realized that financially it would be impossible for me to finish the course, and fulfil my family responsibilities as well. Whilst I was still struggling with this unpalatable fact we broke up for the summer holidays. We were set various subjects to study during the vacation, plus a précis which we had to produce on return to college. All this I immediately put on hold, in favour of employment with the Missions to Seamen. We broke up on a Friday, and I started work the following morning. Term recommenced on a Monday, and I finished at the Mission on the Sunday evening before!

On the last Sunday afternoon of the holidays I collected together all that I needed to take with me the following day, and came across the details of the précis I was required to hand in on the morrow. I hadn't even thought about it yet alone put pen to paper. I finally arrived home from the Mission about 9.30 pm and, after a strong cup of coffee, started work on the precis. I worked through most of the night, and although come the morning I had something on paper I knew in my heart that it was a woeful attempt to deal with the subject set, and in no way satisfactory. I debated whether or not I should submit it, or 'come clean' with the new Warden. As I waited to be admitted to his study I thought of the occasion when I waited outside the CO's office to learn my fate regarding whether or not I was to be commissioned. Once again I prayed that all would be well, but it wasn't! The Warden told me that the only place for my precis was in the waste-paper basket, I felt as if the walls of Jericho were crashing down all around me. There was now no option but to 'come clean' so I did. Presumably because he was new, the Warden didn't seem to be fully aware of my background, and certainly did not know of my employment with the Missions to Seamen, which was taking up all my spare time. He at first suggested that I gave up this employment to concentrate on passing my exams. I pointed out to him that, without the money earned, I wouldn't be at college at all. Furthermore that my meagre savings were almost gone, which meant there was no possibility of me being able to finish the course. He told me that he needed to think about it, and would see me again in a week's time. That week was one of the longest of my life. I desperately wanted to finish the course, but with my other responsibilities weighing heavily upon me, I could see no other option but to leave St Michael's and take up full-time employment.

One week later I presented myself to the Warden's study with very mixed emotions. On the one hand, I could see no way out of the impasse, yet on the other I believed passionately that God was calling me to the ministry. I secretly hoped that there was a fund or grant that the Warden may have discovered which would tide me over. His opening remarks put paid to any such hope. He told me that although he had searched there was no help available. He then outlined the problem as he saw it. What was unalterable was that I couldn't be ordained without passing GOE. True, I had passed five subjects, but that meant that eight remained. Normally that meant another two years' study. I then countered by asking, 'But if I could follow the graduates' timetable and qualify in a shorter time, what then?' There was an awkward silence before he replied.

'Well,' he said, 'if you could complete the course in a shorter time and pass with the necessary grades then I would be prepared to recommend to your Bishop that you be ordained.'

I left him with the feeling that I had been thrown a lifeline, although I was still in the midst of a very stormy sea. My life to date however had convinced me that 'where there's a will there's a way.' So there and then I decided to 'go for it'. Burning the midnight oil became the norm. The college chaplain, John Poole Hughes was tremendously supportive and gave me extra tuition and coaching. To cut a long story short, I did succeed in matching the graduates' timetable as well as gaining the necessary grades – well almost! The one epistle with which I was most familiar was I Peter. I found I could answer all the set questions, so tended to give specialist answers. When the results came out I was told that I hadn't presented a full enough coverage of the subject so would have to take it again.

They say that 'pride comes before a fall'. As I came out of the examination room I felt confident that I had done enough to reach the necessary grades. In those days we had to use pen and ink, and so confident was I that I had passed that with great glee and passion I smashed the bottle of ink against a wall. When the results came out and I found that I had to retake I Peter, I had to buy another bottle of ink as well!

This meant that my three years had been reduced to eighteen months, and as a consequence we were able to last out financially, although only just. My debt to John Poole Hughes soared to new heights when he called me to his rooms shortly before I left, and gave me a cheque for a considerable sum of money. Although I had no reason to know it at that time, our paths were to cross again in the future – John became Bishop of South West Tanganyika, and I was posted to Dar es Salaam as port chaplain. Many years later it gave me huge satisfaction to be able to return that money to him for use in his diocese, as so many of his people were desperately poor.

The events I have just described meant a sudden change in direction. Instead of well over another year in college I now had a date for my ordination. Trinity Saturday, the 31st day of May 1958. Because I had assumed that my ordination was still a long way ahead, I hadn't given my future ministry even a passing thought. The Bishop, on the other hand, had, because, apart from anything else, he was responsible for the salary of deacons until they are priested, which can be any time from a year onwards. My Bishop told me that there were vacancies in four parishes, and he was happy for me to make the choice. Remembering the vow I made at my ordination to go wherever I was sent, I replied that I would rather him make the decision. I pointed out that I knew nothing about any of them so would like him to send me to the parish where he thought I would fit in best and do the most good.

Within a week I was back in his presence. He said there was one parish in the Rhondda Valley that hadn't had a curate for about eight years, and although he didn't say as much I got the impression that he thought that my going there might reactivate movement that had possibly gone a little stagnant. He said that Caerau and Cynfelin, for that was its name, was one of those parishes where Cynfelin had been added on to Caerau a few years ago and that the daughter church had since been very much the poor relation. He hoped that I might be able to rejuvenate it. There and then I accepted his offer. He told me to expect a call from the vicar, which indeed came a few days later. So, with no little apprehension, I made my way by train and bus to the vicarage in Caerau. The Reverend Evans greeted me warmly. Over coffee he gave me some background knowledge about the parish, including the fact that he had been there for very many years. Although he didn't actually say it, he certainly implied that he had been somewhat overlooked. It was possibly for this reason that the sparkle had somewhat gone out of the parish, but if I was hoping for my appointment to be greeted with enthusiasm I was sadly mistaken.

In fact what he implied was 'don't rock the boat'. He nearly rocked my boat however when I said I would like to see the curate's house. 'Oh, we haven't got one,' he said. He pointed out that my appointment had come out of the blue, so they hadn't had an opportunity to purchase one. This came as a bitter blow. Having been separated from Rose for eighteen months, we were both obviously impatient to be together again, and had assumed that, come my first appointment, we would be.

He promised that it would be his top priority to rectify the situation, but in the meantime, Mrs Davies (the secretary of the Mother's Union in the parish) had agreed to put me up. So, instead of going to see the curate's house, I went to see Mrs Davies, who lived in a typical miner's terraced house only a few minutes walk from Cynfelin church. I also met her husband, a retired miner, and both made me very welcome. As was the norm in the valleys, the first question was, 'Would you like a cup of tea?' I noticed that the best china had already been brought out for the occasion, and in any case I could do with one, so replied, 'Yes please.'

Then followed rather strained conversation while the kettle boiled, with me doing my best to put them at ease, which was easier in the case of Mrs than Mr. But he it was who made the most impact a few minutes later once the tea was poured. He obviously forgot protocol by taking his sugar from the bowl first before offering it to me, which I could see from the look on Mrs Davies' face wasn't what had been planned! It wasn't him taking it first, however, that worried me but rather what he did afterwards. He put two spoonfuls of sugar into his cup, stirred it well and then put the spoon straight in his mouth, and sucked it clean. I watched in amazement as he then put the spoon back in the bowl and, under the scrutiny of Mrs Davies, offered the bowl to me! I had learnt in college about John the Baptist eating wild bees and locusts in the wilderness, but this was something else! I considered saying, 'No thank you, I don't take sugar,' but realized that if I did I was doomed to sugarless tea for the duration of my stay. So, putting on a brave face, I took the offered sugar bowl, and indulged in two teaspoonfuls.

I have often reflected on my thoughts that day. Since then I have celebrated Holy Communion times without number in churches, hospitals, nursing homes, prisons and houses, to varying congregations. They included the dying, the infected (including those with AIDS) and in every case consumed what remained of the sacrament without even giving a thought.

I returned to Cardiff in a sadder state than when I had left. Despite putting on the bravest of faces when Rose opened the door, she knew immediately that all was not well. It is to her eternal credit, however, that after hearing it all through she accepted the disappointment regarding the curate's house and our prolonged separation, and agreed that it was to Caerau and Cynfelin that we would go. I duly notified my Bishop that, despite the lack of a house I would accept, and that was that. We consoled ourselves with the thought that no house at least meant that we had a little longer to try and get some furniture together.

The great day of my ordination was growing ever closer, and there was still much to be done. Rose's parents had very kindly agreed that she could move back with them for the expected very short time before the curate's house was purchased. We therefore gave notice to our landlord, who was as sad to see us go, as we were to be leaving. Sadly we lost touch with him afterwards but were always grateful that we had been able to live in his house during my time at St Michael's. I sent notification to all my friends and family of the date I was to be made a deacon at Llandaff cathedral, and hoped against hope that my father would come, but he didn't.

I sent a special invitation to my Roman Catholic friends, Francis and Ken. I was shattered to learn that she had approached her priest for permission to attend an Anglican service, only to be refused. One can only thank God for the progress that has been made since then in seeing the best and not the worst in other religions. I was reminded again of my Chinese friend from Hong Kong, Chui, who had become so confused and disillusioned over the infighting between the Christian churches that he had gone back to worshipping his joss sticks. I made a vow there and then that in my future ministry I would do everything in my power to work for unity among the churches.

There was also a reception to be arranged for after the service, which thankfully was taken out of our hands by other members of the family. There was also the necessity to obtain such things as clerical shirts and a cassock. My mother, who was a seamstress before she was married, not only made my cassock but also a priest's cloak, which I still proudly wear to this day. Then came the preordination retreat, for which I shall always be profoundly grateful. After all the drama of recent months, I would be able to withdraw from the world and 'to be still and know that I am God'.

The retreat conductor was holy, very down to earth, set the highest standard of morality, full of understanding and compassion, deeply profound yet able to express himself simply and beautifully. Again the silence was like manna from heaven, and proved the best preparation possible for what was to follow.

Saturday the 31st May 1958 finally dawned. In solemn procession we filed across from the college to the cathedral for what was surely one of the most momentous days of our lives, the day we were to be admitted as deacons. As we waited in our special places the cathedral filled up behind us and I was conscious that in the congregation were all my loved ones, but especially Rose, who had encouraged and supported me on every step of the way. My thanks to her mingled with my thanks to God and, as one would expect, there was ample space for both.

As I knelt in Llandaff cathedral waiting for that service to begin, I came to see that this (and not when I first went to see the Archbishop of Wales) was truly the moment of truth in my life. Nearly thirty years of it had been spent, one way or another, in preparing for this hour. The vows I was shortly to make, as with the first disciples, would set me apart for ever to serve him in this most special of ways. As I continued kneeling it was with the knowledge that I was just one of a vast congregation. In a few minutes time, however, I would have to rise from the anonymity of my pew and advance before the Archbishop. To stand there exposed and vulnerable as the archdeacon started the service with the solemn words, 'Reverend Father in God, I present unto you these persons present, to be admitted deacons'.

That moment came to pass, and we stood in all our weakness and frailty as the Bishop replied, 'Take heed that the persons whom ye present unto us be apt and meet, for their learning and godly conversation, to exercise their ministry duly, to the honour of God, and the edifying of His church.' I, together with my colleagues experienced a great sense of relief as the archdeacon's reply, spoken with authority and clarity, resounded to every corner of the cathedral, 'I have enquired of them, and so examined them, and think them so to be'.

Then we waited in silent apprehension (just as in the wedding service when the priest says, 'If anyone knows any cause or just impediment why these two people shall not be joined together') as the Archbishop put a similar question to the congregation. A blessed silence signified that another hurdle was over. But all this paled into insignificance as the Archbishop addressed us candidates in the following terms. 'Do you trust that you are inwardly moved by the Holy Spirit to take upon you this office and ministration? ... Do you think you are truly called according to the will of Our Lord Jesus Christ? ... Do you unfeignedly believe all the canonical scriptures?' And so the questions and answers continued. 'Will you apply all your diligence to frame and fashion your own lives, and the lives of your families (I would dearly have loved to turn and meet Rose's eyes at that moment), according to the doctrines of Christ; and to make both yourselves and them, as much as in you lieth, wholesome examples of the flock of Christ?'

After affirming all these vows, I moved, in obedience to the rubric, and knelt 'humbly' (surely an unnecessary word at such a moment!) before the Archbishop to hear the solemn words, 'Take thou authority to execute the office of deacon... Take thou authority to read the gospel ... and to preach the same...'

I rose to my feet in the knowledge that the past had been superseded by the present, and that the future was no longer in mine as much as in the Lord's hands; that I had been set apart in this most privileged way of all to be a servant of the Lord. Because

133

of all the training, the retreat and blessings, I felt (in the words of Isaiah) high and mighty and lifted up. No thought of failure, not even any doubt that I could fulfil the demands that would be required of me. True, that at times came later, but as I rose to my feet and returned to my place, all I knew was that I had been blessed beyond all understanding, and as a consequence I was truly one with the Lord.

The service came to an end and, after the formalities were over, we hastened out to be embraced by our loved ones, and receive their congratulations. To others the shining white dog collar signified a change in status yet in the eyes of those nearest and dearest I was exactly the same (even if now the Reverend) John Rowland Taylor. All that had happened to me had happened within and any other difference might emerge later, but as I joined them after the service I was no different than I was before. A son greeting his mother; a husband embracing his wife and child; a brother surrounded by the rest of his family, and all this in the presence of his nearest and dearest of friends. Both spiritually and emotionally, I was at that moment enjoying the happiest day of my life. The following reception although enjoyable, was almost an anticlimax, especially as I shortly had to depart for my new parish for the princely sum of £320 a year. On my first Sunday, apart from assisting with the chalice, I was due to preach my first sermon. It was so hard to say goodbye yet again to Rose, and put baby Michael back into her arms, but in keeping with my new status I kept a stiff upper lip, kissed them both goodbye once again and departed.

Chapter 13

My First Parish: Caerau and Cynfelin

As I boarded the train at Cardiff Central station I suddenly realized that something was very different. The last time I had stood at this station I was a layman going to visit two villages in the Rhondda Valley. Now I was the curate of Caerau and Cynfelin, on my way to my new parish.

Last time I stood in this spot no one gave me a second glance, but not so now. People caught my eye and gave me a gentle and friendly smile. Why? Then it struck me. It was because I was wearing a dog collar! A huge amount of water has flowed under the bridge since those days. Ministry has, many would maintain, changed beyond all recognition. But what has not changed is the effect the dog collar has on certain people regarding the person who wears it. Without it one is just an anonymous person in a crowd. With it one is set apart just as in the ordination service and treated somehow differently ... but not always! In Buddhist Thailand (where I later served for eight years) the vast majority of the population had never even seen one! I remember being taken to a very expensive air-conditioned restaurant, which necessitated the wearing of a jacket and tie. In honour of the occasion I donned my best suit complete with clerical shirt and collar, only to be turned away at the door because I wasn't wearing a tie!

On the other hand, when wearing my cassock in Thailand, I was sometimes mistaken for a Buddhist monk, with very positive results, details of which I will reveal when I reach that stage of my story. For now back to the present. I was, I remember, wearing a mackintosh because the weather was damp and chilly. The events of the past day had somewhat drained me, including my eye-opening experience on Cardiff station. To this day I am not sure that when the train neared my destination and I closed the lapels of my coat tight around me I did so because of the damp and chilly night or because

I craved a time of privacy, which I had already learnt would not occur very often when wearing a clerical collar. Indeed, my mind flashed back to the day when my friend Steph Roberts had taken off his collar and replaced it with a tie. At the time I wondered at his action but now I wondered no longer.

As it happened, by the time I left the station it was dark already so I had an uneventful journey to my lodgings at the Davies household. Once there I quickly made my excuses and retired to my bedroom to prepare for the morrow. It was Trinity Sunday and I was preaching at the two morning services. Of all the Sundays in the year to have to preach one's first sermon, Trinity is surely the worst! Equally daunting was the thought of assisting with the chalice for the first time. As a deacon one is not authorized to conduct a wedding; funerals and baptisms are allowed, although usually parishioners would rather they be taken by the vicar. It's because a deacon is so limited in what he can do (largely just being of assistance to the vicar) that the unwritten law is that he has to give at least as long serving in the parish as a priest as he did as a deacon, which (depending on how long it takes to pass the priest's exams) can take up to two years.

As Sunday morning broke, however, I was only concerned with getting through the first day. Because of the knots in my stomach breakfast was a non-starter (which is just as well considering what happened the next day!) I would have given almost anything to have Rose there as a friendly face in the congregation, but that was not possible. In actual fact, as far as I can remember, the morning passed without incident. Alas it proved to be 'the lull before the storm'. During my preordination visit I had met 'Dai, the Pithead' as he was universally known. He was and had been the Sunday school superintendent at 'the daughter church' for longer than anyone could care to remember. The fact that he was illiterate seemed to bother no one, although it surprised me. His first words to me signalled danger ahead. 'I suppose you're going to take over the Sunday school, are you?' he said.

My first attempt at a diplomatic answer went something like this, 'Well, let's see how we go shall we? I tell you what, you start off the Sunday school in the normal way,' (which I had learned was with a hymn). 'Once the hymn has started I will come in to the church, and then you can introduce me. On the first Sunday I will just observe all that's going on.' I seem to remember that

Sunday school started at about 2.30 pm, so decided I would get down there about 2.15 and discreetly watch proceedings from afar. I was very agreeably surprised with the number of children who arrived, but immediately became aware of just how boisterous they were in the grounds of the church. I waited with some apprehension for the ringing of the bell, which summoned them into the church. 'Probably a good thing,' I comforted myself, as I watched their behaviour worsening, 'at least they are having an opportunity to get rid of their excess energy before school starts.' I became increasingly alarmed, however, when I saw two of them (encouraged by cheers from their respective supporters) going at it hammer and tongs as they disappeared into the church. I gave a silent prayer of thanks for 'Dai the Pithead' who, with his years of experience, would I felt sure soon sort them out.

The singing of the first hymn told me that it was time to make my appearance. Like an actor in the wings waiting to go on stage I took a deep breath and entered at something approaching a run. Very appropriate as it turned out because before I had barely entered through the porch I ran into trouble. I could not believe my eyes. There were about forty children in the pews. Dai (John, I found out later, was his real name) was up in the sanctuary singing his heart out, but he was effectively singing a solo. Whether or not the aisle separated two rival gangs I am not sure, but what I do know is that as I advanced down it I was bombarded with hymn books, which were flying from one side of the aisle to the other. Mayhem reigned! John was so engrossed in his singing that he noticed neither the chaos nor the fact that the curate had arrived. Neither, might I add, did anyone else! Expertly dodging two more hymn books I decided enough was enough. I have often thanked God that I had been blessed with a powerful voice, and now was the time to put it into effect. 'STOP!' I shouted at the top of my voice. Miraculously they did. The organist must also have heard for, just like a record player breaking down, the music slowly ground to a halt too. Over the years I have found that wearing one's cassock not only gives a sense of security, it also gives a sense of authority. I was so grateful that I was wearing it on that first afternoon, as I continued striding down the aisle of the church. I gave no chance for John to introduce me, and in any case he was looking so bemused that I don't think he could have. Even his presence seemed to slide away into oblivion. I immediately saw the two who had been fighting outside the church, assumed (correctly as it turned out) that they were the ringleaders, and created history in the parish by throwing them out!

I had an extremely difficult path to tread in supporting John and the three other teachers, whilst laying into the little terrors (excuse me, 'darlings'!). Sunday school that day was the shortest in history, but it was followed by a longer meeting of all concerned with the school. Needless to say, I did take over from that moment and one of the first things I did was to arrange for a farewell presentation and party for John, who had served church and school for so long and well, but now felt it was the time to retire. I wasn't sure what the vicar or the parish reaction to all this would be, (accepting that the first rule for any deacon to learn is that you can't please everyone), but surprisingly I came out of it, on the whole, very well indeed.

As I left the scene of battle one of the Sunday school teachers came and said to me in all seriousness, 'Curate, I've often wondered what it's like wearing your dog collar in bed. It can't be very comfortable, is it?' ('Is it' being a very common Welsh expression in the valleys.) I looked for the twinkle in her eye but there was none.

'Why would I wear it in bed?' I asked her.

'Well,' she said, 'I have always understood that once you are ordained you have to wear it at all times.' For the second time in my first day as curate I had to be very diplomatic with my answer.

As I finally sank into my bed that night (minus dog collar) I reflected on how much they didn't teach you about being a curate at theological college!

I was due to attend my first staff meeting the next morning, so was up with the lark, said my early prayers, washed and dressed and then presented myself for my first breakfast. Mr Davies was already at the table and kindly enquired after my first day in the parish. Despite the fact that Mrs Davies was secretary of the Mother's Union, he didn't go to church at all. That first morning before breakfast was over I was given the grounding of my very next lesson. Be assured that whatever you said (even if in the strictest confidence) would be all round the parish in five minutes, with any resemblance to one's original 'pearls of wisdom' being nothing more than pure coincidence! And the worst house to lodge in in this regard was surely that of the secretary of the Mother's Union!

That first morning, however, I didn't realize this so was in full flow to Mr Davies when Mrs Davies made an entrance with my breakfast. I looked at it and just couldn't believe my eyes – it was vast! A couple of eggs, four rashers of bacon, tomatoes, mushrooms, three sausages and fried bread. With some pertinent comment like, 'We must feed a growing man, mustn't we?' she placed it triumphantly before me. A few moments later she returned, this time bearing lashings of toast, which somehow she found space for on the table. The only good thing about it all was that, in an attempt to do justice to what I had been given, I stopped talking for the rest of the meal. But it was when I came to the sausages that I met my Waterloo. I have always liked my food well done, but my first bite of sausage revealed that, compared to how I liked them, it was raw! John the Baptist eating locusts in the wilderness was nothing compared to this!

It was Mr Davies who came to my rescue. 'I can see you are struggling,' he said, 'and that's a pity because I want you to try some of this home-made marmalade.' I seized the opportunity to tell Mrs Davies that, because of the magnificent ordination reception, I was still rather full so please forgive me if I didn't finish my breakfast. Courage completely failed me in telling of the real reason, the uncooked sausages, and as a consequence they continued to be served in the same raw state. It took me over forty years before I could ever face another, and even then it had to be burnt almost to a cinder!

My agony was not yet over. Mr Davies had already buttered his toast and, even as I was buttering mine, he took the spoon to the marmalade, put an ample amount onto his plate, then proceeded to lick the spoon clean before putting it back in the jar and passing it over to me! This, plus the still vivid memory of the sugar spoon, made me certain of one thing. Whatever the vicar had on the agenda, I was going to raise the urgency of a house for me and my family.

The first meeting went fairly well. He had already heard of the drama of the Sunday school, about which he was fairly non-committal except by saying 'take it easy and don't rock the boat.' In an attempt to assure him that I had no intention of so doing I told him that in fact I was still trying to get used to wearing the dog collar. I said that, although during my time as a lay reader I had done a great deal of visiting, somehow it all seemed different now that I was ordained. That made everything I did seem much more important, and I was very aware of the sense of responsibility that came with being his curate. I had expected to receive some directions about what he wanted me to do, whom and where to visit, etc. I had already heard that the vicar wasn't a very ardent visitor, and this seemed to be enforced when he repeated that I should take things easy and not, repeat not, rock the boat! I, however, being full of the enthusiasm of youth, plus a very strong sense of vocation, pressed him for something concrete he wanted me to do.

'Well,' he said, 'there's a couple that live on the council estate that are celebrating their golden wedding anniversary today. Why not go and visit them? They are not church people but I don't suppose it would do any harm to give them a visit!' I then raised the subject of housing for the curate, but received even less enthusiasm than I did about visiting. Consoling myself with the knowledge that I had at least raised the subject, I obtained the address of the couple and departed on my first ever home visit as curate of the parish.

Within a very short time I reached the estate, found the road and then the house number. It was a typical council house, with an iron gate leading into a fairly long front garden. As I had confessed to the vicar, I felt somewhat nervous and apprehensive. My mind flashed back to the first time I went ship visiting in Cardiff docks. Remembering the good advice given to me by the general secretary, I started saying a prayer as I opened the gate and advanced up the path. Despite the prayer I was still apprehensive as I approached the mottled glass front door and rang the bell. My prayer was just going to change to 'Dear Lord, please let there be no one in,' when I saw a body advancing from behind the mottled glass. The closer it came the larger it seemed. Too late now to run, I stood there almost transfixed as the door opened to reveal one of the largest ladies I have ever seen. She must have been around six feet tall, had huge bosoms and a thin mouth.

'Yes,' she growled most suspiciously, 'what do you want?' I felt sure she was going to continue that she didn't welcome travellers, salesmen, or collectors for charity, when she noticed my shining white dog collar. If possible the lip grew even thinner, the bosoms filled out even more as she exclaimed, 'You're not one of those Jehovah witnesses people are you?'

I managed to blurt out in a stuttering voice, 'No, I'm the new curate and I've come to congratulate you on your wedding anniversary.'

'Well, why on earth didn't you say so?' she cried, and with that grabbed me by the hand and literally yanked me into the hallway. As the door shut behind me I expected to see a print on the wall, 'Abandon hope all ye who enter here'. Instead she said in an accusing voice, 'I suppose you want to meet my husband too?'

'Yes please,' I managed to whisper, trying unsuccessfully to keep the shaking out of my voice, 'that would be very nice.'

Her next broadside, thankfully not directed at me but at her husband, drowned my whisper out. 'HENRY!' she screeched, 'come and meet the new curate.' He appeared as if by magic, although I didn't see him at first. He was only half her size and I swear to this day he came out from underneath the table!

'Shake the curate's hand,' she instructed him. I don't know who was the most nervous but the fact was that we were both shaking so much that our hands missed each other by a mile! The lady of the house appeared not to notice because she was off again in full swing. 'We've had a wonderful life together,' she informed me. 'I've been a wonderful wife to him,' she volunteered and then with her voice rising to a crescendo exclaimed, 'What is more, we've never had a cross word in fifty years, have we HENRY?'

'No dear,' he whispered, 'no, we haven't.' I sensed the interview was over so, with a great sense of relief, escaped through the front door. A last backward glance as I left saw, I swear, Henry disappearing back under the table!

My first venture at visiting, then, was not a huge success, possibly just as well, as I soon found many other activities in which I could be better engaged. Remembering that my brief from the Bishop had been to try and install new life in the daughter church, I decided to direct my energies in that direction. The church itself was in reasonable condition, but the church hall situated in the grounds was in a woeful state, and likewise the grounds. I decided to tackle the hall first and straightaway put my previous training as a civil engineer into good use. An inspection revealed that although it was run down and dilapidated, a few holes in the walls and windows broken, structurally it was sound. I had already found out that there was a local builder in the parish, and that he attended church occasionally. So off I went to, as they say, 'make my number'. He had also heard about last Sunday's Sunday school

141

fracas, and I knew his fate was sealed when he congratulated me on what I had done, and wished me all power to my elbow – the perfect opportunity therefore for me to talk about renovating the hall. He was obviously impressed that I knew something about buildings and before long was as enthusiastic about the project as I was. Providing we worked according to his slacker times, he would lend us the equipment we needed. Furthermore he had some paint in stock that he wanted to get rid of, and providing the colour was acceptable... 'Perfect,' I replied without even asking what colour it was!

The next task was to gather an army of volunteers, which again met with an immediate response. It was pretty obvious (as well as probably true) that the daughter church congregation regarded themselves somewhat as the 'poor relations' so jumped at the chance of turning things around. In an amazingly short time a transformation occurred in the hall's appearance and, by obtaining sponsors for nearly every item, from a bag of cement to panes of glass, the cost was kept to the minimum. The church treasurer was one of the few who opposed the idea on the grounds of cost, but was swept aside in a wave of optimism. But even he was converted when the final bill was so low he thought at first that there must have been a mistake! The activity was also reflected in a rise in the congregation. In no time at all the old choir was resurrected, the number of children attending Sunday school increased (including receiving back into the fold the two boys whom I had earlier ejected) and some new young families swelled the congregation even more. Riding on a wave of euphoria I started a youth club, mothers and toddlers group, and a branch of the Church of England's Men's Society.

At the next PCC meeting, at which I was eagerly awaiting to learn of progress towards the curate's house, I was to be bitterly disappointed. The small subcommittee simply reported 'no progress'. The highlight of the evening came instead during the treasurer's report. Not a word about the renovation of the hall at almost no cost to the PCC. Instead, 'I have a very serious situation to report,' he said. It's amazing how electrifying such words from a treasurer can be, so everyone without exception waited with bated breath for what was to follow. Out came the bombshell, 'the electricity bill for the Church hall has soared,' he announced in a voice of doom. 'It's gone up by about two hundred per cent.'

Not a word about the renovation. Not a word about the Men's Society, the youth group or the mothers and toddlers, only and simply the electricity bill has soared! I looked for support from the vicar, who merely looked away. So I rose to make my maiden speech. 'Of course it's gone up,' I exploded, 'the hall is now being used for one afternoon and four nights in the week instead of lying dormant, it's being used for the very reason it was put here in the first place.' Red-faced and amazed at the ferocity of my outburst I sank back to my chair. There was an embarrassed silence, before the treasurer continued in a much more conciliatory tone, 'However I must admit that the church collections have also gone up by about two hundred per cent.' Crisis over. Defeat turned into victory, which was made even sweeter when the new Sunday school superintendent reported on the increased numbers and improvements in the organization.

Rose understandably was more interested in any house purchase developments. Living back again with her mother renewed some of the old problems, now of course made worse because of the presence of baby Michael. That apart, she missed the freedom she enjoyed in 'our Cardiff residence' as we fondly called it, to say nothing of the lovely garden, which was just not there in Newport. But above all else was our mutual desire to be together in our own little house, united as a family. She was bitterly disappointed that I had nothing to report and I sensed a growing frustration over the whole situation. Then, as so often happens, help came from an unexpected quarter. I had made good friends with the local Methodist minister, who was very ecumenically-minded. He had been attending a rally in Cardiff and whilst there met my archdeacon. He related to him what he considered to be a disgraceful situation over the fact that the curate had no house. The archdeacon was stung into action, and as a consequence the subcommittee were summoned to give a report. I learnt later that they were told in no uncertain terms that unless they found us a house shortly they would have no curate to put in it!

About five days later the vicar told me that a house had been found, and that the PCC was in the process of buying it. I was in no way privy to the transactions nor to any of the details, nor in fact did we even know which house it was until after it was purchased, which as it turned out was a great pity. We were, though, overjoyed that our long separation was almost over, and busied

143

ourselves with removal arrangements, and other relevant matters. Two days before we were due to move in Rose come up for the day and we went to inspect our new home. It could accurately be described as, just like the curate's egg, good in parts.

Like most of the terraced houses in the valleys, there was no front garden, the front door opening straight onto the pavement. No matter, we thought, because there is a back garden, but then came the second snag. On opening the back door we were faced with about five steep and uneven brick steps with no railings on either side, which even to the uninitiated spelt problems with getting the pram down into the garden. But that was only part of the problem; at the bottom of the garden ran an angry stream with no safeguard of any sort. Not ideal for our son once he began to crawl or walk. The back door opened into the kitchen, which was all right, but what was decidedly not was the toilet that led directly off from the kitchen, minus a door. Totally unhygienic with no privacy as a bonus! We looked in vain for an oven or indeed for any other modem convenience. The rest of the house seemed normal and had obviously just been freshly painted, although to my experienced eye this could at best be seen as a 'botched-up job'. Nevertheless, it gave us a key to our own front door. I confidently promised Rose that I would soon sort out the problems we had discovered, so thus assured she returned to Newport. As I kissed her goodbye at the station I had an awful feeling that what we had already discovered about the house was just the tip of the iceberg, and that worse was to follow.

I discovered later (too late) that the house had belonged to two elderly spinsters, both of whom had recently died in their nineties. Nothing had been done to the house for years, but on their death it had been bought up by a 'cowboy' builder, who had intended to do it up and then sell for a profit, which he certainly did. Part of the modernization plan was to replace the outside loo with an indoor toilet that he started but never finished – hence the little room with no door on it staring straight into the kitchen!

I went straight to the vicar, who was not amused at my complaints after they had 'moved heaven and earth' as he put it, to get us a house. When I pointed out that there was no oven he said, 'What do you think the hob's for?' Regarding the stream at the bottom of the garden he said, 'but your baby can't even walk yet!' The missing door on the toilet received similar short shrift. 'If you have visitors you can always shut the kitchen door.' It was only when I returned the next day to say that the hob was broken and therefore dangerous that he reluctantly promised some action. In the meantime we moved in and settled down. Rose was, in the circumstances, marvellous, and in an incredibly short time had the house ship-shape, clean and running. The one thing she found very difficult to cope with was the broken hob. In fact it finally proved to be the straw that broke the camel's back. But more of that later.

At first we used to have a weekly staff meeting, but after a while this was amended to meeting only when the vicar had something special he wished to discuss. Things plodded along for about a month with nothing particular happening, although as far as I was concerned I learnt something new every day. One's time as a deacon was always intended to be just that – a steep learning curve when mistakes would be made and excused. Hopefully lessons leant during this time ensured for a smoother ride in the next posting. Two examples spring to mind.

Because as a deacon I was not authorized to take a sacramental service, the vicar was always present at the Eucharist. Other services, such as morning or evening prayer, I was able to conduct alone. During the last hymn the choir and the incumbent retired to the vestry. The cue to leave was the beginning of the second verse. As this moment arrived I moved in front of the altar ready to follow the choir as they filed out from their stalls. They moved into the aisle, bowed to the altar, and turned towards the back of the church, which was the route taken to the vestry. I then followed on. After about a fortnight of this procedure the choir director said to me. 'The choir object most strongly to bowing to you in the sanctuary at the end of the service.' It had never occurred to me that by standing where I did I was in direct line between them and the altar, right in the way of their acknowledgement of it. I was horribly embarrassed by this gaffe, apologized profusely and needless to say never made the same mistake again.

The second example was far more serious, and concerned hospital visiting. Whenever I visited I followed the normal and accepted procedure, which was to see the sister in charge of the ward, explain who I was, and then ask if there was anything special I needed to know about any of the patients. On this particular occasion the sister told me that I would find a young girl (whom she pointed out) tearful and upset. The reason for this was because she had tried to commit suicide earlier that day, so was understandably in a distressed state. I reached her bedside and sat down beside her. Despite her tear-stained face she was an extremely pretty girl, and I wondered what on earth would lead her to attempt such a drastic step. She then proceeded in no uncertain terms to tell me that it was entirely her parents' fault, they didn't understand her; they cruelly denied her the normal life of a young girl of her age. And so it went on. I say now in shame that her beauty as much as her story won me over, and indeed the longer the list of woes increased the more incensed I became. Seeing myself as a sort of knight in shining armour, I patted her hand and said, 'Leave it to me. I will sort everything out'.

I went straight from the hospital to her house, and rang the bell. Her tear-stained mother answered the door, was obviously pleased to see me and invited me in. There I met father, who likewise thanked me for coming. But their thanks turned to dismay as I ranted at them for being so cruel to their daughter. They were completely taken aback by my outburst but said nothing. Taking this as a sign of guilt I then added a few more 'appropriate' words before taking my departure.

I had not arrived back at the house more than five minutes when the telephone rang. It was the local doctor; 'I want you in my surgery inside ten minutes,' he said and slammed down the phone. I was there in five! He then proceeded to give me the biggest roasting of my life. I couldn't have got the facts more wrong. It was the girl, the doctor told me, and not the parents who was the problem. The parents were two of the kindest, thoughtful and most loving parents he had ever met. The daughter was a thieving, lying troublemaker who had been a constant burden to her parents ever since she was a young girl. They were devastated at this latest turn of events and to top it all I had gone to their house and cruelly attacked them. Unless I went back to their house immediately and apologized he told me he was going to report me to my Bishop. I came to see there and then that I had been stupid in the extreme, no doubt swayed by the girl's attractive looks, and had ignored the cardinal rule of not making a judgment until having heard both sides of the story. Furthermore that it was not my job to make judgments at all. The whole incident was one of the hardest yet at the same time most useful lessons I learnt during my time as a deacon. It was a very chastened curate who retraced his steps to their house and very shamefacedly admitted that he had been completely 'out of order', offered apologies and begged forgiveness.

It was shortly after these two incidents that the vicar called another staff meeting and it was with a great sense of foreboding that I made my way to the vicarage. Actually I wanted to tackle him about the house, which we had discovered during some recent heavy rains leaked like a colander – but not only through the roof! The woodwork of the window frames was completely rotten, despite the camouflaged coat of paint that had been put on to hide its true state. As a consequence the wind and rain poured in. In fact we had to abandon two of the upstairs rooms altogether. There was no central heating, which made drying out almost impossible to achieve. Despite the urgency of this matter I decided I had better wait to see what the vicar had to say before raising the subject.

What the vicar did have on the agenda really threw me.

'Now that you have a nice home and are happily settled in,' he said, 'I'm off on holiday.'

My immediate reaction was to say, 'Not, I hope, until you've authorized the necessary work for improvements on the house,' but I didn't get a chance.

'Everything's arranged,' he said, 'we're off at the end of the week.' The rest of the meeting dealt with various actions that needed to be taken, which I very carefully wrote down in my diary. No sooner were the details completed than the meeting was called to a close, and I prepared to leave. Just as I was going the vicar said ,'Oh by the way, there's a wedding in the daughter church on Saturday week at 11 am, but it needn't worry you because I've arranged for the Reverend Jones from the next parish to take it.'

The Reverend Jones was universally known as 'Jones the Rope'. This was because he was thought to be a communist, extremely unpopular, regularly had the windows of his vicarage broken and, it was rumoured, received numerous threats that he would one day find himself hanged. Not unsurprisingly he was a somewhat strange character, and although I was relieved that as a deacon I was to have no part in the ceremony, did feel for the couple who were to be married. I prayed all would go well, and then forgot all about it.

On the way home from the meeting I was aware that Rose would be asking if there was any good news regarding the house? I really felt so sorry for her, and knew that my negative result from the

147

meeting would upset her. So much so that I contemplated having the work done myself, and paying the bills. When I arrived home she had gone out so I sat down and worked out the state of our finances. Warning bells should have rung at the last youth club meeting. There was a young lad who had just left school and was so excited because he was starting work the following Monday. The youth club met on a Friday, and one week later he turned up and proudly and excitedly showed me his first pay packet. As I looked at it I noticed that, in his first week as a tea boy down the mines, he was earning more than I was! All the time I was at college I consoled myself with the thought that, providing I could keep going, even if with the aid of our dwindling savings, once I was ordained our money troubles would be over. I was wrong. As I studied the accounts I could see just how tight our finances were. One thing was certain; there was no way that I could pay for any repairs on the house. It was a sobering thought as I looked at my present income, compared to when I was a civil engineer. Then I claimed as much in expenses as I was receiving in salary now.

Looking back now I marvel that, although we struggled financially throughout my early ministry, it never really upset us at all. The only negative effect was that it limited us in what we could and could not do. Throughout my life I have always found that if the good Lord doesn't give, he sends. Many members of the congregation were miners, and one of their perks was that they could go to the coal tips and pick up what was called the slack. Slack was a mixture of small pieces of coal plus dust, which was usually made into briquettes, and burnt well on the fire. I believe I am right in saying that they were only allowed to collect enough for their own consumption, but whether that was true or not, we seldom had a week go by without a sack of it appearing outside our front door. On another occasion we found a large parcel outside the door, and on opening found it contained, of all things, toilet rolls! Some time later I found out by chance that one of our parishioners worked in a factory that produced them.

Despite all these acts of kindness there were many occasions when, with three or four days to payday, we were literally out of money. On one such occasion my younger brother turned up unexpectedly to visit us. Rose made him a cup of tea, but apologized that she hadn't got a biscuit to go with it. I came in a few minutes later, and we had a good old chinwag about many things, but not money. Nevertheless he must have sensed that things were tight, because when I saw him to his car, he said. 'Oh, by the way, I've left something in the bowl on the mantelshelf.' When I returned to the house and looked in the bowl it contained a five-pound note! That was indeed manna from heaven, and enabled us to end the month without going into debt.

Another family visit occurred shortly afterwards, which was entirely different. This time my elder brother turned up unexpectedly and we were delighted to see him. Then, to our amazement, a knock on the door heralded the arrival of my father! It was the one and only time he ever visited us, and to this day I do not know why he came. Rose's experience of my father was limited to the time he went to her parents' house and tried to get them to stop our marriage. His sudden appearance caused a complete flap, but luckily my elder brother Peter took over. One of our farewell presents from the staff of the mission in Hong Kong was a magnificent silver teapot, milk jug and sugar bowl proudly residing on a silver tray. We hadn't used it; in fact, I think it was still in the wrappings from Hong Kong. 'Let's show him we're not poor,' said Peter. 'We'll make tea in it.' Whilst all this was going on in the kitchen, I was engaging Father in conversation in the front room. I wondered what was taking them so long so made my excuses and went out to find out. By now everything was ready including our best teacups. Peter poured the hot water into the pot, but just before we took it in Rose lifted the lid to give it a stir. There was a muffled scream from Rose, who then blurted out, 'There's a dead cockroach floating on the top!'

'No problem,' said Peter, 'father will never know,' and then, with the aid of a large spoon, he expertly removed the offending article. So we all proceeded back to the front room and Rose poured Father a cup of tea.

'Thank you,' he said. He then noticed that there was only one cup. 'Aren't you going to have one as well?' he asked.

Quick as a light Peter said, 'No thank you, we've all had a cup just before you came.'

We watched in fascination as Father downed his drink without further ado, before leaving shortly afterwards. Once he had gone we all dissolved into tears of laughter, did indeed have a cup of tea, but not from the offending teapot!

Actually some of our bits and pieces painted a very false picture of our true financial position. Rose had been presented with a wonderful Tin Sin carpet from her firm as a farewell present. We had brought one or two pieces of carved furniture back with us, so our front room became a talking point in the parish. Indeed parishioners insisted on taking their shoes off before walking on the carpet, and were enthralled with some of our carvings, bits and pieces.

We didn't have a car, but thought nothing of it at the time. In those days, of course, buses and trains were more abundant than they are today. Rather like the cry for more bobbies on the beat, the great advantage of having no car was that I walked everywhere in the parish, so was constantly seen. The exception was when I visited the daughter church of Cynfelin in the hamlet of Nantyffyllon, about two miles down the road. Then I took the bus.

On the Friday morning before the vicar and his wife left we met for a final briefing. 'Oh by the way,' he began, and I immediately experienced a sense of foreboding, 'I've just heard of a death in the parish, so you'll have to deal with it and take the funeral yourself.' Memories of my first encounter with such matters, when I was a lay assistant at the Cardiff Missions to Seamen came flooding back, but as I realized that the circumstances were now very different, I pulled myself together and, with more confidence than I actually felt, said, 'No problem. I can cope'.

Actually the funeral went very well. The only difficult moment was when the eldest son who had made all the arrangements, confided with me, 'I'm very nervous, curate, because this is the first funeral that I have been involved in!' I felt like saying that he wasn't half as nervous as I was, but managed to resist the temptation. If the truth be known, after it was all over I felt rather proud of myself, which only goes to show that 'pride comes before a fall'.

The days after the funeral passed comparatively uneventfully and as we approached the second weekend of the vicar's holiday I was in high spirits. Came the Saturday morning and, after a pleasant breakfast, I told Rose that I was off to visit a few families in the area. Luckily I told her where I was going because no sooner had I left than the telephone rang and a voice said, 'I need to speak to the curate immediately'.

'He's out,' Rose replied, 'but I'm expecting him back in about an hour.'

'You need to get hold of him straightaway,' was the response, 'because he's got to take a wedding in Nantyffyllon.'

Rose patiently explained that the neighbouring vicar was taking it.

'I am the neighbouring vicar,' he interrupted. 'I did agree to take it but I've just remembered I've got to take one of my own! So the curate will have to take it instead.' With that the phone went dead. I nearly had a fit when Rose found me about twenty minutes later and gave me the unwanted news!

Because I knew that as a deacon I wouldn't be involved in taking weddings, I had never studied the marriage service. So when Rose told me that I had to take the wedding, that it was at 11 am, and that it was now five past that hour, there was only one word to describe how I felt – panic. I flew back to the house and grabbed my cassock and surplice. By now it was well gone ten past and I realized that the next bus wasn't until half past, which meant I would be at least three quarters of an hour late! Desperate situations require desperate measures. Like a colossus I strode into the middle of the road and waved down the first car that came along. The startled look on the driver's face told its own story, but I had no time for niceties. 'Take me at once to the church in Nantyffyllon. It's a matter of life and death!' I ordered. Giving him no chance to argue I opened the door of the car and sank into the passenger's seat. A bemused driver reversed the car and we were off. As he drove I explained what had happened, and once he knew he couldn't have been more cooperative, so much so that within about five minutes and with a huge screech of brakes we drew up outside the church.

To the background of some ironical cheers I flew up the path to be met by an indignant best man who demanded to know 'Where the hell have you been?'

'I'll explain later,' I replied, in what I hoped was a conciliatory tone, but in any case didn't wait to hear what he said. I flew round the side of the church and through the vestry door. Once inside I tried to collect my thoughts, but was given no chance, because immediately the organist started up 'Here comes the bride'. Actually she was not an organist at all. She told me afterwards that she could only play three pieces of music suitable for a wedding, and by the time I arrived she had played them all four times already! So once she was given the signal that the curate had finally arrived she immediately burst out into 'Here comes the bride'.

I had intended to go into the church, make my apologies for being late, explain what had happened, and then prepare for the service. But as I entered the chancel the bridegroom was already in place and the bride three-quarters of the way down the aisle. I attempted to give her a reassuring smile, but it froze on my face when I saw her condition. Even to my inexperienced eye I could see that she was at least eight months, thirty days, and twenty hours pregnant! The fact that she was dressed in a traditional white wedding gown only added to the overall effect. The fact that she had been waiting almost half an hour for luckless me to arrive hadn't helped either, and she looked (and I can only explain it in one word) 'awful'. One step away from her increasingly nervous groom she faltered, stumbled and fell. Keyed up as I was, my reaction was instant. I jumped forward and caught her even before she reached the ground. She had obviously fainted so I laid her on the front pew and called for a glass of water.

I must say that after I had drunk it I felt much better! Whereas everyone else was hoping that she would recover very quickly, I was praying that she would take longer. The unexpected break enabled me at least to find where the service was located in the prayer book, and have a quick look at its contents. I also had time to dash into the vestry and find the marriage register. Somewhere in the back of my mind was the thought that I had overlooked something very important. Just at that moment there was a knock on the vestry door, and I was informed that the bride had recovered sufficiently for the service to continue. Continue it did, because as a deacon and not qualified to conduct a wedding anyway, whatever I did would be wrong. However, finally and mercifully the service came to an end and we proceeded into the vestry to sign the register. Unfortunately I was in such a state myself that I signed the register in the wrong place, and of all the wrong places, where the bridegroom should have penned his signature! To this day I am still not sure whether, legally or not, I am married to that pregnant Welsh lady!

Even more warning bells should have rung when the persistent photographer complained that he hadn't been able to take a photo of the bride and groom signing the register. I murmured something unintelligible and ushered them out of the vestry. The organist struck up the remaining piece of her repertoire and, to my immense relief, they returned from whence they had come, and disappeared out of the door.

The reception was being held in the local pub, which was situated right opposite the church, but in honour of the occasion there was the bridal car waiting for them, although it had to drive up the road for at least a mile, before it could turn round and drop them back outside the pub. I had moved out into the churchyard to try and clear my brain, so watched the car draw up, the bride and groom alight and to the compliment of clapping and confetti, disappear into the building. As if to add to my sense of deep brooding, heavy clouds rolled over the valley and down came the rain.

I retreated once again into the vestry and my eyes were immediately drawn yet again to the open register showing where I had signed instead of the bridegroom. To make matters worse what had been nagging at the back of my mind came into vivid and frightening clarity. There should be three registers (not just one) completed and signed, including the copy that is given to the bride and groom. Unlike the bride, however, that copy was still in a virgin state!

I realized that action, rather than feeling sorry for myself, was needed. My first priority was to eliminate my name from the space reserved for the bridegroom. In my civil engineering days, if there was a mistake on a plan, or a line needed to be altered, the alteration was achieved with the aid of a razor blade, which scraped off the offending lines. It needed a gentle touch not to go through the paper. I decided to apply this knowledge and skill to eliminate forever the incriminating evidence. I was so agitated, however, that I applied the blade far too heavily, so went through the paper altogether. At that time the fine for defacing HM documents was £500 or six months' imprisonment! Be that as it may, the next task was to fill in the other two registers, which thankfully I achieved without any further mishap. The problem was of course that they weren't signed. If only I had been thinking clearly I could have taken them over to the pub for the bridal party to sign, but in my turmoil that line of reason escaped me.

The only thing for it, my befuddled mind told me, was that they would have to come back to the church. Taking a deep breath, I entered as unobtrusively as I could into the pub, where the celebrations were in full swing. I searched diligently until I found the best man and then in the most persuasive manner I could muster informed him that the bridal party would have to return to the church to complete the necessary documentation. In a voice so loud that it brought the whole proceeding to an immediate halt, he cried out, 'Bugger off, curate.' The more I tried to explain the louder he repeated his refrain. 'You kept us waiting for over half an hour,' he screeched, 'so bugger off now and leave us alone!'

This of course I couldn't do. So I delivered my bombshell 'You've all got to come back,' I exclaimed, 'because the bride and groom are not yet married!'

Pandemonium reigned for about five minutes, during which even more drink was hastily consumed. What amounted to a council of war was entered into before finally I was able to convince them that return they must. By now the heavens had opened, as the sorry looking party (this time without the aid of the bridal car) remade its way across the road, and back into the church. It's one thing to see a bride who is eight months, thirty days and twenty hours pregnant dressed in a bridal gown, but to see the same person soaked to the skin with the gown clung tightly to the body, so revealing every contour, is something else. To make matters worse, the rain had turned the path into a mud bath so the virginal white was transformed into a muddy brown.

The first thing I did was to make the bridegroom sign in the right place, which was quite difficult because of the hole in the paper, then to complete the other two registers. I gave them their copy and wished them luck as I waved them goodbye. I then sank into a chair exhausted and a complete mental wreck, especially as I contemplated what the reaction of the vicar would be when he returned and saw the hole in his register. I later found out that at regular intervals one of the registers had to be sent off to Somerset House. In theory the registers were alternated so that the authorities viewed both from time to time. But to the best of my knowledge it was the same (and unspoilt) book that made its way to Somerset House for very many years after the incident took place.

I was thankful for the few remaining days before my vicar returned from his holiday, which enabled me to regain my equilibrium. I very much hoped that my first curacy would be a success, and that I would be able to develop a closer rapport with him. But in actual fact future events were taken out of my hands. The same minister from the local chapel who had earlier had a word with my archdeacon about the fact that there was no curate's house, attended the next ecumenical follow-up meeting in Cardiff, this time attended by the Bishop. The minister had earlier visited us in our new home, seen its condition, especially the fact that two rooms were so wet we couldn't even use them, and expressed his disgust to him when they met. Apparently the Bishop replied that he would look into it, and no more was said.

The vicar duly returned from his holiday, and at our first meeting enquired how things had gone. 'You'd better come and see,' I replied, and without further ado we jumped into his car and travelled to the church. Whilst on the short journey I told him about the 'Jones the rope' telephone call on the morning of the wedding. 'But as a deacon you're not allowed to officiate!' he exclaimed. Silence followed until I showed him the register with the hole in it, at which he exploded, 'You're not allowed to do that either!' This opening exchange rather put me on the defensive, which was a pity as I had intended to broach the topic of the necessary improvements to our house. Rose was finding the situation increasingly tiresome, indeed frightening as she looked forward to the future. We fully expected to be in the parish for at least two years, by which time baby Michael would be running around exposed to the dangerous steps outside the back door, to say nothing of the stream running through the back of our garden. He would need his own bedroom, plus the fact that there was still no door on the inside toilet which was a cause of concern. The most pressing need of all, however was for the repair of the hob over the kitchen fire, which at present was outright dangerous, and actually proved to be the straw that broke the camel's back. So, rather than a full-frontal attack, I humbly stated that I would be most grateful if the improvements could be regarded as an urgent priority. A muttered 'oomph' had to suffice.

Apart from the wedding and the house, however, things were going well. Because there had been no curate for many years it was not surprising that I was able to make some impact. I found that a large number of children needed to be baptized. So many in fact that a mass baptism was the only answer! One Sunday afternoon about a month later came the day when no less than twelve candidates plus parents presented themselves around the font for baptism. Unlike the wedding, everything went perfectly. Not a single child cried throughout the whole of the service; I

155

managed to give everyone the right names, and all the children were remarkably well behaved. Everyone went home in high spirits, complete with their correctly filled-in certificates.

I also went home in high spirits, was greeted warmly by Rose, who said, 'I'm sure you would like a nice cup of tea,' to which I replied in the affirmative. As I looked around the kitchen I saw that I was not the only one who had been fully occupied. Everywhere I looked were clothes; some drying on the clothes airer; others beautifully ironed piled up on empty chairs, to say nothing of the table, and anywhere else that there was an available space. I carefully lifted one such pile from 'my chair' to enable me to sit down, and then waited in pleasant anticipation for the kettle on the hob to boil.

Then disaster struck. The kettle, which was on the broken hob, suddenly toppled over and poured water on to the fire beneath. The first thing that happened was a mass of steam hissing into the air. That wasn't too bad but what followed will forever remain a nightmare in my mind. Ash, black, slimy and in huge volume rose from the fire, and continued to rise until everything in sight, but especially the clothes in whatever state they were in, were covered in its clinging embrace. To crown it all, Michael, who was lying peacefully in his carrycot, underwent a colour change as a combination of soot and ash covered his hands and face. A wail rose from the depths of Rose's body that ended in a screaming crescendo that I thought would never end. At first I sat transfixed as the horror of the situation became increasingly apparent. This changed into a need for action, but I didn't know which way to turn. My first inclination was towards Rose, my second towards Michael. As I sat trying to make up my mind, my hand instinctively reached out to a pile of ironing by my side. I tried to flick off the offending ash, but this only made the situation worse, as an ugly smudge covered what was left of anything white! As Rose saw the result of my handiwork her cries of anguish turned to tears of frustration and anger that nothing I could do would pacify.

I too grew increasingly angry and determined that as soon as I possibly could I would go to the vicarage and let the Reverend Evans have a piece of my mind. This suggestion met with Rose's wholehearted approval, so whilst hating to leave her in such an inconsolable condition, that is what I did. The vicar was surprised to see me on a Sunday afternoon, and looked at his watch in some distaste as he answered the door. The lady, as they say, was not for turning, and I more or less forced my way into his house. It was one of the few times I met his wife, and proved to be the only time she ever entered our house. But as I related all that had happened, and the state in which I had left, the vicar turned to his wife and suggested that it might be better if she returned with me, which she did. I had an evening service to attend so left them together, and if the truth were known, it was with a sense of relief that I escaped out of the door.

My outburst at least had the desired effect, as three days later the hob was replaced. But to the day we left that was the only improvement that was made to the house.

Fired up with enthusiasm over the success of the last multiple baptisms, I soon found many more who needed to be christened. In no time at all I had an even larger number of babies and children (fourteen to be exact!) so a date was duly arranged for about a month ahead. At our next staff meeting the vicar informed me that the archdeacon suddenly seemed to be taking an interest in our parish, and that he was going to visit us soon. I knew that archdeacons were responsible for the maintenance of churches and parsonages, as well as the discipline of the clergy. From time to time they conducted what was known as an archdeacon's visitation, so the fact that he would be visiting the parish didn't strike me as anything unusual, and aroused little or no interest as far as I was concerned. In any case, I assumed that all his business would be with the vicar, and wondered whether as a new and lowly curate I would even meet him. Before the meeting ended the vicar repeated that I should take things easy, making mention especially at the comments my mass baptism had aroused.

He also informed me that the Easter collections went to the vicar, and he gave me a huge pile of special envelopes to deliver to every house so that people could enclose their offering in them. Like most things I undertook I looked forward with satisfaction to completing this task, seeing it as a good opportunity to knock on every door. I must say however, some of the comments I received – 'Oh, someone from the church, is it? It must be that time of the year again!' Or 'where's the Vicar then? Getting someone else to do his dirty work is he!' – were disquieting. On the other hand regular members of the congregation gave me a warm welcome, and accepted the envelopes without any adverse comments.

157

The weeks rolled by, then two things happened. The first was that Rose had a miscarriage, which her mother claimed was as a result of the damp house we lived in. I then caught a very bad cold that turned into bronchitis and forced me to my bed, including the Sunday planned for the baptism. My vicar immediately solved the problem; the archdeacon says he wants to visit, so this Sunday presents the perfect opportunity, what's more he can take the curate's services, including the mass baptism. So it came to pass, but not alas without incident as related to me later by one of the doting parents. Unfortunately just as the service began one of the babies started crying. As if on cue, four or five other babies followed suit, so within a few minutes the archdeacon's voice was almost lost completely. He struggled manfully on until some of the older children got thoroughly bored with the whole situation and started playing up. At this moment the archdeacon lost his temper, and as a result more children started crying. Chaos reigned, which wasn't improved when in his agitation he got the children's names wrong, which meant two of the mothers started crying also! Finally and mercifully the service came to an end. The archdeacon's parting words were something to the effect that he was going to introduce a new canon stating that no more than four children could be baptized at any one time!

News of this disaster was conveyed to me on my sickbed (exaggerated of course), which I am sure set me back another few days. But just as I was getting better and taking an interest in the affairs of the parish once again I received a curt letter from the archdeacon to say that he was coming to visit me in a few days' time, and to make sure that I was at home. Naturally, I feared the worst and had visions of being defrocked even before I was priested! In many ways the archdeacon role is similar to the sergeant major in the army. Not only that but he is next in seniority to the Bishop. The fateful day arrived and with it the archdeacon, who to my utter surprise and relief was extremely pleasant, and didn't mention the baptism at all. He asked for a cup of tea, and seemed to take particular interest in the new hob. He chatted about things in general, and then asked to have a look around the house. He poked his pocketknife through the first window frame he inspected and grunted in disgust as a huge chunk of rotten wood fell to the floor. When we came to the two rooms that were uninhabitable, his face visibly paled. When he asked to use the toilet and found that it boasted no door, I thought he would have a fit! From the toilet he went to the garden, but by now no words of explanation were necessary. We returned to the kitchen, where I waited for the outburst that to my surprise didn't come. After a few more minutes he made his excuses and left. But just before he did, almost as an afterthought, he said, 'you will be hearing from me shortly'.

Rose and I debated just what we might be hearing, but having no idea of the workings of the hierarchy of the church, decided the only thing to do was to wait and see. Two things did happen; the vicar and PCC received a letter from the Bishop, which I understand said something to the effect that if you can't look after your curate properly, you don't deserve to have one. I received a letter from the archdeacon telling me that I would shortly be hearing more about my present situation, and the possibility of a move. All this was somewhat overwhelming, and made it difficult to carry on as usual. But some events were already planned, including the youth club's first trip to the seaside, so carry on I did.

I was apprehensive about taking some thirty-five teenagers to Barry Island but in actual fact they were all remarkably well behaved and the day went perfectly (well almost!). You will know from my time in Hong Kong that I could swim and was qualified as a lifesaver. Everyone was eager to get to the beach and have a swim, so I changed into my costume, complete with lifesaver's badge on it, which obviously impressed. But as I stood there in my costume I soon became aware of just how cold it was. My previous swimming had taken place in the subtropical waters of Hong Kong. When I 'tested the water' as they say, my toe nearly froze! Making a dignified retreat from the water's edge I sat down on the sand and tried as surreptitiously as possible to protect myself from what was actually a slight breeze but to my freezing body seemed more like an arctic gale.

Then it happened. 'Come in and swim with us, curate,' said an eager group of youngsters. Using all the tact within my power I mumbled something about staying where I was so that I could keep an eye on everybody, but my words were brushed aside as they picked me up and bodily carried me down to the water's edge. Then, amid great excitement, they threw me in. Surrounded by members of the youth club I endured about ten minutes of torture before escaping back to my welcome towel. That was the first and last time I organized a youth club outing to the sea!

In case I am painting too dismal a picture of my time in my first parish, I must say that I retained many happy memories and friends for almost the last half century. To give but one example I returned on a sentimental journey to the parish forty-five years after I left it. I pulled up outside a house where during my time a lovely couple called Stan and Peggy Cox lived with their delightful children. They were not only pillars of the church but kindness personified to Rose and me. I knocked on the door and an old lady in her nineties opened the door. 'You won't know who I am,' I began, but even before I had finished the sentence, she said, 'Come in, John Taylor!' Although both parents have now died I still hear from the rest of the family.

With all that had been going on I had spent far too little time preparing for my priest's exams, which were fast looming on the horizon. They necessitated going down to Llandaff to sit them under the supervision of the Warden of Ordinands and the Bishop's chaplain. They covered two full sessions. The first day went fairly well, but it was the second that I was dreading because it included Christian ethics, which all through college (and since) I had found extremely difficult to get my mind around. The morning session went fairly well but as we filed back into the hall after lunch I dreaded what was to come. My worst fears were realized. As with most examination papers, one looked through them all to decide which questions to answer. I can say with hand on heart that as I looked at them I didn't find a single one to which I could do justice.

I wrote my name on top of the paper, and came to a full stop. I was debating what to do next when the door burst open and the Bishop's chaplain came tearing into the room. He approached the adjudicator and a whispered conversation followed. My colleagues had their heads down and were busily writing, so hardly noticed what was going on. I, on the other hand, was glad for the diversion, but not prepared for what came next.

'Mr Taylor,' called the adjudicator, 'will you please bring your paper up to my desk.' Completely bewildered, I approached him. 'The Bishop wants to see you straightaway,' he said. He wrote the time on the top of my paper, signed that I was leaving the examination room, and told me to go with the chaplain.

The Bishop's palace was less than five minutes away, and although on the short journey I tried to pry out from the chaplain why he wanted to see me, he wasn't saying anything. A few minutes later

I was ushered into the Bishop's study, to find him furiously pacing up and down. As I entered he bore down on me, furiously waving a sheet of paper.

'What's this?' he asked, before shoving it under my nose. 'What's this?' he repeated a second time, and put the offending sheet into my hand.

I looked at it for a moment and said, 'It seems to be a list of names, My Lord!'

That's exactly what it is,' he replied, 'It's a petition from your parishioners saying they don't want you to leave. We just don't have petitions in the Church in Wales,' he exploded, 'so what have you got to say for yourself, eh?' And with that he poked me in the chest.

'It's the first time I have heard about it, I have never seen it, and I know nothing about it,' I replied. There was a silence, during which time he sank into his chair and I remained standing just where I was.

The silence was finally broken when he pressed a button on his desk, the chaplain appeared, and he was asked to bring in a pot of tea. I took this as a sign that the ordeal was over, and so it proved. Once convinced that I had nothing to do with the petition his mood changed, and the next quarter of an hour or so passed pleasantly. Then, in a way that those in authority make it known without actually saying so, I knew that the interview was over. I therefore took my farewell, and left.

It was only when I was back outside the palace that I remembered that I had been removed from the examination room, and to there I must return.

Out of the frying pan into the fire, I thought as the chaplain escorted me back. Just as I entered I heard the adjudicator call out, 'Time's up, gentlemen. Please put your pens down and leave your papers on your desk.' He initialled on my paper the time I returned and told me to do likewise. As I did I wondered what would happen, as I had only been in the room for about five minutes of examination time! In fact, when the results came through about ten days later I had been given passes in every subject including Christian Ethics. If there ever was a case of divine intervention in my life, then this was surely it!

I have said before that on my ordination retreat I made a vow that I would never apply for a job, but wait to be invited. When

161

I was appointed to Caerau and Cynfelin I had given no thought to what might follow, and in any case I knew that as a deacon I was expected to serve for at least two years, so that no immediate move was possible.

I was shocked to the core, therefore, when a letter came through from the vicar of Aberdare. In it he said the Bishop had asked him to interview me regarding a possible move to his parish, and asked me to contact him for an appointment. The parish of Aberdare was known in the Church in Wales as equivalent to the parish of Leeds in England. It had four churches and was famous for its most illustrious vicar becoming the revered Archbishop Green of Wales. Many of its other vicars had risen to positions of authority and leadership in the diocese so it was regarded as one of the stepping-stones for aspiring clergy. It was therefore with no little apprehension that I duly made my way to Aberdare to meet the Reverend Charles Arthur, the present incumbent.

I could see from the first moment I met him that the Reverend Charles Arthur was an entirely different character from my present vicar. He was charming and kindly, although very much old-school. No Christian names were ever used, and I found it quite difficult to be known as Mr Taylor, after years of being just John. He showed me where, if I were to be appointed, we would live. It was one of three clergy flats on the top of Lord Aberdare's old mansion. It was large and spacious, and compared with our house in Caerau, very impressive. The ground floor housed the local income tax offices, which in fact created no problem for me, as on a curate's salary I didn't have to pay any.

I also met Mrs Arthur and family, and was very warmly welcomed into the vicarage when we went back for tea. What I couldn't decide was whether or not the choice of moving rested with me, or the hierarchy of the church. I was not long left in doubt, as shortly after my return to Caerau I received a letter from the archdeacon telling me that my move had now been finalized, and I was to make immediate arrangements for the move. My vicar must have been notified at the same time because he expressed no surprise when I showed him the letter. We in fact left about six weeks later, but not before kind parishioners organized various presentations for us, which amazed me, as we hadn't even been there for a year. The following month's parish magazine simply stated, 'The Taylors have let us flat for a flat'.

Chapter 14

The Parish of Aberdare

So we moved to Aberdare. Our small possessions were a little lost in the larger size and extra rooms of our new flat, but this didn't worry us at all. Our flat was actually on the third floor, but we had space on the ground floor for our precious pram, and quite extensive grounds for Michael to enjoy as he started walking. A school had been built on part of the estate, but because of the size of the gardens this didn't affect us at all. The headmaster was one of the churchwardens, the other being the owner of the biggest and most expensive shop in town. At our first staff meeting (at which I met my three fellow curates) we were reminded that it was at this store that the curates were expected to do their shopping. I don't know about the others, but we very rarely did. No one tackled us about this, however, and the subject was never raised again.

My fellow colleagues fascinated me. One was an ex-Nonconformist minister, and much older than the normal run of curates. He seemed to be a bit of a loner, did his own thing, and in any case moved on shortly after I arrived. His advice about coping with the stresses of Sunday services was to get away from the parish completely on the day before. Being an older man was an advantage as he had more experience to call upon, and whereas we accepted the Reverend Arthur (at first any way!) as being the last word in all things liturgical and canonical, he knew there was another world out there, and being an ex-Baptist minister, was not afraid to say so!

The second curate was Welsh-speaking, with at least two degrees, and obviously very highly rated. Being Welsh-speaking was a huge advantage, especially as one of the Aberdare churches held only Welsh-speaking services. Needless to say, being a Londoner in the valleys for the first time, I never once took part in a service there! During our college pastoral lectures we were told that every morning

163

should be spent in our studies, and that is exactly what he did. I knew this because we had to pass through his flat on the second floor to get to ours on the third. Time and time again as I returned from my morning's work I would find him at home in his study, and this set me thinking very seriously about the future pattern of my work.

The third curate was a typical product of the theological sausage machine. One felt that his mother should still be behind him, making sure that all was OK. In my colleague's case it wasn't his mother, however, but his new bride. She utterly adored him. She attended everything he did, and always sat entranced in the row immediately under the pulpit as he preached. She made sure he had a clean surplice for every service he took.

Sometimes two curates were called upon to take part in a funeral service. If he was one of them, it was as if there were three, for his wife stuck closely by his side, as I found the first time we shared a funeral service together. The valleys could always be relied upon to provide a fair share of rain, and this particular day was no exception. Indeed, it had rained for the best part of a week. This meant that the graveyard was waterlogged, to say nothing of the grave itself. As we approached it we saw it had about six inches of very muddy water in the bottom. That apart, the ground around it was very muddy, very slippery and, quite honestly, very dangerous. No wonder the funeral procession picked its way very carefully to the open grave. Because I had taken the service in the church he was to carry out the burial. As the service began and his adoring wife tried to get even closer to her beloved husband, disaster struck. As he moved over to make more room for her, the ground gave way beneath his feet and, to the accompaniment of a great shout, and with his surplice flowing out around him rather like a parachute in full flight, he disappeared from view. There was a horrified silence for a few moments, after which everyone looked at me, including his adoring wife, whom I noticed made no attempt to be by his side now! Nothing in pastoral training had prepared me for this. I advanced very carefully and gazed into the depths below. Covered in a sea of mud, and with an incredulous look on his face, my colleague stared up at me. Rather like when a golfer stands and waits by the hole when his ball has stopped right on the brim, hoping that it will topple over, I waited too. I threw up a dart prayer that the funeral director and his men would come forward to rescue him, but my prayer was not answered! Indeed in a miraculous way they seemed to have disappeared altogether. There was nothing for it but for me to kneel down and try and help him out. Rather like a buffalo coming out of a mud bath (that I was later to see so many times in East African game parks) and accompanied by a large squelchy sound he slowly but surely appeared over the top of the grave and after much more slipping and sliding plus help from me, finally made it to what by no stretch of imagination could be described as dry ground!

By the time I had completed the rescue there wasn't much to tell between us. His doting wife rushed forward and, without even a glance of gratitude in my direction, produced a handkerchief and made a vain attempt to clean his face. The whiteness of his face contrasted vividly with the brown of the mud on his otherwise spotless surplice. I must admit he looked ghastly, so against my better inclination, I heard myself volunteering to finish off the funeral. No sooner said than done, and supported by his ever-loving wife, he disappeared from view. His disappearance coincided with the reappearance of the funeral director and his men. The grieving funeral party still looked shell-shocked, but after waiting a few moments for them to gain some sort of composure, I continued with the service. To crown it all, Rose (who also made sure I looked nice and tidy before taking a service) berated me when I got home for being in such a filthy state!

To return, however, to thoughts about how my future ministry might develop: having changed career horses in midstream, and at a time of my national service to boot, meant that my education had been severely interrupted. Spending the next four years as a lay reader didn't help either. I did wonder if my ministry might be hindered because I had no degree. Since then I have come to see that promotion in the Church is not what position you hold, but being where God wants you to be.

As so often happened in my life, decisions seemed to be taken out of my hands. Within six months of being in Aberdare I had built up a clientele of about fifteen very sick people who could no longer get to church. I believed passionately that if they couldn't get to church then the church needed to go to them. So I arranged a monthly rota of sick communions and this alone took up two or three mornings a week. At my first retreat I reviewed my ministry to date. It became obvious to me that I was called to be a 'worker', rather than an 'academic' priest, and that I could best serve the Lord in the daily round rather than in the study. So I gave up the idea of working for an external degree, but instead concentrated on developing a practical ministry. In this, of course, I had a four-year advantage through my work with the Missions to Seamen, plus just under a year in my first parish. As a result I felt I had already had a good groundwork in such things as hospital and sick visiting.

Charley Arthur (as by now we had nicknamed him) had other ideas. To his great credit he took very seriously the responsibility of training his curates. Shortly after I arrived he told me that he was going to take me with him to our local hospital to teach me how to visit. I respectfully pointed out that I had been hospital visiting on a regular basis for some five years, so didn't really need instruction, but he would have none of it. 'I'll meet you, dressed in your cassock,' he firmly instructed me, 'at two-fifteen outside the hospital grounds.' We met exactly on time and advanced towards the hospital.

There had been a very serious pit accident a few days earlier, involving fire underground. We knew that one ward had been set aside for the miners who had been injured, and it was to this ward that we went first. I was shocked by what I saw. I was reminded of one of those cartoons showing a patient bandaged from head to toe, both legs in raised splints, with slits in the head dressings for the eyes. There were about twelve men in the ward, so after a short prayer outside we entered and made our way to the first bedside. I felt even sorrier for the patient as he saw two men, dressed in black, gazing down at him. Being the pupil I waited for my teacher to speak. He did. 'Do you know who I am?' he asked the unfortunate patient.

'No, mate,' came the muttered reply and in a tone that signified to me that he couldn't care less who we were.

'I am the vicar of Aberdare,' he informed him in a slightly pompous manner. I squirmed as the patient closed his eyes. After a few more words we moved on to the next bed, and then on to two further wards. At this point the vicar decided that I now knew how to hospital visit, so we split forces to cover the rest.

Two days later I returned alone to the miners' ward and stood in the middle of the room but this time without my cassock. 'I'm a scout from Cardiff City football team' I told them, 'and I'm looking for a goalkeeper and a centre forward. Any takers?' After only a few moments (whilst I wondered whether mine or the vicar's approach was right after all) came chirpy replies from all over the room. 'Yes me – put me down as centre forward,' and other similar replies. I have long since found that, for me and those for whom I have had the privilege of serving, laughter is often the best medicine.

Seeing and visiting those badly injured men had a profound effect on me, and from that day on I have never ceased to pray for all those with whom I will come in contact as I enter any hospital, and to thank God that I am able to walk out as I leave. As my ministry developed I followed the same practice in visiting prisons and hospices too.

Although, after my experiences of mass baptisms in my last parish, I was very wary of going down the same road again, I still pursued any who had not been christened with great enthusiasm. I still rate the privilege of holding a baby in my arms, and baptizing that infant 'in the name of the Father and of the Son and of the Holy Spirit' as one of the most rewarding of my ministry. Possibly this became obvious from the way I conducted such services because in a surprisingly short time I acquired a reputation for taking baptisms, and as a result I was constantly being told of new arrivals into the big wide world, which merited a visit from me. One such baby, however, I found through personal contact.

Our young milkman proudly informed Rose one morning that he had just become the proud father of a lovely baby daughter. Rose told me the good news when I returned from an early morning communion, so I determined to visit his house as soon as possible. I actually met the milkman about an hour later when doing my rounds. I offered my congratulations and promised to visit mother and baby shortly. Because he was our milkman I knew him fairly well and thought him a nice enough fellow, although he never had much to say for himself. I was surprised when, on knocking on his door a few days later, I found his wife to be extremely attractive, highly intelligent and brimming with fun and vitality. The baby was simply gorgeous, and in no time at all the baptism was arranged for about two weeks' time.

As it happened there were three babies to be baptized on the same day. It proved to be a very successful service as everyone knew each other, and the service was completed without a hitch.

The milkman's baby was the last of the three to be christened, and although up to that moment all the babies had been as good as gold, she did start crying just before I christened her.

I thought nothing of it as everyone went their separate ways. On the Monday morning a very distressed milkman informed us that soon after the service the baby had become very ill, and had been taken to hospital. I immediately went to visit her and was told that she had meningitis and was desperately ill. Her mother was absolutely distraught, and although I offered what comfort I could she was inconsolable. I left feeling totally inadequate, helpless and extremely distressed. Because I had just baptized her I felt in a very special way deeply involved. I visited the hospital every other day for as long as she was there, and kept up seeing her once she was brought home.

In visiting houses there are three scenarios. The first is being invited into the front room (grandly known as the parlour!). The second is being invited into the kitchen (which was usually the most used room in the house, and the best place to get a cup of tea) and the third is being told, 'don't bother to knock on the front door, just come round to the back and let yourself in!' In a very short time I progressed through all those stages, and ended up letting myself in through the back door.

The baby never recovered and died about six months later. She must have been in a lot of pain and cried continually. My heart bled for the baby and her mother as she desperately tried to manage. I don't blame the poor husband at all, but the truth was he just couldn't cope at all, and increasingly distanced himself from the scene. This of course upset his wife even more and, as can so easily happen, made her rely more and more on me.

I found coping more and more difficult, especially when she started saying things like, 'you understand me much better than my husband does'. I knew that I had to remain perfectly professional and in this I succeeded, although on one occasion I came to realize how easy it could be to cross over the boundary between the two. I had made my way round to the back door and as usual let myself in. I was used to hearing the baby crying but what met my eyes and accosted my ears on this day was something different. Mother was cradling the crying baby in her arms, but she too was sobbing her heart out. She must have sensed that I had come in, for she turned and saw me, put the baby down and rushed towards me, tears cascading down her face. I put my arms around her, and held her tightly, whilst she proceeded to break her heart. I do not know how long I comforted her, but gradually she calmed down and the tears subsided. As she gained her composure she lifted her tear-stained face up to me and gave me a very tender look. As she did I was suddenly aware that I was holding a young and very attractive woman in my arms.

These days, clergy are told never to put themselves in such a compromising position, but in those days no such advice was forthcoming. I became acutely aware that I was in a potentially dangerous situation, so as soon as I could I disengaged myself, suggested she make a nice cup of tea, which she did, and after a short while took my leave. I had a word with her husband, encouraging him to be more supportive, which in fairness to him, he did. The baby died very shortly after and that funeral ranked as one of the most difficult I have ever conducted.

Another difficult service, but for entirely different reasons, came about as a result of my work with young people. There was youth work of a sort in the parish, but no one had taken it under their wing, and as a consequence there was huge potential waiting to be harnessed. I took it on, and the results were remarkable, certainly in terms of numbers. Aberdare, in line with so many other Church of England parishes, had never really sorted out its policy regarding youth work. Should the 'Church Youth Club' be for the committed Christians from within the congregation, or be opened up to all young people within the parish? I saw it as the latter, because it embraced the opportunity for outreach into the community. Because it had become 'my baby' I was given a free hand at first. We had excellent facilities and I soon learnt that, provided the club was open to everyone and that the organization itself was prepared to pay half towards the cost of items obtained, considerable grants could be obtained from the local council. In no time at all we had first-class equipment including two table tennis tables, gym equipment and football gear.

The club went from strength to strength, not only socially, but also through what I called 'The God Spot'. The first part of the evening was devoted to something constructive such as drama, cooking, woodwork or art. Then we had the 'God Spot', which lasted about quarter of an hour and gave me the opportunity to introduce a little homily or some religious teaching. Refreshments followed before the final session, which was social activity or dancing. I was so thrilled that the 'God Spot' seemed appreciated and even enjoyed that I decided to hold a special youth service in St John's Church, which was the original parish church, and situated in a prime position right in the heart of Aberdare.

The vicar supported the idea, and said he would come along to give the blessing, for which I was very grateful. The service was planned for a weekday evening, and I was agreeably surprised at the enthusiasm that surrounded the organization and young people's participation. At the staff meeting before the service the vicar announced that, as well as giving the blessing, he was going to address the congregation at the beginning of the service. The great night came, and the young people flocked to the church. There must have been over 100 young souls in St John's. As I waited for the service to begin I couldn't help but reflect that in all its hundreds of years this was very possibly the only time that it had been totally filled with young people. There was a real buzz in the air as we sang the opening hymn and the clergy processed into the church. Then the vicar spoke. As he did I wanted the earth to swallow me up and let me die! Just like a headmaster at a school assembly he berated his young congregation. 'I don't want to see you here just tonight,' he began, 'but I want to see you in church every Sunday'. He continued in a similar vein telling them that if they hadn't been baptized then that must be their next course of action. And then after that confirmation!

In the course of about five minutes of pontificating he destroyed five hard months' work. I totally despaired, but what was more to the point, so did the young people. That was the first and last service of its kind. The Church in Wales at that time included in its baptism service the placing of a white chrisom on the baptized person. They were also given a lighted candle to hold. The Vicar insisted that if a couple wanted to be married in church then they both had to be baptized. This meant that we had a whole series of what I would call baptisms of convenience. In many cases there was no sincerity at all in the service, and as the chrisom was placed on the young man and he was given a candle to hold he could barely contain himself from laughing. To me the whole service was a farce and I squirmed whenever one took place.

I mentioned that one of the previous vicars of Aberdare was the Reverend Green, later to be the Archbishop of Wales. There were still in the vestry his handwritten notes setting out procedures for various preparations and services. From these it was obvious that he was a stickler for even the smallest details, which may have been in order in his day, but were more than outdated by my time. But to the vicar of Aberdare they were sacrosanct, and had to be implicitly obeyed. To my mind, he moulded his present ministry along exactly the same lines as Green before him, not taking into consideration the years that had passed.

Every person is different, of course, and what works in one time and for one person does not necessarily work for another. As a consequence I felt the ministry at Aberdare was stinted, which was a huge pity as there was so much potential, as my work amongst the young so ably demonstrated.

Not only is every person different, but also so are their circumstances. OG Rees the previous incumbent (and the warden of St Michael's during my last months), was different in every way from Charles Arthur. So were his finances. OG Rees either had no children or they were grown up and no longer a liability. Mr and Mrs Arthur had three young children who were very much a financial liability. Their eldest son, Richard, unfortunately had a very difficult birth (I believe being starved of oxygen). Whatever the reason he was a source of constant worry and expense, which all meant, that as with most clergy, money was very tight. The Church in Wales became disestablished in 1928, by popular acclaim of the clergy, but the very act of disestablishment meant a huge drop in salary for the incumbents, from which the church has never fully recovered even to this day.

During my time in Aberdare most of the funerals were burials, and no matter who took the service, the fee went to the vicar. The same applied to weddings. Cremations, however, were now becoming more and more popular, and if the crematorium was outside the parish, whoever took it received the fee. At the weekly staff meeting during the Reverend Rees's time there was great excitement when at the appropriate moment, everyone got down on the carpet and OG Rees threw in to the circle all the money he had received for fees during the past week. It was then shared out equally amongst all present. When OG Rees left, his curates remained, so when the new incumbent stopped this practice, they were not at all pleased.

But things sadly got worse! It was the vicar who delegated all the services and if one was called upon to take such a cremation it was great, because curates especially were even poorer than the incumbent. The fee in those early days was ten shillings. Whenever I took a cremation I always bought Rose a present with the money. It was the only time she ever got nylon stockings!

Then we suddenly noticed that we were no longer taking cremations. Burials, yes, and lots of them, but cremations, no! Then we realized why. It was because the vicar was taking them all. From that moment on he was known amongst his staff as 'Cremation Charlie', and if the truth be known I don't think he was ever forgiven.

It was around this time that I witnessed another misuse of power. Ever since my Nonconformist minister befriended me in my first parish over our house I had a very soft spot for the ecumenical movement. So when we were informed at our weekly staff meeting that there was to be a meeting of all the clergy in the valley, to see how we could better work together, I was really thrilled and looked forward with great enthusiasm to the forthcoming meeting. It was held in one of the local church halls and by the time the meeting was due to start there must have been about thirty priests and ministers milling around the hall.

Everyone seemed to be getting on very well and conversation was flowing. Then someone jumped up on the stage and called for order. It was our rural dean. He began by thanking everyone for coming (the wisdom of which I mentally queried as I knew the initiative had come from the chapel ministers and not him). Then he said, 'Well let's get on with the meeting. As I'm the rural dean I am the obvious person to chair the meeting.' The response from the assembly proved just how wrong he was. Within a few seconds chaos reigned. No less than a dozen irate clergy climbed onto the stage, all trying to speak at the same time! As a consequence nothing could be heard either from the stage or from those left on the floor. Within five minutes the meeting was over, in fact it was really over before it even began, and we all went home.

What I didn't realize, of course, was that despite some of the failures I have recorded during my first two curacies, the experience gained would stand me in good stead in years to come, as I hope to show. As in all situations there is always some light relief. This came in the person of Richard Arthur, the vicar's eldest son. He was obsessed with church matters, and claimed to know who was to be appointed to where, almost before the vacancy had been announced! He could tell you who was to be the next Bishop, or to be appointed to one of the stepping stones of the church, for which the Church in Wales was famous. His father being vicar of Aberdare (which was itself a stepping stone), no doubt discussed some of these issues round the dining table, but funnily enough Richard never forecast further promotion for his father. It was surprising however that Richard, from whatever source his information came, was usually accurate, and it became a common saying that if you wanted to know what was on the move, ask Richard!

He attended the local school, which was housed in the grounds of Lord Aberdare's estate where we lived. The headmaster, who was the vicar's churchwarden, was a very strict disciplinarian and I was appalled at times by his vicious use of the cane. There is no shadow of doubt that if Richard had been anyone else but the vicar's son he would have been at the receiving end of punishment on very frequent occasions, but it was generally recognized that he was handicapped, so got away with indiscretions on more than one occasion.

I soon became as one of the family, and sometimes ended up looking after the three children whilst the vicar and his wife attended a function. Richard had a sadistic streak in him, which was on occasions vented on his two younger sisters. I found this extremely hard to cope with, but having been beaten as a child, knew this wasn't the right way to cope with his sometimes shocking behaviour. The vicar told me he would support me in whatever way I controlled him, but being one of his curates obviously made things very difficult. I think at the heart of the matter was the fact that, all other things being equal, Richard would have liked to be a priest, but that obviously was impossible. It was in this area that the biggest problems arose.

Probably because of his disability he tended to mix with children younger than himself. The fact that he was tall for his age anyway gave him a position of leadership and authority over his peers. He set up his own chapel in one of the rooms in the vicarage, and used to hold services there for his 'followers'. Nothing wrong with that, except that in his enthusiasm what started off as baptizing dolls then progressed to baptizing children. Baptism can be conducted by anyone, whether ordained or not, which meant that those baptisms were legal. It may well be that some of the children were baptized already, or if they hadn't been before, their parents would have no

Our top floor flat in Mardy House, where Michael escaped onto the roof!

doubt preferred a more traditional baptism service. The whole thing was hushed up so I never knew the outcome, but for Vicar Arthur, following in the steps of Archbishop Green, a stickler for correctness, the whole matter must have been a terrible cross to bear.

Then a crisis of a much more personal nature occurred for Rose and me. Because we lived on the third floor of Lord Aberdare's old house there was a problem of hanging out the washing. It was obviously too much of a hassle to go all the way down to the grounds, but our predecessors had found a solution which we continued to use. A door had been inserted into one of the corridors of our flat that opened up onto the roof at a point that gave access to a gully at the meeting of two roofs. Our predecessors had added pallets and a washing line, which solved the problem of drying the washing. Because they had no children the question of danger wasn't an issue. Michael by now, however, was crawling and walking, and like every child of his age was into everything. We therefore had a wooden barrier made, which was put into place immediately the door was opened so providing a safeguard to stop him venturing forth onto the roof.

On the day in question I had gone to the school to take morning assembly. Rose was, as usual, busily engaged in the normal household chores including washing. She had emptied the washing machine of its first load then filled it up with the next wash. She put the washing machine on for the second time, and then took the first load out onto the roof for drying. As she turned to pick up some more clothes from her basket she saw that the washing machine, which was visible through the window, was spilling out hot soapy suds all over the kitchen (unfortunately she hadn't closed the door properly). Understandably she panicked and flew into the kitchen to repair the damage.

In her haste she omitted to put the barrier back in place. She did what she could to minimize the mess in the kitchen and then returned to finish off putting the remainder of the washing on the line. The first thing she saw was the barrier not in its proper place. She immediately thought of Michael, called his name but there was no answer. She looked out onto the roof and horror of horrors saw him right at the far end of the gully and looking down to the ground some forty feet below. She was almost paralysed with fear and just didn't know what to do. She saw one of the schoolchildren in the grounds and called out to her to go and fetch me immediately and to say that Michael was out on the roof.

As it happened I was on my way back anyway. Having just been given the message my eyes were glued to the roof as the house came into view. And I immediately saw Michael standing completely unfazed right on the edge of the roof, gazing down to the ground beneath. I am sure I created a world record for running upstairs, at the same time trying to work out what was the best course of action to take. Like many children of his age one of his favourite games was to run away when we called, 'Come to Mummy, or Daddy', before being swept up into our arms. That obviously was not on. I know I prayed for divine help and decided to sit on the doorstep at one end of the gully with Michael at the other and as casually as possible call out, 'Hello Michael, come and see what Daddy's got.' I pulled out my bunch of keys and pretended to examine them minutely. Michael grinned at me in the most disarming manner but made no move. What horrified me was that I had no idea whether Michael was expecting me to chase after him, when he didn't respond to my call. There was nothing for it but to sit tight and continue enthusing about my keys. After what seemed like an eternity, I sensed, rather than saw, that he had taken a step towards me. Yet again I extolled the keys' virtues but this time I dared to look out of the corner of my eye and to my immense relief saw that he had indeed taken a few more steps away from the edge of the roof. It took an effort of supreme willpower not to rush and pick him up, but I knew that could result in disaster. So I sat tight, prayed, and continued encouraging him to come and see what Daddy had got. Finally he was by my side and examined my keys, whilst I grasped him tightly in my arms. Seconds later Rose was also by my side and the three of us joined in a mutual embrace. Because we didn't want to frighten him we made very light of the incident but for Rose and me it was probably the worst half hour of our lives. I certainly had nightmares about it many times in the months ahead.

One of my weekly duties was to take the school assembly in the church primary school. The headmistress had held the post for years and years so was known to many generations as a tyrant of

The nearest Michael came to following in my footsteps!

176

discipline. It wasn't the pupils alone, therefore, who held her in awe, but the parents too because so many of them had passed through the school themselves. If the truth were known, the curates who were detailed to take the assemblies were also a little scared of her. I was warned beforehand of what I might expect but nothing prepared me for what followed. I was introduced as the new curate who had come to talk to us and 'we will listen very carefully to every word he says, won't we?' she said. The children replied in no uncertain terms: 'Yes miss'.

Before the assembly began she told me how long I was to talk for, what I was to say and how I was to end. I don't know who was the more nervous, the children or me. I cannot remember a thing I said, but I do remember suddenly being aware that her beady eyes were upon me, and conveying more strongly than any words could command, that my time was up. It was, so we then sang the psalm, 'I will lift up my eyes unto the hills'. We sang it the first time I took the assembly, and we sang it every time I took the assembly. Parents told me that they sang it every time in assembly in their day too! The fact that there are 150 psalms to choose from seemed to have completely escaped her notice! There was, however, one great advantage: every child knew it by heart and sang it with great gusto. Nevertheless, above the sound of singing I heard another sound that at first I couldn't identify. I looked up from my book (because on that first occasion I, unlike the children, did not know it by heart) and noticed that the headmistress had left the stage and was, with amazing agility, gliding among the children like a knife through butter. It was then that I identified the sound. It was Mrs Davies slapping the legs of the children as she moved around the hall. It was bad enough during the singing of the psalm, but once it was over and we moved on to the Lord's Prayer, the noise of the slapping seemed to drown out everything else. Almost every phrase of the prayer was accompanied by a SLAP. 'Our Father' – SLAP. 'Who art in heaven' – SLAP. 'Ouch' – SLAP. 'Ouch!' then often three more slaps in rapid succession followed by some really serious crying. Occasionally she herself uttered some comment, such as 'stop fidgeting/turning round/talking during assembly'. She made her way majestically around the room before finally returning to the rostrum on the stage. I remember instinctively cringing back as she walked past me for fear that I would be attacked too!

I relayed my experiences at the next staff meeting and the general consensus was that the vicar should speak to the headmistress. Whether or not he ever did I will never know, but even if he did, it made no difference.

I did actually get into trouble over one of the assemblies but for an entirely different reason. I was talking to the children one morning about my experiences in Hong Kong. One of the children asked me if it was true that Chinese people had slit eyes? 'Oh yes,' I replied and intending to be funny, continued, 'and so do the birds!' In one of the lessons later on in the day the children were asked to draw a picture reflecting what I had told them about the colony, and almost without exception they all drew birds with slit eyes! When they took their work home to show their parents, they immediately picked up on the slit eyes.

'That's wrong,' the parents told them.

'Oh no it's not,' the children replied, 'the new curate told us so.' The next day I was accosted by an angry group of parents for giving such false information. It taught me a very valuable lesson. It also just goes to show how things have changed since the early sixties when, unlike today, anything a clergyman said was literally taken as gospel!

That incident apart, most parents were very supportive in everything

Aberdare's Sunday School

the church did. I have mentioned elsewhere that finances were always very tight, but we experienced some wonderful and thoughtful acts of kindness. During a particular cold spell the local coal man delivered sacks of coal to some other residents at Mardy House. As we were completely out of money I had not ordered any myself, but the coal man must have noticed as he filled up the other sheds that ours was completely empty. He came up to me and whispered, 'I have put some coal in your shed; just pay me when you can.'

We used to travel to Newport about once a month to visit Rose's family, and we never came back empty-handed. Rose's mother always went to the local market, returning with a joint of meat, fresh vegetables, and fruit. We were often given small gifts of money and told to buy Michael, and in due course our daughter, Elizabeth, a little present. That money always went on food or some other vital commodity, although Rose kept a very accurate account of how much had been given, and once we had got on our feet she reimbursed them with savings certificates.

During our time at Aberdare our daughter Elizabeth was born. Although in those days fathers were not allowed to be present at the birth, I was in the next room and heard the birth and Elizabeth's first cry. Unlike with the birth of Michael I was the first to be allowed in and on my own too! Such moments live in one's memory forever. Unlike when I saw Michael for the first time, I made sure that I said, and meant, what a beautiful baby she was. It was one of the proudest moments of my life when, together with Michael, who was now three years old, I went to the hospital and brought them home.

Aberdare then was an extremely happy time. It was there that I was ordained a priest, and celebrated Holy Communion for the first time in St Elvin's magnificent church. I was then given charge of one of the daughter churches, a huge privilege, in which I revelled and just loved being able to minister to the people who worshipped there.

I had given no thought to the future. In the first place because we were so happy, and in the second place, only having been there a short time, thinking about a move hadn't even entered my mind. On top of this I was convinced that the vow I made never to apply for a post, but wait to be invited was absolutely right for me. I was absolutely bowled over, therefore, when a letter arrived from the Missions to Seamen saying (to use a common expression at

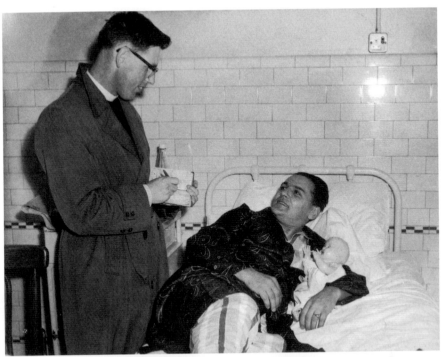

'Can it be true? Is she really yours?'

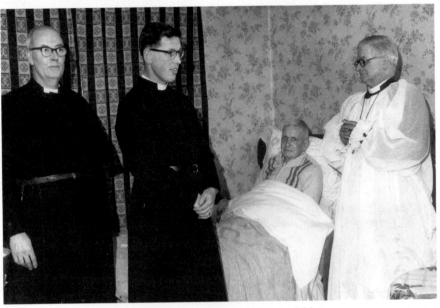

The confirmation of a bedridden parishioner

that time) 'We've got our beady eyes on you and want you back in the Society as soon as possible'. The letter continued that, although where I would be posted depended upon when the Church in Wales would release me, they would certainly be sending me abroad to one of their foreign stations.

Because the letter was so completely unexpected, I needed time first of all to take in its contents, to talk it through with Rose, and to decide whether in accepting this call I would be fulfilling the will of God. I also had to decide how to approach my vicar, and then inevitably the Bishop. I was also aware that, because the Church in Wales had accepted me, and put me through one of their colleges, I was obliged to serve them for a certain period, to repay, as it were, all they had done for me. How long I had to serve I had no idea. There was another factor to consider: if this was a call from God, should such conditions apply?

The necessary time to think and pray came from an unexpected quarter. To hospital for an ear operation! My mother had been deaf from a very young age and unfortunately I seemed to have inherited the same problem. The specialists had decided to implant a wire in my inner ear, and in fact I was to be almost one of the first to have such an operation. I was to be in hospital for about five days, and then I would be sent to respite home for another week to give me a chance to fully recover. Rose and I agreed that we would make no decision until after I returned, and that's what happened.

The operation in the hospital passed without incident, and then it was off to the recovery centre, which turned out to be an ex-hotel on the cliffs near Portsmouth. I arrived quite late at night, after 10 pm, so was quite surprised when the night porter told me that the matron was waiting up as she wanted to see me. He told me to sit in the hallway whilst he went to fetch her, and in the meantime gave me a brochure to read which set out all the conditions to which the patients had to adhere. I read with interest the rules of the establishment, which seemed pretty strict, including such details as what time patients had to be in before the doors were locked for the night.

Then Matron appeared, looking every inch the part. I rose to greet her, intending to thank her for waiting up for me, but I didn't get a chance even to open my mouth. She poked her finger towards my clerical collar and said in the voice of the inquisition, 'What are you?' It had been a long day, I admit to being tired, I wasn't

181

completely with it, so wasn't really sure what she meant by her question. The urgency by which she repeated it focused my mind. She wanted to know of what Christian persuasion I was. Of one thing I was certain, upon my answer depended how much I would enjoy the following week. I looked at her for a clue to her persuasion, decided she wasn't a Nonconformist, and so was either a RC or an Anglican. 'Well?' she demanded in a tone of voice that would brook no more waiting, 'Well what are you?' Cornered, I replied, 'I'm C of E'. Immediately her face softened and I knew I was on to a winner!

'Come and have a nice cup of tea,' she said, signalled to the porter to pick up my bag and led me into her private quarters. Over tea she told me she was the sacristan at the parish church at Portsmouth, that she would tell the curate to come over the following morning to take me out and show me around, and that if there was anything I wanted just to let her know. I was still grasping the brochure in my hand. She noticed it and said 'Oh don't worry about that, I will let you have a key so that you can come and go as you please!' Needless to say I had a wonderful week, including watching Portsmouth play football on the Saturday, and made good friends with the curate, who was kindness personified.

Now was time, however, to consider the decision that had to be made about any future move. Rose told me on one of our frequent telephone calls that she was going to leave the decision to me, and whatever I decided was all right with her. I decided that God did want me to resume my work with the Missions to Seamen, the proof being if it came to pass. The week passed very quickly, and was certainly beneficial, so I returned to Aberdare feeling fit and ready to face the future.

The first step was to tell the vicar. He was quite distressed and couldn't understand why I would want to leave Aberdare. All I could tell him was that I believed it to be God's will, so I really had no option. I am not sure that he was very much convinced by that argument, and retreated behind the authority of the Bishop.

A few days later the Bishop's chaplain rang me to arrange for an interview, and remembering the last time I was in his presence over the 'we don't want you to leave petition', I certainly was not looking forward to the experience one little bit.

The interview turned out yet again to be rather like the curate's egg. The first matter that came up was that I needed to serve in the Church in Wales for a minimum of five years to repay the time I spent in college. Although I could see the reasoning behind this I countered by saying, 'I believe it is to this vocation that God is calling me now. If so, then answering that calling must be right. In any case, surely the Church in Wales will not be losing a priest, but gaining a Missionary!' This answer somewhat flummoxed the Bishop, but I sensed that it had struck home. As we discussed the matter further, and on two other occasions as well, I sensed that doors were being opened for this new stage in my ministry. The Missions to Seamen joined in the debate, saying that they needed me in Ceylon, as it was then called, as soon as possible. Vicar Arthur, on the other hand, said that with Christmas coming up, he couldn't possible do without me over that period. I was profoundly moved when in my next interview the Bishop told me that he did accept that this was a call from God, that the Church in Wales would regard me as one of their missionaries, but that he wouldn't release me until after Christmas.

I myself was looking forward to Christmas in Aberdare so was perfectly happy with the decision that was made. The Church in Wales had at that time very few priests in the mission field, so to my surprise I became something of a celebrity. My old theological college at Llandaff set up a special prayer group to pray for its college's missionaries, a link that was maintained for many years. So Christmas came and went, and progress towards my new appointment continued. Not everything went smoothly, nor did my move meet with everyone's approval. Rose's parents were horrified that once again I was taking their daughter away, and again overseas. I was also a bit miffed that I had to be interviewed again by the Missions to Seamen candidates committee, having been before them seven years earlier, prior to being appointed as a lay reader. They had written to me asking me to rejoin them! It was only a formality, I was informed, and so it turned out. There were about five other young priests being interviewed on the same day, and I found it fascinating to hear their comments as they waited their turn. I did not let on that I had been with the Society before as a lay reader, although I could have answered many of the questions they raised amongst themselves! My interview was only to abide by Society rules and regulations, I was informed, but in any case they wanted to see me again. Before I left it was made abundantly clear to me that 'I was in' and they then wished me every blessing in my new appointment. After the interview I met with the general secretary who told me that they were sending me to Dar es Salaam in Tanganyika. It was a very interesting time, as Tanganyika was shortly due to be granted independence.* Because of this, however, I would need a work permit, which might delay our departure date a little. When they told me originally that they wanted me to go to Ceylon I went to the library and devoured many books on the country. I now decided that I would wait for confirmation of the Tanganyika posting before brainstorming similar books on East Africa. In the end the difficulties to be overcome simply faded away and before we knew it our passage was booked and, after a round of farewells, we were off.

---

*Three years later, Tanganyika merged with Zanzibar to form the new country of Tanzania.

EAST AFRICA

Chapter 16

On Board SS Uganda, *En Route to Tanganyika*

'We're off!' usually refers to the start of a race, with horses or athletes, tuned up to perfection, straining at the leash, impatient for 'the off'. Our departure to Africa was rather different. We arrived at the London docks on a chilly November afternoon, not so much 'straining at the leash to be off' as full of apprehension about what the future held for us. Last time we had set sail for distant lands there had just been the two of us; we were newly married, with not a care in the world, and life stretched before us like an exciting adventure waiting to unfold. And so it proved to be, as our three years in Hong Kong were enriching beyond description, religiously, culturally, and in the raw experiences of life. We arrived rather like 'babes in the wood', we returned with a much greater sense of maturity, my vocation firmly fixed on ordination, and with our first baby on the way!

Now it was altogether different. First and foremost, we were four souls, not two, with all the extra responsibility that entailed. Secondly, I was going out not to test my vocation but to exercise it. Thirdly, we knew we were going to a country that had just been given independence, which ensured a climate of uncertainty, to say the least. Indeed in my briefing at Head Office before departure, I was advised to 'make haste slowly', which I knew was exactly the opposite of how I normally worked! My very first words with the chairman of the port committee in Dar es Salaam would bring this fact into sharp focus, as will be shortly revealed.

Inevitably, there were last minute details to be finalized, and essential shopping to be completed. 'You never know what you will or will not be able to get in Africa,' we were informed by anxious parents. Luckily we were given a clothing allowance, which Rose particularly enjoyed spending, but that was not the only positive side of the coin. When we sailed to Hong Kong we went on a tramp steamer. Our journey to East Africa would be on the British India Liner, the SS *Uganda*, a very popular and, by the standards of the early sixties, luxurious passenger liner. Furthermore in view of the fact that I was now a Missions to Seamen chaplain, the company had upgraded us to first class. Included in the crew was a children's hostess (who actually became a very good friend over the years, and was the first woman ever to become a member of the Flying Angel Fellowship, about which I shall write later). Nevertheless, it was with some trepidation that we boarded the *Uganda*, and were shown to our cabin, which, although in the first class accommodation, was small for four. I remember that, while Rose busied herself with getting the children settled and the cabin shipshape, I explored the ship to find out the layout. Just before I returned to the cabin I felt the throb of the engines as they burst into life. Then came the announcement over the tannoy, 'The ship is very shortly to depart. Would all non-passengers please disembark now?' A few minutes later, as if in obedience to the ship's siren and with a barely perceptible movement, we slipped our moorings and were off. A new chapter in our lives had begun.

It was by now the children's bedtime, so we were very relieved that the changed environment didn't seem to worry them at all. Within a very short time they were both tucked up and asleep. There was a good system of baby-sitting on board that allowed us to have our meals together, and so we made our way to the dining room. We were shown to our seats and felt very honoured that we were seated at the table of the Chief Officer, John Young. He too became a very good friend of ours over the years, and we were delighted for him when he eventually became the commodore of the fleet. The company and food on board were excellent, and we were thoroughly enjoying them both when suddenly the ship started rolling and pitching. The Chief Officer assured us that it was nothing to worry about; it just meant that we had left the Thames, and were now out at sea. John Young told us one thing but our stomachs told us something else! Within a very short time we made our excuses and returned to the cabin, where we were both violently ill. I know of nothing worse than being seasick except what followed ... both the children became ill too! The next three or four days were probably the worst of our lives. We took it in turns to look after the children. fed them with drinks and biscuits brought to the cabin, and waited to die!

Then, mercifully, we awoke one morning to realize that the ship was comparatively calm. The steward advised us to get dressed and go up on deck, which we did. The fresh air was a tonic in itself, the sun fought to break through the clouds, and within a short time we all felt a great deal better. The children too became much sprightlier, so the previous days' experiences quickly became nothing more than unpleasant memories.

That proved to be the end of the rough seas, and although there were a few more spells of unsettled weather, having found our sea legs, we were not bothered any more. For most of the passengers the voyage was a time to relax, but I realized it was a golden opportunity to meet as many of the crew as possible, which I did. I was delighted to oblige when the Captain asked me to take Sunday services, and this again proved very useful in getting to know the Christian crew members.

As the *Uganda* was a regular visitor to the East African coast I eagerly sought the crew's views on the Missions there. 'Dar's not bad,' I was repeatedly told, 'but not a patch on Mombasa' (the next port along the coast). On enquiring why, the answer was the same every time: 'because they've got a swimming pool'. Ten days out from the UK, I informed Rose that the first thing I was going to do when I got to Dar es Salaam was to build a swimming pool. I shared this information with the ship's purser, who promised that some of the money raised on the ship for charitable causes would come to me. He was as good as his word, so when I disembarked in Dar es Salaam I was armed with a considerable donation towards it.

We left the UK on a cold, dismal autumn day and we arrived in Dar es Salaam on a wonderfully hot and sunny late Sunday afternoon. Dar is a beautiful harbour, as its name implies, its translation being 'the haven of peace'. One of the crew pointed out where the Mission was, which made us even keener to get ashore. No sooner had we berthed, however, than I received a message from the chairman of the Mission's committee to say that, due to a previous engagement, he couldn't greet me, but that he would come down first thing in the morning to take us to the Mission. Actually this proved to be a good move as it took away the worry of transport, etc. and also meant that the staff would know when we were arriving.

As every passenger knows, once a ship arrives in port it becomes a different animal. Swarms of stevedores and other workers, agents, ship chandlers and visitors appear to take over, and the serenity is replaced by organized chaos. In the case of Dar this meant that for my son Michael, for the first time in his life, he was confronted with African natives. I was horrified when, in a very loud voice, he came running up to me and said in the presence of about fifteen people, 'Daddy, there are lots of men who look like black monkeys running all over the ship!' I had visions of being deported even before setting foot on Tanganyikan soil! I frog-marched him off to the cabin to tell him the error of his ways, although I must say that he couldn't understand what he had done wrong, and was indignant about being reprimanded. The whole episode made me realize that coming to a newly independent country presented many difficulties. I was aware that in similar countries a degree of 'apartheid in reverse' was the practice. I would need to be very sensitive in dealing with Tanganyikan staff and colleagues. I needn't have worried about the children though. They settled in very quickly to a new way of life, made friends with the local children, so much so that I don't think they even noticed the different colour of their skins.

Chapter 16

Dar es Salaam 1961–1973

The last night on board ship was, I realized, the end of one era and the beginning of another. This I found both challenging and exhilarating, and so it proved to be. Equally so was meeting the chairman of my committee the following morning. Captain Church, who was also the Harbour Master, so an important person in his own right, greeted me very warmly. He proved to be a very pleasant and likeable person, although as with anyone who has risen to a position of authority, he obviously had a strong will and mind of his own. I am not sure that I got off to the best start, by presenting him with the ship's donation and volunteering the information that it was to be put towards the new swimming pool. 'What swimming

SS *Kenya* entering Dar es Salaam Harbour

191

Its Swahili translation 'The Haven of Peace'

pool?' was his startled reply. I passed on the comments of the ship's crew about the superiority of the Mombasa Mission because it boasted a pool, but he did not seem convinced. I found the same opinion to be common to quite a large number of the committee when I met them at our first meeting. The treasurer (who was also the manager of the largest bank in Dar es Salaam) spoke out very strongly against it. 'This is a time,' he said, 'to lie low and see what the future holds for expatriate institutions.' He was of the opinion that the Mission might well be taken over as an army officers' club.

I, on the other hand, argued that whatever the future held we should do the very best possible with the Mission whilst it was ours; that any improvements, even if held for a short duration, would benefit the seamen for that time; that we should definitely 'go for it'. The second argument against was 'Where is the money going to come from?' I optimistically replied that if the project were right, the money would come. I also said that I was quite convinced that the ships' crews themselves would contribute very generously and this source of income, together with grants and fund-raising, would meet the cost. Not surprisingly the committee

192

Dar es Salaam's Missions to Seamen

The pool

were divided but, even as I argued I sensed that there were some who were now on my side. I suggested that we put the matter to the vote, and to my great joy, and no little surprise, by the narrowest of margins the 'ayes had it'! The treasurer immediately resigned in protest (along with two colleagues) but others agreed to form a fund-raising committee. I left the meeting in high spirits, but with the knowledge that the talking was now over, the hard work about to begin.

My first clash then was with the faint-hearted on the committee, my second was surprisingly with the church establishment in Tanzania. News of the intention to build what would be the first pool in Tanzania created a lot of local interest, which was reflected in increased church attendance. Every Mission had a chapel, and ours, with St Peter's, was no exception. There were some local expatriate families who lived in the area, and a few of them started coming to the Mission services. But not only locals, other expatriates who lived in other parts of Dar es Salaam also started attending services at St Peter's Chapel.

The main Anglican church in Dar was St Alban's, and being also the pro cathedral, its senior priest was titled the Provost. The priest concerned, one Edmund Capper, had lived for many years in Tanzania and was very well known. He also was on the Missions to Seamen's committee, so I assumed he would give me every support. As my congregation increased I realized that, as a matter of priority, I needed to find an organist to play at the services. I discovered that apart from the regular organist at St Alban's they had three or four other musicians who also played from time to time. I went to him confident that he would be prepared to help me by letting one of them play at St Peter's. To my dismay he not only refused to cooperate but also started complaining about the number of souls (including some of his own congregation) who were now attending my services. My task, he told me, was solely to minister to visiting seamen. I tried to explain that I was trying to establish a normal congregation, so that seafarers attending found not just other seamen present but also a congregation similar to that of their parish church back home; that I encouraged shore-based members of my congregation to make friends with the visiting seamen, including inviting them to their homes for a meal; that this was in fact happening, to the intense joy of the men, who thereby witnessed family life away from home and loved ones.

There was sadly at that time a misconception amongst seamen about the expatriate community, whom they considered to be rather 'stuck up and aloof'. It was normally only the ship's captain and senior officers who would be entertained in a foreign port. As for the others, on the whole, no one wanted to know. The expatriate community on the other hand seemed to think that all the seafarer wanted was to drink in the nearest bar! The truth was of course very different, and I felt it was important that this ignorance should be broken down as quickly as possible on both sides. This was another reason why I started shore membership, which became very much sought after (especially after the pool was built!). I explained to those who applied that there were strict rules to be observed which could be simply summed up as 'they, and not the seafarers', were the visitors to the club; that they were at all times to offer friendship to 'those who go down to the sea and occupy their business in great waters' (to quote a well-known Missions to Seamen prayer). They were also expected to help in fund-raising and other activities. This scheme in fact became very successful, and I consider it to be one of the most useful things I have ever done. I know of friendships that were formed as a result of this scheme which exist to this very day.

To return to my meeting with Provost Edmund Capper, not only did he refuse to let me have an organist, but he told me in no uncertain terms that I was not to try and promote my church into parish status. Also, that if anyone came to me for counselling or enquiries about marriage or baptism, that I was to refer them to him, and that I was not licensed to conduct marriages, and any baptisms needed to be carried out at St Alban's. I was incensed. I pointed out that my ordination was as valid as his was; that I was not prepared to become a 'second-class citizen' as regards my priesthood; that I would be writing to Bishop William immediately, saying that unless I was allowed to conduct my ministry to the full I would ask my Mission Society to recall me to the UK. I requested a meeting with him and all concerned as soon as possible. The meeting came about very shortly afterwards. The Bishop, who was based upcountry, informed me that he was coming down to Dar on another matter and would see me at the same time. We met at St Alban's and as I walked in I felt rather as if I was a prisoner entering a court of appeal! The Bishop, flanked by the Provost and the archdeacon, sat on one side of the table, and I on the other. Formalities were soon over and the debate began. I was reminded that I was a young priest fresh in Holy Orders, and that they had years of experience, plus the authority of the hierarchy of the church. Nevertheless I stuck to my guns and slowly but surely I sensed that I was gaining support from Bishop William. To cut a long story short, I left the meeting feeling far happier than when I entered. The Bishop promised to write to me with his verdict and, although I couldn't swear to it, I felt sure he gave me a wink as we said goodbye!

I was not surprised, therefore, when his letter duly arrived completely upholding my request, raising the Mission to a parish status, and giving me authority to conduct weddings and baptisms at St Peter's. There was one more very important outcome as a result of my new status in the diocese. I became a member of the chapter (the regular meeting of all the local clergy). My predecessor had not attended so was not all that well known to the other brethren, whereas I very quickly got to know them all, and they me. I found my involvement with the indigenous clergy to be highly rewarding, and was surprised, especially as I was a Mzungu (foreigner), how quickly and genuinely they accepted me. At that time, of course, I had no idea how close the links were to become, nor that we were to spend the next twelve years of our lives in East Africa.

In all this I have somewhat 'jumped the gun'. When we arrived we found a very pleasant Mission building but little else. It reminded me of an empty shell. My first priority was to rectify the sad state of the Mission transport. Apart from my own car, transport was also needed to ferry seamen from ship to Mission, and also to places of interest. I soon found out that the majority of the men hardly ventured beyond the dock gates. This I considered a great pity, especially as so many tourists came to East Africa just to visit the game parks. Mikumi, the nearest to Dar, was about 140 miles upcountry, so although this meant a round trip of some 280 miles, I considered it possible, providing the transport was good.

The mission transport was anything but! It consisted of three vehicles, two cars and one small lorry. All three could best be described as 'old bangers'. The older of the two cars they had for a long time been unsuccessfully trying to sell (and that's saying something, for in Africa there is usually a market for anything!). Apart from turning the engine over occasionally to charge up the battery it lay forlorn and alone in an unused garage. The other car, although running, was badly in need of a major overhaul. Timing its servicing to coincide with what looked like a comparatively quiet period in my diary, I booked it in. Alas 'the best laid plans of mice and men' – not more than ten minutes after I had returned to base after taking it to the garage, an emergency cropped up that required my presence immediately at the bank in the centre of Dar. There was nothing else I could do but resurrect the remaining car back into active service. It took me to Dar (just!). After finishing my business I prepared to return and was immediately concerned that the steering seemed even more erratic than on the journey in. Just how much, I was shortly to find out. There is a very sharp corner near the Mission, which I had navigated successfully on my way to town, but coming back my luck ran out! The car refused to navigate the bend and ended up halfway up a telegraph pole.

I cannot remember whether or not I lost consciousness, but I do know that when I looked around me I was lying on the floor surrounded by coins. It was as if pennies had rained from heaven (at the bank I had purchased a lot of change for the Mission tills and it was everywhere!). I was frantically trying to pick them all up when help arrived. In no time at all I found myself being stitched up in the outpatients department of the local hospital. Careful observation reveals the scars on my face to this day. Rose arrived shortly afterwards, and after further treatment I was discharged into her care. Ten days of loving care and attention did the trick, after which I was able to resume duties. I have recorded this incident for two reasons. The first is that the car was a write-off, and the insurance paid out over twice the amount that we were trying unsuccessfully to sell it for. As I became better known it was suggested that I crashed it on purpose to obtain the money!

The second reason is that the Governor of Tanganyika, who was still in residence at that time, came to hear of my accident and that the Mission now had no transport, as the other car was still being overhauled. He immediately put his own official car plus driver at Rose's disposal whenever transport was needed. Rose was most grateful and took full advantage of this generous offer. She was immediately named 'Queen Rose'! She was very amused one day when all she needed to go to town for was to get an iron repaired. The driver ceremoniously laid it in the boot, and drove Rose to town. The shop she wanted was in the main street of Dar.

The driver drew up outside (no fear of a parking ticket with the Queen's Crown instead of a number plate on the front of the car), opened the boot, then the car door for Rose to alight, saluted her, and then opened the door of the shop. The shop attendants meanwhile were convinced that a VIP was arriving, rushed to greet her, only to discover it was Rose with an iron that needed repairing!

Chapter 17

Developing the Mission

During my enforced time off work I investigated further the possibility of taking seamen to the game park. I calculated that, provided we left about 3.30 in the morning, we could arrive at the park soon after dawn (which is one of the best times to view the animals as they are then on the move). Then we could spend all day in the park, not leaving until just before nightfall, which was the second best time to view game. I knew I could rely upon the ships to provide the food. This meant that I only had to meet the cost of the petrol and the park's entrance fees, which divided amongst ten men was a sum well within the reach of all. I was determined, therefore, that one of my first endeavours on returning to duty would be to organize a game park safari. Everyone wanted to come; indeed I could have filled the seats ten times over! This was despite my explaining that it would be on an open lorry with benches as seats, not built for comfort, that it would entail a very long journey, and an even longer day. 'No problem,' I was assured. Indeed, the grimmer I painted the picture the keener they became, so despite the misgivings of some of the committee members, the great day arrived when we set off on the first ever safari to Mikumi Game Park.

When we left at 3.45 on that first morning, not only were the passengers present, but many envious well-wishers as well. Apart from a certain apprehension – 'had I bitten off more than I could chew?' – I had one other concern. Amongst my ten passengers were deck and engineer officers, as well as some members of the crew. Would they all get on well together? I wondered. There is a well-known saying in shipping circles, 'Oil and water don't mix!' On that score I needn't have worried at all. Everyone got on like a house on fire. In fact I found out afterwards that some long-standing disputes were settled on the journey! We hadn't gone far before banging on the roof of the cab told me something was wrong. The benches had come loose. Having seamen on board, however, meant that particular problem was soon fixed, so off we went again.

The whole day was a tremendous success. We arrived just as dawn was breaking and were immediately rewarded with a herd of elephants complete with young actually blocking our path. Including them we saw all the big seven game: buffalo, rhino, giraffes, hippo, wildebeests and lions. We also saw warthogs, monkeys, wild dogs, deer and of course the birds. It really was an unforgettable experience, and not only for the men. I rate it one of the most memorable and worthwhile days of my life. It epitomised for me what the Missions to Seamen stood for: 'The spiritual and material welfare of all seafarers irrespective of nationality, colour or creed'. When we finally arrived back at the Mission some twenty-four hours later, my suggestion that before we separated I should give a prayer of thanksgiving was well received and honoured. During the next twelve years I took many more parties to Mikumi, but that first safari will always stand out as something very special.

The poor state of the Mission finances meant that we were living from hand to mouth. I had an awful fight even to buy a new table tennis net! This helped me to better understand why some of the committee were reluctant to branch out on a major project such as a swimming pool, when there was barely the wherewithal to keep the Mission running. I, on the other hand, became even more convinced that a major project was the answer. It creates enthusiasm and support, not only for the project itself, but also makes waves in other directions. A swimming pool in Dar es Salaam in 1961 was an ambitious project by any standards, so once the news got around, many offers of help, as well as donations came pouring in. My trump card was to appeal to ships coming into port to take up a collection, and almost without exception they did. I had a large board erected at the entrance listing the names of all the ships that had given, how much, and also the state of play of the ships in port. In this way I built up a sense of competition, and the results, to put it mildly, were astonishing. I even received complaints from missions in other parts of the world who said that if they tried to get a donation off a ship they were told, 'Sorry, we're collecting for Padre John in Dar es Salaam'!

It is a matter of record that by the time the pool was finished and opened, it was paid for. Apart from ships' donations, we had many other fund-raising efforts, varying from fêtes to concerts, wrestling and boxing matches, dances and first night films at cinemas. Because of all this the Mission became the focal point of Dar fund-raising activities, and our popularity and support grew. To give one example. Every Christmas for a twenty-four hour period, people were invited to ring in to the local radio station and request a special tune or song, in exchange for a donation to their favourite charity. When we arrived the Missions to Seamen was at the bottom of the pile – within three years we were at the top. Apart from naming one's favourite charity one could also donate to the 'charity box'. This amount was then divided amongst all the charities named in proportion to their popularity. We obviously benefited greatly from this source as well.

The first fête was held on the Mission football pitch, from 2 pm to 4 pm on a Saturday afternoon and boasted ten small stalls. Over the years this grew to a three-day affair, and proved to be the biggest fund-raising event of the year of any charity in Tanzania.

As a consequence of all this support, we built during our time

The shop

201

A satisfied customer

The library and writing room

The renovated lounge

there: the swimming pool complete with changing rooms, etc, a kitchen, restaurant, cinema, shop, library, floodlit tennis courts, a four-table snooker room, a nine-hole crazy golf course and a bowling alley. We doubled the size of the chapel, and built a souvenir shop and a library.

It wasn't, however, only the Mission that was enlarged. When we arrived in East Africa there were three berths alongside. Before we left there were twelve, plus an oil terminal. Dutch firms undertook the civil engineering work, and I got to know them very well. As a consequence we received a huge amount of help. Many diggers, bulldozers, loads of concrete, and workers, etc. were miraculously diverted into the mission compound to aid our expansion projects, and at no cost.

The great day came when work started on the swimming pool. The first thing we discovered was a great plus. The Mission and grounds were built on top of sand. Excavation was therefore quick and easy – sadly too easy! I returned one day to find that they had almost finished excavating, the only problem being that they had dug out with the deep end where the shallow end needed to be, and vice versa! So came the first (of many) confrontations with the contractors. 'It doesn't matter which end is the deep end,' said

The Rev. Tom Kerfoot (General Secretary of the Missions to Seamen) and Bishop John at the official opening of the new library

Doubling the size of the chapel

Adding a vestry

the contractor. 'It matters a great deal,' was my reply. I won the day but a lot of extra work was required to put matters right. Work continued apace and it was not too long before the concrete base was laid. To avoid leaks it all had to be put down in one continuous operation. The task began early in the morning, and was finally finished (with the aid of flood lights) late at night. Being the first pool in Tanzania it attracted a great deal of attention. We had many visitors, including a Chinese delegation of engineers, who were in the country planning the Tan Zam railway. To my amazement I found myself (with the aid of an interpreter) explaining to them some of the principles governing the building of a swimming pool. I'm afraid I couldn't help but include into my explanation the importance of water as the means of initiation into the Christian Church! The speed of construction was matched by the donations from ships and other sources of fund raising. So much so that its costs were covered by the time it was completed. Needless to say, this was a cause for great celebrations. I was particularly pleased when those members of the committee who had objected and resigned over the project came to congratulate us and admit they had been wrong.

Ships' crews in port donating towards the new swimming pool

Some more of the same

Such was the impact of the pool that President Nyerere himself agreed to open it. This was a tremendous plus in many ways, not only because it gave us an official stamp of approval, but it also augured well for the future. It also turned out to be an historic occasion in an unforeseeable way.

As can be imagined, we planned to capitalize on the opening in every possible way. The official opening was to be in the afternoon, to be followed by a demonstration of swimming and life-saving by one Helen Eggert,who was elected to swim for the UK in the 1954 Melbourne Olympics. Unfortunately she misbehaved on the ship going over; and with rules being so much stricter in those days, her actions caused her to be dropped from the team. These days they would have been put down to nothing more than high spirits, which is in fact all they were. She was a ball of fire, fun and energy and had the vast audience in stitches as she pretended to be drunk and fell into the pool.

I obviously wanted as many seamen as possible to be present for the opening. There were about twelve ships in harbour at that time, and I managed to visit them all with invitations to the opening. Experience had taught me who was the best crew member to notify if I wanted to make sure that everyone knew what was going on. I would carefully select 'my victim' and the conversation would proceed something like this.

'I do hope you are coming to the official opening.'

Often a half-hearted response, 'Well I will come if I can, padre,' and then would follow possible excuses as to why he may not be able to make it.

'That's a great pity,' I replied, 'because Elizabeth Taylor is going to be present, and at ten past three she is going to dive into the pool topless. I obviously can't tell everyone because there won't be space for all who would want to come, but I had singled you out particularly to represent your ship.'

Suddenly great interest takes the place of indifference. 'You're kidding me, aren't you Padre?'

'No,' I would reply, 'with hand on heart I tell you that she will be there at ten past three, and will be diving into the pool topless.'

'Hey, padre, I've just realized that I can make it after all, so I will be there.'

I hadn't finished yet. I pointed out that because there wouldn't be space for all his shipmates he should keep the news to himself,

The President and Mrs Nyerere on the occasion of the opening of the
new swimming pool

Bishop William blesses the pool

except possibly telling his best mate. Knowing full well that it would be the worst kept secret of all time, I departed to follow the same tactic on every ship in port.

The result exceeded all expectations, and I think for the first (and last) time ever we had every available seaman in port at the Mission on that day. At ten past three precisely, just as promised, Elizabeth Taylor did make her appearance, and dived topless into the pool. The only difference from what the men expected was that the Elizabeth Taylor in question was my own three-year-old daughter!

That apart, the official opening went extremely well. President Nyerere duly arrived and was welcomed and introduced.

The Army military band under the command of one Captain Green played the national anthem and then entertained us with stirring music. President Nyerere, who was an Edinburgh University graduate, was a staunch Roman Catholic. I had met him before, through church circles, but even so I was overwhelmed by his friendliness to me, and his obvious enjoyment of the occasion. He gave a very complimentary speech about the work of the mission in Dar es Salaam and assured us of his support in the future. After about an hour he said his goodbyes and left. I had organized a ball in the evening and Captain Green kindly arranged for the dance band section to play for us (without charge) at this event. This too was a great success, and finished just after midnight. The band members asked if they could leave their instruments at the mission overnight. Although I readily agreed, I thought it a rather strange request, as they had all the transport there, so could easily have taken their instruments with them.

Chapter 18

The Army Mutiny

The next morning I found out why the band had made their unusual request. For the children it was school as usual, which, as was common in the tropics, meant an early start. We had a duty rota of parents to take the children to school and sure enough at about 7.30 the duty parent arrived with hers and other children in tow, to pick up my son Michael. Being the day after the official opening there was an awful lot to do so I took very little notice of their coming and going. About a quarter of an hour later, however, I was surprised to see her return to the Mission with all children still on board. She was in a very distressed state, understandable after what she had just been through. She was, she told me, approaching one of the roads leading into Dar when soldiers, who had erected a barrier across the road, forced her to stop. They approached the car, and one of them then pushed a rifle into the back window and threatened to shoot the children. To make matters worse, she realized they were drunk. They made her hand over her money and jewellery, and after shouting at the children in a most frightening manner, made her turn the car around and return from whence she had come.

The port offices were next door to the Mission, so I ran over to see if they had any news. They had. The Tanganyikan army had mutinied during the night (which explained why the band did not want to take their instruments with them when they left), and taken over the city. President Nyerere had gone into hiding, and there was chaos everywhere. Everything was closed down, and incidents such as the stopping of cars and demanding money were commonplace and made everyone extremely apprehensive. The Mission had, because of its church services and other activities, become the local centre for the expatriate community, so I was not surprised when some of them arrived, assuming that we would be a sanctuary. Indeed when, later on that morning, firing began in the vicinity, we all retreated to an inside corridor in the building, which, having no windows, gave us protection. The next few days were traumatic in the extreme, and I felt a great sense of responsibility for having brought my family to such an unstable situation with the prior knowledge that this kind of incident was a distinct possibility. Because the Mission was out of town we actually saw very little of the troubles, but I became involved in other ways.

The port authority's offices, like all other official and government institutions, were closed down. At least twice a day army patrols came to check that no activity was taking place. In fact an awful lot was going on. There were very powerful radios used for contacting ships at sea in the offices, and unbeknown to the soldiers two of the harbour pilots were locked in the radio room keeping contact with the outside world. During the hours of darkness I took them over food and other essentials, and by this means heard that they were in contact with the Royal Navy. I learned that the 41 Royal Marine Commandos were standing by waiting for the order to come ashore. President Nyerere himself had requested that British forces come to restore order to his country. This must have been a bitter pill for him to swallow, seeing that it was only a short time since Tanganyika had received independence. In the meantime there were other pills that had to be swallowed.

A few days after Saturday's pool opening, I received a phone call.

'This is the band master speaking,' came an obviously Tanganyikan voice, 'put me on to Padre Taylor.'

I knew for a fact that Captain Green and the other British officers who served in the Tanganyika army had been taken to the airport on the Saturday night and flown out of the country. I pretended not to notice the local intonation, however, and said, 'Hello Captain Green, how are you?'

'This is not Captain Green,' came the reply, 'this is Ambrose, the new band master.'

I started to mumble a suitable reply but was cut short by the voice of Ambrose once again.

'The band's musical instruments are still at the Mission,' he said, 'and I am sending down two army lorries to pick them up shortly.'

'No problem,' I replied, 'I'll have them all ready for you.'

Ambrose then said, 'Give the officer in charge the fee for playing at the mission last Saturday.'

'But Captain Green said that there was to be no fee, especially as President Nyerere was present,' I replied.

'Ah,' said Ambrose, 'that was in the afternoon. I'm talking about the fee for the dance band section that played in the evening.'

'Oh no,' I replied, 'it was made abundantly clear that the whole of the day was part of Tanganyika's involvement in the celebrations, and therefore there would be no charge.'

Now the mood turned ugly. 'I'm sending armed troops down shortly and they expect to pick up the instruments and the money. Have it ready or else!'

I was determined not to give way so I countered by saying, 'Then bring me down an official invoice, signed by Captain Green and I will pay.'

'That's not possible,' he said. 'Captain Green is no longer here.'

'Then I can't pay you,' I replied. 'I'm sorry but that's how it is.'

One of the committee members had come in during the course of the phone call, and became extremely agitated by the gist of the conversation. 'You must pay him,' he said, 'or the consequences don't bear thinking about.'

I was determined, however, not to give in to bullying or blackmail but I did take what precautions I could. First of all I made all the family and any visitors retreat to what I called the safety corridor. The next step was to put on my cassock! I always felt that when I had it on I was under special protection! I was too angry to be afraid, but whilst I was waiting I did nip into the chapel to pray. I came out just as two army vehicles swung off the road and onto our football pitch. Out jumped about fifteen soldiers, all armed with rifles, and they started to advance towards the Mission.

I strode out to meet them and called out 'Simama', which means stop. To my surprise they did. I explained that, the Mission being a house of God, I could not possibly allow them to bring arms inside. Remembering my national service days I showed them how to stack their rifles in a circle. I then told one of them to stand guard over them, and welcomed the others in. The officer in charge demanded to collect the instruments and receive the payment for the band. The instruments I had all ready, the money, no. I explained that I couldn't possibly pay out without an official invoice signed by Captain Green. We stood eyeball to eyeball for a seeming eternity. Then he spoke. 'I will take the instruments now,' he said.

A Royal Navy helicopter carrying marines landing on the Mission's football pitch following the mutiny of the Tanganyikan Army

'I will report to the bandmaster what you have said. But be sure we will return for the money shortly.'

I breathed a sigh of relief as they left, telling myself I lived to fight another day. I returned to the chapel to give thanks and to pray that it would be sooner rather than later before the marines landed. On reflection I wonder whether I would have been so adamant in refusing to pay if I had not known that relief was not far away. The trouble was I couldn't share this knowledge with anyone else, so others thought I was just being stubborn if not downright stupid!

Relief reigned when, a few days later, a British Army helicopter landed on the Mission football pitch, and out sprawled the liberating troops, who in no time at all organized themselves into units, and spread out from the Mission, especially into the port area. Rose was so elated that she went out to the jukebox, which was located in the swimming pool area, turned the volume up to its loudest and then played *Rule Britannia* and *Land of Hope and Glory*. The music blasted out all around the surrounding area. The relief to those who heard it was immense, as they knew it would have been suicide to play those tunes whilst the mutiny was still in force. I was immediately appointed chaplain to the marines, and met Colonel Nick Carter, the commanding officer, to examine the best way I could be of service.

213

Michael inspects an armed carrier!

Within a few hours of the landing, the mutiny was over. The British troops advanced to the Tanganyikan Army barracks, surrounded the guardhouse, and then gave the guards inside an ultimatum: 'Five minutes to surrender'. After the five minutes were up a mortar was fired into the guardhouse, and that was that. Troops, as well as some of the police. who had also joined in the mutiny, abandoned their uniforms where they stood and fled into the bush. The following day, a Sunday, the marines proceeded to 'Show the Flag' by parading their band along the sea front in the centre of town, playing all the traditional military tunes. This thrilled the expatriate community, but infuriated the President to such an extent that, although he had asked them to come in, he never forgave them for holding what he called a victory parade the very next day.

The marines were housed in the local stadium that had only recently been built to house the Independence celebrations. It was very basic, however, and as the troops had been diverted from their way back to the UK for leave after overseas service, understandably morale was not very high. The British Ambassador suggested that the President should come out and visit the troops at the stadium. He at first refused but under extreme pressure was forced to agree, although he drew a line at actually thanking the troops for coming! His visit was planned to take place in three days' time, and I was impressed just how much effort the troops put into making the stadium spick and span. He was to arrive in his own car but then be taken around the stadium in an armed carrier. I was on parade with the troops and standing next to the vehicle that was to take him on tour when he arrived. A few moments before he was due to board the carrier, an officer gave a final check on the vehicle to see that all was well only to discover that someone had stuck some drawing pins under the seat he was due to sit on! They were hastily removed, but for the record the culprit was never discovered. Looking back, I am not sure how much effort was made to find out who the guilty party was! As it turned out, the visit went off without a hitch, to the great relief of all concerned.

The orders to the troops were, once the mutiny had been put down, to play down their presence as much as possible. This meant that, unless on patrol, civilian clothing was to be worn. But this had its drawbacks. One of them being that not being in uniform they came under the jurisdiction of the Tanganyikan judiciary. This led to a so-called 'serious incident'.

Dar es Salaam boasted only one 'nightclub', a rather sleazy place which, after the incident was put firmly out of bounds. Understandably the troops were by now thoroughly depressed, as by rights they should have been back in 'good old Blighty', enjoying some well-earned leave with their families. Instead they were billeted in a sports arena, under very basic conditions, and feeling unwanted into the bargain. To alleviate their discontent a group of them went down to the nightclub, not with the intention of making trouble, but certainly of having a few drinks and letting off steam. At one stage during the evening a dancer appeared on the stage, and in a most provocative manner started to strip. This proved just too much for some of the men, who invaded the stage and surrounded her. The management, who had sensed trouble as the marines became more and more boisterous, had alerted the police, who were in fact standing by. In no time at all the men on the stage were arrested, the other marines thrown out, and some sort of order restored. Other marines were also in Dar that evening, and in an incredibly short time the word got around that a group of their mates had been arrested and taken to the nearby police station. Some thirty

215

marines congregated outside the station, held a council of war, and decided that they were not going to allow their comrades to be incarcerated one minute longer. They advanced into the station, took it over, and had the prisoners released. They then bore them off (like heroes!) in triumph back to the stadium.

The first task delegated to me was to hasten to the police station on a damage limitation exercise. Fortunately I knew some of the officers concerned, and was able to convince them that all that had really happened was that 'high spirits' had got out of hand, and that in the best interest of all concerned it would be wise to play down the incident. I assured them that the offenders would have to account for their actions before their own authority. After offering profuse apologies on the men's behalf it was agreed to let the matter drop, although it certainly left a bad taste in the mouths of all concerned. The commanding officer, whilst reprimanding his men severely, for political reasons also played down the incident.

Someone who didn't get off so lightly however was a marine who was found sleeping on guard duty. This was considered a very serious crime, because it was only the day after the marines landed and the troops were still in a state of high alert. He was sentenced to three weeks' imprisonment, which although only in a makeshift cell, was nevertheless pretty uncomfortable. He became extremely depressed, with guilt feelings of having let his fellow soldiers down. I visited him and found him to be a nice lad, used to church going, who said he missed being in church on Sundays. My Mission chapel had become the church for the marines, and a goodly number attended our services. The prisoner asked me if it would be possible to attend. I took his request to Colonel Carter, who summoned the RSM to the meeting.

This RSM was a typically formidable man – he looked every inch of what one expected and was well over six feet in the bargain. I had already received an insight to his character and personality over another incident. It was 41 Commando who made the original landings, only to be relieved by the 40 Commando shortly afterwards. In the landings there was only one casualty. A crane, which was unloading equipment from a lighter, swung and hit a marine, causing fractures to his arms and legs. He was taken to the local hospital, where I found him. By now his comrades had departed to be replaced by 40 Commando. To my surprise he told me that he knew their RSM and would very much appreciate a visit from him.

My experience up to that time of RSMs was that they would be the last people in the world that I would want to visit me! I passed the message on to him nevertheless. He immediately stopped what he was doing, commandeered a jeep, and went to visit the injured man in hospital.

But back to the prisoner and his request. The CO granted his request, but said under that, Queen's Regulations, he would have to be taken and kept in handcuffs whilst outside the camp's perimeter.

'Permission to speak, sir,' barked the RSM.

This was granted, so he continued, 'I am prepared to take him to church and bring him back afterwards. If you are prepared to let him out under my charge, I guarantee that he won't escape, and that's without the aid of handcuffs.'

His request was granted, so on the following Sunday morning the two of them came to church, and no one else was even aware that one was a prisoner. He sat in the pew with the RSM by his side, made no attempt to escape, either on that Sunday or the two that followed. As a result my admiration and appreciation of the RSM increased even more.

One of my duties was to conduct a weekly 'padre's hour'. This was a compulsory session for all serving men, but I was aware that it was not popular, so feared I was in for a rough time. The first session took place at the stadium. It was a very hot day, there was little shade, and the men were fed up even before I began! Despite my best efforts tempers were no better – indeed probably worse – by the time the session came to an end. I knew I had to do something, so went to see the CO.

'Rather than me come to the stadium,' I suggested, 'they could come to me at the Mission. We could meet in the open-air restaurant, overlooking the swimming pool on one side and the football pitch on the other. I could see no reason,' I continued, 'why after the session was ended, they couldn't have a swim in the pool.' To my delight he agreed.

Thereafter 'the padre's hour' became the most enjoyable 'run ashore' of the week. The sergeant would march them up, see them all seated, report them all present and correct, and then ask permission to leave.

'Granted,' I said, and off he went.

Once he had gone I said to the assembled men, 'I'll do a deal with you. You're here for one hour. You give me your undivided attention for thirty minutes and then you can go swimming. If you don't, the session up here will last the hour!' I have never had a more attentive congregation in my life. If a single one of them deviated from perfect behaviour all those around him gave him such glares that order was restored even before it had been lost.

I was true to my word, and once the allotted time had passed I dismissed them and down the stairs they went and into the pool. This pattern continued without a hitch for about four weeks. One day, however, I was delayed for about five minutes, but by now the drill was so well rehearsed that the sergeant marched them up as usual, saw them seated and left. When I arrived I was puzzled because instead of being spread comfortably over the whole area, all the men were hugging the side nearest to the swimming pool. I looked over and saw the reason. There were two lovely girls swimming in it! The next thirty minutes seemed an eternity, both for the men and for me, but eventually the moment came when I was able to dismiss them. which I did. Instead of making for the stairs, at least half a dozen of them vaulted over the banister around the restaurant and within some five seconds were in the pool with the girls! The girls (actually seamen's wives) took it all in good part, and if the truth were known enjoyed the episode as much as everyone else!

An experience I didn't enjoy one tiny bit was boarding their aircraft carrier, which was anchored some little way out at sea. The wounded marine had been transferred on board and was asking to see me. A group of men were going out in a launch, so I went with them. Unfortunately our arrival coincided with the arrival of President Nyerere, so instead of boarding by means of the gangway, we were diverted to the other side of the ship, where the means of access were rope ladders hanging over the side. There was a considerable swell, which meant that one moment the rope ladder was within reach but the next moment it was five to ten feet above or below you. The marines were used to this but I wasn't!

Furthermore, from sea level to the deck of the aircraft carrier was a very considerable distance, requiring a lot of energy and effort to reach the deck. To be honest I was petrified, and the nearer it came for the moment for me to reach out and grab the swaying ladder, the more weak-legged I became. When my turn came I had no option but to leap and grab it, which I did. I made contact but after a few faltering steps upwards the ladder swayed alarmingly, after which I hung on for grim life, unable to move either up or down. The hymn 'For those in peril on the sea' came to mind, but didn't help me one little bit! Luckily for me the marine below me on the ladder came to my rescue. He put his shoulder under my bottom and more or less carried me to the top! Never have I been more relieved than when I finally reached the deck. A deep-felt thank you to my rescuer brought a cheerful answer. 'No sweat, padre,' and off he went.

I went to the sick bay feeling and looking far worse than the man I was visiting! I made sure when the time came for me to depart that there were no VIPs blocking the main gangway.

I had one other very nerve-racking experience, which came about after another visit to the CO. The main military barracks for the Tanganyikan army was just outside Dar es Salaam, but there was a second upcountry at Tabora. There the troops were housed in even more basic conditions than in Dar and were still on full alert, as there were pockets of resistance in the surrounding area. 'It would be a good for morale,' said Colonel Carter, 'if you were to go up there for a few days, take a couple of services and try and cheer them all up.'

The next day therefore saw me boarding a naval chopper and being whisked away to Tabora. I was warmly greeted and looked after very well. I had a meeting with the Major in charge, who wanted to know if I had any suggestions to diminish tension and raise morale. I noticed a group of the men kicking a football around, which gave me an idea.

'Why don't we challenge the Tanganyikan Army to a football match?' I suggested. This was considered to be a good PR move, and so a match was duly arranged. Because I was a padre (so would be impartial!) and also because I could speak Swahili, it was decided that I should referee the match. The Tanganyikans readily agreed to this and so the details were finalized. Originally it was intended that most of our troops would come along and cheer us on, but at the last minute an incident arose which meant they were needed elsewhere. In the end just the team and I went on our own. Soccer is popular all over the world and Tanganyika is no exception. When we arrived at the local 'stadium' (a slight exaggeration!) where the local top matches were played we found the stands on either side of the pitch packed with local supporters, and more on the touchlines. There must have been at least 1,000 people present. There was a tremendous cheer when the Tanganyikan team ran onto the pitch, but whistling and jeering when our lads joined them!

I then ran on, trying not to show my apprehension as I whistled for the start of the match. The marines had been told to keep it clean and were remarkably restrained, whilst the opposition became more and more dangerous and brazen in their tackling. I too had been advised to use the whistle as sparingly as possible, but as the standard of play deteriorated I was more and more forced to blow for fouls, the vast majority being committed by the local team. This of course made me more and more unpopular. Rough play apart, the game was very exciting and with only a few minutes to go the score was two all. I was rather hoping that would be the final score, but when the marine centre forward was blatantly fouled in the penalty area, I was forced to award a penalty. The opposing team swarmed around me protesting that I was biased, but I held my ground, insisting that the spot kick be taken. A few more minutes elapsed before the ball was finally put down on the spot. A glance at my watch told me that the penalty kick would be the last of the match. The centre forward who had been the player viciously brought down, ran up, shot and scored a sizzling goal. I signalled a goal and then blew the final whistle! The booing and hissing, which greeted the result, increased in volume. I then noticed that one section of the crowd was beginning to advance in an extremely menacing manner. The senior NCO noticed it too and immediately took charge. 'Retreat in an orderly manner,' he commanded, and with me shielded in the middle that's exactly what we did. Our driver had also noticed the disturbance so had the engine running by the time we arrived and clambered aboard. Within a few seconds we were off, after turning on the pitch and narrowly missing some of the advancing crowd. I was extremely relieved to return to base, although no little miffed that the Major seemed pretty unperturbed by our experience.

After a few weeks things settled down. The ringleaders of the mutiny were arrested, and peace and stability were restored. The time came for the troops to leave, and I felt a personal loss at their departure. Colonel Carter sent for me one last time, thanked me for what I had done, and suggested that I ought to consider becoming a naval chaplain. He said he would give me the highest possible recommendation. I was tempted but by now Africa was in my blood, and in any case I knew there was a great deal more to be done both in the Mission and within the diocese, so I never did apply. To this day, however, I consider the CO, the Major in charge of the troops in Tabora and the RSM of 41 Commando to be three of the finest men I have ever met.

Arrived. 25/4/64   Dar es Salaam
3rd April

Dear Padre

Thank you for coming in last night. It was good to see you again but just my sort of ill luck that it had to be so brief. I had looked forward to seeing you in your Mission and I had hoped that you would be able to spend a bit of time with t· Company. Never mind — you have earned your holiday as much as anyone else and I sincerely hope you enjoy it.

I don't think that I have ever met a parson who was able to make such an immediate and lasting impression on men as you did in Tabora. Your visit did me a power of good

Major Horston letter

221

Chapter 19

Back to Normal

It was only after the marines had finally left that I realized how much of my time had been taken up by my involvement with them. There was a great deal of catching up to done, new bridges to be built, and fresh projects to be undertaken. The pool had been constructed and was a great success, but I soon found that maintenance was, in two distinct areas, going to be a huge challenge. The first was to obtain the chemicals, etc. needed to keep it in pristine condition. Equally daunting was finding someone capable of operating the machinery and monitoring the state of the water. One of my staff was designated pool engineer, but the title did very little to expand his knowledge to the desired level.

Providentially, we received wonderful practical help from the ships' crews themselves. The filtration plant particularly needed constant maintenance and repair. I soon developed a very simple but effective technique in obtaining help. I feigned complete ignorance about how anything worked! Here follows a typical conversation, which usually took place in the Chief Engineer's cabin on the ship that happened to be in port at the given moment of need.

'Hello, Chief, how nice to meet you (or see you again).' Then, depending upon the time of day, would appear a cup of coffee or a cool refreshing beer. Then either he, or if he didn't, I, would quickly turn the conversation around to the pool, leading to the inevitable, 'How's the pool going?'

'Well,' (spoken rather hesitatingly) 'it's OK; the only problem is the pump seems to be spouting all over the place!'

'It obviously needs packing,' came the knowledgeable diagnosis from the chief.

'Packing,' I would reply. 'It's not long since it arrived from the UK. I don't want to send it back again!'

The 'Malu' ... donated to the Mission

An indulgent mutter followed from the Chief. 'I don't mean that sort of packing. I'll tell you what; I'll send the second engineer and a couple of apprentices up to the Mission to sort it out for you.'

Problem solved. It was often claimed that if all ships' stores (paint, electrics, ropes, etc) were returned to the ships, the Mission would collapse like a house of cards.

A large number of ships berthed in the harbour, which necessitated a launch to visit them. The Mission didn't have one and although the pilots and ship agents helped me whenever they could, it sometimes meant that valuable time was wasted, as I had to fit in with their timetable. I was thrilled therefore when we were presented with a launch, which of course also had to be maintained. It never cost us a penny. Ships in port would lift it on board, do the necessary and lower it down again into the water. All this had the effect of creating a bond between the crews and the Mission: 'How's our-Pool/launch or whatever?' became a common expression whenever I went ship visiting. I even got into trouble once or twice by not waiting for a ship to return that had helped me before because they were miffed that another ship or company had taken over their maintenance slot!

Another way I received help was over a hobby of mine which began during my time in the Port of London Mission – keeping a fish tank. I set up a large tank in the main hall and it wasn't long before seamen were bringing me fish from all over the world. I also received help for the Mission shop. Ships crews coming from the Far East would bring me such items as camphor wood chests or other items from Hong Kong that I knew would sell well. They did.

It's time now to turn to my increasing involvement with the diocese. As already mentioned, giving me parish status automatically meant much more involvement with my brother clergy, and I became a regular participant at chapter meetings. It was there that I first learnt some very exciting news. Dar es Salaam, which at present was part of a larger diocese, was to become, together with Zanzibar, a diocese in its own right. One John Sepeku was to be the new

Bishop John Sepeku enthronement as the first Archbishop of Tanzania

224

Bishop. I met him shortly afterwards and took to him immediately. I felt very honoured when I was invited to take part in his consecration. The service was inspiring, in part because it was so different from a consecration in the UK. Gone was all the pomp and ceremony, instead I was amazed to see the Bishop elect lying face downwards on the floor for a large part of the ceremony. The occasion was especially moving as John was their first Tanzanian Bishop.

Because my work was with visiting seamen (who wouldn't speak Swahili) and also because of the short time between my appointment and my departure, there had been no chance for me to master Swahili. Once I became involved with the diocese I regretted deeply that I had not had the chance to do so. All the clergy in the chapter understood English, however, and so that became the language spoken whenever I was present. I nevertheless recognized the need for me to conquer it, so was very pleased when the Anglican nuns undertook to teach me. I must confess that, although I made some progress, I never fully mastered the language. Apart from anything else I became extremely busy and found it increasingly difficult even to attend lessons. I will never forget taking my first service of Holy Communion in Swahili, actually for the sisters in the convent. I did my best, knowing and being comforted by the fact that I had a sympathetic congregation, but was completely unnerved when during the prayer of consecration I heard distinct noises of laughing and giggling coming from the nuns. After the service they told me why. Instead of using the correct words for the Virgin Mary, I apparently called her 'the tea pot'! – in Swahili 'birika'. I should have said 'bikira' (virgin).

During all my time in East Africa, Bishop John never once complained about my poor Swahili, although I was constantly conscious of this weakness. It made what followed even more remarkable. With the formation of a new diocese, apart from a new Bishop there were other positions to be filled, the most important being that of archdeacon. As is usual in such situations there was much speculation as to whom he would be. Being the Missions to Seamen chaplain, so very much an outsider, it didn't really concern me, so I wasn't very interested in who would be chosen. It was different however with the other expatriate clergy, who had been missionaries in the country for many years. They spoke the language like natives and had a wealth of experience of the workings and ways of the church in East Africa. Canon Sydenham was the hot favourite and fully expected to be named as the first archdeacon.

There was another school of thought and that was that a Tanzanian would be appointed. Tanzania being newly independent, many reasoned 'Africa for the Africans'. I used this argument when some time later I was approached regarding further promotion myself, but, as I have said, over the appointment of the new archdeacon I hadn't even given it a thought. As I became more deeply involved in the diocese so I had more and more contact with Bishop John. He increasingly sought my opinion on many matters so I was not surprised when I received a message asking me if I could please go and see him at his house. To be honest, it was at a very inconvenient time as I already had another engagement planned. I rang him and asked if I could come a little later and to this he readily agreed. It turned out to be a memorable evening, and a turning point in my life.

Bishop John lived in the African sector of the city, where tarmac roads gave way to dusty tracks. I parked my car as near as I could and headed for his house. It was that time of the day when the evening quickly surrendered to the night, bringing with it a soothing coolness after the searing heat of the day. As I approached his house I heard the sound of children singing to the accompaniment of a drum. I turned a corner and there in front of me was a ring of children dancing and singing as only African children can. The drum turned out to be a biscuit tin (but that didn't matter, the rhythm was fantastic). I watched spellbound as their faces reflected the enjoyment in what they were doing. Their movement was effortless, the moment enchanting beyond words. I was profoundly moved by the whole episode, and it stirred within me a longing to become more and more involved with the indigenous population in this fascinating country that was now my home.

The bishop's summons called however, so I tore myself away from that idyllic scene and made my way to his house. He greeted me warmly and led me to his study, where refreshment awaited. After the normal Tanzanian greetings (one never got down to business until after one had asked after all the family, friends and events of the day) he came to the reason for the visit. He wanted to discuss with me the outstanding appointments to be made in the new diocese. I waited, expecting to be asked my opinion about Canon Sydenham – 'Slippery Sid' as he was universally known! I could hardly believe what I was hearing when Bishop John said, 'Father, I want you to be my new archdeacon.'

Because his words were so unexpected, I actually turned around to see who else was in the room, but there was no one, he was talking to me.

There was a stunned silence as I tried to absorb what he had just said. I finally composed myself enough to venture to speak. After thanking him for the great honour he had bestowed upon me, I did my best to make him change his mind. By Canon Law I knew I hadn't even been in orders long enough to be appointed archdeacon. The archdeacon is addressed as 'the Venerable'. I always looked young for my age, but in any case at only thirty years old I looked anything but venerable. I didn't pursue that line of argument however, because mercifully in the mission field one tends to get on with the job, and if Canon Law gets in the way, 'then ignore it!'. I did argue strongly, however, that some of the senior British clergy could serve him far better than me, and mentioned one or two obvious names. He wouldn't even be drawn into that line of discussion, so I then brought out what I considered to be a very strong argument.

'Bishop,' I said, 'Tanzania has just become independent, and Tanzanians are being appointed throughout all aspects of the economy to leadership posts. You yourself, being the first Tanzanian Bishop, are a good example. I am quite sure that amongst all your African clergy you have someone who could amply fill this post, and such an appointment would make you very popular with all your peers.'

'Father,' he replied, 'of course I have thought about this and prayed about it a great deal too. You don't know this but last week I summoned all the African clergy and told them that I intended inviting you to be my new archdeacon. To a man,' he continued, 'they all knelt down on the floor and prayed that you would accept.' I experienced at that moment a huge conflict of emotions. Amazement that I had been invited to be promoted in this way, but above all else a feeling of intense humility that my brother clergy wanted me to be their archdeacon.

I had one last chance of a 'get-out' and that was that, unlike other clergy in the diocese, I was in the employ not of the local church, but the Missions to Seamen. I would have to seek their permission to accept this appointment, I told him. To this the Bishop readily agreed. I also said that before finally deciding I

227

needed to pray about it and also consult my spiritual mentor, Bishop John Hughes of South West Tanganyika (who was the chaplain of my theological college when I was a student there).

Bishop John happened to be in Dar at that time so without further ado I went to see him. His advice, as always, was sound. 'Before the bishop asked you,' he said, 'he obviously thought and prayed about this matter deeply. Furthermore, he has also consulted his African brethren and received their support. It is not a matter of whether or not you think you are worthy, because none of us is worthy! The only reason for turning this appointment down is if your health won't allow it. That is not an issue in your case, so subject to your head office approval, you should accept.'

Head office's reply came by return of post. **Yes**. So it was that,

The Rt Rev John Sepeku
P.O.Box 2887 DaresSalaam
Tanzania
16 th July 1965

To

The Rev T.P.Korfoot . M.B.E.
Missions To Seamen
4 Buckingham Palace Gardens
London S.W.1.

My dear Father ,

You may be amazed a little if not very much, to receive a letter from me , but from now I shall be writing to you from time to time, I did not write to you in the past days , because it was not in my province to do so. You may be pleased to know that I was enthroned to be the Bishop of DaresSalaam on 10 th July , may I ask for your prayers to support me .

During my enthronment I have made some appointments within my Diocese, but I have reserved one appointment until I hear from you. It is my intention to appoint Rev John Taylor to be Archdeacon of DaresSalaam. this appointment is strongly supported by the African Clergy , because he carrys on well with Africans. Terefore it will be great joy to all of us here to receive your favourable early reply .

I am very grateful indeed to you for the arrangement you made last time when you came here to allow Father Taylor to help us in Parish work , he has won the hearts of so many people in this City .

Your brother in Christ

+ John DaresSalaam

My installation as Archdeacon of Dar es Salaam

at the next chapter meeting, I sat with head bowed whilst the Bishop announced that I was to be the first archdeacon of the new diocese. I sensed that my expatriate brother clergy received the message almost in unbelief, but the indigenous clergy broke out into spontaneous clapping and crowded around to congratulate me. Their encouragement carried the day, so I left that meeting head high and proudly returned to the Mission as the Venerable Archdeacon of Dar es Salaam.

Pride is one of the cardinal sins, which the devil can use with devastating effect. For the record, I was one of the youngest archdeacons ever to be appointed. In fact, strictly speaking, one had to be in holy orders slightly longer than I had to be appointed at all. My appointment raised no little public interest, and as a consequence my photo was on the front page of the local paper, and the nuns made me a wonderful purple girdle. This was because, apart from being appointed as archdeacon, I was also named as the 'Vicar General'. This is a title that is hardly ever used in the Anglican Church today, although it is still used in the Roman Catholic Church, admittedly with a slightly different remit. In their

229

case the office is almost completely tied up with the discipline of the clergy, whereas in Anglicanism one acts for the Bishop, whenever he is out of the diocese. In the early missionary days all the Bishops were expatriates, which meant that when they returned to their own country for leave or other business they could be away for several months at a time. The vicar general held the reins while he was absent.

As a result of my appointment I returned to the Mission resplendent in a new cassock, complete with purple buttons and girdle. Rather pompously I went to my office via the main hall of the Mission, so ensuring that as many people as possible witnessed my arrival! There was a group of American seamen who had returned from town considerably worse for wear. As I approached, one of them staggered to his feet and advanced towards me in a very uncertain manner.

'Say, chaplain,' he managed to stutter in a very blurred voice, 'I hear we've got to congratulate you.'

'Congratulate me?' I replied, at the same time giving my purple girdle an enthusiastic twirl. 'Why have you got to congratulate me?'

'Because they've made you the Venereal Archdeacon of Dar es Salaam,' he replied. My pride received yet another blow when a misprint in the paper referred to me as the Venerable Archdemon of Dar es Salaam! God works in a wondrous manner his miracles to perform!

The duties of the archdeacon included: the discipline of the clergy, the maintenance and building of all properties, and the granting of faculties, which were necessary before any new works or major repairs could be undertaken. For my sins I was also appointed chairman of the Diocesan Finance Committee, so any new project seemed to fall very neatly into my lap. Actually this gave me immense satisfaction, for on more than one project I drew up the plans, as archdeacon approved them, issued a faculty, then supervised the building itself, as well as raising the money to pay for it.

Another of my duties as archdeacon was unique to the office of Dar es Salaam. It concerned a large area of land known as Mtoni Shamba. I was very proud to be part of what happened because of the history that lay behind it. 'Shamba' is a very common word in Swahili, and means a plot of land that could be an allotment, a farm, or an even larger area. The church had acquired Mtoni Shamba over one hundred years before my time, but had done very little to it. It covered a large area of land, just outside Dar es Salaam, so was potentially very valuable. The government had recently decreed that, unless the owners of land did something constructive with it, it could be taken from them. This is where I came in!

But first its history. A hundred years earlier the slave trade in Africa was rife. Slaves were taken from their villages upcountry, brought down to the coast, taken across the sea to the island of Zanzibar and sold on the slave market. From there they were taken by ship to many parts of the world. When the slave trade finally came to an end the church became involved in two ways. They bought the plot of land on which the slave market was situated and on it built an Anglican cathedral. The freed slaves were taken back over to the mainland, some repatriated, but not all. Those who knew not from whence they had come, or didn't want to return, were given plots of land on Mtoni Shamba. The church built houses for them and also planted cashew nut trees so that they could harvest and make a living.

By 1960 all the original occupants had either died or moved on, being replaced by squatters. With the threat of losing Mtoni Shamba to the government something had to be done to reclaim the land. We decided that the squatters should be moved on, after being compensated by the church, calculated by the number of cashew nut trees on their plot. It was my responsibility to ascertain the exact number of trees so that they could be correctly paid. There was, of course, the problem of making good use of the land so that it would remain in our hands once we had reclaimed it. Lots of rice paddies were planted. On more than one occasion the Bishop and I stood side by side in about three inches of water planting the rice shoots, with him (1 must admit) far more at ease than I was. It wasn't only my mother who was petrified of snakes!

I gave a lot of thought to how else we could best develop Mtoni Shamba to our advantage. I discovered that it was extremely difficult to open the cashew nuts without breaking them, so much so that there was nowhere in Tanzania where this could be done. As a consequence the nuts were shipped to India, to a factory there which had the necessary machinery and the skill to open them. From there some were sent on to markets around the world, others returned to Tanzania for onward marketing. I did my research and then approached the Bishop with my suggestion. Why not build a factory to break the nuts free from their kernels in Mtoni Shamba? We could not only process our own nuts, but from all the cashew nut plantations across the country. It would obviously be cheaper for them to have them processed in Tanzania than send them down to India and back. We could create employment for our own people, and the income generated would allow us to develop the work of the church right across the province.

The Bishop was very taken by the idea, but there was a problem. He knew of no one (other than me) to whom he could or would entrust such a project. I had already been in Tanzania for eleven years, and as the work of the mission had by now been extended to its full potential, I had to think and pray very deeply about my future. I knew that if the project was to proceed then I had to commit myself to another three years at least in my present post. The Bishop was aware of my dilemma, and hinted at further promotion were I to stay.

On the other hand there were others (including the British High Commissioner) who told the head of my Mission when he came out to visit, that I ought to be moved on to bigger and better things! He was singularly unimpressed when the head of my Mission told him, 'The trouble is we have no one to replace him.'

There was another occasion when it was decided that I was the right person to fulfil a mission, when quite honestly I would have preferred it to be someone else! It was to do with the coup in Zanzibar, which overthrew those in power. News reached us on the mainland that there had been bloody clashes, with all those in authority being targeted for attack. Zanzibar was by now part of our diocese, with the cathedral sited on the old auction site for slave traffic, and obviously of great importance to us. We had a resident priest called John, who was in charge of the cathedral and lived in a house adjoining it. Despite many phone calls and other enquiries we were unable to make any contact with him, and the Bishop particularly was desperately concerned for his safety. Because I was white and the archdeacon, it was decided that I was the best person to go over to Zanzibar and find him. It was with no little trepidation that I boarded the plane, which landed shortly afterwards on Zanzibar soil.

Things were still very chaotic, but eventually I managed to reach

232

the cathedral, which I was relieved to see seemed undamaged. Of John there was no sign. I then went to the priest's house, which at first sight appeared empty. As I made my way around the various rooms I started calling out his name, again with no reply. I reached the top bedroom and called out his name, this time adding, 'John, it's me – Archdeacon John'. Then to my great relief I heard a reply, which came from somewhere above me. 'I'm up in the roof,' he cried. A few minutes later we were reunited. He told me that after the uprising mobs were running everywhere killing anyone in any sort of authority, so he took refuge in the roof and, not knowing what was happening, hadn't dared to leave his sanctuary. I was able to get him a flight back to Dar, where he arrived to a hero's welcome.

After the coup Zanzibar became one with Tanganyika, with the new name Tanzania, incorporating both the mainland and the island. One of the advantages of being archdeacon (I hoped) was to be able to improve the lot of my African brother clergy. As was inevitable they were on a very different pay scale from the expatriate priests. Expatriate expenses, cost of education, etc. was in an entirely different bracket from theirs, as was the expense of maintaining accommodation, holidays, travel, etc. Furthermore, our time in the mission field was limited, and at the end of it we had to return to the UK and resume its standard of living. Strangely enough (although on reflection maybe it wasn't as strange after all), whenever I suggested improvements for the indigenous clergy, whether that was in housing, working conditions, or salary increases, I had to overcome Bishop John's reservations first. He reasoned, correctly, that their standard of living, housing and working conditions compared very favourably with most of their parishioners, and was higher than anything they had experienced before they were ordained.

In these matters I lost some and won some! Being archdeacon obviously increased the workload, and incidentally my expenses too. I never once claimed a penny, however, and this little sacrifice on my part gave me an empathy with my poorer African brethren. One of the main differences between working in the mission field and in the UK was that, no matter your rank, it made no difference to your salary, which remained the same. I was quite happy about this, as it gave me another link with my brother clergy. Indeed, during the whole of my time in East Africa I didn't cost the diocese of Dar es Salaam a penny, as the Missions to Seamen paid my salary and expenses.

The difference in equality between the expatriate and indigenous clergy was a problem that I was never fully able to overcome. To give but one such example. On occasions I had to organize conferences and retreats for the clergy. I always arranged accommodation and catering with the expatriate members in mind, which was obviously of a higher standard than many of my African brethren, were used to. But did they enjoy it! Never have I seen eggs and bacon, toast and marmalade devoured with as much enthusiasm and enjoyment. It was at such a retreat, incidentally, that I had another vivid experience of the difference in living standards between 'them' and 'us'.

I had arranged for our retreat to be held at a new Roman Catholic hostel that had actually been built to accommodate senior Catholic delegates coming to Dar as Salaam for synods, conferences, etc. Being new, it was equipped with all the latest and best of fittings, so was very much in demand. I happened to know the priest who was running it, so was successful in booking it up for fifteen of us for the duration of our retreat, being held from the Tuesday to the Friday.

'There is only one problem,' he told me. 'There is a meeting of all the Bishops in Tanzania, beginning next Thursday, and possibly three of them will be staying here. If they do come you will have to vacate three of the bedrooms for those last two days.'

It was an easy matter for me to decide who the three clergy should be. They would, I decided, all be married men, especially Dick Martin (an American who had only very recently been married and joined us). I duly told the three potentially lucky men (as none of them really liked being away from their wives) that I would let them know if they had to vacate their rooms.

On the Thursday morning, we were all together in the chapel listening to Bishop Sepeku, who was conducting the retreat and giving the addresses. The priest in charge of the hostel signalled to me that he wanted to talk to me, so I excused myself from the chapel and joined him outside. He was relieved to tell me that the three bishops weren't coming after all, so that all our clergy could stay for the duration of the retreat. I thanked him and rejoined the rest of the clergy in the chapel. By now the Bishop had finished his address, which I had found interesting, so was sorry to have missed the end of it.

Later on in the day I went to tell the three clergy concerned that they were, after all, there for the duration. The first two were rather indifferent, but I expected more reaction from young Dick, who was, I know, missing his beautiful new bride. Rather hesitatingly I knocked gently on the door of his room, remembering that the retreat was in silence. 'Come in,' roared the unmistakable voice of Dick. I opened the door to be greeted by waves of smoke, which were not unpleasant to the nostrils. My first thought was that the room was on fire but as the smoke billowed down the corridor, I could see where it was coming from. It was from a very large fat cigar that Dick was, with great enjoyment, smoking. He was sitting at his desk, not working on, but resting his feet on it! Instead of the bible, prayer book or reading material there was a large bottle of scotch, and an even larger box of chocolates!

'Come in, John,' he roared, 'and help yourself to a scotch and soda.' He then pointed to an open box of cigars and the box of chocolates and indicated – help yourself! Rising to my full five feet eight inches I reminded him, that, 1. We were supposed to be in a silent retreat, 2. We were supposed to be fasting, and 3. There was a notice on the wall that said no smoking in the rooms. He either didn't or chose not to hear me, but instead repeated his offer of a whisky, at the same time proffering this fabulous box of chocolates before my twitching nostrils, saying, 'Help yourself, pal.'

There was only one thing to do. If you can't beat them, join them! I did. A few moments later, with a stiff drink in my hand and a large cigar in my mouth, and the box of chocolates very close at hand, I broke the news that he was to be away from his lovely young bride for another two nights. This provoked the pouring of another (two drinks) and the lighting of a fresh cigar. I should add that at that time such luxuries in Tanzania were very scarce, except if you were an American with doting parents. But to return to more pressing matters. 'Dick,' I said, 'when I had to leave the meeting to speak to the priest in charge of the hostel the Bishop was talking about expatriates working in Dar es Salaam. I am wondering what he said after I had left the chapel.'

Dick thought for a moment, reached out for another chocolate, took another sip of his drink, and said, 'Oh yes, I remember. He was talking about the hardships of being a missionary in East Africa'!

Not long after he was consecrated Bishop, John Sepeku became the first Archbishop of Tanzania. As such he was called upon to attend a meeting of all the primates in Africa, held in a different country each year. This particular year the lot, as they say, fell upon Uganda. Relationships between the two countries were at a very low ebb, so much so that Bishop John feared that if he attended the conference his life would be in danger. President Idi Amin ruled Uganda at that time, and his wickedness was common knowledge. We called him General Amen because he claimed that all his instructions came from God. Archbishop John wrote to the presiding Archbishop, at that time in South Africa, requesting that, because Tanzania and Uganda were to all intents and purposes at war, the meeting be transferred to another venue. But on the personal assurance of Amin that no harm would befall him, the venue remained in Uganda and John agreed to go. He was very unhappy about it nevertheless. In my capacity as vicar general, I had a long meeting with him, who made me aware of his wishes should he not return. The nearer to departure date the more nervous he became, and by the time I saw him off at the airport, he really was in an awful state. No news was good news, however, although it was with a great sense of relief that I picked him up from the airport a few days later, to take him home. He couldn't wait to tell me what happened.

He said that the flight to Entebbe was uneventful, but just as they were preparing to land, the pilot's voice came over on the tannoy. 'I've just received a message from the control tower,' he said. 'Once we have landed I am to taxi the aircraft to a distant part of the airfield, and then await further instructions.'

Once there the captain spoke again. 'No one is to move until they have been given permission to do so.' There was a further delay and then the door of the aircraft was opened to admit four Ugandans who boarded the plane. Bishop John described them as looking just like American gangsters at the time of prohibition. They all wore fedora hats and dark glasses. They walked up and down the length of the aircraft twice without saying a word to anyone. Then they stopped in the aisle by the Archbishop's seat. 'Are you Bishop Sepeku?' one of them asked.

As the Archbishop was dressed in his purple cassock with all the trimmings this was an unnecessary question. 'Yes I am,' John replied.

236

'You are to follow me,' said one of the four.

With two in front of him and two behind, he was led to the door of the plane and down the steps. They were in a deserted part of the airport, and as John descended and was pushed towards a large car, with all curtains drawn, he really thought his end had come. He was so petrified he confessed that he was unable to control his bladder. He was bundled into the car and off it sped. Apart from the original question no one said a word to him and so in complete silence he sped off to he knew not where. Finally the car came to a halt, the door opened, and John alighted from the car. Waiting to greet him was General Idi Amin himself, who acted as if nothing untoward had happened.

I duly handed back to the Archbishop all the papers and instructions he had given me, thankful that I had not had to implement them. Needless to say, what those instructions were I would never reveal, although I will say that my admiration and respect for him reached a new high as a result of the whole incident.

The Archbishop liked a glass of beer and cashew nuts. He became a regular visitor to the Mission, often leaving (as was the African custom) his wife in the car! We would proceed to the open-air restaurant that overlooked the swimming pool on one side and the football pitch on the other. He loved football and used to get really excited as he watched a game in progress. The seamen, who were somewhat bemused at seeing an archbishop enjoying a glass of beer and cheering on a good move, were nevertheless thrilled when I introduced them to him. John was marvellous with the men, and had the great gift of putting them at ease. As a consequence he was an instant hit with everyone. Indeed he endeared himself to all who met him.

Two incidents stick out in my mind, which illustrate his common touch with others. During my time in Dar es Salaam the Franciscans established themselves in the diocese. They built their church and other buildings on Mtoni Shamba. Through my many contacts with the expatriate community, I was able to help a great deal in the construction of their complex. The Archbishop was thrilled to have them in his diocese, and we were frequent visitors as the building progressed. The historic day came when the church was ready for use. The Archbishop and I were to be present, with him celebrating the first Mass. This came to pass, and afterwards we adjourned to the refectory for a most enjoyable breakfast. A tour of the site followed and then it was time to leave. The senior brother was all set to thank Archbishop John for coming (and me too incidentally!) when he was pre-empted by the Archbishop's words. He thanked them for inviting him, allowing him to celebrate the first Mass, and for the wonderful breakfast that followed, turning around completely the notion of who was the giver and who the recipient.

The second incident was much more personal, because it concerned my mother who came out to visit us. Because of internal problems with the governments concerned, she had to fly to Nairobi in Kenya, rather than Dar es Salaam in Tanzania. As a consequence I had to travel by road to pick her up. This was the first time that she had travelled on such a long journey, on her own, so I was naturally concerned that she would be all right. I needn't have worried because in due time she appeared, charmingly dressed in a summer dress, hat and gloves, rather as if she were going to a tea party at Buckingham Palace! It was stinking hot so the first thing I did was to make her remove her hat and gloves! We started back on the long journey home with me surreptitiously glancing at her from time to time to see she was all right. Despite the windows of the car being wide open to provide a cool breeze, I became alarmed at the perspiration that was pouring down her face. I stopped the car and asked her if there was anything she could discard?

This is what she told me. Someone had warned her that when the aircraft climbed into the sky the air outside became very cold, so to make sure she had something warm to put on. Mother's answer to all this was to wear no less than three vests, which she still had on! Needless to say once these were discarded she felt much better!

I naturally I took her around as much as possible, including a trip to Mtoni Shamba. I was due to go out there anyway to have a policy meeting with the Archbishop. Like very many people, my mother had a horror of snakes. We met on a well-worn path, but then decided to move to another area not too far away. It meant leaving the path and walking through a very dense copse. My mother froze.

'I couldn't possibly go through there,' she exclaimed. 'It could be full of snakes!' My mother was about 5 feet 2 inches tall. The Archbishop was 6 feet 2 inches tall.

'Don't worry, Win,' he said, 'hold my hand, and I will look after you and see that you come to no harm.' Without hesitation she did so, and he led her through the thicket, with her now perfectly at ease. I will never forget walking behind them, seeing the Archbishop dwarfing my mother at his side, she now seemingly without a worry in the world.

All this shows that Archbishop John, whilst being a very good and holy man was also very human too. This I saw vividly in a trip to Mikumi Game Park. He was aware that I used to take seamen on safari to the park, and one day he volunteered the information that, although he had lived all his life in Tanzania he had never seen 'the big five' in the wild. So I promised that next time I took a party, he would be in it. And so it came to pass.

Chapter 20

Archbishop John's Visitation ... to a Game Park!

One of the problems of course of visiting a game park is that you can't guarantee seeing everything, indeed anything! Although we saw lots of game in the distance, for the first half an hour we saw nothing close, and I sensed a certain disappointment from all on board, but particularly Archbishop John. By now I knew the park very well, and was aware of certain areas that were usually prolific for game. The problem was to get to them one had to leave the tracks and 'cast out into the deep.' There was one particular copse that seemed very popular with the game, as it provided both cover and shade. I knew exactly where I had to leave the track which was just as well, because the elephant grass was at that time of the year at its highest – in fact taller than the minibus itself! Undeterred I swung off the track and straight into the grass. The first to exclaim in some alarm was the Archbishop. 'Don't worry,' I assured him and any others who were listening, 'I know exactly where I am going.' Sure enough a few minutes later we came to the end of the long grass and entered the copse. There we found what we were looking for. A large herd of elephants complete with young were there in abundance. Coming out of the long grass meant that they had not seen us, so were startled as we suddenly appeared. With one accord, they all turned and ran.

But not very far! To make matters worse the young had been separated from their parents. I could see a circle of angry elephants around us and could tell by the signs that they were preparing to charge. That's exactly what they did! In other circumstances it would have been an enthralling sight. But none of us on the bus sensed anything other than acute danger. All the Archbishop could do was to scream out, 'Funga Milango!' (shut the window), which

240

would have done no good at all! I did the only thing possible. Put my foot hard down on the accelerator and headed out of the copse. As I did I had a vivid picture in my mind of watching an army motorbike display at a tattoo when every rider headed towards a central point, missing each other by inches. My situation was similar but different. We were in the middle and the elephants were all charging towards us! To make matters worse, we were in a copse, so I had trees to miss as well as elephants! By the grace of God and no little luck I managed to clear the copse, and escape between the charging animals.

From then on our luck changed too and we saw an abundance of game. The only animal we didn't see was leopard. The lions took no notice of humans in vehicles, and we came across a pride of them resting under trees in the heat of the day. We got so close that one could almost reach out and touch one, which thrilled everyone on board including the Archbishop. Despite the scare with the elephants he was thrilled with the safari, and spoke about it for a long time after the event.

The most dramatic safari incident of all, however, came not in the game park, but on the way home from it. On this particular

A pride of lions

Safari to Mukumi Game Park

occasion I had taken a party of cadets from the SS *Chantala* to Mukumi. We left as usual just before 4 am and got within about 40 miles of home when we came across a ford in the road ahead. It was not usually there but was the result of the monsoon season, which brought lots of rain. To get back to the Mission we had to pass through a valley with hills on either side. The road ran near the bottom of the left hand range of hills. It was the rain coming off these that was responsible for the water on the road. There were traffic wardens on duty who waved me safely on through the ford. I thought no more of it, had indeed forgotten all about it until the return journey some twelve hours later. It had been raining heavily ever since we set off for home, which meant that our speed was slower than usual. It then changed to a crawl, as we joined a queue of traffic before us, including a convoy of large oil tankers that plied between Tanzania and Rhodesia.

The reason for the queue was the ford, which was now much deeper than it had been twelve hours earlier. I didn't like the way the water was cascading across the road in a very angry fashion. I anxiously watched the tanker before me as it navigated safely across the water. I realized of course that it was a much bigger and heavier vehicle than my mine, which helped it a great deal.

But I was in a quandary. This was the only road that could take me back to Dar. Furthermore, I knew the ship was due to sail the next morning so I had to get the cadets back in time. I decided to tackle the ford.

Slowly we inched forward and as we did so the height of the water outside rose steadily until the lower body of the van was now below water level. Despite the obvious danger I knew that I had no option but to keep going so I did, although the depth of the water continued to rise. Then to my horror I realized that the force of the water was pushing the minibus across the road. There was only one thing I could do. I called out to the cadets to jump out (which luckily was on the left hand side of the bus) and push the bus to the right. Without hesitation they did. As I wrestled with the steering wheel I heard them calling, 'Two, four, heave'. Their combined weight and power, plus me turning the wheel into the swirling water, allowed us to inch forward, but I knew it was touch and go. Then suddenly and with a huge sense of relief I sensed that the van was no longer going deeper into the water; that we had passed the lowest point of the road and were on the way out. 'Keep it up chaps,' I shrieked and slowly but surely we continued our way forward until mercifully the road was clear before us. Ten yards clear of the ford I stopped the bus, so that the cadets could come back on board. At that moment there was an almighty roar behind us. The headlights of vehicles going in the opposite direction lit up a horrific scene. The road, which only seconds before we were on, had been swept away by the force of the raging water. We had been only feet away from certain death. I suggested that we had a prayer of thanksgiving for our safe delivery. I have never had a more attentive congregation than during it. For me personally I had some conception of how the Israelites felt, when by divine intervention they crossed safely to the other side of the sea.

The rest of the journey was without incident, so a little later than planned I returned the cadets to the ship. Just before she sailed a delegation of the crew came to the mission and presented me with a brass plaque, which they had just created in the engine room. It said quite simply, 'Two, four, heave'. Whilst in the game park they had purchased a skull of an eland, which was to have adorned the wall in their mess room. This they also gave to me. I have them both to this day, but with or without them I will never forget that drama. Neither, I suspect, will any of those who accompanied me on that trip.

Trips to the game park apart, my work with the diocese continued to grow. It was good therefore that in so many ways the Archbishop and I were compatible. We both enjoyed a similar sense of humour. We both had a simple faith, and were optimistic about all that befell us. There were two areas, however, where we had nothing in common. One was in office routine, the other in timing. I had regular meetings with the Archbishop, to discuss developments or strategies, and to deal with correspondence. Needless to say, many important letters were received, sometimes with me getting a copy but not always.

'Now, Archbishop,' I would begin, 'what do you want to do about the letter from State office?'

'What letter?' he would reply, 'I don't remember receiving it.'

I knew he had because I had received a copy. So would begin a search. I came to learn that his favourite 'file' was in the leaves of the telephone directory! On many cases the missing letter was discovered only after shaking it out!

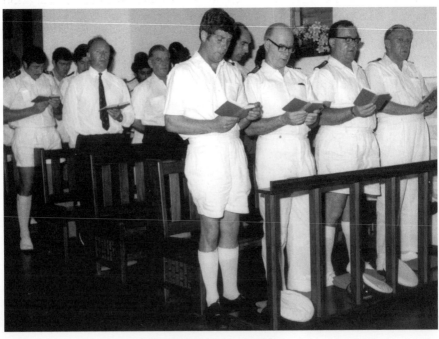

A service in the chapel

244

He had, however, a very practical approach to most things. 'I haven't got these grey hairs for nothing' was one of his favourite expressions. Most problems were dealt with by the simple use of common sense, and in a non-aggressive manner, which endeared him to all. I never did succeed in making him a model of efficiency, although he did become a bit better as the years rolled by.

But his greatest failing (which was a common fault amongst East Africans) was not having any concept of time. 'Bado Kidogo' (in a little while) was probably the most common expression in East Africa. This was not a great problem when dealing with fellow Tanzanians, but when it came to meeting with expatriates, or people in high positions it could be highly embarrassing!

I remember on one occasion when we were enjoying a beer and watching a football match at the Mission a ship's Captain approached. I introduced him to the Archbishop, and could see that he was extremely flattered by this. Later on that day a cadet brought me a letter from the Captain inviting the Archbishop and myself to lunch on his ship. The Archbishop was thrilled by this and accepted the invitation. Knowing the Archbishop's weakness about arriving in time I unashamedly told him to get to the Mission at 12 noon sharp (one hour before we were due on board). 12 o'clock came and no Archbishop. 12.30 and 1 o'clock also passed without any sign of him. By now I was really worried because I knew that the Captain had every member of the crew lined up to meet him, that he had ordered them all to wear mess kit, and that in the middle of a working day. I wasn't too worried when he hadn't arrived by 1 pm as I knew this allowed for a drink before lunch but when 1.30 approached with no John in sight I really panicked. Just as I was contemplating suicide he appeared in his car. I jumped in and told his driver to go straight to the ship. Sure enough as we arrived a welcome party was lined up on the quayside and with much ceremony we were ushered on board at five minutes to two!

The Captain didn't turn a hair and proceeded to show the Archbishop around as if time was of no consequence. I knew that the food had been ready for an hour, however, and was acutely embarrassed on the Archbishop's behalf. The Archbishop thankfully didn't seem to sense any tension at all and thoroughly enjoyed the whole experience. For my part it was all's well that ends well, although I must admit I didn't encourage many more lunches on board with the Archbishop as the principal guest!

245

The last few pages have all been about my relationship with John Sepeku. I will return to him time and time again but, important as he was, I need to stress that actually I was appointed to Dar es Salaam as the Missions to Seamen chaplain, and it is to record some of my work in that capacity that I must now return.

But before I do; it was around this time that a representative from the war graves commission came to Tanzania to complete some unfinished business. Going back to the time of the First World War there were British and Commonwealth soldiers' bodies scattered over various parts of the country, and the decision had been made to create a new cemetery for their remains. To me fell the privilege of planning and organizing the dedication service, which was attended by Christian and Muslim clerics, as well as representatives from the various countries concerned.

What I loved most about the work of a chaplain was the length and breadth of its scope. I have already referred to my work with the SS *Schwabenstein*, the German ship that broke down in Hong Kong during my time there. The crew of that ship were all West

Clergy from different denominations at the dedication of a
new war graves cemetery near Dar es Salaam

Germans, but many East German ships also visited Dar. Their crews were mainly young men, very fit and very keen on football. Countless numbers of games were organized on our football pitch, very often against a British crew. Sadly there was one notable difference between them, and that concerned what happened after the match was finished. Football in Dar was a very hot business, and a glass of beer afterwards was like the nectar of the gods! Unfortunately the East Germans were strictly rationed as to the amount of foreign currency they were allowed to come on shore with. On many occasions, because the team had no money, they came straight off the pitch and went back to the ship. On very rare occasions someone had the money to buy a couple of beers, and then it was literally 11 straws, as the beer was shared amongst the team. Shortages of money apart, the East Germans were extremely nice people, and most grateful for the service we supplied. They were of course all communists, so unfortunately none of them ever came to church. On more than one occasion, however, I was asked for and provided Bibles in German. I was also presented with many little presents, such as photos or paintings of ships. One I particularly treasure because all the members of the ship's football team signed their names on the back of the picture.

We also had ships from communist China, but although I went on board, the crew was almost never allowed ashore, except as an organized party with a commissar in charge. He was stationed at the head of the gangway, and very rarely allowed anyone to get past him. He would, however, take the mission posters and welcome sheets that we gave to every ship when they entered port.

I particularly remember an incident concerning a Russian seaman who was actually the ship's doctor. He had a heart attack out at sea and, Dar being the nearest port, his ship was diverted so that he could be brought ashore and hospitalized. The ship then continued on its journey. I had an arrangement with every hospital that I was immediately informed of any seamen admitted and as a consequence I was usually at their bedside within two hours of admission. On this occasion time was not so important because he was unconscious so unaware of my presence then or for the next few days.

It was with good reason that I made hospital visiting one of my top priorities. It's bad enough being in hospital in one's own country, with loved ones visiting and bringing those little things that make all the difference, and make you feel loved. But to be in hospital in a strange country, often with a foreign language being spoken; to see people streaming into a ward at visiting time, knowing that none of them would be coming to your bedside; shipmates gone on to the next port, the nearest loved ones thousands of miles away was most depressing. I was often the only regular visitor a seaman would have during his time there, so I pulled out all the stops to try and make his stay as pleasant as possible. I was also on many occasions able to ring home on his behalf, to relieve anxiety and convey messages back and forth.

The Russian doctor had obviously had a very severe heart attack, as he was unconscious for a considerable time and in intensive care for well over a week. At first I would just sit by his bedside and hold his hand, trying to be mother, father, wife or friend, as well as a priest carrying out his ministry. I remember experiencing a huge sense of relief the first time I found him conscious. The problem was of course that I could not speak Russian nor he English! I arranged for a member of the Russian Embassy to meet me at his bedside, who explained to him who I was. At first he was very weak and did nothing more than lie there but as the days went on so he began to improve. I remember the first time I walked in to be greeted with a lovely smile, which made it obvious how pleased he was to see me. After a few more days he started speaking, but of course in Russian. I couldn't understand a word he said! He didn't seem to notice this, however, and once he started talking didn't seem to know how to stop! I concentrated on his face, and sort of made clucking noises from time to time, nodding my head as if in agreement with what he was saying. I knew his recovery was almost complete when one day he signalled to me that he wanted to show me something from his locker. It proved to be his wallet. With great tenderness he opened it and brought out, yes you've guessed it, photographs. It needed no language to work out who were his wife and his children. Half an hour passed whilst he told me (I presume!) of their virtues, how much he loved and was missing them.

Then came the day when the Russian Embassy rang me to report that he was being discharged in two days' time and would be flown back to Russia. The ambassador had particularly requested that I went to the airport to see him off, so naturally I did. When I got there I was surprised to see the ambassador himself in attendance. I was even more surprised when he made a speech. He thanked me for visiting him so frequently in hospital, and said the doctor particularly wanted to thank me for talking to him about his home and family. My conversation had of course actually been limited to clucking noises and grunts, plus nodding my head at what I hoped was the appropriate moment! It taught me the great value and importance of listening as an aid to counselling. The talking was now over but something else was yet to come! The ambassador then presented me with some bottles of vodka and caviar, before saying goodbye.

Chapter 21

The Dimensions of Ministry

What I found so fascinating and exciting about my ministry was that it not only brought me into contact with seafarers from different cultures, but also those of different branches of the Christian faith. I particularly remember one occasion, when I was preparing my chapel for a service of Holy Communion, when three seamen walked in and asked me what time the Mass was going to start. Their use of the word 'Mass' told me that they were probably Roman Catholics, which indeed they were. It was our policy to admit anyone to receive the communion, provided they were entitled to receive it in their own church. I told them that they were most welcome to come if they wished. Sadly, the Roman Catholic faith does not admit the validity of the Anglican orders, and as a consequence Catholics were not allowed to receive communion from us. One of them replied, 'The trouble is, padre, we kick with the other foot'. They asked if there was a Roman Catholic church in the neighbourhood. The nearest was actually the RC cathedral in the centre of Dar. It was too far for them to walk, but a glance at my watch told me that I just had time to run them into town and return in time to take my own service. So I did.

On the way I explained that the only problem was that the service would be in Swahili. This worried them greatly as they said they wouldn't know what to do. 'That's easy,' I told them. 'Just sit about five rows from the front and watch what the people before you do. If they stand up, you stand up. If they kneel down, you do so too.' Thus assured, I dropped them outside the cathedral and returned to the Mission. To be honest, I then forgot all about them, as other duties demanded my attention. Some time later I saw them enter the Mission, and was somewhat surprised when they advanced to me in an aggressive manner.

'Did everything go OK?' I asked.

'No it didn't,' one of them most emphatically replied. 'You told us to sit about five rows back from the front, and copy what the people in front did.'

'That's right,' I replied, 'what's wrong with that?'

'We'll tell you what's wrong,' the spokesman said, 'the priest came in and stood in front of the congregation and started to speak. After he had finished there was a pause, after which a man in front of us stood up, so we did too. To our embarrassment the congregation erupted into laughter. Apparently there was to be a baptism and the priest had asked the father of the child to stand up!'

On another occasion I was conducting Evensong in the Mission chapel in the presence of a good congregation, which included an American who came from the Bible belt in the USA. I always tried to involve visiting seamen if I could, so I asked him if he would take the collection. To this he readily agreed. All went well

A Tanzanian nativity scene

251

until the sermon. Even if the congregation hasn't fallen asleep, sermons in the Anglican church are nevertheless heard in silence. But not in the church that he attended back in the States. As I preached so came the 'Alleluias', interlaced with such phrases as 'you tell 'em, padre. Praise the Lord.' No one fell asleep at that service, I assure you! Similar outbursts erupted during the prayers, so to be honest it was a relief when the service drew to an end. I announced the offertory hymn and signalled to my American friend that this was the time to take the collection. This he did, while I approached the altar in readiness to receive the offering. Then to my amazement I saw him disappearing through the back door of the chapel! The hymn came to an end and the congregation knelt for the blessing. I was about halfway through it when once again I heard the now familiar Alleluias, and he entered the chapel holding the collection bag high in the air, triumphally proclaiming, 'I've been all round the Mission and I've got 'em all, padre!'

On yet another occasion I attended the funeral of a Roman Catholic local resident, which took place at the cathedral. In line with local custom the coffin was brought and left at the steps of the cathedral, whilst all the mourners gathered round and indulged in the customary wailing and crying. This continued until the priest arrived on the scene complete with holy water and incense. He liberally sprayed and censed the coffin, the wailing stopped as if by magic, and after this part of the ceremony was completed, the coffin was carried into the cathedral with everyone following on behind. I joined the queue and entered the cathedral. The combination of coming out of the bright sunshine into the dimmer interior, but even more because of the swirling incense that threatened to choke and blind, meant that I couldn't see a thing. My groping hand found what was obviously the end of a pew, so I thankfully entered it and sank to my knees in prayer. After a short while I opened my eyes expecting to see others around me, but there was no one! I saw that the cortege party had moved on to another part of the cathedral, and the service was happily continuing without me! At this point I decided that enough was enough, so after a short prayer, I arose and left!

I also attended Muslim weddings and funerals. Although the customs were different in all these experiences yet in them all I felt the presence of Almighty God. No wonder that I am so ecumenically minded today and abhor arrogance on the part of any single section of the whole body of Christ.

I remember on another occasion a ship came into port at the beginning of November. The ship had been away from the UK for a very long time so everyone on board was ecstatic that the ship was at last on its way back to the UK, which meant that they would all have Christmas at home. At the last minute, to the bitter disappointment of the crew, the schedule was changed. Two of the crew found their own way of drowning their sorrows – by drink! As the evening wore on they got more and more inebriated, but worse was yet to come. They consumed what they had in the cabin, and looked around for a means of replenishing their stocks. One of them remembered that the ship was unloading crates of gin, which was exactly what they had run out of! No problem, they reasoned, we will go down and get a few bottles ourselves. Needless to say they didn't succeed. They were quickly apprehended by the security police and spent the remainder of the night, plus many more days, in police custody. Pilfering from the dock area has always been a problem, so was considered an extremely serious offence. They were found guilty of stealing and sentenced to a term of imprisonment.

I spoke up for them in court but to no avail. One of them was particularly devastated because not only would he now miss Christmas at home, but Easter too, when he was due to get married. They were taken to prison whilst I, through telephone calls and letters, did my best to ease the pain of everyone back in the UK. Before they were led away I promised I would come and see them as soon as possible, which I did. A priest traditionally enjoys certain rights regarding visiting, including being able to see the prisoners alone, for confession, etc. I knew this prison fairly well so expected no problems. Two things had happened, however. Tanzania's independence meant that in some quarters 'the boot was now on the other foot'; the 'big white chief' was no more. If a European found himself in trouble his discomfort was not always helped by the switchover in power. The second problem was that there seemed to be a changeover in the warders, and as a consequence I didn't recognize a single friendly face.

Whilst on remand and waiting for trial, prisoners were allowed certain items to be brought in, including food. Before, when I had done this, there had been no problem, but 'the old order changeth' as I soon found out. I was required to taste every part of the meal, to prove that it wasn't poisoned. Why I would want to take poisoned food into a prison I never was able to make out. I had brought the food in containers that kept it hot. But by the time it had all been examined and tasted by me, it was neither hot nor presentable. But more was to come. When I asked for somewhere private so that I could talk to the men I was led to one of the huts where prisoners slept. The prison radio was blaring away at such a high volume that it was almost impossible to hear oneself speak. Furthermore, the hut was full of other prisoners, some of whom knew me from previous visits. They all wanted to talk to me, or seek my help, which gave me no opportunity at all to speak in private to the two men I had particularly come to visit.

1 had on previous occasions used a small room set apart from the rest of the buildings, which was ideal for private talks or taking services. I approached one of the guards and asked him if I could use it please. 'Sorry, Bwana Mkubwa,' he replied, 'but we've lost the key.' By now most of the prison inmates seemed to be following me around, not wanting to miss any of the excitement. I was wondering what to do next when one of the Tanzanian prisoners came up to me and whispered in my ear, 'I'm in for safe robberies, I could open that lock without any bother if you want me to?'

So I turned to the warder and said, 'If I can get the lock open can I go in?'

He, thinking I had no chance, said, 'Yes'.

So I signalled to my newly found friend to take over. He, like all Tanzanians, had lovely thick black curly hair. He advanced towards the offending lock, and studied it in silence and deep concentration. Somehow the word got around what was happening, and a deathly silence took over. Presumably by complete coincidence the blaring music stopped also. After a few minutes spent studying the lock he put his hand into his hair and pulled out a small sliver of wood. He approached the lock and inserted the piece of wood. Nothing happened, but undeterred he replaced it in his hair and withdrew another, slightly larger, sliver. The same process was repeated but this time and with a loud click the lock opened, to be greeted by a huge cheer from all the spectators!

Like a colossus I swept pass the bemused guards, signalling for the two seamen to follow me. The trouble was, everybody else came too! The room was packed with men like sardines, which again meant that I had no opportunity to talk to them. Then I had a brainwave. I told the assembled congregation that I was going to hold a church service, if any one wanted to leave, please do so now. No one moved, in fact even as I was talking some more men crowded in around the door. I explained to them all that because the two English men couldn't speak Swahili the service would be in English. Again no departures. I then told the seamen to listen very carefully to what I said and join in where appropriate. A Church of England service includes such lines as 'The Lord be with you' and the reply 'And with your spirit'. The first words are intoned by the priest, the answers by the congregation. This service, however, was different!

Instead of the normal words, I intoned, 'Is there anything that you want?' Startled looks came on their faces but they soon cottoned on. 'Yes, we need toothpaste and brushes,' came the reply.

'Is there anything else that you need?'

Back came the answer, 'Yes, we need some writing paper'. And so it went on until, by the end of the service, I knew all their wants. After it was over I wished them all goodbye and left to a background of clapping from the men. I did make an official complaint to the governor about not being allowed my visiting rights. The combination of my letter plus the events just described seemed to do the trick, as the next time I visited I had no problems at all.

There was, thankfully, a very happy ending to this incident. One of the prisoners was due to get married back in the UK at a time that coincided with my own home leave. He not only invited us to the wedding, but also requested that, if possible, I should take the service. An understanding priest in his home parish agreed to this, so arrangements were finalized. The sentence actually finished only days before the wedding was due, but with the cooperation of the shipping agents I arranged that, on leaving prison, they would immediately be flown home. Rather unkindly (I thought) just before being released they were subjected to a typical prison hair cut. So they arrived in the UK looking like convicts. Neither of them was happy about this, particularly the potential bridegroom, who was very upset indeed. Then I had a brainwave! 'If I have my haircut as short as yours I can mention in the service that this is typical in hot climates. No one will think any more about it.' So I did, including making a passing reference to severe tropical haircuts, which everyone accepted, so the incident passed without comment.

The most harrowing prison incident of all, however, actually had nothing to do with seamen, but with a man called Sholto Douglas. The Douglases were an extremely well-known family, one of them being Air Chief Marshal of the Royal Air Force during the war. Before independence, Sholto Douglas held a very high position with the government. He was so highly thought of that the government asked him to stay on after independence. He agreed, on condition that he was not to be given any job that involved money, as he admitted to being a kleptomaniac! This condition was accepted and he was put in charge of prison administration.

I should explain here that, some time after independence, the government introduced a law to try and stamp out stealing. Anyone caught taking even a comparatively small amount of money from the government or a charitable organization was sentenced to a mandatory term of two years. On top of which they received twelve strokes of the cane at the beginning of their sentence, and another twelve strokes when they came out. Sholto Douglas was one day visiting the Dar es Salaam prison shamba, which grew vegetables for use in the prison. He apparently picked some of the vegetables and put them in the boot of his car. When leaving, his car was routinely examined and the vegetables discovered in his boot. The value of them was over the designated limit, so he was immediately arrested, charged and sentenced to two years in prison, plus the twenty-four strokes. He was so petrified at the thought of being beaten that he couldn't even walk. I went to see him the day before he was due to be beaten, and he was in such a state that the warders had to carry him into my presence. I was shocked when I saw him, and thought him to be no more than a blubbering jelly. I was convinced that he had become (if only temporarily) insane. I immediately contacted the British Embassy, including their doctor, and explained my fears about his health. To my immense relief he was indeed certified as insane. This meant that he would not be beaten, and also that he was transferred to another prison upcountry that had a mental hospital wing. There he was treated and gradually he improved. I went to visit him as he neared the end of his sentence, and was greatly relieved to see the improvement. The problem now was that if he was declared sane at the end of his sentence he would have to receive the mandatory twelve strokes.

Somehow a deal was struck and the day he left prison he was whisked out of Tanzania to neighbouring Malawi, where, as a personal friend of the president, he was saved from Tanzanian officials.

Of all my dealings with the processes of law in Tanzania, however, the one that stands out most in my memory was the case concerning an American seaman. It was my practice to visit an incoming ship as soon as possible after it had berthed, especially if it was alongside. On this occasion I was standing on the quayside as it came to rest, so was one of the first on board. Actually there was always a slight delay as the customs officers went on board first to seal the liquor store, in accordance with government regulations. This did not take long however so very shortly after berthing I climbed the gangway armed with the normal Mission posters, plus one advertising a dance we had on that night.

There were usually about four noticeboards on every ship, and I made it my business to put up my notices on them all. The last one on this day was just outside the mess room. I was busily engaged in pinning them up, when a steward passed by and stopped to talk. I couldn't help but notice that he was grossly overweight. He wasn't very tall either so reminded me almost of a ball! He appeared to me to be as wide around the waist as he was tall! Nothing daunted, I enthused about the dance we were having in the Mission that evening and expressed the hope that I would see him there. 'I'm sorry, chaplain,' he said, 'but I have already made other arrangements for this evening.' I was not surprised therefore that he didn't turn up, and if the truth be known thought no more about it.

He certainly did have other plans for that evening, but they did not turn out as expected! He went up to one of the local bars in town, where he met and agreed a price with a prostitute. They went in a taxi to her house, and he instructed the taxi to wait for him as he went in. Once inside, however, the lady upped the price for her favours. The American was furious but had no option but to agree. He paid up and they went to bed. After it was all over they both fell asleep. He awoke in what was now the middle of the night, still nursing deep resentment that he had been forced to pay more than the agreed price. He had noticed that there was a very nice radio by the side of her bed, which he decided to take as compensation. The room was in pitch darkness but he felt around the floor by the bed, and was relieved to find his shirt, socks, shoes and trousers, but not his underpants. He quickly dressed, picked up the radio, and tiptoed out of the house. The taxi was still waiting and took him back to his ship.

All this was relayed to me the following morning when the local police inspector rang me to say that he was shortly on his way to the ship to arrest the offending party. There had also been a *'shauri'* (a lovely Swahili word for a problem) the day before with the ship's master, who had queried the right of a Tanzanian official to act in the way he did. The master said on board ship the official was on American soil, so therefore had no jurisdiction over him. The master was wrong of course, but the official being young and inexperienced didn't feel able to stand up to him, so left. When he reported the matter to his superiors, they were incensed and decided that they would return the following morning to confront the Captain.

In the meantime, however, came the second complaint. The good lady awoke to find her client gone, together with her precious radio. She found the missing underpants but understandably considered they were not fair exchange, so went to the police. She knew the taxi driver very well having used him many times before, so it was easy to ascertain to which ship he had taken him.

The police inspector told me that he was bringing armed men with him, but they didn't want any trouble. He suggested that I went on board and informed the Captain of what was to happen and to advise him that he should do nothing to worsen the situation. This I did but the Captain (despite my earnest pleas) was having none of it. He swore he wouldn't let them place one single foot on his ship. With that his Chief Officer appeared, to inform him that a section of police armed with rifles was advancing down the quayside, and heading for them. The Captain put on his uniform hat and made his way to the top of the gangway. The inspector also made his way up the gangway to be met by the Captain (with me hovering behind him).

'You can't come on my ship,' said the Captain.

'Captain, I arrest you,' came back the reply! And arrest him he did.

Unceremoniously he was bundled down the gangway and away to the police station, where he was charged with offences against the state. He was then bailed to appear before the magistrates the following morning. In the meantime, the other officers who were investigating the theft of the radio had immediate success. Because of his huge girth, identifying the suspect was easy. The radio was recovered very shortly afterwards. He had in fact sold it to a shipmate for just a few dollars. The steward likewise was arrested and taken to the police station. He too was charged and kept in custody.

The Captain received a very hefty fine and had to apologize publicly to President Nyerere; the steward remained in custody after the ship sailed and was duly brought before the judge. The situation I have already described came out in evidence, with the most damning piece of evidence being his missing underpants. The prosecutor made a great show of displaying these huge underpants in court, and there was only one person to whom they could possibly belong, and that was the man in the dock. One good thing that came out of the whole saga was that he lost some weight whilst serving his sentence!

Football is as popular amongst seamen as with any other group of men. Most ships had their teams, complete with all the gear, and hardly a day went by without at least one match being played on the Mission pitch. I became quite expert at refereeing matches, as well as filling in for teams that were short of a player. As a consequence I was extremely fit. On more than one occasion I refereed a match, and then made up the numbers in the next game, finishing up by refereeing a third – all this, remember, in the tropics! Apart from playing, most men had their favourite football team back home, and I am not only talking about British seamen, but men from every country. The same applied to a country's international side, and I particularly remember huge interest being taken in the 1966 World Cup, which was held in the UK. There were none more enthusiastic than the Germans. Many of the ships were on regular runs to East Africa, which meant that they visited Dar es Salaam about three times a year. This meant that I got to know the ships and their crews very well indeed. As a consequence I was invited for many meals on board their ships. On one occasion I was having a meal, and as the World Cup was only about three months away, the main topic was all about who would win.

The men on board were all convinced that Germany would win

it, but needless to say, I rooted for England! The Chief Officer in particular was fanatical about it, and as a consequence a bet arose, which was witnessed by most of the crew. By the time the ship was due to return, the World Cup would have been over for about a week. If Germany won I agreed that dressed in my clerical robes, I would dive off the top of the Mission's diving board. If England won (it was always assumed that the two teams would meet in the final) then he, dressed in his mess kit, would do the same. Well, England won, so I waited with great glee for the ship to return. The Chief Officer was as good as his word, and duly climbed to the top board, saluted, and then dived into the pool! I had widely advertised the event, so there was a large audience present (including the press) to witness his dive.

Looking back on the huge amount of use the pool enjoyed, it is remarkable that there was not one serious accident during the ten years it was in use. In fact the only incident concerned my young son, Michael, who could swim like a fish, and dived off the top board continually. On this particular occasion he somehow managed to land not in the water but on the edge of the pool. I saw it happen and was horrified as he hit the ground. To my amazement however he jumped up, shook himself, climbed straight back to the top board, and performed a near perfect dive, this time safely into the water.

My two children, Michael and Elizabeth, had a wonderful time at the Mission. The men, especially those with children, made a huge fuss of them, and they on their part enriched the lives of many seamen. Although of a very young age they were perfectly at ease with the men. On more than one occasion I saw them sitting at one of the tables with half a dozen men around them, talking away and often leading the conversation. One man told me that on one occasion he was looking through the glass doors of the chapel, which led off from the main hall of the Mission, when Elizabeth came up to him and said, 'You can go in if you want to, my daddy won't mind!'

Michael became very adept (at eight years of age) at refereeing football matches, and would stand no nonsense either. I remember on one occasion he gave a penalty, and when the player protested very strongly, Michael sent him off – and off he duly went!

Apart from football, cricket was also popular, and matches were arranged against local teams. The same with rugby, although it was

260

very difficult with the average size of the crew, to raise fifteen men from one ship. This often meant that I played these games too. Just before we left the UK I was given a set of golf clubs. I had never played but hoped to take up the game once I arrived. Sadly I never did find the time to take up the sport, but my clubs came into good use, as I used to lend them to seamen who wanted to play. In fact, in the twelve years I was there, they became completely worn out.

It was not, of course, only sports fixtures that we arranged, although that was an essential part of the work. In James' epistle he says, 'Faith without works is dead'. Some have called it an epistle of straw, but I consider works to contain the essential elements of the gospel. Needless to say, however, it is only part. One can equally say, 'Good works without faith is dead'. I hoped and believed that my work as Missions to Seamen chaplain embraced them both.

Every day began with prayer. I had a lovely dachshund called Judy. She used to follow me wherever I went, and that included the chapel. It was my practice to go to the chapel as early as possible because once the day swung into action there was little time for solitude and quiet. Judy used to sleep outside our bedroom door, and when I staggered out (often half asleep!) first thing in the morning Judy would greet me with obvious joy, and then lead me (rather as a verger in church precedes the minister to his pew) down to the chapel. She would then settle down quietly by my prayer desk, and not move until I had finished my devotions.

Because of the nature of the work, especially the long hours, a great deal would come to pass before the day ended. The Mission facilities were open every day from 8.30 am to 10.30 pm, although the men didn't leave until they were ready, which was usually much later! Then, after they had all gone, there was the Mission to put to bed, including counting the takings from the shop, the bar and the restaurant. More often than not there were seamen whose ship was a long way from the Mission (especially when the port expanded to twelve berths alongside, plus an oil terminal at the far end of the bay), who needed transportation back to their ships. Then there were those jobs that one just didn't have time to tackle during the day. As a consequence one hardly ever got to bed before midnight, sometimes even later. It was no exaggeration therefore to say that on occasions I made my way in the early hours of the morning to the chapel almost by instinct.

The particular day to which I am now referring occurred after a very late night. I made my way down to the chapel, Judy as usual leading the way. I advanced to my prayer desk and was mentally preparing to kneel down when Judy started growling which was not like her at all. I then noticed that the hairs on the back of her neck were raised. This all brought me out of my half asleep state, which was just as well for coiled all around my desk was a very large snake! Like all buildings in the tropics, every wall had louvres to encourage airflow, which also of course allowed access to snakes and the like. I called out to my shamba (gardener) Mohamed to come immediately, which he did. 'Get rid of it at once,' I ordered him.

Mohamed looked at the snake, which seemed unfazed by all this and hadn't even moved. 'Don't worry, Bwana Mkubwa' he told me, 'he's friendly.'

'Friend or not,' I said, 'get rid of it!'

I gave Judy a big thank you hug, decided to abandon my prayers for the time being and went back to my flat above the Mission to enjoy a cup of tea. I never did enquire how the shamba disposed of it!

Usually then, the day began with prayer, and continued in a more practical way. After breakfast it was down to the office (which Rose ran). A quick look at the mail, in case there was anything that needed immediate attention. I was so lucky with Rose that I could say to her, 'the answer to that letter is "Yes" or "No",' as the case may be, and later on in the day, when I returned from visiting or meetings, there would be a letter ready for my signature written exactly as I would have dictated it. Things did not, however, always go smoothly! She did not always agree with my point of view. She hated, for example, the felling of trees to make way for new buildings, with which, as both Mission padre and archdeacon I was constantly involved. I could tell from how she addressed me whether or not I was in the doghouse. If she began, 'Darling, no problem,' it was OK. If it was 'John' that meant I was on a slippery slope. If 'Padre' – then in real trouble! In the end, when everything else failed, my punch line was, 'Well, I'm the padre, and that's that.' She would sweep up any papers she had with her, and storm out of the office! I knew from experience that before long she would return with a cup of coffee or the letter typed, and peace and harmony would be restored. Before going ship visiting I always kissed her goodbye, with the familiar phrase, 'I don't know when I will be back'. We never arranged a lunchtime (except on special occasions) because as likely as not I would end up having lunch on a ship. All this before the days of the mobile phone!

Before I left, Judy seemed to sense when I was going out and would jump up onto one of the two chairs I had in front of my desk. She would look at me and give a little yap. She was asking permission to advance across my desk to receive a cuddle. 'Come on then,' I would say, and come on she did. A sloppy lick from Judy, and a pat on the head from me signalled the end of that little episode, and then I was off.

Apart from Judy I also acquired a parrot. He loved to sit on my shoulders, and was a great favourite with all, especially the seamen. Because he seemed so tame we used to leave him to roam at will in the lounge at night. That was until disaster struck. Elizabeth had some budgerigars, which she adored. They also lived in a cage in the lounge. We entered the lounge one morning to find that the parrot had attacked them, killing some and injuring others. By poetic justice the parrot caught distemper (very common in young parrots) and died shortly afterwards.

Snakes were very common, and some of them very dangerous, especially the cobra. I remember on one occasion I was in a great hurry and decided to take a short cut into the Mission. This entailed going through some bushes and longer grass. Suddenly a cobra reared up right in front of me, its hood up, hissing, and poised to strike. It all happened so quickly, that I hadn't got time to be afraid, but just froze where I was. I then heard the voice of Mohamed the gardener, who had obviously seen the danger. 'Don't run,' he called, 'and don't move.' Because my eyes were glued to the snake I sensed rather than saw him advancing. The seconds passed and then suddenly he was behind the cobra, with a panga in his hand. As quick as a flash it swung through the air and in one clean strike decapitated its head. I broke into a cold sweat, and thanked God and Mohamed that he was on hand to rescue me. I remember on another occasion going down a path in my car, intending to visit an expatriate who lived all on his own miles out in the bush. The path was very rough so I was travelling slowly. There was long grass on either side of the path, and suddenly, about five feet in front of me, appeared the head of a large snake, which I believed was a python. It took no notice of me but advanced across the path and into the grass on the other side. I stopped the car and waited. The head had now disappeared but the body kept coming! It must have been at least twelve feet long. I stayed where I was for a long time before slowly moving forward down the path. The expatriate I was visiting seemed unfazed by my experience, but I was so grateful that I witnessed it from the safety of the car.

We were very fortunate in that the chairman at one time of the Mission's committee was a very kind man called Claude Robinson, who was managing director of Tanganyika Cotton. The company had a beach hut just outside Dar, and Claude used to let us use it for little breaks. It was basic but contained one's entire needs. The only problem was that the sea was so warm, it was almost like having a hot bath. Nevertheless it was wonderful to get away from

3/6/68

My dear Archdeacon ,

Thank you very much for your two letters ,the post card, and for the Lambeth Magazine,

It is very nice to hear that you are enjoying your holiday very well.

We are all very well hear , every thing is going on also very well,

May the 12th we blessed the Ukonga Church at4 pm in the Afternoon , many peole came to attend the Service ,

We hope to bless the Kinondoni house and Parish hall June 23rd,

The Diocesan Office is finished,we are now buying Faniture,

Please excuse me for these few lines, but the aim of this letter is

To Well Come You Again to Our Diocese/DaresSalaam. You will continue to be Archdeacon of DaresSalaam, and as I promised you you will be looking after this Diocese in my absence to the Lambeth Conference as Its Vicar-General.

Give my best wishes to your wife & the Childern.

Your sincerely

+ Jon D'Salaam

264

it all. The children loved it, and what with the sea and the Mission pool they were both excellent swimmers. Rose never learnt to swim, and was afraid of the water. Near to the hut were some salt flats and it was there that I first taught Michael to drive. Strangely enough, Rose never learnt to drive either. lacking the confidence to venture onto the roads.

Because I was, for most of the time, a one-man band, holidays were very infrequent, so all the more pleasurable when one came along.

It was almost impossible to get on top of one's work, because apart from running the Mission (with a total staff of about 40) there was a constant changeover of ships, which meant there were always new ships to visit. A great deal of my time was spent in ship visiting. My usual practice on boarding a new ship in port was first of all to ask God's blessing on my visit as I climbed the gangway. My first task was to make myself known to the ship's master, so that he would know that 'the man from the Mission' (as I was called) had been on board. The master was always very busy on entering a port, with lots of official visitors, so unless he invited me to stay I quickly moved on. The next person to visit was the Chief Officer, who was also very busy as he was responsible, apart from anything else, for the loading and unloading of the cargo. But he was also a key person as far as I was concerned. He controlled the crew, so his permission was needed before I could arrange activities. He was a mine of information about the length of stay, of any sickness or hospitalization, or of anyone with a problem. All these factors determined what I could or could not arrange. I, on the other hand, could supply him with local knowledge, which could be a great help and enable him to take short cuts, and find the right person to contact. I could hand over my Mission posters and he would arrange for them to posted on the various notice boards. He would usually be aware of any practising Christians amongst his crew, which was invaluable to me and saved me a great deal of time. Most of the life on board ship was spent at sea, and the routine on a Sunday was the same as any other day. As far as I was concerned, therefore, every day in port was like a Sunday. By that I mean that I would arrange a service on board, or at the Mission any time, any place if there was a need.

There were occasions when the harbour was full of ships so others had to drop anchor outside. I remember on one occasion arranging a service of Holy Communion for a Bank Line ship. The master was one of the communicants so he arranged for me to take the service in the officers' dining room, using his table as the altar. Although he had everything beautifully set up, there remained a problem. In a chapel there would have been a cross on the wall. Instead there was a picture of the owner of the Bank Line, Lord Inverforth. He had a very stern-looking face, and gazed down on the altar rather like a wrathful God! There was only one thing to do. I took a spare purificator from my case and reverently laid it over the picture frame. There was a horrified gasp from the Captain. 'You can't do that,' he spluttered, 'that's the owner of the company.'

'He may be your God,' I told him, 'but he's not mine.' The purificator remained!

From one source or another I would on occasions hear of a seaman who had a personal problem. It could range from receiving a 'dear John' to family problems, sometimes very serious. A financial problem could have arisen at home, or news of sickness or even worse had come with the mail. Very often the man concerned would come to me of his own accord, and in many ways I was

Archbishop Ramsey talking to the sisters of the Community of the Resurrection, during his visit to Tanzania

able to help. Problems, which are fairly easily solvable if one is at hand to deal with them, become magnified and extremely acute if you are the other side of the world. The telephone is a wonderful link and times without number seamen from my office at the Mission made contact with loved ones back at home. Just as I was contacted in Cardiff from missions in South Africa and South America, so I too on occasions contacted a priest in a seaman's home town asking him to visit a family and help whenever possible. Seamen who were discharged into hospital (or prison!) obviously received top priority, not only in visiting the person concerned but also making the folks back home aware of the situation.

Sometimes the requests for help were very mundane, such as having a film developed, or buying toothpaste. But each and every one of these occasions provided an opportunity to show the love of God for all creatures both great and small.

The Mission's ministry is, to my mind, perfectly summed up in the following daily prayer, used by all Mission chaplains:

The Mission's prayer

Bless the Missions to Seafarers and all who work for them.
Keep their welcome warm, and their love and care unstinting.
May their ministry to seafarers express the love of Christ for
   all people.
Amen.

Over the years, of course, I built up contacts with the regular crews who came to Dar, and this made my work much easier. It also meant an ongoing ministry with those I had counselled before. A vicar in a parish has plenty of time for dealing with a problem. A padre in the Mission sometimes only has a ship in port for twenty-four hours; often not long enough to deal with difficult situations. This was particularly true in the case of building up another's spiritual life. But seeds sown months before sometimes had developed or even blossomed since the last meeting. A talk about being confirmed, for example, can harden into a desire for it to actually happen. But how could you prepare a person for confirmation in one lesson? That was impossible. So a basic teaching programme of twelve confirmation lessons was set up for use by all chaplains. I would possibly give the first, and then contact the padre at the next port of call, who would give the second, and so on. I remember particularly the joy of preparing one seaman in this way, and then arranging his actual confirmation in Dar some eighteen months after the lessons first began. He had received lessons in nine different ports!

There also existed the 'Seafarers Fellowship'. To be a member one had to agree to a simple rule of life, which included making contact with the padre of the Mission once you arrived in port. On occasions it was possible to find three or four members in port at one time, which created a wonderful opportunity for a meaningful meeting with them. You may recall that on our maiden voyage to Dar on the SS *Uganda* there was a woman officer whose sole job was to look after the children on board. Not surprisingly she became a firm friend over the years. I had the great privilege of enrolling her as the first ever woman seafarer into the 'Flying Angel Fellowship'. In the same week we had a confirmation, which shows the variation in my ministry. One candidate was a seafarer, the other a member of my local congregation.

Confirmation of a parishioner and a seaman at St Peter's

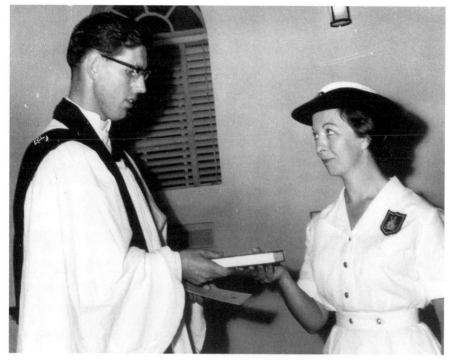

The first ever woman seafarer being admitted to the Seafarers' Fellowship

One of the major changes in life at sea during my time as a Mission chaplain was finding an increasing number of women going to sea. When a ship was in port, the radio officer had less than most to do, and it was for this reason that 'Sparky', as he was always called, was often nominated as the sports organizer for the ship. I will never forget my surprise the first time I was told to contact 'Sparky' about arranging a football match to find that he was a she!

Because seamen away from home missed so much being there, we used to do as much entertaining as possible in our own home. Many is the time I have gone onto a ship and invited say six of the crew (picked at the Chief Officer's discretion) to come and have dinner with us. Inevitably more wanted to come than we had space at the table for, which meant that there were also some disappointed crew members. We had a restaurant at the Mission, of course, and times without number, crew members who had not been nominated asked me if they could please order a meal from

269

the restaurant, but eat it with those who had been invited to our flat. There was only one answer, and that was, 'Of course'.

It was quite common, therefore, to have more people eating sitting on the floor (once the armchairs were all occupied) than around the table! I never pushed religion, but have always insisted that grace was said before every meal, and that we all held hands whilst it was being said! I remember 'a morning after' that became very special. Among the guests the night before was a ship's bosun. The size of his stomach suggested that he was very fond of his beer. He was not a very talkative person, but seemed to be taking everything in. He came to see me the next morning, and told me there was something he wanted to discuss. With very little encouragement he confessed that he was not a very religious person, and almost never ever went to church. When I had said at supper that we all had to hold hands for grace, he was embarrassed and, felt totally out of place. But as we all held hands and the grace was said, he became conscious of a great gap in his life. He was extremely moved and affected by the experience, and longed for what he had briefly experienced to be a regular part of his life. So began a new Christian pilgrimage, which blossomed. We kept in touch for very many years, and whenever we met he was wont, given the slightest opportunity, to tell of his conversion through holding hands and saying grace at the meal table.

Chapter 22

The Mission Staff

Another very rewarding aspect of the work was my relationship with the staff. After independence, the government built many hotels in and around the coast and in the game parks. This meant that anyone who had any experience in the hotel or catering business was snapped up, so there were very few left. Because we were open every day and evening (never once for even a single day during my twelve years at the Mission in Dar did we close) we needed a staff of about forty souls. Two shifts, plus days off, ensured this number.

Immediately after independence a basic problem arose that took many years to resolve. For very many, Africa became 'Africa for the Africans'. The expatriates, who, before, were the masters, were now the main guests at the hotels. But there arose reluctance from the indigenous to wait on them. In addition the tourists were by African standards very rich, the staff very poor, and understandably this caused resentment. I had in a much smaller way exactly the same problem with the staff at the Mission. Although the seamen were generally speaking very generous in tips, nevertheless it must have been very galling to see a seaman spend as much on an evening's entertainment as they earned in a month.

To give but one example. Empty beer bottles had a refundable value. We used to return all empties for credit which, by the end of the month, added up to a considerable sum. Despite the most rigorous checks however we were never able to return as many empty bottles as we had purchased full! The staff almost considered it their right to take a couple of empty bottles away with them. Although I sympathized with them in my heart, we obviously couldn't allow this so I had to stop it somehow. In the end I worked out a bonus scheme based on the number of returned bottles, which went a long way towards solving the problem.

There were other problems, however. No one considered it his or her duty to put the rubbish out for collection. After independence every firm or institution introduced what we would call in the UK a shop steward. Our steward was called Anontoni. One day he came to me with the news that the staff were going on strike because of their reluctance to carry the refuse bins to where the lorry came to pick them up. They had all gathered together near the offending bins. I asked them what was the problem, and without hesitation and all at once they began to tell me. I let them finish and then I said in the most disarming voice I could muster, 'No problem, I will move the bins myself.' I advanced with a firm step towards the bins and started to pick the first one up. But before I could do so at least half a dozen of them rushed forward shouting, 'No, Bwana Mkubwa, I will carry them for you.' After that I had no more problems.

Anontoni came to see me afterwards, and I told him that I didn't think he had handled the situation at all well, and that I was disappointed with him. He turned to me and said, 'Father, you mustn't be upset. You are our father and we are your children. No father with forty children can expect them to be good all the time, so please don't be upset any more!'

One of the exciting things about being an expatriate at this time, was you never knew what the morrow would bring. For instance, I picked up the daily newspaper one morning to learn that the government had passed a law stating that every Tanzanian had to have an identity card, with the appropriate details on it including a passport-type photo; that the law was to come into effect in about one month's time, and that it was the responsibility of the employer to ensure that every one of his staff had the card by the required date. There were only three photography shops in Dar at that time, and simple statistics told me that they wouldn't be able to cope with the numbers, so I decided to take the staff photos myself. This I duly did.

Unfortunately one of the staff was away on holiday, and when he returned there was only just over a week to go. I was completely tied up and in any case had no films left. There had been such a demand that it was almost impossible to buy another. There was only one thing left to do and that was to send him down to one of the three shops in town to have his photo taken. I dispatched him and thought no more about it. With only three days to go I suddenly realized that he had not given me his photo, so I sent for him, and told him to go down at once to the shop, and not to return without it! I had been told that there was absolute chaos in the shops concerned, with piles and piles of photos waiting for collection, so was very surprised to see him returning about an hour later clutching photos in his hand. It was with great pride that he handed them over, whilst I received them with a sense of relief, as heavy fines were promised to any firm that failed to meet the deadline. As he turned and left, I glanced casually at the photo, only to recall him immediately.

'Justin,' I exploded, 'that's not you on the photo!' He gave me the most charming smile and said, 'I know, but he's got a wonderful shirt on. Far better than any of mine!'

There was a real sense of my being a father to them, which endeared them to me and me to them. But as anyone knows loving makes one vulnerable too. I was so pleased that a large percentage of the staff remained with me for the whole of my time in Dar es Salaam, but there were casualties too. As I have already written, the major hotels naturally absorbed the best of the available labour, which meant that the staff I recruited often had little or no experience of the work, so had to be trained from scratch in even the most mundane of duties. I well remember when a young man called John joined the staff. He started off as a waiter but quickly rose through the ranks, and it wasn't long before I put him in charge of the shop. Because of shift work, and the very large stock held, apart from basic safeguards, one had to rely to a large extent upon the honesty of those handling money. For a long time everything seemed in order, but then the income from the shop decreased for no apparent reason. I was forced to the conclusion that John was stealing money from the till. I set a simple trap, which proved conclusive, so I had no alternative but to sack him on the spot. There was a problem however: under the labour laws it was not possible to sack a person unless one had indisputable proof of their dishonesty. The only way I could achieve this was by calling the police. They came and in the face of indisputable proof John admitted that he was guilty. I had not bargained however for what came next. With the proof verified by the police I just intended sacking him, but the police had other ideas. As referred to earlier in the case of Sholto Douglas, if an employee stole from the government or a charitable institution more than nineteen shillings, then the mandatory sentence was two years in gaol, plus twelve strokes of the cane at the beginning of the sentence, and twelve as you came out.

The young inspector who arrested John seemed to have great pleasure in telling him that tomorrow he would be taken in front of a magistrate, would receive the mandatory sentence and then be beaten. As John was led away I was mortified, and became deeply distressed. The inspector told me that I needed to go down to the station to make a statement, and it was with a heavy heart that I shortly afterwards went down to the station to do just that. When I arrived I was shown a book where John's arrest was recorded and that he had been charged. All that was needed now was for me to make and sign a statement confirming that I had called for the police. John had been with me for about six years, he was little more than a lad when he first came, and in many ways I had helped and seen him develop. He was a charming boy and, as with the other members of the staff, was very precious to me. I realized that I just couldn't let him be beaten and spend two years in gaol; so there and then I said I wanted to withdraw the charges. This caused huge consternation in the station, and the senior officer tried to make me change my mind. But I was adamant I could not allow him to be beaten, so he was released.

That, sadly, was not the end of the story. About three months later, who should appear at the Mission, accompanied by two hard-looking individuals, but John. The two men, it transpired, were union officials, who had come to investigate what they claimed was an unfair dismissal. My initial reaction was one of apprehension. More than one expatriate had been deported for alleged mistreatment of staff. But any clash with the unions could be a very long, unpleasant and possibly expensive experience, which no one cherished, least of all me. Apprehension quickly turned to annoyance as I relived in my mind John's arrest and my consequent withdrawal of charges.

'How can you possibly do this, John?' I asked him.

But the union officials signalled for John to be silent, and said, 'You must address all your questions through us'. From the start they assumed a very threatening attitude, which annoyed me intensely, and made me even more determined to stand my corner. As it happened their appearance clashed with a weekly event that I had come to cherish. Not far from the Mission was the Mgulani Salvation

Army camp. I have always admired and supported the work of the Salvation Army, so having them almost as neighbours was a golden opportunity to help in practical ways. A section of the camp housed crippled children. I was a regular visitor and also raised funds for them so got to know them well. About ninety per cent of them wore callipers and moved only with the aid of crutches. They were nevertheless an incredible bunch of cheerful children, and I loved them to bits. It was common knowledge that being in water gave them a sense of freedom of movement so invited them to use the Mission pool on a weekly basis. It proved to be one of the highlights of their week, which I enjoyed also. I made it my business to greet them and then help the children to take off their callipers, then carry or help them into the water. Their excited screams as they splashed around under the watchful eyes of their carers was wonderful to behold.

The arrival of the excited children and the union officials coincided. I told them that whatever happened I was going to maintain my weekly ritual and that they would have to wait therefore until I had seen all the children 'safely gathered in'. I arranged for one of the staff to bring them coffee, and left them to it. Whether or not they thought I was going to escape, I know not, but they apparently were determined not to let me out of their sight. So they followed me over to the pool. The children greeted me as usual in a very enthusiastic manner; I did my usual stint in preparing the children for the water, stayed a short while to see that all was well and then turned towards the office. The union officials blocked my path. Gone was their arrogant manner, as one of them spoke, 'We have been watching you with those children,' he said. 'It is obvious from what we have seen that you do not hate, but love Tanzanians, so we are dropping the case.' I nevertheless insisted that we all went down to the local police station to prove that John had been arrested and charged but that I had withdrawn it so he could not be prosecuted. The inspector remembered me well, and quickly produced the book containing the evidence. A sheepish John departed, I bade the union officials farewell, and that was the last I saw of John or them.

Apart from John, the vast majority of the staff remained with me, and were still there until I left. I got to know them very well, and learnt a lot about them and their families. Not infrequently a member of the staff would ask to see me and, almost without

275

exception, they came with the request, either for a loan, or an advance of wages. I was torn between the desire to help, and the knowledge that lending them money wasn't necessarily the best solution to their problem. In fact it could be disastrous! I overcame the problem by establishing a discretionary fund. Needless to say I had to keep a very tight rein on this fund, but it did prove to be a godsend, not only to the staff, but also to me, as it enabled me to help out in deserving cases.

From time to time seamen too came to me with financial problems. The difference between them and the staff however was the amount involved. Whereas a comparatively small amount could make a huge difference to a member of staff, the size and amount of the seamen's financial problems was usually beyond my scope. However, because of my contacts with the shipping managers, most of whom were on our committee anyway, I was able to 'have a quiet word' with the manager concerned, who was sometimes able to help. The vast majority of problems that were brought to me by the seamen, however, were the sort that any parish priest would have to cope with. The difference was that, whereas in a parish the vicar could call a meeting between all concerned, with me that was impossible. As anyone involved with counselling will tell you, 'there are two sides to every story'. It is unwise and difficult to come to a conclusion after listening to only one of the people involved. Nevertheless I was, on occasions, able to clarify the situation by helping the person concerned to separate the 'wood from the trees'. The usual turnaround for ships on the regular East African run was about four months, and the next time the ship returned I was usually updated with the latest developments.

There was one more area where I was concerned with counselling, and that was with any expatriates with problems. My duties as archdeacon also included dealing with diocesan problems. At that time anyone wishing to be divorced had to meet with church officialdom before the process could go ahead. I remember having to deal with one expatriate who I only knew vaguely, but because I was by then a well-known priest, he knew me. Amongst the community in general I was best known for my work with seamen, so unless those concerned were churchgoers they wouldn't even know that I was also the archdeacon. I was due to meet with the expatriate concerned at St Alban's church, and this duly came to pass. But before we met officially, I bumped into him in the

276

grounds. He came up to me and said, 'Am I glad to see you! I've got to meet with the archdeacon of Dar es Salaam in about ten minutes. Can you tell me what's he like? And do you think he will give me a rough time?' I didn't at first let on that I was the archdeacon, and his face when we met officially was something to behold! But whoever was receiving counselling it is always with a great sense of privilege and the realization that 'there but for the grace of God go I'. Included in every confession are the words spoken by the priest, 'Pray for me a sinner'.

Another aspect of my role was working with priests and ministers of other denominations and nationalities. There existed in Dar a 'ministers fraternal', which used to meet monthly to discuss matters of common interest. Because I ministered to all seafarers irrespective of race, nationality, colour or creed I found the fraternal most helpful, especially if there was a priest or minister from the same country as the seaman I was trying to help. So I regularly attended the meetings. Not surprisingly, I duly found myself elected as chairman, a post I held until I left. Actually an Anglican chairman was a very sensible choice, as a brief look at the history of the church will show.

For the first one thousand years of Christianity, there was only one church, the Roman. A division arose between Roman and Constantinople Christians over the date of Easter and other matters. Constantinople thought itself equal to Rome in every matter, and refused to submit to Rome's claims. Although they duly separated, their doctrine and teachings were basically the same, so they remained part of the main stream of orthodox Christian doctrine.

The break with the church in England in the sixteenth century, however, was far more serious, resulting in the whole church in England being excommunicated by the Pope. Round about the same time Martin Luther in Germany was also having problems and he too was excommunicated, so was born Lutherism on the continent, and the Church of England in the British Isles. There were many who thought the break with Roman Catholicism should go further than it did, and as a consequence Nonconformity was also born when various Christian sects broke off from the Church of England.

Especially in the mission field, the division of the Christian church is very sad and confusing, and it should be the prayer of every Christian that one day we will present a united front to the rest of the world and other faiths. But this brief outline suffices to show that reunion would seem to centre around the Anglican

277

Church. The Nonconformists are more likely to return to the Church of England from which they broke off, than treading the huge gap between them and the Roman Catholic Church. What is more, the Anglican Church continues to have close links with Rome, with the emphasis these days on finding what unites rather than separates.

To return to the ministers' fraternity, after a great deal of negotiation we were able to present a common syllabus for teaching religious education in the schools. No matter who took the assembly and instruction, the children would receive exactly the same teaching. This worked extremely well for about eighteen months, but then storm clouds started to appear on the horizon. It appeared that the Lutherans were injecting material that had not been agreed by all, and in no time at all a serious division arose between members of the fraternity. Then someone had the 'brilliant' idea that I, as chairman, should invite all members to a dinner party, and then in the mellow atmosphere created sort out the problem!

Reluctantly I agreed and a date was set. Unfortunately, in setting the date I had forgotten that Rose would be in England sorting out our children's education, so would not be there to organize the food! I admit to being the world's worst and least domesticated creature, and although it would be an exaggeration to say that I didn't even know where the kitchen was, it would not be an exaggeration to say that of the mysteries of that part of the house, I was completely unaware. The day of the dinner drew nigh, and if the truth were known the event had entirely slipped my memory. So when Mohamed, our cook, collared me in the office, asking what he was to prepare for that evening, I hadn't got a clue. Then I had a brainwave. 'Let's have roast chicken with all the trimmings,' I enthused, 'Just like Memsahib would prepare.'

He looked less than happy and then asked, 'What about the first course and the sweet?'

By now I was warming to the task. 'That's easy,' I replied. 'We'll have tomato soup to start, and ice cream to finish. Buy some blocks of ice cream and just cut it into portions.' What I did know about Mohamed was that he took ages to get anything done, and even with Rose in the background pushing him along the meal very rarely started on time. Armed with this knowledge I said, 'I want to sit down to dinner at 6.15 sharp'. Actually I had informed all the guests that dinner would be at 7.15, so thought I would be safe in allowing him an hour's grace.

The guests duly arrived, and as they did I hesitantly offered them a sherry. I say hesitantly because many of the ministers' churches frowned upon drink, although I noticed that no one refused a drink on the evening! It came to 7 pm and still no sign of the meal, so I excused myself and went to the kitchen to find Mohamed in a real state, and still not ready even for the first course. I told him to be as quick as possible and returned to my guests, some of whom were looking rather eagerly at the laid table. I explained that there would be a slight delay but in the meantime 'have another sherry'! In fact it was two sherries later before Mohamed announced that the first course was now ready.

We moved to the table and I asked one of the ministers to say grace, which he did. It was while I had my eyes shut for the grace that Mohamed put my soup plate in front of me. When I opened my eyes I couldn't believe what I saw. Not tomato soup but two boiled tomatoes adorning the plate! Mohamed had disappeared to the kitchen, for further plates of the same stuff. There was nothing for it but to put on a brave face, which I did. 'This is a special English way to make soup,' I told them. 'What you do is to take your spoon and give the tomato a good whack.' By way of illustration that's exactly what I did. I was somewhat perturbed to see bits of tomato flying all over the place. This actually became as nothing compared to what followed when everyone began the same exercise! I sensed that one or two were venting some frustration over the increasing lateness of the meal, by the venom they put in attacking their tomatoes.

I took the opportunity to fill up their glasses with my remaining sherry. This definitely seemed to help relax the atmosphere, which was just as well, as soon after the first course was disposed of, on came the second. There were two complete chickens and when I say complete I mean complete. Everything was there including the heads and the feet. The crowning indignity came with the vegetables. All there was was just one huge plate of baked beans! I no longer had the nerve to pretend that this was another English delicacy so humbly apologized for what was before them. Miraculously the drink had succeeded where the meal hadn't. No one seemed to mind any more and I felt sure that when the topic of the syllabus would be raised, all would be well. The straw that in any other circumstances would have broken the camel's back, however, came with the sweet. No blocks of ice cream cut up in slices on the plate, but ice lollies delivered to the hand .'I couldn't get any blocks,' he told me, 'so I got iced lollies instead.'

Any vestige of pomposity or hard feelings vanished as we sucked our lollies, and when a few minutes later I raised the problem for which we had met, apologies from the guilty party, plus renewed vows to stick to the script in the future, were quickly agreed and on that happy note everyone left. All that was left was for me to explain away the tomato stains when Rose returned from the UK, and to sack the cook!

Apart from having fellowship with other Christian denominations it was inevitable, living in Africa, to also have contact with other non-Christian groups. As a consequence I became very friendly with an Asian called Vino Vanza. He became a wonderful Mission helper, especially during our three-day fêtes, when he acted as treasurer. He worked tirelessly for weeks before, including erecting all the stalls, which in the end covered the whole of the football pitch. Wherever one is in the world and organizing an outdoor event, the biggest imponderable is the weather. I have always been incredibly lucky with the weather, never once ever having an event rained off. I was always given the credit for this, but according to Vino it was not the result of my prayers alone. On the night before the fête he would with great reverence, dig a small hole in the ground and then bury a large nail. He would fill in the hole and then stand for quite a while in silence and presumably prayer. Never once in eleven years did its influence fail!

After a few years we employed an Asian clerk, who progressed to become a sort of manager. I say 'sort of' because Rose was really the driving force behind most of the administration. It would have been impossible for me to do all the other things I did without her help and expertise. He soon became one of the team, and fitted in very well with all the rest of the staff. We were thrilled when he met and fell in love with a beautiful Asian girl, which led to their marriage, which we attended. The ceremony was entirely different from a Christian service, but very moving and meaningful.

I also had experience of an African witch doctor at work. There was an African village not far from Mtoni Shamba that I had dealings with from time to time. They became very distressed when it became obvious that they had a thief in their midst, and to find out who it was they called in the local witch doctor. He made every single person in the village stand in a large circle. He then entered into the middle of it, laid out various items on the ground and performed ceremonies around them. He then told the gathering that he was going to walk around the circle three times, and on the third circuit the identity of the thief would be revealed. He actually danced rather than walked and as he did one could sense the tension rise. The first circuit completed he began his second. As he did, the villagers started swaying in time with the witch doctor's gyrations, and the atmosphere became electric. So he started around the circle for the third time, one just knew that something was going to happen and it did. A man just ahead of him broke away from the circle and fled! He was immediately chased by other men from the village and caught. I feared for his life but the village elders then took charge and took him away to the local police station, where he admitted his guilt and was charged.

Unfortunately, there came a time when it was decided (especially in rural areas) that the local populace were the best people to combat this sort of crime. The Swahili name for thief is Mwizi. If anyone saw a thief in action they immediately shouted out 'Mwizi' and then started chasing the culprit. Everyone around joined in and inevitably the thief became cornered, when he was then stoned to death. An African friend of mine who was the son of a bishop, had experience of this whilst still a young man. He told me the cry 'Mwizi' went up and he immediately took chase picking up a large stone as he ran. The thief ran towards a house where relatives lived but they saw the mob chasing so locked the door. John described how the baying mob surrounded him and then stoned him to death. John had his arm raised to throw his stone when he suddenly realized that this could not be right. He dropped it and moved away. Apparently after the victim had been killed (the police kept out of the way whilst this was going on) the crowd dispersed. Later on the police came and took the body away, making no enquiry, asking no questions – end of story. The weakness in the system was that it could lead to innocent people being killed. It was also a wonderful way if one had a grudge on another person to call him a Mwizi, and let the crowd do the rest. Thankfully this practice was eventually halted.

When we first went to Tanzania it was on a three-year contract. This first period flew, and before we knew it we were on our second tour. There was good elementary education for our children, but nothing suitable once secondary education needs came along. This meant that, if we were to continue serving in Dar es Salaam for further tours, our children would have to return to the UK for their ongoing education. The difficulty in making the right decision was aggravated by the terms of our mission contract. What it meant in effect was that if we stayed and our children went, we would only be able to have them out once in three years. After a great deal of agonizing we decided to stay for at least one more tour, so arrangements were made for Michael to attend St Edmund's School, Canterbury. Three years later Elizabeth would also have to follow the same route, and indeed that's exactly what happened.

Then a miraculous thing happened. I was counselling an expatriate who ran a small air charter company. Travel inland was very limited by the lack of roads, but in any case the vast distances involved meant that for the top people both in government and commerce, air travel was the only practical method of getting around. Unfortunately, although his business was thriving, his personal life was in tatters. His wife had run off (together with their two children) with his chief pilot to South Africa. Because he had once flown into South Africa illegally to fly someone out who was in conflict with the ruling powers he was deemed 'persona non grata'. This meant that he couldn't enter South Africa to see his children, or make any viable arrangements with his wife over future visits.

He was terribly distressed and at our weekly counselling session would pour his heart out, whilst I tried to lift his spirits. One day he came to see me when his spirits were even lower than usual. As was and always has been my practice, I greeted him with a smile. At this he exploded. 'It's all right for you,' he cried, 'everything in your life is perfect. If my life was as carefree as yours I could smile too!' He continued in this vein for some little while, and I let him continue, as I knew all his frustration and venom needed to be released. As he finally paused to regain breath I cut in and said, 'Right, now you listen to me. I have just decided to stay in Dar for another three-year tour. This means that Michael will have to go to boarding school in England, and as a consequence, because of the conditions of my contract, we will only see him once or twice in three years! And if, as everyone wants us to, we stay even longer, Elizabeth too will have to follow the same route, so we won't see her either. Unlike most other expats, we can't afford to fly them out. So don't tell me that everything in my life is perfect. I find it very difficult to smile myself sometimes.'

A poignant silence followed and very shortly afterwards he made his excuses and left. The next day he rang me and said he wanted to see me as soon as possible as there was something very urgent that he wanted to discuss with me. He duly arrived and, as was his manner, came straight to the point. 'I want to make you a director of my air company,' he said.

I was tempted to reply, 'I may be a sky pilot, but that doesn't qualify me to be a director.' But before I had the chance to open my mouth he continued, 'You won't get any salary, but as a director you and your family will be able to travel for quarter fares on any of the recognized airlines.'

I immediately saw the implications and was overwhelmed. It meant that we could travel home or bring the children out for a quarter of the normal fare. As we were entitled to be flown home and back at a full fare at the beginning and end of our tour, our children or we could in fact have three extra flights without any direct costs to us. I said I would have to clear it with my Mission (which I successfully did), and as a result our whole situation altered from then on. We, in fact, were able to have our children out for every Christmas and summer holiday, thanks to this generosity. Furthermore, Rose was able to fly home and see them at other times as well. It also had a far-reaching effect on our future lives, which I will unfold at the appropriate time.

Rose and I were both tremendously uplifted by this change in our fortunes, and as a consequence I had renewed energy and desire to move forward positively wherever possible, both in my work for the Mission and the diocese.

Chapter 23

A Trip to Mtwara

The country at this time was negotiating the building of a railway from Tanzania to Zambia, to enable exports to be shipped from Tanzanian ports rather than Portuguese East Africa, which was still in colonial hands. Consideration was therefore being given to developing the port of Mtwara, which was right on the southern border of Tanzania. Mtwara was where the infamous groundnut scheme was launched, and the Missions to Seamen acquired a plot of land at that time, because if the groundnut scheme did materialize and with it the expansion of the port, then they wanted to be there too. The rusting heavy equipment, which clutters the area to this day, records the failure of that plan.

With the possibility of the Tan Zam Railway came renewed interest in the development of the port, so head office asked me to go down to investigate the possibility of opening up a new Missions to Seamen station there. President Nyerere (by now a good friend) was keen for a Mission to be built there, so I went down armed with a letter from him telling all concerned to offer me every assistance.

On arrival I studied the plans for the port development, which had been changed considerably from the original concept at the time of the groundnut scheme. This meant that the original plot of land acquired at that time was not now in the best spot. I envisaged that most seamen would have to walk from ship to club, so set out to walk the distance myself to see how long it would take. There was no road as such so I decided to take the shortest route, which actually followed the coastline. It was a stinking hot day and in no time at all perspiration was pouring off me. Furthermore, the going was very tough, as I was more or less blazing a brand new trail. Three times I nearly gave up, but by the third time I was very near to the proposed site, so I decided to continue.

I came to a particularly thick hedge, which I had great difficulty getting through, so emerged the other side covered in scratches, and looking extremely dishevelled. I came out into a clearing that was obviously man-made, and soon found out why. I had unwittingly broken into the local army camp! In no time at all I was surrounded by some very excited soldiers, some armed with rifles, but unsure what to do. I heard the words 'spy, terrorist, enemy' being bandied about freely, and suddenly the situation turned ugly. I produced my letter from the president's office, which calmed things down somewhat. The senior NCO present said, 'OK, but you can't go any further. You must turn around and go back.' My heart sank, not only because my destination was almost within touching distance, but also the thought of retracing my steps along the tortuous route I had travelled was too much to bear. Grasping at straws I said, 'Please go and ask a senior officer to come and see me'. After some mumbled conversation among themselves they agreed and a party of them departed to fetch him. The few soldiers remaining seemed to lose interest in me also, and more or less faded away. As I was waiting I had a brainwave! I figured that the officer would take the same line as the others, so I turned and faced in the opposite direction. I now had my back to where I wanted to go. Sure enough this worked. On production of the letter he accepted that I was no danger but repeated that I had to go back the way I had come. But because I had turned around and was now facing in the opposite direction (of which he was unaware), I moved on in what was for me now the right direction! I came to a similar hedge on the other side of the compound, which I scrambled through, and with a huge sigh of relief moved on to my destination. I now knew that the position of the old site wasn't suitable, but in the end it didn't matter because the port wasn't developed, nor did we build a mission.

The journey was not completely wasted. I wanted to visit the Makonde tribe famous for their carvings of wooden figures of animals and people. Their work was prominently displayed in every tourist shop. I wanted them to carve a large crucifix to place in a new church that we had built. The village chief greeted me very cordially, and listened patiently as I told him of my need. 'There's only one man to carve this for you,' he said, 'I will take you to meet him.' As good as his word he led me through the village and to a typical African house, with an aged gentleman sitting in the shade outside. After the customary African greetings, which seemed to go on forever – 'Habari Gani,' etc. (How's your work, your father, your mother, your children, and everyone else!) – we got down to the matter in hand. I explained exactly what I wanted.

He listened very carefully, then rose and moved to piles of wood that surrounded his house. As he inspected piece after piece, feeling the texture, studying the grain, feeling the weight, I was reminded of a pipe smoker preparing his bowl before lighting up – almost caressing the bowl, lovingly filling it up with tobacco, and firmly prodding it to the right consistency before actually lighting up and enjoying the smoke. He picked up no less than ten branches before a smile of satisfaction appeared on his face, and he lovingly presented it to me saying, 'this is it'. I thanked him very much and said I would return in about three months. I only wish now that I had taken a photo of that branch before he transformed it into a work of art. The crucifix was stunning in every way and I would have loved to keep it rather than to hand it over for the purpose for which it was created. I determined to return at some time to ask him to make something similar for me, but alas I never did.

Shortly after my return I embarked on another safari, but this time on diocesan business. I knew that part of my journey would take me very close to the famous Ngorongoro crater, an extinct volcano that was now one of the most prolific game areas in Africa. Michael was out on school holidays at the time, and he jumped at the opportunity to come with me. I too was thrilled to be able to spend time together. The business side of the journey all went well and then it was off to Ngorongoro. The camp was housed at the top of the crater, but because we arrived in the evening we couldn't see any game. The first thing one noticed was how much cooler it was at camp level. In fact we were not all that far from the equator at one of the hottest times of the year. It was a fantastic treat therefore to sit before a glorious log fire and enjoy its warmth. It was early to bed and early to rise, and we had a truly fabulous day viewing the game, seeing all the big five in large numbers. Darkness fell and once again it was back to the campfire for good food, and then a good night's sleep.

Chapter 24

A Horrendous Accident

I was due at my next port of call the following afternoon so we arranged for an early call and left the camp just as dawn was breaking. The road down the crater was pretty hairy to say the least, in many places only wide enough for one vehicle to pass, so everyone travelled very carefully indeed. I had driven about halfway down when a local frantically flagged me down to tell me that a tourist bus had gone over the edge and fallen down about a hundred yards below the road. I pulled in as close as I could at a spot where another car could pass, told Michael to remain in the car, and clambered down to where the bus lay. It was fairly obvious what had happened. A tree had at first broken the fall then collapsed under the weight of the bus, causing it to roll a further forty feet or so down the slope. I was horrified by what I saw. There were bodies everywhere, some obviously dead but others still alive. I ascertained from one of the injured men what had happened. They were a party of newly retired Canadian schoolteachers, having the retirement holiday of a lifetime. There were about seventy of them altogether, travelling around the various game parks in a convoy of two coaches. There were, I was informed, thirty-three people on the bus when it went over the edge. The coaches had left the camp the previous evening, the destination being the next game lodge on the tour. They were on the second coach, and left a few minutes after the first. He said that the driver seemed to be travelling very fast, didn't successfully navigate a bend and the bus left the road. He knew nothing more until he regained consciousness some time later. He said he couldn't move and I soon saw why. He had, apart from anything else, a badly broken leg. I assured him that help was on the way, although I hadn't yet worked out a course of action. I took another look around and decided that the top priority was to get further help, even though it meant leaving them all where they were. I climbed back to the road to find that a group had gathered. I asked two of them to go as quickly as possible back up to the camp, report what had happened and radio for help. Also to send helpers back down to me with any equipment and first aid, etc. that they could muster.

I had no sooner finished seeing them off than a coach approached from below. It turned out to be the first coach of the ill-fated convoy. The driver told me that the previous evening, because his people were on board before the other coach was ready, he set off with his passengers onto the next stage of the journey. Arriving at the destination he unloaded his passengers, by which time he expected the other coach to have arrived. When half an hour passed he realized that something was wrong, but assumed it was something minor, such as a puncture. It was by now pitch dark, so he decided to wait at the lodge, fully expecting the coach to arrive any minute. The hours went by with no coach so finally he decided to retrace his steps back towards the Ngorongoro camp.

I was tempted to wait until help arrived from the camp, but knew that time was of the essence. I was aware that there was a maternity clinic not too far away, and although it would not be geared up to cope with such an emergency, it was the best place available. But how to get them there? It then occurred to me that we should turn the coach into an ambulance. So I told the driver to drive to the nearest place where he could turn around so be facing downwards, to take out the seats of the bus, and remove the luggage racks, which we could then use as stretchers. With willing hands to help, by the time the party from the camp arrived, the coach was transformed into an ambulance and facing in the right direction. I know that it is very dangerous to move badly injured people without medical supervision, but there was no option. They had already been lying in or out of the bus for some twelve hours. I was amazed that, in one of the most game-infested areas in Tanzania, no wild animals had appeared on the scene. And it was obvious that proper medical treatment was needed as soon as possible unless more lives were to be lost. I suppose because I was first on the scene and had taken apparent charge from the word go, my decisions were accepted and my plan was adopted.

The first priority was to get the injured and the dead back onto the road, the injured by using the roof racks as stretchers; the dead by any means possible. We split into two groups, one to deal with the wounded, and the other with the dead. So, armed with racks, some blankets and rope we descended down to the scene of the accident. It was backbreaking work but everyone worked as if inspired. I helped to bring the first few injured people up to the road, and once there we laid them out on the grass. Shortly after, others arrived carrying dead bodies, which they laid also on the grass verge. I decided that I should now probably remain up on the road to organize some sort of system for laying out the injured and the dead, as well as transferring the injured onto the bus. One of the ladies we had brought up was in great pain but even greater distress. 'Can you tell me if my husband is all right?' she said. I asked her for a description, which she gave, and to my horror I saw that he was lying very close to her, but dead. I made some excuse about not knowing until we had got everyone up from the wreckage and started moving the injured into the bus.

All things considered, we did remarkably well time-wise, and within about two hours we were ready to move. I arranged for the dead to be loaded into Land Rovers and then to follow our little convoy to the clinic. Once we were on the right road I stopped the bus and told the driver that I would go on ahead to warn the clinic of the impending arrival. Michael had all this time been waiting in the car, but had seen enough to know the seriousness of the situation. He was remarkably calm however, and although he remembers the incident well, it seemed to leave no long-term scars on him. When we arrived at the clinic I told Michael to remain in the car while I let them know what was coming. The head nurse started to protest. 'I don't have the staff or the facilities,' he started to tell me, but I cut him short. 'They're coming here – end of story.'

Michael had another very nasty experience. A Land Rover containing some dead bodies came into the compound and parked next to my car. They opened up the back and some of the bodies fell down on the ground right before Michael's eyes.

It was a great relief to me that I could now leave the organization to medical staff but there was still a great deal to be done. I was allocated the task of removing clothing and washing the arms of the injured so that they could be given intravenous fluids. As in any medical centre, there were holders for the bottles but not enough. I had to improvise with anything I could find, which included coat hangers and even picture frames! I still needed more, so tore round the clinic seeking other suitable props. I dashed into one room only to realize that it was the delivery room. There amid all the carriage and injury I had been involved in for the past few hours I witnessed the miracle of a baby's birth.

Once my task was finished I went around giving what comfort I could, including praying with those who wished me to. I was relieved to learn that more medical help was on the way, so I said my goodbyes and left. In fact I was due to be about eighty miles away for a meeting first thing in the afternoon, so drove non-stop to get there in time. I knocked on the priest's door and couldn't understand the astonished look on his face as I extended my arm to greet him.

'Are you all right?' he said. 'You've obviously been in a bad accident.' I wondered how on earth he knew, until he pointed to my shirt and shorts, which were covered in blood.

That was the last meeting of my tour, which meant that shortly afterwards we were back home in Dar. I was anxious in case the scenes that Michael had witnessed might have some long-term adverse effect on him, but there were none. I was delighted to learn that every person we found alive lived to tell the tale. The Flying Doctors (a magnificent organization that flies doctors to inaccessible places) transferred all the patients to a hospital in Nairobi, before they were eventually repatriated back to Canada. Because there was so much going on both in the diocese and the mission, the whole matter might have ended there, except for two things.

The first was that two days later I was driving my car in the docks, when suddenly I felt an excruciating pain in my back. I stopped my car and tried to get out of the car, but couldn't. My back had completely seized up. I was well known in the dock area, so before long help was at hand. An expatriate character who worked in the docks and was known as 'Jones the Crane' appeared and asked what was the matter? When I told him he somehow managed to move me into the passenger seat and drove me to the hospital. The pain had by now worsened and I couldn't move at all. Despite the best efforts of the nurses I just couldn't get out of the car. In the end a doctor appeared and gave me an injection in my back. It took about half an hour to take effect, after which they were able to move me into a ward. X-rays showed that I had

Organizing the fête from my sickbed

The Dutch community running the fête bar

put my back out in two places. They surmised that this probably happened when I was lifting and pulling the wounded up the sheer sides of the Ngorongoro crater, but because of the adrenaline generated at that time I was able to ignore my damaged back. After about a week I was allowed home but only to bed rest, from where, incidentally, I organized the next fête.

The second event happened whilst I was still bedridden. Some representatives from the firm in Canada who had organized the safari trip for the retired schoolteachers came out on a fact-finding tour. They interviewed some of the patients, who were by now in Nairobi hospital, and apparently I was mentioned by many of them, although no one knew my name or where I came from. Investigations soon revealed who I was, so they came down to Dar to see me. I gave them what information I could, and they for their part thanked me for what I had done. I thought that would be the end of the matter, but I was wrong. Some time later other representatives came to see me, bringing the gratitude of all those involved. Furthermore they wanted to reward me in some way, and wanted to know what I wanted! I said 'nothing' but they were insistent. At that time we were adding another extension to the Mission. It was a large pool hall, and my ambition was to have one of every sort of snooker, billiards and pool table in existence, so that no matter where the seamen came from they would find in the room the sort of table that they were used to playing on at home. I hadn't got an American pool table so said if they were insistent then that is what I would like. No sooner said than done. A magnificent table duly arrived from Canada, and was installed along with a plaque acknowledging the gift. But that was not all. They also gave me a plaque (in the shape of Canada) acknowledging my involvement at the crater. This I treasure to this day.

My first stay in hospital was when I crashed the old mission car shortly after my arrival in Dar. My second stay in hospital was due to the accident at Ngorongoro crater. I had one more stay in hospital during my twelve years in Dar, which was nothing to do with accidents at all, but to have my appendix out!

There was a lovable but rather mad Irish doctor at that time who was also a very good friend. I had complete confidence in him, so went down to the operating theatre with no worries at all. The next thing I remember was waking up in the ward. As I began to come to I sensed rather than saw that people surrounded my bed. There is a rather wonderful time when coming out of an anaesthetic, when you are neither in one world or the other. As it passed and I fully regained consciousness I thought I was in the other! And by other I mean heaven! Clergy and nuns surrounded me, and by my head was my beloved Archbishop John. Then, in descending order of rank, were all the clergy of the diocese including the sisters who tried to teach me Swahili. I don't know if it was because they were waiting in order to speak, but no one said a word. So I had to make all the conversation! Not very easy when you have just come out of an anaesthetic.

I was beginning to panic because I was running out of small talk when I heard the unmistakable voice of the Irish doctor as he advanced down the corridor.

'Where is he?' he bellowed. 'Make way for some special medicine!' With that he burst into the room accompanied by another good friend of mine; one John Hobbs, who apart from anything else was managing director of Tanganyika Breweries. Walking behind them were two of John's staff carrying a 24-bottle crate of beer! These they expertly thrust under my bed, causing robes and cassocks and habits to fly in disarray. Doctor Paddy came up to the bed and started tickling my feet. This caused me to bellow because it hurt, but as I did even more cassocks disappeared from view! To those who were left he then proudly produced a bottle, which contained the offending appendix, and invited everyone present to have a look. This all but finished off the rest of my visitors.

There was a mission supporter who used to play the organ occasionally for us in church, who worked for a local firm of solicitors. He was rather a strange but lovable person, who offered to help in our forthcoming fête. The trouble was he wasn't the sort of person you could even put in charge of a stall, yet alone an administrative task, so I didn't really know what to do with him. In the end I gave him some mundane task in one of the stalls I think it was washing up in the bar. Something cropped up which meant that he had to return to South Africa on a business trip at the time of the fête. He wrote me a letter apologizing, and wished me every success. I had a large pile of mail that day so really did no more than glance at it at the time. Later on in the day when I had more time I turned to the pile of letters awaiting my attention. I picked up his letter and something fell to the floor. I picked it up and to my amazement saw that it was a cheque for £1,000!

This was in the early sixties when £1,000 was a great deal of money. The press printed the story with the headline 'Padre laughs all the way to the bank!'

Chapter 25

Mother Superior and the Coming of the Holy Spirit

There were also great characters amongst the clergy and nuns (or sisters as we were more inclined to call them). I particularly remember one incident regarding the mother superior of a convent I went to for retreat. I was due to attend a meeting with the Archbishop in a town nearby, but was feeling the need for a retreat after a particularly hectic time.

'Why don't you go up five days before the meeting,' he suggested, 'and have a retreat at the convent nearby? I will come and pick you up at the end of it, and then we can go on together to the meeting. I will make all the arrangements for you; all you need to do is to turn up!'

He was as good as his word, as I discovered when I duly arrived. I say duly because the convent seemed miles off the beaten track. It was at the end of a long valley, in a wonderful place for quietness and peace, which I craved. The Mother Superior greeted me warmly, and showed me where I would be staying. I had decided to have a solitary retreat in silence, so all arrangements for this were put in order.

Unless a person has experienced going from a busy environment into solitude and silence, I do not believe it possible to convey adequately by words the transformation that occurs. I will merely say that it was heavenly in every sense of the word and I loved every moment of it.

Came the last day but one and by about 6.30 in the morning I was in my usual place in the convent chapel. The charismatic movement was beginning to 'take off' in America, and being of a rather conservative, middle of the road nature in my churchmanship, I wasn't sure that I liked what was going on. Nevertheless,

I believed in the power of the Holy Spirit, so this day I decided to pray for a renewal of the Holy Spirit in the diocese, but in a more conventional way.

I embarked upon a meditation based on Acts 2 (describing when the disciples first received the Holy Spirit on the day of Pentecost), when suddenly there was the sound as of a mighty rushing wind. I realized that this was not as a result of my meditation but was actually happening. Then there were tongues as of fire. These too were for real. As the roof was blown off so electric wires were exposed and damaged. As a result sparks were flying all over the place. I have never risen from my knees more quickly than I did that morning. I left the chapel and moved out into the open to see the Mother Superior running towards me with robes flying, and in great distress.

'Oh, archdeacon,' she cried, 'the roof's been blown off the convent. What's happening? I don't know what to do!'

'I don't know either,' I confessed. 'I was in the chapel praying for the coming of the Holy Spirit, when suddenly there was a sound as of a mighty rushing wind and tongues as of fire as the roof disappeared!'

She looked at me for a moment and then burst out, 'Please don't pray as hard as that in the future!'

Retreat time was obviously over, as was the wind. I realized that it was what we call in East Africa a 'Tufani', the Swahili word for a typhoon. The wind picks up speed and rapidly advances, especially up a valley, by the end of which it can be very powerful indeed. It then tends to blow itself out, but in the meantime the damage has been done.

As with most buildings, the roofs were of corrugated iron. The first task was to locate as many as possible of the sheets and repair any damage before fixing them back on the roof. With sisters searching all over the place it wasn't too long before a large number of them had been retrieved. Then began the task of fixing them back on. I knew that at best it would be temporary repairs only, but that it was imperative to get some sort of cover back in place as soon as possible. So I worked with a will, and if the truth were known thoroughly enjoyed what I was doing. By the end of the first day I had (more or less) got the roof back on the chapel, and learnt a lot in the process of the best way to go about the repair. Encouraged by my achievements on the chapel roof I started the next day on the convent. This was much more difficult. Apart from anything else, the chapel was a one-storey building whereas the convent was three. Nevertheless, I warmed to my task and by mid-morning was making good progress. Came the lunch break and with it a break from the rather meagre food I had been having on my retreat: I was treated rather like the prodigal son, with the killing of the fatted calf!

After a very full lunch I then resumed my position high in the sky, and continued my work. As I gazed at some of the cells below me I couldn't help thinking that I was probably the only man in the world to have looked in those rooms since the nuns moved in. The afternoon wore on and the work progressed, intermingled with helpful comments from the mother superior, who continually begged me to be careful. I not only enjoyed what I was doing but also felt so elated that I burst into song. I was singing away at the top of my voice when I heard the sound of clapping. Clapping one's hands in Africa is a way of commanding attention. I looked down far below to see none other than my Archbishop.

'Archdeacon,' he cried, 'I expected to find you in retreat not sitting on top of the roof singing your heart out! What on earth do you think you are doing?' Thankfully at that moment the dear old mother superior appeared and, after explaining what had happened, took him in tow. This enabled me to complete the necessary temporary repairs, and shortly afterwards we departed. Mother Superior had the last word: 'Please, Archdeacon,' she repeated, 'please don't pray so hard in future.'

The meeting Archbishop John and I were to attend was an ecumenical gathering. Because of the various traditions (including the Roman Catholics'), it was not possible for us all to meet around a common altar. Each denomination therefore met together for their early morning prayers or celebrations, after which everyone came together for breakfast. For the Anglicans this meant meditation, morning prayer and a celebration of Holy Communion before breakfast. The Nonconformists didn't share the same rules of life as us, which meant that, whereas we had been in prayer for well over an hour before breakfast, others could jump out of bed and still be there in time! A different denomination minister was selected before every meal to say the grace. Because they had already been at it for some time the Anglican and Roman Catholic 'grace' was inevitably short and to the point. For some of the Nonconformist ministers the breakfast grace was their first prayer of the morning. They therefore tended to make a meal of it – excuse the pun! One particular morning the minister concerned excelled himself, and as a consequence he went on, and on, and on! I was standing next to Archbishop John at the table and I sensed a movement beside me. Sure enough the Archbishop, with patience exhausted, reached out, picked up a piece of toast, and took a bite out of it! I don't know whether it was his crunching or my giggles that did the trick, but seconds later the prayer came to an abrupt end and we all sat down to eat.

On another occasion I accompanied the Archbishop on a visitation. Our journey took us to a remote village, which could only be reached by leaving the road and travelling along what was nothing more than the equivalent of a farm track in the UK. The track went on and on and on, so much so that I was beginning to wonder whether we were not lost forever, when we turned yet one more bend to find the path blocked by a group of women, obviously dressed in their brightest and most colourful clothes. As they saw the Land Rover approaching they advanced to meet us singing as only Africans can. I then noticed that on either side of the track were cut palm leaves, which decorated the path all the way into the village. They excitedly surrounded the vehicle, forcing us to stop. The Archbishop left the Land Rover and, then surrounded by dancing and singing villagers, advanced triumphantly into the village to be met by the elders, who greeted John with great joy and enthusiasm. I was completely forgotten in the excitement, but was content just to soak up the atmosphere, and feel so happy to see just how much he was loved.

Whilst there we had baptisms, confirmations and meetings interspersed with food and giving gifts to Archbishop John. It was one of my most memorable experiences ever, partly because of the contrast with a bishop's visitation in this country.

I never ceased to be enthralled by the devotion the indigenous people put into their worship. During my time in Dar we made many alterations and additions to the Mission. On one particular occasion we doubled the size of the chapel, which meant of course that it was out of use for some time. We also made other improvements at the same time, which meant that during this period church services were held in three different locations, the last being the general office. No matter where the temporary church was, there was a local lady who used to come faithfully every day to pray in the chapel. Her worship included singing hymns as part of her devotions. It was obvious that she was completely absorbed in her prayers and seemed oblivious to all outside noises or activities. It was a great relief when the chapel was finished and we could get the general office back into use. So literally one day it was the chapel, the next, back again to the general office.

My faithful lady came as usual the next morning, and not knowing of the change, came into the office. There, oblivious to the noise of typewriters and people moving all around her, she knelt and prayed and sang her hymns. There was only one thing to do and we did it! One after the other we left the office to her and the Lord!

We arrived in Tanzania in 1961, and left in 1973. Twelve years is actually the longest time I have ever lived in the same place and remains so to this day. The years spent there saw our son and daughter grow into teenagers, our siblings get married, and our parents get older. We had three months' leave after a three-year tour, and every time we went to the UK we saw many changes in our extended families, as no doubt they saw in us. I remember our first leave, which coincided with the winter months. We awoke one morning to find that snow had fallen, giving a three-inch carpet to the garden. Michael and Elizabeth had also seen it; actually for the first time in their lives. In Dar the children often used to go out into the grounds without any shoes on, and this is exactly what they did in the UK. Their excited cries awoke us to the fact that they were out there, and with no shoes on to boot! Before we had a chance to call them in, in they rushed complaining that their feet were burning; a hard way to learn about the winter climate in the UK!

Although we loved our holidays in the UK, it was nevertheless a very trying time. The biggest problem was that we had no home to go to, so spent the whole time going from one member of the family to another, living out of suitcases all the time. Carrying everything around with you for a family of four for three months, moving from one place to another was exhausting and extremely stressful. To make matters worse, if we spent more time in one parent's house than in the other, that upset the other parent! At first we used to come home, not having a complete timetable for the three months, so literally did not know for certain where we would be in, say, ten days' time. After the first two leaves however we learnt our lesson. We worked out our timetable for the duration of the leave, letting everyone concerned know exactly what it would be. This tended to ease matters with the parents, but it didn't take away the hassle of being constantly on the move, with heavy suitcases to lug wherever we went.

We enjoyed our leave, but it was always a relief to get 'back home' to the Mission in Dar. For the first two leaves we went home and returned by ship. I always thought the Mission to Seamen were mean in this regard, because the day we embarked they deducted from my salary an amount to counter the fact that on ship we were on free board and lodging. As anyone knows, leaves and holidays are expensive times, especially if you don't have your own home to live in. To pick up one's salary greatly reduced was not the best start to a holiday. Luckily, after the first two leaves flying became the norm. And no, they didn't deduct the cost of the meal on the aircraft from my pay!

After our first two leaves we arranged a picnic family reunion at a site central to most and these proved highly popular occasions. It not only ensured that we met every one, but that everyone met everyone else!

On one occasion whilst on leave and driving my car I got hopelessly lost in the middle of a town. To my huge embarrassment I suddenly realized (after being flagged down by an angry-looking police officer) that I was driving the wrong way down a one-way street. His anger was slightly muted when he saw my dog collar, and even more so when I apologized profusely offering as an explanation the fact that I had only just come into the country from Tanzania where I was a missionary. By now he was all sympathy for my predicament, and said, 'I expect, sir, that in Africa they drive on the wrong side of the road!'

'Well not exactly,' I replied, 'in Africa we drive on the best side of the road!'

After this he told me to be more careful and watch the signs. He then helped me to turn around in a restricted space, and with a great sigh of relief, and a wave of the hand, I was off.

Leaves once every three years apart, I have always believed that life is not about holidays but the rest of the year. As our time in

East Africa lengthened so did our ties with the local community and friends. Friendships made all those years ago have survived unto this present day, not only from Tanzania, but also from Hong Kong and Thailand (which turned out to be our next port of call) as well. It's amazing that one can meet up with friends of yester year and, no matter how long the timelapse, after a few minutes it's as if one has never been apart from them. How true it is that old friends are the best friends, although that in no way detracts from friendships new.

We arrived in Dar as they were celebrating independence, which was a very exciting time for all concerned. Until the day we left it continued to be exciting. As the inevitable results of independence worked their way into the system we noticed many changes in the law and practices of the country, although not to the same extent as in Uganda, where the Asian community was affected far more than the white expatriates. Possibly this was because most of the white expats were in top management, whereas many of the Asians were involved in middle management. Inevitably, indigenous people took over some of the jobs, which up to then had been the domain of the Asian work force. Understandably this led to a period of readjustment, which didn't always go smoothly.

Examples of this became apparent in funerals and related matters. There was a much loved harbour master called Jimmy Mackie, who was on the committee, and a terrific worker and supporter of our work. His was, incidentally, the first wedding I conducted at the Mission after obtaining parish status. Sadly he died a few years later and a very large congregation turned up for the funeral at the appointed time, including, of course, his widow. The time for the undertaker to arrive with the coffin came and passed, and so did another quarter of an hour, still with no sight of the cortége. I took the widow into my vestry and offered her a cup of tea. I apologized profusely for the hold-up, to which she replied, 'He was never on time for anything,' (actually quite true!). 'I always said he would be late for his own funeral, and now he is!' In the meantime I asked Rose to ring up the undertakers. 'Oh dear,' came the reply, 'we've forgotten all about it. Pole Sana!' (I'm sorry!)

There was another occasion when I was asked to conduct a service at the graveside. The family had made a request to me that the wedding ring could be removed from the deceased's finger, as they wanted to keep it. I passed on this request to the undertaker when arranging the funeral, and was assured that they would bring the ring with them at the time of the service. We all duly met at the appointed time and place, but waited in vain for the hearse to arrive. After half an hour I suggested that we postponed the service for two hours, during which time I would investigate what had gone wrong. The distressed families made their way back from whence they had come and I went to the undertaker's office. There I discovered that the person on duty had no instructions whatsoever regarding this funeral, indeed that as far as he knew the body was still in the hospital morgue! This, when I got there, I found to be true. Nor could I find anyone prepared to do anything about it! So it fell to me to remove the ring, dress the body, and arrange for a hearse, complete with coffin, to help transfer her into it and then dash back to the cemetery, arriving just in time to meet the mourners before the coffin arrived. It was extremely difficult to concentrate on the job in hand without reliving all that had gone on in the last two hours, but somehow I managed it, including passing over the ring.

The most stressful event of all however concerned a young mother who was involved in a car accident. She was thrown out of the car and broke her neck. The family was new to East Africa, so understandably her husband wanted his wife's body to be flown back to the UK. This was possible but required many regulations including the fact that the body had to be encased in a lead coffin housed inside a wooden one. All regulations were duly met, but before the coffin was sealed the husband asked if I would conduct a short service. He was naturally extremely upset by his loss, and stressed out by all the regulations that had to be met, so I was aware that the next half an hour could be very difficult. Just how difficult I had never imagined.

Once I arrived the attendants discreetly moved out of the room so we were alone. I started the service and came to the point when I wanted to sign her forehead with the sign of the cross. It was only then that I realized that her head was slightly protruding above the sides of the coffin, which meant that it would not have been possible to put the lid on and seal it! As surreptitiously as possible I pushed her head down below the level of the side only to see that the feet were now protruding at the lower end! Without trying to show my concern I continued praying whilst at the same time trying to make further adjustments to allow the lid to be closed.

It proved impossible! As gently as possible I had to inform him that there was a problem. Understandably this added greatly to his distress, to say nothing of mine. In the end a larger lead coffin had to be produced, so that it could be sealed. I remember standing with him on the tarmac as the coffin was loaded onto the plane, and feeling a great sense of relief as it eventually took off.

Another stressful funeral I conducted involved a baby. A young couple came out fresh from the UK, complete with their little baby, still only a few weeks old. The baby had a severe attack of diarrhoea, which can (especially in the tropics) cause dehydration. They sadly were not aware of this, and as a consequence the baby died. Their devastation and grief were overpowering, and I found it very difficult to offer meaningful comfort. They wanted the baby to be cremated, which at that time meant a trip to Nairobi. A tiny charter plane was hired, and there was just space for the pilot, the two parents and a pathetic tiny white coffin, and me. It took many hours to reach our destination, during which the atmosphere in the tiny cabin became almost unbearable. Eventually we arrived at Nairobi Airport and from there a short journey to the crematorium, and the service. In seemingly no time at all we were back on the return journey. Thankfully the atmosphere was a little more relaxed and the conversation more general. We were passing over one of the large plains below when the pilot pointed out that there was a huge herd of wildebeests crossing the plain, and would we like to go down low and see them? They said they would so down we went. It was one of the most thrilling experiences of my life. We were so low that one felt it would be possible to reach out and touch them. As we arrived so they seemed to scatter in all directions, wherever one looked they were running in their hundreds. A truly amazing sight and experience I will never forget. It also incidentally lightened the atmosphere in the plane; nevertheless we were all relieved than when the journey came to an end.

President Nyerere continued to be a good friend of the Mission and actually seemed quite proud of the set-up. We received a request to hold an International Medical Conference at the Mission, to which we readily agreed. The day of the conference arrived and with it the news that the President was coming to open it. Because the conference itself was nothing to do with me, I kept very much in the background. The President duly arrived surrounded by bodyguards and made his way to the conference hall. I was standing well out of the way, but he must have noticed me because he broke off from the official delegation and (much to the consternation of his guards) came over to where I was standing. He greeted me with a huge smile, gave me a hug and said, 'How are you, Father?' followed by, 'it must be very hot wearing a dog collar in this heat!'

After the normal niceties I said, 'I want to ask you a huge favour. Would you please open the new extension that we are building at the Mission?' (and then gave him the date).

He looked at me very earnestly and said 'Father, I am very hot under the collar with your government at the moment,' (this was in connection with problems over South Africa).

I replied, 'I tell you what. Come to the Mission early; dive in the pool that you kindly opened for us. That will cool you off and then you can open the extension.'

He roared with laughter, gave me another hug and turned to members of his escort, who had by now caught up with him, and asked his secretary, 'What am I doing on that day?' He was told

The second Vice President of Tanzania, the Honourable RM Kawawa, officiating at the opening of the new extensions at the Mission

that a visiting president would be with him so he wouldn't be free. 'I'm so sorry, Father,' he said, 'but I'll tell you what I will do. I'll send the Vice President in my stead.'

He was as good as his word, and that's what happened. Vice-President Kawawa duly came with his wife and did the honours.

Chapter 26

The Tan Zam Railway

President Nyerere was very friendly with Bishop Trevor Huddleston, who was at that time Bishop of Massasi. On the occasions when the Bishop came to Dar he would make contact with the President to pass the time of day. President Nyerere had only recently returned from a visit to China to tie up details regarding the Tan Zam Railway, which the Chinese were to build. The World Bank had also been interested, so there was some surprise that China instead of them had been awarded the contact. I spent a fascinating hour with the President and Trevor Huddleston, while he explained that he wasn't a communist but felt that the Chinese way was the only way for Tanzania to climb out of the poverty gap in which his country was so firmly embedded.

The building of the Tan Zam railway was another fascinating chapter in the history of Tanzania. Whilst I was not party to all the details, I do know that Tanzania had to pay in part by buying Chinese goods. This did not always have the desired effect. Two examples will suffice. The first was to do with Dar's public transport system. The fan belts, without which the engine cannot run, were giving up in so many of the buses that the public transport was in danger of grinding to a halt. In the terms of the railway agreement, replacements had to come from China, so an urgent order was dispatched for them. To the great relief of the authorities concerned they eventually arrived and were put in place. They were no sooner put in place however than they broke, so even more urgent alternatives had to be ordered.

The other instance affected almost everyone. It concerned light bulbs. No replacements had been ordered for a long time, which meant that stocks in the shops at first dwindled and then dried up. An urgent order was again sent to China but by the time a shipload arrived many more light bulbs had ceased to function. The situation became quite desperate; in some cases householders having to take operating live bulbs from one room to another, where light was required. Being Missions to Seamen, thereby getting a list of all ships' movements, I became the contact for many people and in the end gave a daily update on the ship's progress. The long awaited day came when the ship entered port, and was given top priority alongside berth number 1. There were, of course, official processes to be gone through but finally came the moment when I could tell my enquirers that tomorrow (yes, tomorrow) light bulbs would be for sale in Seifi household stores. For the first time in its history queues formed outside the shop long before opening time as people lined up to ensure that they could replenish their stocks. The bulbs went on sale; they were sold in great numbers, and in great joy taken home. Only to discover that the Chinese had sent screw-in bulbs, when bayonet bulbs were the norm in the country!

Another remarkable fact about the Tam Zam railway was the men who built it. A Chinese ship would come alongside the quay and discharge the workers. They were all dressed in exactly the same uniform. To the casual eye at least they all looked exactly alike. Every one of them came ashore with one small brown suitcase. They were taken straight to their heavily barbed wired camp (which it was rumoured was to keep them in rather than others out) and were not seen again, except when working on the railway. Then about six months later another ship would arrive with a similar discharge of identical men, to be replaced by the previous group of workers, who boarded exactly as they had arrived with just one small suitcase and nothing else. To the best of my knowledge there was no fraternization of any kind between them and the local populace. The general opinion was that to be that disciplined they must have been military personal, but no one actually knew.

There was a sad ending to the whole scheme. Portuguese East Africa, although much nearer than Tanzania to Zambia, was still held in colonial hands and was not considered as a viable exit port for Zambian exports. However it did receive its independence shortly afterwards, which meant its port could now be used and, being so much closer than Dar, this was obviously much cheaper. This is what came to pass and the railway was under used. Another purpose for building the railway was of course to open up the hinterland of Tanzania, although how successful that became I am not sure.

It wasn't only the Chinese who came to Tanzania to help its people. The Canadians sent a team of its Air Force experts to train Tanzanian pilots so that they could operate internationally. There were initial problems because the government wanted the various procedures, orders and codes to be translated into Swahili. They were persuaded, however, that such codes and procedures were internationally recognized, whereas Swahili wasn't, so English had to be the language. I became involved with the Canadian servicemen as honorary chaplain, and offered them the facilities of the Mission while they were with us; an offer which they gratefully accepted. On one of my evening visits to their camp, I found the men watching a film show. Much to my surprise it turned out to be one of the latest Hollywood films. Their welfare officer told me that it was their government's practice to send out the latest films as a morale booster for the troops. I was delighted when he told me that I could borrow them to show at the Mission. They proved immensely popular, not only for the visiting seamen, but also for our shore members. In next to no time, to cope with the numbers who came, I had to show them outdoors, and still the numbers grew. Then, alas, came a snag. The cinema owners in town objected to us showing films long before they could get hold of them. They complained to the authorities, who then wanted to charge us import tax. Sadly we had to stop, but it was good while it lasted!

There was another avenue for watching 'new films' and that was at the British High Commission. The High Commissioner (in similar circumstances to the Canadians) used to be sent films and show them up in the grounds. Select persons used to be invited to watch, but it was timed like clockwork. You had to be there five minutes before the film began to find your seats by aid of the lights in the garden. Right on time the film began, and when it finished the lights in the garden were switched on for five minutes only, so that you had to leave immediately before darkness swallowed you up! However, it was considered a great honour to be invited, and when we were, we always tried to attend.

There was great excitement when the first drive-in cinema was opened, and it proved extremely popular. For us it was a great treat to go as a family. As you entered you were given a machine similar to a small radio, which contained the voice track of the film. It was huge fun to sit a considerable distance away from the giant screen, and watch the movie from the comfort of your own car. The children particularly appreciated the interval, when you could obtain refreshments including chips, which the children loved. It was a time when many of the wonderful musicals were produced, such as *The Sound of Music, Chitty Chitty Bang Bang* and *My Fair Lady*. It was not very often that we had the opportunity to be together as a family, which made the open-air cinema such a special treat for us all. Then an unexpected problem arose. The cinema was built on the side of a hill, which gave one a tiered effect, so that everyone had a perfect view. One could go further up the hill and look down on the screen but couldn't of course hear the sound track. Then some Asians had a (brilliant?) idea! They would go to the cinema on the first night of the new film. Their car there would not be full of passengers but tape recorders! These they would then hire out to their friends, who could watch the film the next and subsequent nights from higher up the hill without paying an entrance fee. I do not know whether this brought about the demise of the cinema, but I do know that when I revisited Tanzania some time later the open-air cinema was, alas, no more.

Because of my work at the Mission and as archdeacon, I became fairly well known in Dar, which didn't always work to my advantage. Although there weren't all that many, beggars started appearing on the streets and became very persistent in asking for money. As a matter of principle I never gave to them (possibly memories of clothing that nude baby in Hong Kong, only to find the next day, and in the same place, the same child completely unclothed in the arms of its mother, influenced my reasoning!). Someone saw me refusing to give and reported me to the authorities as being anti-African. The press came down on me like a ton of bricks, demanding to know if this was true. Luckily for me, I had already made representation to the city council about the undesirability of having beggars on the street. I said that if a person couldn't work it was degrading for him to have to beg for a living. If there were such unfortunate people then the council should provide a proper hostel where they could live. To give to a beggar who could work was to encourage him to become a blot on society, and was not really helping him at all.

I offered to become involved in fund-raising if necessary. The publicity from the press actually helped the cause, and in due time a hostel was opened for such unfortunate people. Ironically, however, some of those who were offered accommodation shunned it in favour of begging because it was more rewarding than sitting in a hostel!

My (good?) name was restored when shortly afterwards a hostel for the poor was partly destroyed by fire, and I organized a collection on an American ship in port to help with the rebuilding. A photo appeared in the press of the mayor being handed a generous cheque by members of the crew, with me in attendance.

One of the great blessings of being a priest is meeting so many different people, from royalty, presidents, ambassadors, and ministers of the crown, ministers of other faiths, down to the cabin boy on a tramp steamer. Yet all are equal in the sight of God, and therefore all the same in the eyes of the priest. That does not mean that one does not respect them or their position, but that respect is as valid for the cabin boy as for anyone else. I could write a separate book on some of the characters I have met and enjoyed.

Take for instance a cockney stevedore called John Ward. Before independence most of the stevedore foremen were expatriates, but after independence they were almost the first group to be replaced by indigenous personnel. But not Johnny Ward! He had a typical cockney sense of humour, and an equally typical language to go with it. But he had a wonderful way with the Tanzanian workforce, and although both before and after independence he swore prolifically at his men, they didn't seem to mind, indeed loved him to bits, whilst everyone else marvelled at how he got away with it!

I was also full of admiration for my brother expatriate clergy, especially those who were in the main, like me, newcomers to Tanzania. The Reverend Paul Hardy (later to become Canon) was about the same age as me, but whereas I was mainly involved with visiting seamen, Paul's work was almost completely tied up with Tanzanians. The way in which he wholeheartedly immersed himself in his work I found inspiring. One or two of the clergy who had been out there for many years were in danger of becoming 'princes of the church' but Paul remained humble throughout. Not all the long-serving clergy of course fell into the same trap, and some were amongst the most saintly priests I have ever met. I was most grateful to Paul Hardy, who stood in for me on one of my home leaves from the Mission, although I don't think he enjoyed the experience very much! Especially when the manager suddenly became ill and died.

Because of the nature of my work I also had a lot to do with other ministers of religion, especially the Roman Catholics. Many of the ships' crews from such countries as the Philippines were Catholics and providing I let one of the priests know, he would go on board ship to celebrate Mass for them.

Chapter 27

Cardinal Rugumbwa

There was great excitement throughout Tanzania, but especially amongst the Catholics when one of their bishops was elevated to be the first Tanzanian Cardinal. Cardinal Rugumbwa's see was upcountry, but after his appointment he was translated down to the cathedral at Dar es Salaam. A very special service was arranged with Archbishop Sepeku and President Nyerere being guests of honour; indeed the Archbishop was to be seated in the sanctuary, so that he would be the first person with whom the new cardinal would exchange 'the peace' during the service. Unfortunately the date clashed with a very special anniversary service of the USPG

Cardinal Rugambwa, the first African to be so exalted, at his enthronement

312

being held in London, where John Sepeku's presence was desired. So the privilege of representing him (as Vicar General) fell upon me. It was a wonderful occasion, the highlight for me being exchanging the peace with the new Cardinal.

I was vaguely aware of flashlights going off, but thought no more of it until the following morning and the delivery of the daily newspaper. There on the front page was a photo of us exchanging the peace, which I didn't mind, until I read the caption. In fact I was horrified. It read something like, 'The picture shows Cardinal Rugumbwa exchanging the peace with the Anglican Archbishop of Tanzania, the Right Reverend John Taylor'! I deliberated long and hard about what I should do next. To point out the error to the editor was easy, but what to do about Archbishop Sepeku in London was another matter. In the end I just cut out the article and the picture, added the briefest of notes – 'don't bother to return to Tanzania, there's been a coup' – and sent it off! John being the person he was enjoyed the joke as much as anyone else.

Indeed he went further. Shortly after he returned I was taking part with him in another service in the Pro cathedral. He was wearing a magnificent cope. Suddenly he interrupted the service, called me up to where he was standing, made a little speech, then took off his cope and put it on my shoulders!

It was, I remember, during the run-up to Christmas, and I returned to the Mission to find a real problem on my doorstep. I have said elsewhere that, as the festive season approached, there was only one topic of conversation on board ships. Where are we going to be for Christmas? There was a ship alongside that had been delayed whilst waiting for a berth, causing great anxiety as the delay gave rise to the real possibility that they would miss Christmas at home. However, the berth finally became available, so it now seemed certain that they would indeed be home for Christmas. The crew had used the Mission a great deal during their time in port, so I had got to know them very well. They were a cheerful crew, and now in very high spirits as in two days' time they were due to set off to the UK. Then disaster struck. The captain received fresh orders from his company. The plans had been altered and they were now to proceed to another port to pick up a cargo destined for Australia. The grief and anger among the crew members was tangible. During the next twenty-four hours I did all I could to appease their anger and grief, and I thought I had achieved some measure of success. On the evening before they were due to set sail a large number of them came to the mission to use the facilities and say goodbye. The conversation amongst them grew more and more heated, with tension rising perceptibly. Then one of them asked me if I would join them, which I did. The second officer, who was obviously their spokesman, said, 'Padre, we have decided that we are not going to rejoin the ship because we want to be home for Christmas. Can you please arrange accommodation for us for tonight and inform the agent of our decision?'

What they were planning was a disastrous move, apart from being criminal. I pointed out to them that the Captain held all their passports on board, which meant that they would be in Tanzania illegally; that they had insufficient funds available, with no likelihood of the Captain providing any; that their careers would be ruined, and that they would never get another job at sea.

Gradually the tension lessened and more reasoned words came from some of the crew. After about an hour I realized that the tide had turned, and they agreed to rejoin the ship. It was, nevertheless, a very unhappy crew that said goodbye on the quayside, whilst I watched with huge relief as the last of them ascended the gangway and disappeared into the accommodation on the ship.

The very next day I escorted a seaman back to his ship in very different circumstances! We had a dance that night at the mission, which were always very popular, especially because of the nurses from local hospitals who came along to support. We also had some of the ladies who were shore members of the mission, which meant that we usually had enough partners for the men. This particular night we had a Union Castle passenger ship alongside, and as they had an all-white crew I knew we would be busy. We used to sell beer at the bar, so we were well stocked up as a consequence. This meant a larger order than was usual, which when it arrived brought with it six very nice glasses advertising the brewer's name. We knew from past experience that people collected such glasses as souvenirs so we told the staff to keep an eye on them, and collect them back as soon as possible.

A steward from the ship had other ideas however and attempted to hide his glass in his back pocket. Somehow he slipped and landed right on his bottom! Screams of anguish filled the air, which brought me hastily to the scene. Once having ascertained the problem I led him into my office to closer examine the damage. His bottom was peppered with glass, and the blood flowed merrily. I was sympathetic, yes, but not too much so. It was a self-induced accident, including one of my six lovely glasses that had now been reduced to five. At no time is a bottom a very pretty sight, but one looking rather like a pin cushion with bits of glass rather than pins sticking out of it, coloured by bright red pools of blood did not endear me to him one little bit. I pensively tried to pull a few pieces out, but the screams put me off. There was only one thing for it – get him back to the doctor on board ship. I told one of his mates to run down to the ship to warn the doctor about what was to descend upon him, and then tackled the problem of how I was going to get him there? I decided my car was the only possibility. I drove it as near as possible to the office, and then led him bent double to it. The only possible way was to have him standing, bent over the passenger seat. So he made this extremely undignified exit from the Mission back to the ship. As luck would have it our arrival coincided with a group of passengers, who looked on in amazement as bent double and exposed to the elements, he ascended the gangway and disappeared towards the ship's hospital.

During my time in Dar es Salaam, head office sent me out three lay assistants. I have already spoken about the first who arrived at the same time as the army mutiny. I remember going out to the airport to meet him and checking with the airline that he was indeed on board. I gave them his name, prefacing it with the word Mr. 'No, Sir,' I was told, 'there is no one by that name on board.' I asked them please to double check and back came the answer: 'There is no Mr by that name, but there is a Master!' In the midst of an army mutiny with all the problems that affected me as chaplain, the last thing I needed was a young boy to be responsible for! The scheme of taking on young students who wanted to take out a year before going on to university, by employing them in some capacity, may have worked in some situations, but certainly not in Dar es Salaam at that time.

My next assistant was superb. His name was Ken Good. He was a theological student breaking his studies for one year to obtain some practical experience before becoming ordained. He was hard-working, had vision and enthusiasm, and was totally supportive to me. He could be relied upon to complete successfully whatever task was set him in a sensitive and responsible manner. I was supposed to teach him, but I learnt as much – if not more – from him, than he did from me. I was always being accused of having unworkable ideas. He was worse than me! Needless to say we got on very well together, and it was a real wrench when his time with me came to an end and he returned to the UK to be ordained. We kept in touch thereafter and I was not the least surprised when once his first curacy was over he joined the Missions to Seamen as a priest. I was very humbled to learn that during his interview by the examining board, when asked what his vision of a Mission should be, he replied, 'like Padre John's in Dar'. After serving as a chaplain in Japan he was appointed to Head Office in an administration post. From there he returned to parish life and was duly appointed archdeacon in a northern diocese.

The third helper was an unmitigated disaster! The general secretary at that time (who had better remain nameless) wrote to me enthusing about this person he had found who was prepared to come and work in Dar. This was most opportune because we were due to go on home leave, so it meant there would be someone there to run the Mission for the three months whilst we were away. When he told me that he had a first from Cambridge for Arabic, I couldn't help wondering what good that would be to us at the Mission. When I was informed that he used the title of major, it set me thinking even more. Why would a retired major with a Cambridge degree want to become a lay assistant at Dar es Salaam? He had been working until recently in Saudi Arabia, I was informed, but was not told in what capacity (I was later told that he worked for a Sultan, stocking his harem!). Anyway, what head office decreed we (usually!) obeyed. I was duly informed of his flight number and went out to the airport to meet him. It was actually a rush to get there because of a previous meeting that I had to attend.

There was no time to change so I was dressed in my cassock (complete with my purple girdle) as I waited on the tarmac for his plane to touch down. I advanced to meet him with hand outstretched in greeting. Instead of shaking my hand he passed me his case to carry. 'Oh there you are, my man,' were his opening words! He then attempted to pass me his second case (which I declined to accept).

When all his luggage came through I just couldn't believe my eyes. My immediate thought was surely he must be overweight! I was right. On arrival at the Mission I escorted him to the room in my flat where he was going to live during my home leave. The first thing he did was to produce receipts for the charges for his grossly overweight luggage. My mind flashed back to my first flight back, when I had to take a Bible out of my luggage because it made me overweight. In the mission field excess luggage charges just don't come into the equation. I said to him 'I'm sorry but I just can't reimburse you, you will have to write to head office and get it from them.'

He was at first taken aback at this; but quickly recovered and replied, 'Don't worry I will soon sort them out. Whilst you're here,' he continued, 'you might as well help me with the unpacking.' My eyes came out like organ stops as his cases disgorged their contents. At least three dinner jackets along with shirts and all the paraphernalia that went with them soon filled up the wardrobe space I had allocated! Suits fit for an ambassador, at least twenty shirts, six pairs of shoes, and so it continued until I didn't know whether to laugh or cry! Then came the next outburst. 'Now how do I go about claiming my expenses?' he demanded.

'Expenses,' I weakly replied, 'and what expenses are you talking about?'

'For my entertainment,' he replied. 'I like to do things properly you know,' he said, glaring at me as if to say 'what a stupid question!' Undeterred, he continued, 'For a start, I always like to offer a choice of sherry when my guests arrive.'

Enough is enough, I thought to myself, so I took the initiative.

'You do know that you are here as a missionary?' I exploded. 'Claiming expenses for sherry parties just isn't part of the scene.' I told him that if he wanted to entertain in that way (even if he could obtain bottles of sherry in the shops) then that would be at his expense, and not the Mission's. By now I had had enough, so made my excuses and left.

I had calmed down a little by the next morning and greeted him as cordially as possible. We had a Union Castle ship alongside, and I thought to myself, I'll send him down to visit the crew, that will sort him out and bring him down to size. So off he went and I soon became absorbed in something that required my attention. The next two hours flew by and then I saw him returning.

'How did you get on?' I asked him.

'Oh wonderfully well,' he replied, 'they all loved me!' I was just going to say that in our work it was not so much a question of how much they loved us, as how much we loved them! I didn't get a chance, however, because he was off again. 'I went into the galley,' he said, 'and told them, "I am Major Middleton and have come to take over the Mission".' Apparently they all jumped to attention and said, 'Yes, sir'.

'Who's in charge here?' he continued.

The Chef identified himself.

'Well,' said Major Middleton, 'my daughter is coming out to stay with me next week and bringing a friend with her. Her birthday falls due whilst she is here so I want you to make her a very special cake. I will come and collect it tomorrow.' (That his daughter and a friend would be arriving and staying in the flat, was, until then, quite unbeknown to me!)

At this I nearly had a fit. It was only the fact that I was due to go on leave in two days' time that stopped me from doing something drastic. I compromised by immediately informing members of the port committee of my fears and then concentrated on doing all that I had to complete before my departure. It was with a huge sigh of relief that I boarded the plane, which was to take me to rejoin my wife (who had gone before) and my children. I was not surprised to learn that within a fortnight of his arrival he had been sacked by the chairman of the committee and repatriated to England. He apparently went missing and was eventually found under some trees, unconscious through drink. Although it meant a lot of sorting out when I returned from leave, it was better than having 'the major' as my assistant.

Leaves were not all holiday, because after about six weeks to two months one could be called upon for deputation preaching, although this did not happen very often. One occasion when it did however is worth recording.

I was asked to preach at a certain church on the work of the Missions to Seamen. As it happened I arrived earlier than expected, as it didn't take me as long as I had anticipated getting there. To kill time I looked around the church, and when I had finished I looked around for somewhere to put a donation. I opened up my wallet only to discover that I only had a five-pound note. In a fit of generosity I thought, 'Oh, what the heck' and put it into the wall collecting box. After the service was over the churchwarden thanked me for coming, but then said, 'I'm sorry we can't give you today's collection,' (which was normal practice when a guest

318

preacher spoke about a mission) 'only we've only just bought kneelers for every pew so we've got no money. However,' he said, 'we do have a wall collection box in the church which we open up when we have a guest preacher to help towards his expenses. I'm glad to say that someone has been extraordinarily generous,' and with that he handed me a five pound note!

Due to the complications of having no base for our UK leaves, and having to be very diplomatic about how long we stayed in a particular place, it was almost with a sigh of relief when it was time to say our goodbyes and return to Tanzania. We sometimes felt after our leave that we needed a holiday to get over it! Although strictly speaking we were not entitled to holidays in Tanzania, the local committee decreed otherwise and some nine months later very kindly decided to give us a wonderful break on the slopes of Kilimanjaro. There were charming little chalets on the side of the mountain, which were just perfect for us.

To add icing to the cake, Anton Jansen, one of the port committee members, and a very good friend (and still is to this day), drove us up to Kilimanjaro in his car. Anton drove a Mercedes, loved driving, and actually took part in the famous East African Rally (of Bert Shankland fame). He tried to interest me in rallying and I actually navigated for him once on a mini safari.

Like me he loved to see wild game, and suggested that once Rose and the children were safely settled in to the chalet, he and I could visit a very wild and little known game reserve about thirty miles away. With Rose's blessing we set off, duly found the reserve and were rewarded with some wonderful sightings. At one point a game warden stopped us and said that the road to the camp (where we were due to spend the night) was in a very bad state due to heavy rains, and advised us, as we were not in a Land Rover, to abandon our plans to proceed.

'Nonsense,' said Anton, 'I've driven through far worse than these in rallies,' and so we carried on. Nightfall comes very suddenly in Africa, and the light was just starting to fade when we turned a bend in the track and saw the way ahead submerged in water. There was actually a ford across the track but the heavy rains had turned it into a small lake. 'No problem,' said Anton, 'the weight of the car will take us easily through this.' It didn't. We got just about halfway, with the water far too high for my liking outside, when the car stopped and the engine died! So there we were stuck in a water hole just at the very time that the animals came down to drink, with, as far as I could see, no hope at all of ever getting out again. Anton tried to work out what to do, whilst I said my evensong!

He was used to this from our rallying time together, so didn't make any comment. After futile attempts to get the engine started, even the ever optimistic Anton admitted defeat, and accepted that we were there for the night. I let down the passenger seat which I knew amongst rally drivers was commonly called 'the rape seat' and settled down as comfortably as I could. Just before my troubled eyelids closed I heard Anton say, more or less to himself, 'just my luck to be stranded for the night in a game park, and to have, of all people, a Bible-punching padre in the rape seat!'

About two hours passed, with neither of us managing to get any sleep, when suddenly the pitch darkness was pierced by headlights, which mercifully proved to be a Land Rover manned by game wardens from the camp. They had become worried so came to look for us. In almost no time at all they winched us out of the ford and onto dry land. After drying out the carburettor, the engine spluttered into life, and in convoy we safely reached the camp. A hot meal was awaiting us. What the meat was I never knew, but it was hot and plentiful, and as welcome as the beers that washed it down. We returned to Kilimanjaro the next morning just as if nothing had happened, and after fond farewells, Anton departed back to Dar to leave us in peace. We woke up one morning to find wild deer right outside our window, but even more exciting, there had been a storm in the night which had cleared by the morning, to expose the top of the mountain with a new fall of virgin snow. Without any doubt one of the most beautiful sights I have ever seen. The twelve days passed far too quickly, but the rest had the desired effect and I returned to the Mission raring to go!

There was actually a great deal to do because the Reverend Tom Kerfoot, the new head of our Mission, was shortly undertaking a tour of the stations in Africa, including ours. He was an old and very dear friend (he married us in the port of London), so I was not worried about his visit, although I obviously wanted him to be pleased with what he saw. I wrote and invited him to stay with us during his visit, in the hope that we could repay some of the kindness he had always shown us. We were very disappointed when he replied that it was Mission policy never to stay with the chaplains, because if things were bad in the station it was very difficult to deal with it if one was a guest of the chaplain concerned. I therefore booked him into the only reasonable hotel (that is, according to east African standards in those days!).

His plane was not due in until just before midnight, but I wanted him to see the Mission in all its glory. I had by now got coloured lights all around the buildings, which looked beautiful at night. I also had underwater lights in the swimming pool, so before I departed to pick him up I put them all on. In actual fact the plane was late, so by the time he arrived and cleared customs it was around 1 am. I was so keen for him to see the Mission in all its glory that I brushed aside his suggestion that we went straight to the hotel, assuring him that it wouldn't put more than a quarter of an hour on the journey. I believe he was impressed but he was also tired, so without further ado I took him to his hotel and departed. I went to pick him up the next morning ('not too early please, John' were his parting words), and asked him what sort of night he had had. 'Terrible,' he replied. 'No sooner had I got into bed than there was a knock on the door. I opened it to find a lady of the night asking me if I wanted company!' I was unsympathetic and told him he should have accepted our invitation to stay with us. 'Mission rules or not,' he assured me next time he would.

I didn't know it then but there wasn't to be a next time, as my

Miles from anywhere, the Mission bus picking up seamen from the new oil terminal

321

stay in Dar was on its last tour. I took him to meet the British high commissioner, Sir Horace Philips. He was a great supporter of the work, and readily agreed to see Tom. I was taken aback, however by what he said. 'Don't you think that John has been in Dar long enough?' To my embarrassment he made some complimentary remarks about my work at the Mission, in the diocese, and with the British community. 'He deserves promotion, and in any case he's already been here too long for the good of his career.' I tried to intervene at this point by saying promotion in the church was being where God wanted you to be, but he would hear none of it. To my surprise Tom Kerfoot said, 'I agree with you, but the trouble is we've got no one who can replace him.' The High Commissioner was having none of that either, so I was quite relieved when the interview ended and we departed. Up to that time I had never given a second thought about my future, or whether I should move on.

I did know that the Archbishop wanted me to stay. I have mentioned elsewhere about my vision of a cashew nut factory being built at Mtoni Shamba. The Tanzanian government repeated warnings to the effect that, if owners of land did not make good use of it, then there was a strong possibility that they could lose it. This resurrected the scheme in the mind of the archbishop, and we had serious discussions as to how practical the whole concept was, and what was the way forward if we decided to go ahead with it. One obvious step was to go and inspect the existing factory in India. Because I was a director of Tim Air, so could obtain cheap tickets, but also because I was the chairman of the diocesan finance committee, and because it was my idea in the first place, I was the obvious person to go to India. But because I was not only the Missions to Seamen chaplain, but paid by them, I just couldn't go off and leave the Mission. The way forward seemed to be that I stop off there on my way back from home leave. The Archbishop emphasized to me that he was very keen on the idea, but only on the condition that I remained in Tanzania to implement it. This meant that not only would I have to finish my present tour, but also be prepared to serve for at least another three-year stint after that. He recognized that this was asking a lot, but graciously hinted at further promotion if I agreed. I still had some time to go of my present tour, and felt that I needed more time before making up my mind. I also felt the need to discuss the matter with my spiritual adviser, as well as the staff at head office.

By mutual agreement, therefore, no decision was to be made until after I had gone on leave, and prayerfully considered all the options. In the meantime the work in the Mission, the diocese and the community continued apace.

As a result of Independence, many elderly expatriates fell upon hard times, so it was decided to set up a 'blanket fund' to help repatriate them. There were a surprisingly large number of such people, some of whom came out originally to work in the groundnut scheme. When it folded, some of them remained, picking up what work they could. With independence, however, work permits became much more difficult to obtain, so jobs dried up, and they lived as best they could. Inevitably their savings were eaten into, until in some cases there was nothing left. Because they had been out of the UK for many years they did not qualify for a full pension, so not only were they broke in Tanzania, but had not the wherewithal to get settled down in the UK. One such person was Muriel Hijas. She had a fascinating background. She was a Queen Alexandra nurse during the war, and actually nursed Winston Churchill when he developed pneumonia whilst visiting the troops overseas. She worked for the Oyster Bay hotel as a night receptionist, a post which I suspect was kindly created for her. She lived in a flat right in the centre of Dar, and was well known and respected by many.

One day she answered a ring on her flat bell to find a young Tanzanian on her doorstep. He forced himself into her flat, beat her and tied her up, threatening to kill her unless she revealed where her money was. She couldn't tell him because she hadn't any. She was severely traumatized by the experience, lost all confidence in herself and it became obvious that she needed to be repatriated. I was asked to try and arrange it. She was by now in her late eighties, with no contacts in the UK. I thanked God for the blanket fund, and also for having some very kind and compassionate Jewish friends in London, who actually put her up in their flat until accommodation could be found for her. She settled down very well, and lived well into her nineties. I used to visit her regularly when I eventually returned to the UK. In fact I visited her only two days before she died. I couldn't help feeling, as I included this snippet about her in my book, that she probably had a strong story of her own to write.

In the meantime the day-to-day work continued. We had by now been in Dar for over ten years, and we had experienced many changes during that time in the administration and government, not all, it must be said, for the better! One of the main problems (which exists to this day in many parts of Africa) was that of corruption. Many jobs that had previously been held by better-qualified personnel had been taken over by the indigenous population. This sadly resulted in less efficiency, which led to longer delays, so creating a hot bed for corruption. To give one example: the emptying of cesspits. The system became hopelessly delayed, with dire consequences, not only for health but also for smell. Numerous requests were made for urgent attention, and assurances would be given that the matter was being dealt with. Nevertheless, one waited in vain. With regard to the Mission, we were in danger of having to close it down completely so I made my way to the office concerned demanding immediate action. The trouble was of course that I wasn't the only one! However, I persisted until I saw it recorded in the log book of one of the vehicles (and I recorded its number) that its first task the following morning would be to empty the Mission's cesspit. It was rumoured that as the lorries left the depot with their set orders they were met just outside the gate by desperate potential customers, who gave large bribes for the lorry to come to their residence instead.

I was determined that this was not to be our fate, so just after 7 am I waited, along with many others, outside the gate of the depot for the vehicles to emerge. As they did so, desperate people waving quite large sums of money in their hands blocked their path. After about five minutes another vehicle left the depot, and a quick check on its number plates confirmed that it was the vehicle that was due to come to us. Like the other vehicles, wads of notes, and earnest pleas immediately surrounded it! I arrived just in time to see money passing hands, but was determined to see that no bribe was going to work with this crew. I somehow managed to persuade them that I was a personal friend of President Nyerere (a slight exaggeration!) and that if they did not immediately come to the Mission I would report them to him. After about five minutes of eyeball-to-eyeball contact, the money was reluctantly returned to the person who had just given it (who immediately dashed to yet another vehicle that was leaving the depot), and I escorted my vehicle to the Mission. Many of the staff were waiting for our arrival, and I think for the first time in his life the driver was greeted by clapping and cheers!

As time moved on towards our next leave, Rose and I discussed how we could best take advantage of the special price airfares that allowed us to go almost anywhere we liked. We had always regretted that, when we were on our way to Hong Kong, and spent twelve days off Kosichang in Thailand swinging around the hook as the ship took on rice, that we didn't go ashore. We felt that we would like to rectify that omission one day. We also felt an urge to revisit Hong Kong, our first overseas post that we so much enjoyed. Enquiries revealed that we could indeed fly to Hong Kong, then on to the UK breaking our trip at Bangkok in Thailand.

I wrote to the Anglican chaplain at Christ Church in Bangkok asking if he could recommend a cheap place where we could stay. To my delight he replied by saying that he would be delighted to put us up at the vicarage, providing I took the services on the Sunday, as he would very much like to be off duty that weekend. I immediately accepted his very kind offer, having no idea at that time just how much it would affect my future life.

Apart from the ships that made regular calls at Dar, we also had our fair share of ships just passing through, often for the first and last time. One of my many acquaintances from the former came to me one day in tremendous excitement. He was a second officer on a ship that made regular runs to Dar. He had told me on a previous occasion that his father was also a merchant navy officer, and had been at sea for over forty years. Because they were both at sea, working for different companies, their paths hadn't crossed for fourteen years. Now there was every chance that both ships would be in port at the same time, and he was overjoyed that after such a long time they would meet again. His ship was going up the coast and back again, so was due back in Dar in about three weeks' time, which would coincide with the arrival of his father's ship. I knew the expected date of arrival for both ships and, through contacts eagerly followed both ships' progress. Sure enough the son's ship arrived dead on schedule. David came up immediately to see me. His father's ship was in Mombasa, and I had to break the news that there was a delay. Nevertheless there was still a good chance that their visits would coincide, giving them a day and a half together. Then two things happened. His father's ship was delayed by another twenty-four hours and the son's ship finished unloading ahead of schedule so left by the morning instead of the evening tide. They missed each other by four hours! I went on board the second the other ship dropped anchor to meet with the devastated father and bear greetings from his son. The cruel sea!

Being at sea created many problems, which for shore folk just wouldn't arise, and even if they did, would be so much easier to solve. They say that 'distance makes the heart grow fonder', but not alas in every case. Seamen received a large number of 'Dear Johns' and many marriages broke up by the strain caused of being away from home for such long periods of time. Counselling in such circumstances was extremely difficult, for, as everyone knows, there are two sides to every story. What one could and did offer was a sympathetic ear, which nevertheless left one wishing that one could do so much more. An increasingly well-used and much appreciated asset at seafarers' clubs all over the world was the telephone. As telephoning home became easier and cheaper, so increasingly did it become an important function in the Mission. A special area had to be made available where conversations could be held in private. At the same time there had to be some control over the length of the call, as it was very easy to get carried away when speaking to loved ones on the other side of the world! As the years rolled by so rules became more and more relaxed regarding having wives on board, and this did a great deal of good. It must be said, however, that depended very much on the wife!

Chapter 28

A Momentous Leave

The weeks and the months rolled by, and the time for home leave drew ever nearer. Being a one-man-band there was always a great deal to set up before going on leave, which seemed to make the time roll by even faster.

I remember it was with a great sense of relief that we finally boarded the aircraft that was to take us back to England, via Bangkok and Hong Kong. The trip was uneventful, and we duly arrived at Thailand's principal airport to be met by (to our great surprise) two welcoming parties. The first, which I suppose was more or less expected, was the chaplain of Christ Church, who greeted us warmly. The second was two of the British Embassy staff. Apparently the high commissioner for Tanzania had written to the ambassador of Thailand asking him to afford us every help, and to make our stay as pleasant as possible.

I was given a letter addressed to the 'Venerable Archdeacon' of Dar es Salaam inviting us to dinner with the ambassador on the Saturday night. Because my main work in Dar es Salaam was to do with the Missions to Seamen I was almost exclusively addressed as 'Padre', so the title archdeacon took me by surprise. So did the chaplain's house where we were to stay. It was magnificent, made all the more impressive when servants took our cases, and showed us to our bedroom. It was very hot but we were used to that, but in any case many fans provided a very welcome breeze. The Reverend Kingston, for that was his name, made sure that we had all we needed, and then made his farewell before leaving for the weekend. Apparently there was a golf weekend when the four British societies – St George, St Patrick, St David and St Andrew – played each other at the famous Rose Gardens complex. At that time I didn't play golf, so didn't feel I was missing anything, but in any case was swept up into the entirely different environment

327

we found ourselves in. By now it was quite late at night, and as we had eaten dinner on the plane, we declined the meal that was offered and collapsed into bed and sleep.

Morning made us even more aware of the magnificence of the house, and as we sat down to a breakfast that contained all the wonderful Thai fruits, apart from everything else, I remember saying to Rose, 'This is how the other half lives!' It was Saturday morning, and after breakfast we explored the house and church, which had somehow become ours for the weekend. We met the ladies in the church who were preparing the flowers for the services, and again were impressed by the exotic flowers in such abundance, which beautified the church. The ladies were enthusiastic in their welcome, and seemed very interested to learn that we were from East Africa. In the afternoon we did a tour of the local shops, and just couldn't get over the difference from those in Dar. Saturday night was equally inspiring when we had dinner at the residence. As we were driven home after a sumptuous supper, we couldn't help but compare the difference in the standard of living between Dar and Bangkok.

So Sunday dawned. I had prepared a sermon before we left Tanzania, although I must admit it had been written in a hurry, and I hadn't looked at it since! Be that as it may, we were warmly welcomed by all those we met, including John Smith, who was a member of the embassy staff and with whom we had shared dinner the night before. He was also, we discovered, one of the churchwardens. There were two services; an 8 am said Holy Communion, followed by the main service of the day, a sung Eucharist. There was the usual coffee after the service, which gave us an opportunity to meet more members of the congregation. I noticed quite a few of the congregation were missing but assumed that they had departed, so thought no more about it. But just as I expected the congregation to thin as people left, it suddenly seemed to swell!

John Smith, who was one of those whom I had assumed had left then approached me and said, 'The wardens would like to invite you out to lunch at the British Club. Our wives will look after Rose, and take her there, but it isn't very far so I suggest we walk.' I readily agreed and off we set.

Then John Smith (who was obviously the spokesman) said, 'Do you know that Patrick Kingston has just told us that he is not going to finish his contract, and is leaving?' I confessed that this was news to me.

'Well,' said John, 'after your services this morning we held an emergency PCC meeting,' (so that's where you all went, I thought to myself) 'and it was unanimously agreed that we would invite you to be our next vicar.'

It is not often that I am stuck for words, but on this occasion I was! Over lunch I recovered somewhat, because I knew I had to make some reply. I took Rose aside and told her what had transpired. She, as always, was wonderful. 'You must do what you think is right, darling. Whatever you decide is OK by me.'

The lunch conversation was taken up by general matters but once coffee time came (and the ladies disappeared as they always seem to do at such times) the main item on the agenda was taken up again. 'It must have come to you as a shock,' they said. 'But have you had the chance to collect your thoughts?' I had of course been thinking of nothing else, but knew it was not the time to make a hasty decision. I thanked them for the great honour they had given me. I said that there was a great deal to think and pray about. I told them that after my leave I was due to return to Dar es Salaam to possibly open up a cashew nut factory at the express wish of the Archbishop (although I didn't mention his hint of promotion). I also explained that I was on the staff of the Missions to Seamen and would have to consult with them because if I did come to Bangkok it would mean leaving the society I had been with since 1953.

All this they appreciated, whilst at the same time pointing out that they did need an answer as soon as possible because if I were not to accept the offer, then they needed to start the process of advertising for a priest. We were due to depart the next day for Hong Kong, so it was agreed that the PCC would write to me officially offering me the post, setting out the conditions of service (of which I had no idea!). I promised that I would make my mind up as soon as possible and let them know. So much had happened in just twenty-four hours that when we arrived in Hong Kong and stayed in the Mission where we had lived and worked for three years, I couldn't help but wonder, was it all a dream? When we arrived back in the UK, however, and found the letter from the PCC awaiting us, confirming the offer, and setting out what seemed to be very acceptable terms, then I knew it was for real.

I went away on a short retreat to think and pray through all the consequences of accepting the post. Apart from seeking God's will there was a great deal to consider regarding my dual ministry in Tanzania. Regarding the Mission I knew that it now had all the needed facilities. They included a swimming pool, complete with changing rooms; a restaurant; a football pitch (which was there before I arrived); an outdoor bowling alley; two flood-lit tennis courts; a crazy golf course; a large snooker hall; an enlarged chapel; a shop, and more office space. Everything was paid for and there was a healthy bank balance. Financially the Mission was a going concern and spiritually it now had parochial standing. There was also a good supporting congregation that helped to create a normal parish atmosphere for the visiting seamen who came to church. It had a good name amongst the visiting seamen, was very popular and extremely well known and used.

I wrote to Charles Mallet (a friend still to this day), the chairman of the port committee, telling him of the invitation I had received, and awaited his comments. They too came by return of post. His main worry was who was there suitable who could take my place, and would it therefore go downhill if I left? Remembering the high commissioner's words to the general secretary at the beginning of the year, I felt that this should not be a deciding factor in making my decision.

Regarding my position in the diocese, the opposite was true. I knew if I returned a whole new challenge would await me. The diocese was still new and there was a great deal yet to be done, including the possible building of the cashew nut factory. There was also the question of promotion. In many cases archdeacons go on to become Bishops, and indeed I knew that this was a possibility. However, for many reasons, I did not feel either the timing or the person was right. I had no religious background (with my father being an atheist), I had no University education, so did not feel qualified to act as a defender of the faith, which is one of the primary responsibilities of a Bishop. Experience-wise, I had only served as a curate for two years in Wales, and as the chaplain in Dar. The other task of a Bishop is to be a pastor and again I felt I lacked the experience to hold such a post. There was, however, the other side of the coin. My confessor, Bishop John Poole Hughes, whom I consulted when I was invited to be archdeacon, said that, if offered a post, unless there was a very real reason why one should not accept it, one should. If I went to Bangkok, then by becoming a vicar I would gain very valuable pastoral experience, which would stand me in very good stead whatever the future had to offer. So I made one of the most difficult decisions of my life. I would move to Thailand.

I immediately wrote to Archbishop Sepeku telling him what had happened since we had said goodbye. I count his reply amongst the greatest treasures I possess. In it he said he would be heartbroken if I were to leave but if this was what God was calling me to then he wouldn't stand in my way.

Regarding the Missions to Seamen, they were emphatic that they didn't want me to accept the post; that my vocation lay in the work I was doing. One of the head office personnel described it as summer madness. On the other hand, the letter from Bangkok set out a vision of what Christ Church could become. I was thrilled with the ideas expressed, and felt that I had the energy to try and make it a reality. Rose reiterated that if I thought it was the right thing to do, then there was no more to be said. So I made the momentous decision to go to Bangkok as vicar, and then notified all concerned of my decision.

The Mission's head office told me that they were going to give me an honorarium so as to keep me on their books. This meant that when I returned to them after I had got this madness out of my system I wouldn't lose any seniority or pension rights. Bangkok was, of course, the main port for Thailand, and I was immediately named as their honorary chaplain.

Because everything had happened so quickly, I knew I had to return to Tanzania for a few months at least to complete a proper handover of my various duties. My mother expressed a desire to come out and visit us one more time, to which we agreed.

We duly arrived back in Dar es Salaam to find that our many friends were already aware of our pending departure, and immediately started booking us up for farewell receptions. Indeed in the last month we were there we were so booked up that on occasions we were out for both lunch and dinner! Believe it or not, in our last week we were even invited for breakfast. We were afforded a huge honour in that the four British societies organized a joint evening for us, at which the British high commissioner presided.

Chapter 29

The Ministry of Edmund John

Around this time great publicity and excitement came to the diocese through the activities of the Archbishop's brother, Edmund John. He worked with the broadcasting corporation until he either reached retirement age, or was made redundant (I am not sure which). He was a deeply committed Christian and, once free of his other work, expressed a desire to enter the ministry in one way or another. Being the Archbishop's brother obviously created problems. Nepotism was sadly a serious problem in Tanzania, so it was difficult to bring him on the staff without arousing some form of criticism. The problem was solved when he was appointed to a real slum area that no one else would want to work! He started holding services in a tiny mud hut, which in no time at all became too small to hold his congregation, so had to be doubled in size.

One day, Edmund John told his flock that he was going to hold a personal retreat in his 'church', beginning after the evening service on the Sunday and going through until the following Friday. But on the Thursday anyone could come and visit him for prayer or counselling. Came the Thursday, and one of his parishioners went to him with her blind son, whom she asked him to bless. Edmund John laid his hands on him, whereupon he called out in astonishment, 'I can see. I can see!' He ran out of the church proclaiming this fact.

The news spread like wildfire and in no time at all huge crowds gathered around him. It was not long before Edmund's fame spread far beyond the diocesan boundaries, and it became obvious that we had to somehow harness this gift for the benefit of all. We, however, had a responsibility to protect him from constant demands on his ministry, so it was decided to organize a healing service at St Alban's, the main Anglican church in the centre of Dar es Salaam. This was scheduled to take place at the end of May 1973.

Crowds gather outside Edmund John's church, after the healing of a blind boy

Within days we received so many enquiries, not only from distant parts of Tanzania, but from Kenya and Uganda as well, that we had to completely revise our plans. We decided to limit those coming to St Alban's, but promised that we would organize a further healing service at Ilala (the main African church) in the July. Although this lessened the number who wanted to participate, we were astonished at the crowds who actually came. For some reason that I cannot remember the Archbishop was absent at the time, so it fell to me to organize the event.

Edmund John prepared by fasting in the church for three days before the healing service commenced. Apart from those who came for healing so many others came to watch and wonder that the situation almost got out of hand. Never before, nor I suspect since, have such scenes been witnessed at St Alban's. The normally staid, prim and proper (originally expatriate) church, where services were conducted in what I call a cathedral-style manner, was transformed into a mass of humanity, the sick interspersed with sightseers standing (yes standing!) on the pews to get a better look. Nevertheless the healing continued as masses of sick people came to be blessed. After he had ministered to one group, he invited the next batch to come to the altar rails. Whilst this was happening Edmund John knelt by the altar to prepare for what was to follow. This went on for two days, during which time I became increasingly concerned

333

about his health, as did also his wife, who begged me to bring him home. This convinced me that the healing session had to stop. He had just retired to the altar in preparation for another group when I went up and knelt beside him.

It appeared to me that he was in a sort of trance. I spoke to him. 'It's Archdeacon John coming to take you home. You've done enough and you've got to stop now.' I tried to sound as official as possible, because I wasn't sure how he would react. In fact he just looked at me, and said 'Thank you'. I parked my car by the vestry door, keeping the engine running, and within a few seconds I had led him from the church, into my car, and away to his house. His wife was waiting for him, and after giving me a grateful smile tenderly took him inside.

After it was all over we tried to assess the results, but it was very difficult through all the 'hype' to truly evaluate what had actually gone on. What was beyond dispute was the demand for more of the same. We learnt a great deal from the session at St Alban's, and put it into practice when arranging the next healing session at Ilala.

As the time drew nearer to the July service, the area around the church turned into what could best be described as a refugee camp. Apart from the healing ministry of Edmund John, we enlisted the help of the local Red Cross. We had to make arrangements for washing and toilet facilities and erect tents for people to sleep in. On top of all this there was the local press and broadcasting media to cope with. All this was for us uncharted waters, and new problems arose every day. One thing we hadn't bargained for was the effect of the recorded music. A tannoy system was necessary to control the huge number of people present, so as an interlude between using it for conveying messages, we broadcast hymns. A large number of those who came were 'demon possessed', and when the hymns came over the speakers, those possessed became violent and out of control. So even before the healing there was a great deal for others connected with medicine to deal with. In the end the effect of the hymns became so dramatic that we had to stop broadcasting them altogether. It became obvious that we had to organize the sick in some sort of order. Some were in wheelchairs; others were so ill that they couldn't rise from their makeshift beds. When we saw how disturbed some of them were, becoming violent at times of stress, we knew that we needed to separate them from the others, for fear that they would cause trouble. Needless to say, everyone wanted to be first in the queue, so all that had to be sorted out as well.

It was not only the sick that we had to deal with. In preparation for the event we had decided that at all times there would be as many Christians praying in the church as people coming to be healed. At any one time then, half the church would be full of members of various congregations, which entailed arranging rotas for about 200 people a session.

We originally planned to admit about twenty of the sick at any one time. As we were ourselves on a steep learning curve, we decided to start with the most able bodied, so this is what we did. They were admitted into the church and put into the empty pews. Edmund John was at this time praying in the sanctuary. Once they were in he called them up to the altar steps, and told them to kneel. He then went along the row laying his hands on and praying for them individually. After he had reached the end of the row he prayed for them all and then told them to go. They left through a vestry door, where the media were waiting to interview them. It wasn't possible to hear from inside the church what they were saying, but an eruption of clapping or cheering told its own story. Inside the work continued but it soon became obvious that the present timetable of events would never succeed in coping with the number who remained. So the numbers admitted at one time was continuously increased until there were just too many to come up to the altar rails. So Edmund John moved among them where they were, laid his hands upon them and prayed for their healing.

My wife Rose, although not part of the operation, came over to see what was happening. She arrived as we were admitting about forty of those 'possessed with demons or evil spirits'. One half of the church was full of people praying, and Rose was kneeling at the back of that side of the church as they poured in. Edmund John then told the demons to do their worst. The atmosphere became electric. Looking back it is very difficult for me to decide how much that was going on was because of mass hysteria, or actual demon possession. The situation became chaotic as those admitted reacted in many different ways. Some started racing around the church screaming and blaspheming. Others stripped off all their clothes hitting their heads on the pews. Others went into fits whilst others even abused the main altar in the sanctuary. I glanced at

Rose and could see that she was very frightened so I moved behind her to assure her that all would be all right.

Suddenly the voice of Edmund John was heard above all the other noise that was going on. 'Simama. Simama' (Stop. Stop), he cried, and almost unbelievably the vast majority of them did just that. There were about three or four who continued screaming and harming themselves. Edmund John confronted them and apart from one woman they also stopped too. The remaining person went into a fit, and was carried outside for treatment.

One moment the church was a screaming mass of humanity, the next there was silence. Edmund John spoke yet again. 'Piga Magoti,' he commanded (kneel down), and they did. He then prayed over them for about five minutes before telling them to leave. Like sheep following their leader they did, in silence that was deafening.

I had many other duties to perform so had to leave the church and return to the Mission, but the sessions continued unabated. As time went on and there were still so many to be admitted, plans had to be changed yet again. In the end enough were admitted to fill all the empty seats at one time. It was obvious that it would be impossible for him to lay hands on them all so Edmund John told them to lay hands on each other. Many miracles were claimed but it was impossible to verify them. I do know of one case involving the mother of one of our priests. She was riddled with cancer, and was so ill that she had to be carried into the church, being too weak to walk. Edmund John laid his hands upon her and, to everyone's amazement, she arose from her bed and walked out of the church. Alas though, she died very shortly afterwards. The time of healing was extended by two days, by which time an exhausted healer was himself in need of attention, so a halt was called.

Apart from these major services of healing, he was also called upon to perform individual healings. There was an extremely famous blind African drummer who always performed on state occasions, and was well known to the President. Whether it was by his request or not I do not know, but Edmund John was asked to lay his hand on him. This he did but with no success. I have mentioned elsewhere the crippled children from Mgulani Salvation Army camp who used to bathe in the Mission's swimming pool once a week. They were very dear to my heart so one day, at the camp's request, Edmond John met them in the Mission chapel. He told them all to take off

Greeting Archbishop Coggan on his return visit to Tanzania

their callipers, prayed for them and then told them to leave their
crutches behind and walk out of the church. I prayed for a miracle,
but although two of the lesser-deformed children did walk, most
remained where they were. To this day I am uncertain in my own
mind about his ministry. Very sadly he died shortly after the events
I have described. What I do know, is that he was a wonderful and
devoted Christian, a saintly figure and, healing powers apart, was
a wonderful servant of the Lord, and brought blessings to countless
number of people.

Around this time the Archbishop of Canterbury returned for a
second visit to Tanzania. During his first visit he laid the foundation
stone of a new church, which was built not far from the Mission.
He had expressed a desire to see the finished building so the day
before he arrived I dashed round to see that everything was in
good order. It wasn't! The outside of the church looked awful. I
told the priest in charge that he must immediately whitewash the

337

outside walls, so that the Archbishop would be pleased by what he saw. The following morning duly arrived and with it the Archbishop of Canterbury. As we drew near to the church I gazed anxiously out of the car window, and to my immense relief saw dazzling white walls awaiting us. The trouble was, when the Archbishop looked for the plaque he had unveiled on his previous visit, he found it had been whitewashed over too!

Chapter 30

'Money is the Root of All Evil'

The Archbishop left, only to be replaced by the visit of my mother. Unfortunately, relationships between Tanzania and Kenya were not too good at this time, which complicated matters considerably. It meant that yet again she had to fly to Nairobi in Kenya, and I would have to pick her up from the airport. There was no exchange of currency between the two countries, which made it difficult for those travelling between the two. Tanzanian currency had little or no value outside the country, which meant that any foreign currency was worth its weight in gold. The Mission was listed as an official money exchanger, but operating under very strict rules. US seamen amongst others used to change their dollars into Tanzanian currency. We had to record every transaction and send copies monthly to the central bank of Tanzania. I was not involved with this, but had staff on both shifts who were competent and able to deal with the transactions.

It was a very difficult time for expatriates who were responsible for foreign currency because they were often kept under surveillance and arrested for the slightest hint of any misdoing. Currency regulations decreed that one could only take 100 shillings across the border. This was not very much considering that I had to drive from the border to Nairobi airport, pick up my mother, who might well require some refreshment or have some other need, and then drive back to the border. I had a 100-shilling Kenya note left over from a previous visit, so hung on to it, knowing that it may be useful.

As it was the best part of a day's drive to the border into Kenya, we were dismayed to find out that the road to Nairobi was having extensive work done to it and was only open from about 3 am to 7 am. This meant that Rose and I had to leave at about 1.30 am to arrive at the roadworks in time to get through. We had been travelling for about two hours, when I saw in my rear mirror that a vehicle was approaching very quickly towards us. I slowed down and moved towards the side of the road, which was just as well, as the large car flew past and then screeched to a halt in front of us causing me to break very fiercely. To my amazement out jumped a policeman armed with a rifle and immediately approached my car and ordered me to get out. Even as I did I saw others alighting from the car. I was relieved to see that they were well dressed, and even happier when I recognized one of them as someone I had seen in the bank. It was he who approached me and said, 'Are you Archdeacon Taylor?' to which I replied, 'Of course I am. You know who I am. What on earth is this all about?'

'We have been informed that you are smuggling foreign currency to Kenya, and we have a warrant to search you and your car for it.'

I was immediately struck by the absurdity of it all. I was on my way to Kenya for only about the fourth time in twelve years. If I wanted to smuggle foreign currency out of the country, it would be far easier to give it to someone on a British ship, to take to the UK for me. But over and above all else, I was in Tanzania to try and do good, not to get involved with currency irregularities.

I tried to keep calm, especially for Rose's sake, who was terribly upset by all that was going on. I was body-searched, including having to take my socks and shoes off. They then searched the car and the case we had with us, all without success. They had taken my wallet and came across the 100-shilling Kenya note. They asked me where the official receipt from the bank was from where I purchased it. I explained that I had kept it from the last time I was in Kenya so didn't have a receipt for it, but possibly because this was the only irregularity they could discover, they latched on to it as evidence that I was smuggling foreign currency out of the country. They took our passports off us and said that we would have to return immediately to Dar, and report to the bank of Tanzania at 10.00 am. I was more angry than scared, but Rose was in an awful state. Despite knowing that there was no truth whatsoever in the allegations there was no alternative but to return to Dar, which we did. By the time we got back it was time to report to the bank where we were immediately separated, to be interviewed by different members of the staff. I said to Rose just to answer all the questions truthfully, as we had nothing to hide, and I would do the same.

Regarding my interview, or should I say interrogation, I had by now become increasingly irate, apart from being very worried about my mother, who as things stood would arrive at Nairobi airport with no one to greet her. I asked them by what authority and with what evidence had they obtained a search warrant and taken our passports. All they would tell me was that one of my staff had reported to them that I was breaking the law regarding the handling of foreign currency. (It later transpired that the member of staff was someone whom I had dismissed for very serious offences, and this was his way of getting his own back.)

It soon became apparent to me that they had no concrete evidence that I had been involved in any way whatsoever, so I decided to take the initiative. I told them why I was on my way to Kenya when they stopped me, and that they must right now either arrest and charge me or return my passport and let me go. If they didn't release me now I demanded to be allowed to contact the British high commissioner, Archbishop Sepeku, and the chairman of my port committee. I was left alone in the interview room for about five minutes, until one of my interrogators returned (I noticed with a sigh of relief) carrying our passports. 'We are retaining the 100-shilling note as evidence,' he said, 'but for now you and your wife can go.' Then as a parting shot, 'You will be hearing from us again.'

I, however, was not finished with them. I pointed out that I had now to leave for Nairobi, cross the border into Kenya without any of that currency at all. What would happen if I needed to buy petrol or purchase something for my mother? As they were holding on to my 100-shilling note they would have to issue me with another! That's not possible, they told me, because then I would have 200 Kenya shillings, which was illegal! At this I exploded, pointing out that as they were retaining my money I would only have one 100-shilling note, which was allowable. After a lot of puffing and huffing they finally agreed and I was taken to a teller who sold me a Kenya 100-shilling note.

Rose was just too upset to start the long journey again, so I took her back to the Mission, where luckily there was one of our very good friends, Esmie Slade (a voluntary helper at the mission), who promised to look after her. After a short while I departed again for Nairobi.

Providentially, by the time I arrived at the roadworks the Tanzania to Kenya section was open once again, so I proceeded without further incident to the airport, arriving shortly after the ETA. Thankfully (and it's not often that we can say that!) the plane had been delayed. As I walked into the entrance hall, so my mother appeared from the customs area, and we greeted each other warmly.

Her first question was, 'Where's Rose?' I made some excuse and whisked her away, because I wanted to catch the roadworks at the right time to get through. I didn't want to upset my mother, so told her nothing of the incidents that had beset us. It was with a great sense of relief that the journey back was completed without incident, except that I felt utterly exhausted by all that had taken place in the last eighteen hours. I had asked Rose to contact the British high commission, and the archbishop, which she did. The next day I was visited by the Archbishop and a representative from the embassy, both of whom were shocked by what had happened. The Archbishop was in tears, and, as I learnt later, immediately went to see President Nyerere complaining of the treatment I had received. The President told him that if someone had reported him for irregularities regarding foreign currency, such was the financial situation at that time that he too would have been investigated in the same way! The Archbishop maintained that to put such a slur on a person's character just on the say-so of a disgruntled ex-employee was very wrong.

The words of the banker interrogator were soon proved to be true. About a week later a team of six employees from the bank, plus a couple of police officers, stormed into the Mission armed with search warrants for both the Mission and our flat. They spent at least four hours looking in every conceivable place. Our beds were stripped and mattresses turned over. Every cupboard was emptied and the contents inspected. In the church even the altar was ransacked, and in the vestry, the vestments and linen were all thoroughly checked out. Our Asian chief clerk was grilled for hours, and most of the books containing the accounts were taken away for scrutiny. Despite all this not a single thing that was in the least bit suspicious was discovered. The team finally came together near the Mission bar, to confer before moving off. One of the team picked up a collection box, which was on the counter with a note beside it requesting seamen to put any loose change or foreign coins in it as a donation towards the Mission. He picked it up, shook it and as he did came forth the unmistakable sound of coins rattling in the box. As one all the team became fully alert and crowded around the offending article.

'What's in it?' one asked me in a menacing manner.

'Money,' I replied, 'which seamen have donated.'

'Open it up,' I was ordered, which I did. I emptied the contents onto the bar counter. Coins and notes from many countries were exposed to view. Included were two US dollar bills and some coins. A whoop of triumph rent the air, as much as to say, 'we've got you at last!'

'So that's where you hide the money, is it?' one of them said to me. 'We knew we'd find it in the end.'

It took me about twenty minutes to convince them that collection boxes in Missions were a common thing, and that there was nothing sinister in the system at all. Finally and thankfully, although still taking the Mission books, they left. About a month later I received a package from the bank returning my 100 shillings plus the books with a note saying that nothing untoward had been found, but that when I left Tanzania I had to take the 100 shillings with me. There was no mention of an apology, but I was so relieved that the matter was now closed, although personally speaking it did leave a nasty taste in my mouth. This slightly marred our remaining time in Dar. Mother never realized the seriousness of the situation, and enjoyed her stay with us as much as on her previous visit.

So the weeks and the days sped past. I almost completed the handover, only to discover that there was something which just cannot be passed on. Ask any expatriate who has lived in East Africa, and they will tell you exactly the same thing. Africa becomes part of you, and when you leave, you leave part of you behind.

Chapter 31

Goodbyes

Of all the farewell occasions one of the most moving was from the crippled children from Mgulani Salvation Army camp. Because they came on a weekly basis to swim in the Mission pool, they had become very precious to me. When they heard that I was leaving, their leader said, 'We don't have any money to give you, but we would like to come and sing for you,' and that's exactly what they did. They also presented me with a wooden inscribed fruit bowl, which I treasure to this day.

The final official function was the farewell party given to us by

The Salvation Army 'crippled children's choir' at a farewell service in the chapel

344

DIOCESE OF DAR ES SALAAM

Telephone :
Bishop's House 63405
Diocesan Office 63151

P. O. Box 25016,
Ilala,
DAR ES SALAAM
Tanzania.

My dear Archdeacon,

Thank you very much for your letter of February 1973, confirming our conversation of that morning of the same day, concerning of what you believe to be God's Call, to serve Him as Vicar of Christ Church Bangkok. My dear John, as I told you, although I find it very very hard to let you go, because of your services here, which have been of great value beyond all measure, to the Diocese, to the branch of the Mission to Seamen here, and to me personaly, even I cannot explain by words of mouth, how I have always appreciated your Love and Loyalty to me, but I feel I shall be doing sin, if I refused you to respond to God's Call. I feel that it is my duty to encourage you, to accept God's Call.

I appreciate your decision to stay on until the end of the third quarter of the year 1973.

God Bless you now, and always, be assured I have been praying for you constantly and shall continue to do so for many years to come.

With love.

+ John Seferku

the diocese. I was very moved by the function, and the presents we were given, which actually created a real problem. Our main belongings had already been sent off to Bangkok, but as the presents continued to pile up I had to arrange for another dispatch. Kind friends dealt with this after we had left, as they continued to come in even on the day we left! Presents were one thing, but they became as nothing at the diocesan farewell when, after a few people had spoken some kind words, the Archbishop rose to his feet. I cannot remember how he began or continued, but how he ended I will never forget. He said, 'When I first knew Father Taylor he was just one of my priests. But as I got to know him better he became a very dear friend. Today, I am saying goodbye to my son.'

I couldn't help but reflect on the attitude of my own father, who when I told him I was going to enter the church, disowned me.

Archbishop John paused and then said, 'Canon Taylor, will you please step forward?' Because we were a new diocese, there had as yet been no canons appointed. By making me a Canon Emeritus he bestowed upon me a rank, which I could take away with me and keep until my death. I have used it with great pride ever since.

The remaining hours were a bit of a blur, but we finally reached the airport to be seen off by a host of friends, before boarding the plane (complete with the Kenyan 100-shilling note!) that was to take us to a new beginning in Bangkok, Thailand.

Chapter 32

On Board the Aircraft Taking Us From Dar to Bangkok

There are times when, whatever one's normal attitude to life, incidents arise when you just have to adapt to the different situation in which you find yourself. A plane journey is one such example. You have no option but to let go, and put your life in the hands of others. Christians are used to putting their trust in Jesus Christ. On a plane journey, however, you have to put your trust in a different pilot! As a consequence time can drag heavily, especially if one is not used to such a luxury. There are various ways of coping with this, including eating, drinking and sleeping. The first time we flew from Dar to Bangkok we were going home on leave, and Bangkok was just one exciting stop on the way. We had no idea that it was to be a step that would change our lives forever, so we ate, drank and slept without a care in the world. As our plane touched down late in the evening we had no idea what Bangkok looked liked from the air, nor what we would find on the ground. This time was very different. We were going to a new appointment, a new home and, we suspected, a very different way of life. So eating and drinking on the plane, yes, but as for sleep, no. The adrenaline was running far too strongly for that so I took the opportunity to look back, take stock, and contemplate the future.

Like all missionaries in the early days, long before air travel, we went both to Hong Kong and Tanzania by ship. This meant a journey lasting weeks or even months. Finally amid great excitement the shoreline appeared, mostly dominated by thick green vegetation, with little signs of life ... our approach to east Africa was exactly along those lines, so much so that it was almost like approaching virgin soil.

How different then as we approached Bangkok Airport for the

347

second time and strained our eyes to see what lay below. There was no sign of the rich greenery seen in Africa, but rather a bright panoply of colour, prominently gold, as the myriad of temples reflected the sun's blessings upon them. The great river Cho Phryana, which appears to bisect Bangkok and forms an essential part of the transportation and life of the people, was a bustling hive of activity, famous for its floating markets, water taxis, to say nothing of the King's Royal Barges, which graced the river at certain times of the year. All this was enough to set the pulses racing, with an urgent desire to explore. This created an infectious atmosphere of excitement and wonder that made us yearn to be out and about in this vast, new and exciting metropolis. My limited research into Bangkok had revealed that it has the longest name in the world! Consisting of no less than one hundred and fifty-two letters that spell out: 'City of Angels, great city of immortals, magnificent jewelled city of the God Indra, seat of the King of Ayutthaya, city of gleaming temples, city of the King's most excellent palace and dominions, home of Vishnu and all the Gods.'

But I have somewhat jumped the gun. As the plane lifted off the tarmac at Dar es Salaam airport, memories of twelve eventful years flashed through my mind. A few are recorded in correspondence, so as we begin the long journey taking us to East Asia, I share them with you.

ON BOARD THE AIRCRAFT TAKING US FROM DAR TO BANGKOK

THE STATE HOUSE,
DAR ES SALAAM,
TANZANIA.

25th July, 1973

The Venerable J. R. Taylor,
Archdeacon of Dar es Salaam,
The Missions to Seamen,
P.O. Box 1179,
DAR ES SALAAM.

Dear Rev. Taylor,

I was pleased to hear news of your success in expanding the facilities at the Missions to Seamen. Unfortunately I do not expect to be in Dar es Salaam on the 7th September, so I must regretfully decline your invitation to open the final project.

I would like to take this opportunity to congratulate you on the way that the Missions to Seamen has been built up during your stay in Dar es Salaam. I hope that you feel a sense of satisfaction and of good service done. I would also like to send my good wishes for successful and happy service in Bangkok.

With good wishes.

Yours sincerely,

Julius K. Nyerere

A MAN WITH A MISSION

Archbishop's House
P. O. Box 167
Dar-es-Salaam
Tanzania, East Africa

22nd August, 1973.

The Venerable J. R. Taylor
Archdeacon of Dar es Salaam
P. O. Box 1179
DAR ES SALAAM

Reverend and Dear Archdeacon,

Thanks for your letter dated 16th August, 1973, in which you
invited us to the Annual General Meeting, on September 7th,
1973, at 7.00 p.m. We regret very much to inform you that we
shall not be able to turn up, because we shall be on safari.

However, we would like to seize this opportunity of saying
how much we appreciated and enjoyed your excellent ecumenical
service you have discharged during the 11$\frac{1}{2}$ years you have
been in Dar es Salaam. Indeed, you have dealt with many
people of various denominations, including Catholics. To all
of them you have been equally helpful and serviceable. We
express our gratitude to you for the great, useful and responsible apostolic activity you have been doing so well. It
is our hope that your successor, whom we warmly welcome, will
follow your remarkable example, so that the ecumenical spirit
so well sustained by you may not diminish but ever flourish
and be strengthened.

With prayerful wishes and hearty greetings,

We remain,

Yours Sincerely,

L. Card. Rugambwa.

ON BOARD THE AIRCRAFT TAKING US FROM DAR TO BANGKOK

CONSULATE GENERAL OF GREECE
TANZANIA

TEL: { RESIDENCE 68425 } { OFFICE 25638 }

P. O. Box 766
DAR ES SALAAM

REF:- 886/73

21st. August, 1973.

The Venerable J.R. Taylor,
Chaplain,
The Mission to Seamen,
P.O. Box 1179,
DAR ES SALAAM.

Dear Sir,

I thank you for your letter dated 17th. August, 1973 informing
me of your date of departure from Dar es Salaam to take up a
new appointment in Bangkok.

In expressing my personal sorrow and also that on behalf of the
so many Greek seamen who have found comfort and a home away from
home in your person and your Mission, I would also like to wish
you happiness and success in your new distant home.

To me personally, it has been a privilege to have known you and
to have observed your untiring efforts to not only build and
expand the premises and facilities of your Mission over the
years, but also the comfort you have offered, particularly to
my countrymen, whenever misfortune lead them to a hospital or
clinic in Dar es Salaam.

I look forward to meeting your successor and will be happy to
be of any assistance to him.

Yours sincerely,

351

A MAN WITH A MISSION

EMBASSY OF THE
UNITED STATES OF AMERICA
Dar es Salaam, Tanzania

August 20, 1973

Reverend J. R. Taylor
The Missions to Seamen
P. O. Box 1179
Dar es Salaam

Dear Reverend Taylor:

I appreciate the thoughtfulness expressed in your letter of
17 August. The Missions to Seamen has provided an unusually
useful service to seamen from around the world, and certainly
to Americans. The extent of the welcome and the program
opportunities available were due in no small part to the
devoted service you rendered, as well as the excellent cooperation of Mrs. Taylor.

We in the American Embassy wish the two of you every success
in Bangkok. Be assured that we will be more than willing to
cooperate with the Reverend Burgess, and please convey this
to him.

Sincerely,

W. Beverly Carter, Jr.
American Ambassador

ON BOARD THE AIRCRAFT TAKING US FROM DAR TO BANGKOK

AMBASSADE VAN HET KONINKRIJK DER NEDERLANDEN

ROYAL NETHERLANDS
EMBASSY
P.O. Box 1174

No. 4066 RN/ar   Dar es Salaam, 24th August, 1973

Dear Sir,

I have the honour to acknowledge receipt of your letter
of 17th instant, in which you inform this Embassy of
your forthcoming departure from this country to take up
a new appointment in Bangkok.
On this occasion I should like to record this Embassy's
high appreciation of your efforts in serving seamen from
the Netherlands, to express our hope that under your
successor, the Rev. Colin Burgess, the existing excellent
relations between this Embassy and the Missions to Seamen
will be maintained, and to assure you of our continued
assistance and co-operation.
I wish you a safe journey to your new destination and a
happy and fruitful stay in Bangkok.

Yours sincerely,

F.P.R. van Nouhuys
The Venerable J.R. Taylor   Chargé d'Affaires a.i. of
Archdeacon of Dar es Salaam   the Netherlands
Chaplain of the Missions to Seamen
P.O. Box 1179
Dar es Salaam.-

353

As our plane winged ever nearer to our new home it became increasingly obvious that Tanzania was now a thing of the past. It is true of many professions but none surely more than the priesthood, that when you leave one incumbency and move to another, you start again from scratch. This is because so much of one's work (just like an iceberg, which has nine-tenths of its mass below water) is hidden from view. As I contemplated my new ministry I could see that things were going to be very different. In Tanzania I was part of a team under the umbrella of the Missions to Seamen, and the diocese of Dar es Salaam. In Thailand I would be quite literally on my own. I would be the only Anglican priest working full time, not only in the huge city of Bangkok, but also throughout Thailand. And, although I didn't know it then, I would shortly be extending my ministry to Laos and Vietnam, as honorary chaplain to the British embassies in both those countries.

On our first visit to Thailand, when out of the blue I was invited to be the new chaplain, certain aspects of the work were discussed. But nothing as mundane as salary! Indeed when after due prayer and consideration, and after finally receiving (even if reluctantly) blessings from those connected with my ministry in Tanzania and the Missions to Seamen, I accepted the post, I really had no idea of what the financial arrangements were. I knew the currency was bhat, that I was to be paid in the local currency equivalent to the salary of an English priest, but I had no idea of the exchange rates or other conditions. It came as something of a shock, therefore, to discover when I had been in Bangkok for only a few days, that there were barely one month's expenses in the church accounts! Furthermore, that Christ Church received no financial assistance from anyone, so was totally responsible for providing my salary and expenses. It certainly sharpened my mind as to what priorities were to be tackled first. Actually this fitted in well with my normal pattern of ministry, which had stood me in good stead in the past, and that was priority number one; to 'put one's own house in order'.

THAILAND

Chapter 33

Christ Church

We arrived to find the vicarage in excellent condition. A reception committee met us at the airport, and yet another when we arrived at the church compound in Convent Road. This included Et our cook, and her number two Nit Noi, my driver Joe, and two gardeners! All this was very overwhelming, made more so when the servants (as was the practice in Thailand) insisted on calling me 'Master'. Master to me meant one person only and that was Jesus Christ! I never fully succeeded in changing this custom, or in convincing them that we were all equal, but doing different jobs. It is a deep-rooted custom in Thailand not to exalt yourself either above or below your station in life. The universal way of greeting was by

**WELCOME TO
CHRIST CHURCH**

A service in progress

the Wai (a salute with the hands). Depending on whom one was greeting so the position of the joined hands was placed: royalty were greeted with the hands in the highest position, actually above the head, children with one's hands level with the stomach. This custom was also reflected in the language: no less than seven intonations depending upon whom you were addressing – just like with the Wai, royalty being the highest.

I came to see immediately that, whereas in Tanzania there were cultural dangers to be aware of, in Thailand it would be even easier to offend. All this called for an immediate and very deep learning curve regarding Thailand and its people. As for the congregation, they couldn't have been more different from Dar's, which to a large extent was made up of seamen. Bangkok was largely made up of expatriates, including diplomats, company executives and permanent residents. There were also Thais, who had either married Christians, or were the product of the two mission school that existed for a short time from the '30s to the '40s. The diversity worried me at first but within a short while I came to see that the only way to cope with it was to be exactly myself. No airs or graces, and as far as possible to be the same with everyone. I thank God that I took this course of action, and looking back I can see that it was right to do so. It has stood me in good stead throughout my ministry.

It must also be said that, despite the challenges of such a different environment, there were many advantages too. One of the losses in leaving Tanzania was that I ceased to be a director of Tim Air Charter Company. I also, of course, ceased to be archdeacon and vicar general! I was thrilled, therefore, to discover that my contract with Christ Church was much more generous regarding home leave than in Tanzania. Most of the PCC were business people, who considered that I was entitled to the same conditions that they themselves enjoyed. As long as the children were in full-time education, allowances were made for them to visit us during at least one of the major school holidays during the year. At the time of the move Michael was 16 and Elizabeth was 13. Furthermore, although my contract (just as in Tanzania) was for three years, unlike with the Missions to Seamen, it allowed for yearly home leave. I was extremely blessed with numerous churchwardens during my time in Thailand (and indeed on reflection, throughout my ministry), who not only supported me in my work, but also took a great interest in our personal lives and conditions. To record their

The church borrowed when taking services in Vientiene, Laos

names would seem like name-dropping, but they included top embassy personnel, knights of the realm and managing directors of some of the leading commercial firms, not only from the UK but the USA too.

To give but one example. In my capacity as honorary British chaplain to Laos I used to visit that country on a regular basis to conduct services there, in the main for expatriates. I always stayed at the house of one of the ambassadors. There were five members on the local church committee, which included three ambassadors, one major general from the United Nations task force, plus a lady secretary. I used to chair the meetings and give them all their orders. They were all as good as gold, and did as they were told!

It was during the time that I was visiting Laos to take services that the country fell to the communists. Shortly before this occurred I was staying with the Australian ambassador. He was invited to a reception at the King's palace. These were very grand occasions, and guests were expected to wear their full white diplomatic uniforms. The court language was French, so when the ambassador suggested that I went with him, I declined. In the first place, I hadn't been invited. In the second place, I couldn't speak French, and finally I had no white suit. The ambassador, however, wouldn't take no for an answer. 'Regarding white, you can wear your alb. Regarding the language, when the King comes around, you can hide behind me, so he won't actually talk to you. As for no invitation, no one will question you if you are with me!'

So to the King's palace I went. It proved to be a wonderful experience. I was within touching distance of the King, and although I didn't know it at the time, it proved to be an historic occasion, because it was the last official reception he gave before his country was overrun by the communists. The King was stripped of all his power and riches, and sent to what was called a rehabilitation camp, to learn a different way of life. As it happened I came away with a lasting memorial of a truly historic time in the country's history. I had timed this particular visit to fall within the octave of Easter. After the service and to my complete surprise the treasurer handed me a considerable sum of money, which, he informed me, was the Easter collection (which traditionally in those days was given to the incumbent). I was acutely embarrassed, and declined to take it, pointing out that I was already paid a salary, and in any case I should be giving them something for all their hospitality.

Despite his insistence I said no thank you, and assumed that that was the end of the matter. It wasn't. The ambassador took the money to the court jeweller and bought me a beautiful silver tray and goblets. It proved to be the last item sold from the court jewellers, as it was closed down by the communists two days later.

I have always been a keen philatelist, and fortunate in being able to pick up stamps in the countries I have visited. Despite the country being overtaken I still went to Laos to take services, because as embassy chaplain I had diplomatic status. Many things were different the first time I returned, including the postal system, as I found out when I went to the main post office to buy stamps. They were no longer valid, I was informed. I told the teller that I collected stamps, and would willingly buy any of the old issues, if she had any. She disappeared to an inner office, returned and went to a shelf where a few books were lying, some of which contained old stamps. Like every country in the world the cost of postage had gone up over the years, but she worked out the price according to the face value on the stamps. Scarcely daring to believe my luck I walked out of the post office with a good collection of old stamps that I had purchased for peanuts.

Although at the time I was the only Anglican priest working in Thailand, there were others employed in a different capacity. One such person was Bill Smith who worked for the United Nations. The Bishop of Singapore licensed him to assist me in taking services. Not only did he prove a great help, but his presence enabled me to extend my ministry to such countries as Laos. On one occasion Bill expressed a desire to visit Laos, so I arranged for him to go on my behalf. Sadly things didn't go well for him, possibly because his documentation wasn't the same as mine, but the fact was that at the airport he suddenly found himself gazing down the barrel of a wicked-looking rifle held by an irate and very excitable soldier. It turned out to be the first and last visit that Bill made to that country.

I had a different hairy experience when visiting Hanoi after it too had been taken over by the communists. A large river runs through Hanoi, with an old and famous bridge spanning it. The bridge had been bombed and badly damaged during the fighting, and as a consequence had a very steep list to port. It was nevertheless the only bridge over the river, so vital to the communication lines of the city. Someone came up with the bright idea that by only using the lane stuck high up in the air, the weight of traffic would in time straighten the bridge! It seemed to me, however, that every time I used it the angle became more acute! It was still standing the last time I used it.

Talking of dealing with parishioners in high places, some of my friends found it difficult to understand why I had left Dar es Salaam as archdeacon and vicar general, and with the distinct possibility of further promotion, to go to Bangkok as a chaplain. I explained that promotion in the church simply meant being where God wanted you to be.

Unfortunately (unlike most personnel who were sent out to Thailand by their companies) I had no chance to study the language beforehand and absolutely no time to take it up once my ministry began. Thai is an extremely difficult language to learn and unlike many overseas countries, very few of the indigenous population spoke English. Most of the firms employed a Thai 'Mr Fix-it-man' who dealt with all official documents and government agencies, which were extremely complicated and time-consuming. In fact, without such a 'Fix-it-man' it was almost impossible to overcome the red tape and officialdom. Furthermore, progress often needed to be oiled by bribes! One of the hardest documents to obtain was a work permit and those who had them guarded them jealously and only passed them on to their successor when finally leaving the country for good. Luckily there were members of the congregation who were able to help me so I was legalized without too much bother. As I contemplated all these things I knew that my future ministry would not only be very challenging, but also full of opportunity. Believing I was in Thailand by the will of Almighty God, I also felt sure that it would be blessed.

Christ Church's beginnings

Before moving on to my ministry, however, it is necessary to share with you some of the history surrounding the beginnings of the Anglican Church in Thailand, only made possible in the first place by the extreme tolerance of the Kings of Thailand towards foreigners residing in their country. It was only when King Mongkut in 1861 gave a plot of land for Protestant Christians to build a church that plans could proceed to build one.

The Portuguese were the first foreigners who came to trade in 1511. The Dutch came in 1601 and the British in 1612. There was a difficult period around 1688, when mainly because of the zeal of Roman Catholic missionaries (who actually tried to convert the King of Thailand!) most foreigners were ordered to leave.

Things changed when King Mongkut ascended the throne. He saw the need for Western trade and influence. Anna Leonowens of *The King and I* fame is but one example. As a consequence, foreigners once again brought trade to Thailand. They also brought their religion with them, which resulted in house groups meeting for Christian worship. On 3rd June 1861 a meeting of non-Roman Catholic Christians (the RC Church already being well established) met at the British consulate to consider the possibility of building a church. They decided to ask King Mongkut for a plot of land. As part of the King of Thailand's title is 'the defender of all faiths' it was not surprising that he agreed. He willingly gave a plot of land on the bend of the river to 'the community of foreigners'. Donations from residents and then (after the first failed attempt) a grant of £400 from the British Government provided the necessary funds. The church was built and opened for worship on 1st May 1864. The church-going community was not large enough to support a chaplain and so the American missionaries (and then later Presbyterians) conducted weekly services of an Anglican flavour. Then, in 1886 the Reverend W Green, an Anglican priest who had been engaged as tutor for the prince (who was later to become King Vajiravudh) took the first services according to the Anglican rites. Finally in 1893 Canon William Greenstock was appointed the first chaplain of Christ Church. Apart from a few gaps and interregnums, an Anglican priest has served the chaplaincy ever since.

Sadly, the days of the church by the river were numbered. Noisy construction around the church for new roads as alternatives to the use of canals, made it difficult to get to church. And increasing flooding meant that it was frequently under water. In 1903 it was decided that an approach be made to King Chulalongkom to see if he would permit the sale of the land on which the church stood to provide funds towards a new building. He not only gave permission but also another site, nearly three times as large, in a position pre-eminently suitable both from the point of view of accessibility and the absence, as the King put it, 'of disturbing influences'.

Some two years later the new church was built. On 30th April 1905 a service of dedication was held in the new church. Christ Church in Convent Road was up and running and has remained so ever since. It is still affectionately known as 'that little bit of England in the midst of Bangkok'.

There was a largely unsuccessful attempt at mission work through St Peter's school for boys and St Mary's school for girls, which folded completely after ten years with the closure of both schools around 1940, mainly because of lack of funds.

This then was the church I inherited in 1973, the only addition being a new vicarage to replace the original constructed at the same time as the church. This brief glance at its history shows that although Anglican in essence, Christ Church was meant at all times to be a sanctuary for all Protestant Christians; that at the heart of its ministry must be a rich outpouring in outreach. If this were not so I would have found it extremely frustrating. The congregation was, like me, an extremely privileged group of people. Most of the congregation had reached the success they enjoyed because of hard work, and I felt convinced that they would support efforts to extend that privileged position through outreach into the wider community. I visualized the ministry developing in two stages; first to the sick, the lame and the blind in and around Bangkok, but not only in the capital. I was concerned that there were no Anglican services anywhere else in Thailand, although there was a sizeable number of expatriates, both in the town Chiang Mai in the north and Pattaya, a coastal resort about seventy-five miles from Bangkok, in the south.

The second (and far more challenging) development would be to open the doors of Christ Church to all of God's children – and that included the Thais. But before this could be possible I knew that there would need to be a full-time Thai-speaking priest who would have to be paid for and accommodated. What is more, although in the early stages Christ Church could be shared by both congregations, the time would come when the Thai congregation would need their own church. More important still, any converts would have to be nurtured and cared for in every possible way. Buddhism is not only a religion; it is a way of life. When a Thai becomes a Christian it is not only the religion that changes, but a whole new way of life. Becoming a Christian can lead to being ostracized, and to rejection from the Buddhist community. That rejection needs to be more than matched by the Christian community and its welcome.

I saw my priorities as

1. Making Christ Church sound financially
2. Moving into outreach
3. Becoming a missionary Church.

From the onset then, this was at the heart of my thinking and planning, the developing of which I trust will become obvious as an account of my ministry unfolds. It lasted for eight years, until sadly my wife Rose died of cancer in 1981, when, feeling unable to continue without her, I returned to the UK.

At only my second meeting of the PCC I unfolded my 'vision'. The treasurer at that time was Chris Stephenson who by coincidence worked in Tanzania at the same time as me. When the PCC decided to invite me to become their chaplain he apparently said, 'If you do, things will never be the same again'. After unfolding my vision, Chris was the first to speak. All he said was, 'I told you so!' I was tremendously impressed and uplifted by the overall response, although I do remember saying to Rose when I got home, 'I wonder where this will all end?'

The first priority was to establish a sound financial foundation. I had long since learnt that whatever you wish to do, it takes money. Another valuable lesson was that although many congregations expect their priest to be able to turn his hand to anything, the truth is very different. Priests like everyone else have their strengths and weaknesses. As I pondered on how best to open generous hearts to this vision, I realized that there were financial experts in my congregation. So I learnt the art of selection and delegation, and with it came success. I spent a long time assessing the various skills of members of the congregation, and once known, it was merely a matter of winning them over to the cause. In Dar es Salaam, with a mainly transient congregation, I had to depend on fund-raising activities to balance the books. In Bangkok, I determined that fund-raising activities would be 'the icing on the cake'; that the congregation through planned and dedicated Christian stewardship would meet the bills.

Another lesson learnt early in my ministry was to use the talents of the people where they could be the most effective. I recall that

in my first parish when I found the parish hall in a deplorable
state I called for volunteers to paint the walls and ceilings. I got
the volunteers all right, the trouble was they ended up with more
paint on themselves than the walls, two members fell off the ladders,
and one spilt a new can of paint all over the floor. Yet another
sprained his back carrying a heavy plank and was out of work for
a fortnight! In desperation I went to a friendly builder who turned
up trumps and turned chaos into order. I ended up with a smartly
decorated parish hall.

Through such experiences I also learnt some valuable lessons
about myself. Like everyone else, I had one or two strengths, but
many more weaknesses. Where possible I strived to do better, but
soon came to the conclusion that, however hard I tried, I would
never become the future Archbishop of Canterbury! So I decided
to concentrate on my strengths, let others move into areas where I
was weak. The same with my preaching, any success came through
simple Bible-based homilies, rather than tackling difficult doctrines.
I found that common sense was the best answer to most problems.
I also learnt that when things became too difficult, I (rather like
Father Christmas with a heavy load of toys on his back) could
hand the whole lot over to the Lord, for him to sort out. So I was
able to deal with people's sorrows and their joys, their hard times
and good fortunes, which often followed one another with alarming
rapidity, sometime even during the course of one single day.

But back to the money! The carefully selected stewardship team
proved to be an instant success, and within a very short time a
sound financial basis was established, which with other fund-raising
schemes, put us into a very healthy financial situation.

My experience with fund-raising in Dar es Salaam had taught
me that it not only raised money, but also, equally importantly,
created a wonderful sense of team spirit and fellowship. Furthermore,
it enhanced 'community spirit'. There were three distinct groups
in Bangkok at that time; the consular corps, the business community,
and the others (although not necessarily in that order!). Although
there was obviously some overlap, it was minimal. In seafaring
circles it was widely accepted that 'water and oil do not mix' (i.e.
deck and engineer officers). To a lesser state this appeared to be
so with the various groups in Bangkok, but fund-raising broke
down such boundaries. Through the church's efforts many people
made new friends and acquaintances, the congregation grew and

more importantly, became more sympathetic towards the plight of others.

There was one huge drawback in all this – the alarming and inevitable increase in the workload! Invitations to Sundowners, cocktail parties and dinners arrived by the bucketful! As I became involved in all three groups so increased the number of invitations which at times reached ridiculous proportions, especially over Christmas. With hand on heart I can say that on some evenings I had no fewer than six invitations, so it was a case of dashing around from one to the other, making sure that at least the host saw you were present. I quickly came to see that having a driver was not a luxury, but an essential. Apart from anything else, if a farang (foreigner) was involved in an accident, it was automatically assumed that he was to blame. The standard of cuisine at such functions was extremely high, and the drinks flowed. I was always careful about the amount of alcohol I consumed, although on such marathons it was not easy. Thailand was an easy place to become an alcoholic! This was one of the reasons why I have always tried to refrain from alcohol from time to time, especially during Lent.

One thing I learnt during such periods of abstinence was how quickly intelligent conversation deteriorated after a few drinks; how drinks make people laugh at the most stupid of jokes, and when they weren't laughing how utterly boring the conversation became! Why go at all? One might reasonably ask. The answer is that these events presented a wonderful opportunity to meet new people, and make important contacts. Not only that, it gave the opportunity for others to open up when they realized they were talking to a priest. Like doctors, I always shied away from talking shop on such occasions, but that did not stop me making a mental note of a chance remark, or a hidden cry for help, and making contact shortly afterwards. There was, of course, also a purely social aspect to such occasions. General remarks with chance encounters such as 'where do you come from?' or 'what are your hobbies?' sometimes brought surprising results. It was at one such event that I got into conversation with a lady only to discover that she was a second cousin, whom I didn't even know existed, and also that we had mutual friends in other parts of the world!

It's amazing how many people want to visit Thailand! Many of only the most casual of acquaintances let you know they are coming and would love to see you again. Luckily, with a large house and servants, this was not too much of a problem, and indeed such hospitality sometimes brought its own reward with kindness reciprocated. One such example was a phone call from the Metcalfes who came from Shapwells in the Lake District. They owned a large hotel, and guests of theirs were friends of ours from Dar es Salaam days. When they learnt that the Metcalfes were coming to Bangkok they said, 'You must look up the Taylors whilst you are there and give them our love'. The Metcalfes came for a fortnight, and then with only a few days to go reluctantly decided to make contact as promised. They were non-churchgoers themselves, so didn't look forward too much to meeting with a priest.

So I received this phone call conveying the message from our Dar friends. I thought the least I could do was to pop round and see them, which I did. As it happened we immediately hit it off, and as a result I offered to put them up for the remainder of their time in Bangkok. This offer was readily accepted and in no time at all they were safely installed at the vicarage. Our friendship deepened and we promised to keep in touch, which we did.

Our friendship also helped to solve the recurrent problem of where to stay when on home leave. On our next UK trip the Metcalfes were at the airport to greet us, and took us straight up to Shap where we spent a wonderful fortnight as guests in their hotel. That friendship expanded to include other members of the family on both sides, resulting in me taking a wedding and a funeral for members of the extended family. On one occasion Geoff Metcalfe presented me with a Bible, which I kept in the pulpit of my church. A guest preacher opened it up to read on the first page, 'This Bible was given by the Gideons and is not to be taken away'! He proceeded to tell my congregation that I was using a stolen Bible! In all, the Metcalfes came out to us for three more holidays, and we likewise spent time with them when in the UK.

Another problem with home leaves for four was the amount of luggage we had to lug around as we moved from one base to another, especially moving from a hot to a cold climate. It's an ill wind however as, after one very trying home leave, the churchwardens urged us to try and purchase our own house in the UK. To find the deposit was a real struggle but various people lent us the necessary money, and the bank came to the rescue with a loan for the balance. So it was that we bought our first house, actually in Truro, where my mother and brother lived. We were able to rent it out, which paid the mortgage and in time we were able to clear the personal loans as well. It turned out to be one of the best investments we ever made, and eventually gave us financial security for the future.

Chapter 34

The Challenges of an Expatriate's Life in Bangkok

Life for expatriates in Thailand was in many ways extremely artificial. The fact that I, a priest, had two servants, a driver and two gardeners is but one example. It was almost impossible for wives to have a job without a work permit, even if they wanted to. So, apart from voluntary work, there was little else they could do ... this was not always a good thing. Thailand is well known for its sex trade (which is the reason why many single expatriate girls disliked coming out to work in Bangkok). As a consequence if a marriage was good then the prevailing circumstances only strengthened it. If, on the other hand, it was not, then through the many distractions and temptations, relationships worsened, often with disastrous results. As my circle of acquaintances grew, so did the call on my time for counselling. As a consequence I became involved with: drug addicts, alcoholism and marriage guidance.

I quickly came to two conclusions. The first was that I needed an inner sanctuary rather than my inherited general office, so that I could talk to people in confidence. The second was the realization that I could easily become swamped with counselling, to the detriment of my other work. Marriage problems apart, there were a large number of desperate people out there, ending in some cases with suicides. There was certainly a need for some form of organization such as the Samaritans.

If all that was not enough, alcoholism was also a prevalent problem. A branch of Alcoholics Anonymous had been formed some time previously, but had fallen into disarray, mainly because those running it had themselves got deeper into the clutches of drink. I discovered that you could not belong to AA unless you were a self-confessed alcoholic, which I considered was one of its

370

weaknesses. It was when more than one Catholic priest came to me with a drink problem that I decided to try and reactivate the existing organization. On top of this, I then discovered that drug addiction was rife, including some amongst members of my congregation. This I discovered when a young man who was a server at communion asked me, 'What advice would I give to someone who was a drug addict?'

'Seek help,' I replied.

'Would you be such a helpful person?' he asked.

'Yes,' I replied.

'Well, I am a drug addict.' He was not only, it turned out, a drug addict but also a homosexual and a kleptomaniac as well!

The British nursing home was next door to the church, and certainly in my early days, it was where most British expatriates went for hospitalization. Most of the English and foreign doctors sent their patients there, and as a consequence barely a day went by without me visiting someone at the nursing home. Dr Colin Britton in particular, a member of the British practice who became a very close friend, would often ask me to visit one of his patients. There was at that time no English-speaking psychologist working in Bangkok, so I was sometimes asked, not to 'psychoanalyse', but at least to try and get the patient to open up, and give a clue as to what was worrying them. In return he was most sympathetic to what I was trying to do, and took in many of my 'lame dogs', who had not the money necessary for treatment in the normal way, and looked after them at least in the initial stages of their recovery. Sometimes it became obvious to me that the person sitting before me needed the help of a doctor rather than a priest, and because of my close relationship with the doctors I was able to pass them on to the right person. The reverse was also true. Doctors sometimes said to their patient, 'It's not me you should be seeing but Canon John'.

But to return to my drug-addicted parishioner. With the help of Dr Britton he was admitted to the British nursing home as the first step in helping him to come off drugs. I visited him a short time afterwards only to discover that he was on a high! I tackled him about this and, after an initial denial, he confirmed that he had indeed just given himself a fix. When I asked him where he got his drugs from he replied, 'One of the major pick-up points for first-class drugs is outside the entrance to the nursing home.' He also told me of other pick-up points in the area. As I had contacts with some police officers, I told them what I had learned. A few days later I found myself in an unmarked police car touring the area. As we passed a certain house, very near to the church, I told the officers that this was where many of the pushers picked up their main supplies. This news was greeted with embarrassed silence, the tour was aborted and I heard no more. Private investigation revealed that the house in question belonged to one of the most senior police officers serving in the force at that time!

Sadly the stay in the nursing home did nothing to alleviate my server's addiction, although he still insisted that he wanted to try and break the habit. There was a very well-known and revered Buddhist abbot who took addicts in in an attempt to cure them. His method was very different from the norm, and followed the lines of 'cold turkey'. My server agreed to give it a go, so I booked him in. As a consequence a few days later he came to my office to be escorted to the Watt (temple) where the treatment was to take place.

The first thing I did was to make him empty his pockets, and sure enough I found he was carrying enough 'dope' for at least four fixes. These I immediately confiscated, upon which he broke down and begged me to let him have a last one before he went in. I debated about this and came to the conclusion that without it he would probably refuse to go. So I agreed, and there and then and in my office I watched him give himself a fix. I picked up the remainder of the drugs and flushed them down the toilet. Then, without further ado, we set off in my car to the Watt which was to be his home for the next ten days. He was one of about six addicts going to receive the treatment at that time. This was so they could give each other moral support through what was undoubtedly a very trying ordeal.

Once they had all arrived the abbot summoned all the monks to assemble together with the addicts. He then preached a very powerful sermon after which he made them take a vow that they would give up taking drugs. After this they sat in a row, whilst the monks brought them a potion to drink. I don't know what was in it but I do know it was absolutely vile. No sooner had they drunk it than they were all violently ill, to the extent that they couldn't look at anything edible or drinkable for days. Acute seasickness was the nearest that I could imagine to be comparable.

Once they came back to life they were chaperoned by the monks day and night to make sure that they didn't take another fix. The abbot preached to them daily, with a mixture of stick and carrot until the course of treatment came to an end, after which they were discharged.

As promised I was there to pick my server up and we went back to my office. Once there he confessed that he was also a kleptomaniac as well as a homosexual. There had been a spate of robberies in the various churches around Bangkok in recent months, causing great distress to the incumbents. Religious items such as crosses, candlesticks, icons and other sacred relics had been stolen. In my office he confessed to being the culprit and asked for forgiveness. I asked him what he had done with the items he had stolen, and he told me he had them all hidden away in his house. I explained that, before he could be forgiven, he had to make amends as much as possible, to which he agreed. So after confession we went to his house, where twenty-five or so sacred objects came to light. I made him list the churches from where they had been stolen and then took them away. I had a wonderful time over the next few days returning the various items to their owners, who accepted them with gratitude. Because of the confessional I obviously couldn't tell them how I had obtained them, but the fact that they had been returned was good enough for them.

Unfortunately, being a kleptomaniac meant that, before long, he stole again, was caught in the act and arrested. I spoke on his behalf to the judge, and suggested the best thing was for him to be repatriated to the UK so he could receive treatment for his condition. The judge agreed, provided that he was released under my care, and that I was totally responsible for him, until his repatriation. The British embassy was most helpful, so thankfully he was a guest at the vicarage for only a comparatively short time, before they arranged for him to go home by ship as a member of a ship's crew, thereby working his passage. It was with a great sense of relief that I took him onto that ship and said goodbye.

My wife Rose was wonderfully supportive in all situations such as this, and readily opened up our home to accommodate 'guests' until their repatriation. In actual fact there were three similar occasions during our time in Bangkok, one of which was particularly challenging. The person concerned had been convicted of a very serious crime, but was released into my care, whilst waiting for

Rose (the powerhouse) at her desk!

transportation back to the UK. Rose knew of his crime, but nevertheless agreed to have him. Staying with us meant that I had to give him a key to our house. When I gave it to him he broke down and cried like a baby. 'For as long as I can remember,' he said, 'keys have been used to lock me up, yet you have given me a key to let myself in.' We had no trouble at all with him, which is more than can be said about our kleptomaniac guest for, after he had left we discovered there were missing items that he had taken from us.

Chapter 35

An Unexpected Trip to the UK

We had not been in Bangkok very long before we were invited to another reception at the British embassy. At first such invitations made us very excited, but after a very short time (rather like in East Africa when visiting game parks, the first sighting of one of the big five was exhilarating, but after several sightings one almost became blasé about it!) we just entered the dates into our social diary and thought no more about it. So, about one month after we arrived, we found ourselves at the British embassy, attending a function. During the course of the evening the ambassador approached me and asked me if I would accompany him to a quiet corner, which I did. Then, and to my utter amazement, he told me that because of my work in Tanzania I had been recommended for the OBE. Would I be agreeable to accept it? he wanted to know. Never at any time had the thought of receiving a 'gong' even entered my head and as a consequence I was completely bowled over – in fact I nearly fainted! The ambassador helped me into a chair and then sent for Rose. 'What's the matter, darling?' she asked. When I told her she nearly fainted too! We both quickly recovered however and agreed that I should gratefully accept the honour. The Ambassador swore us to secrecy until the official announcement was made so not even our children were aware of the honour I was to receive.

Once the official announcement was made congratulations came pouring in, which was very moving. The ambassador asked me if I wanted to go to Buckingham Palace to receive it, or should he present it to me in Bangkok on behalf of the Queen. The thought of going to Buckingham Palace was very exciting, but the cost of the airfares presented a problem, so I asked for a little time to make up my mind. The word must have got around because in no time at all a group of parishioners came to say that our tickets were already booked! UK here we come!

The official notification informed me that I could take two guests with me, which immediately created a problem because we had two children! However, when I explained this I was granted permission to take them both. Michael and Elizabeth were at boarding schools in the UK and, as the presentation ceremony was during term time, they were allowed three days off. What an incredible occasion it turned out to be, although not without one or two hiccups! The first was that I refused to wear morning dress. The second was, because I wanted no fuss at all, I refused to order a taxi to take us to the palace. We can easily pick one up on the day, I assured my family. A friend had lent us their flat in London, so leaving it in plenty of time (so I thought) we tried to flag down a taxi. Twenty minutes went by without success, and even I was beginning to panic. I approached a policeman who was passing by and told him my predicament. I might have exaggerated slightly, saying something like 'we're keeping the Queen waiting!' Whatever I said produced the desired effect as a few minutes later he appeared with a taxi. We did arrive in time, and so began an occasion to remember and treasure.

We entered the palace and ascended a wonderful wide and imposing staircase, lined with guardsmen resplendent in their magnificent uniforms. At the foot of the stairs I was separated from the rest of the family, to be escorted ahead of them to a room where those receiving honours were to be briefed on the ceremony. Came the second embarrassment! My son Michael, who was ascending the staircase some way behind me stopped in front of one of the guards, took out his comb and, using his breastplate as a mirror, proceeded to comb his hair! The soldier did not flick an eyelid, but as Rose told me afterwards, 'if looks could kill...'

The whole organization was magnificent, and despite the number present everyone was made to feel as if it was all in their honour alone. In due time we processed towards the stateroom where the investitures were to take place. The rooms and corridors leading towards the stateroom were adorned with magnificent furniture and beautiful paintings. As we made rather slow progress it gave me a chance to notice others in the procession. Slightly in front of me was someone who seemed to be very well known. Having been abroad for so long I was out of touch with UK personalities, so it meant nothing to me when I was told that he was Jimmy *'Jim'll Fix It'* Savile, who was also was receiving the OBE. There were also a large

OBE Investiture at Buckingham Palace

number of senior officers of the armed forces, all resplendent in their uniforms. Before long we reached the impressive stateroom where the investitures were taking place. The band of the Royal Marines was playing in one corner, and in the centre of the room was a dais with members of the Royal family in situ. All the honoured guests were seated in raised and tiered seats so that everyone had a perfect view. I looked in vain for Rose and the children. Rose told me afterwards that when I entered the room they bobbed down because they were afraid that I would wave to them!

Then came the never to be forgotten moment when my name was called out and I advanced to the dais to receive my award. The officiating Royal was the Duke of Kent. He said to me. 'You were announced as Canon Taylor, whereas on my list you are down as the Venerable Archdeacon.' Quick as a flash I replied, 'That is because I have been fired!' I then explained the reason, which seemed to satisfy him.

After the ceremony there were the inevitable photographs before moving on to St Michael's Paternoster Royal (the head office of the Missions to Seamen) where a reception had been arranged. Many members of my family, plus some very close friends, were there to welcome us, so making a perfect ending to a wonderful day. As regards my children, the highlight for them was not my award, but that they had three days out of school!

Chapter 36

Back to the Grindstone

Altogether we were only away from Thailand for one week. The amount of work that I found awaiting my return confirmed my view that if the ministry of Christ Church was to continue, let alone expand, the old order would no longer do. For a start I needed both an outer and an inner office. A secretary was essential, and she too would need a lot of help. There was a further problem. We were no more than two hundred and fifty yards from the notorious Pat Pong district, which was at that time the centre of the sex and drug trade in Bangkok. This meant that addicts would arrive in hordes looking for a fix, often without the necessary money, so any local building was a natural target for robbery. Unfortunately this included Christ Church, which, at that time we always kept open. It soon became obvious that something had to be done. Although the need for a chapel for the projected Thai congregation was still a long way off, I came to see that having a small chapel, so designed that there was nothing of any value that could be stolen from it, would be a great asset, as it could be kept open at all times, so allowing the main church to be kept locked. The new vicarage was built on stilts, a precaution against the floods that were inevitable in Bangkok because the water table was only about six inches below the ground. In fact the whole of Bangkok was gradually sinking, so the situation could only get worse!

The space under the vicarage was very appealing because it boasted a concrete foundation with slabs. There was no roof needed as the underside of the vicarage formed a natural ceiling. The only drawback was the possibility of flooding, but building a flood wall could overcome this problem. So it came to pass; an outer and an inner office, and a chapel that could always be kept open (and was), came into being. There was another big advantage, as the old vicarage, which now lay empty, could, if needed, be converted to other uses.

Apart from my other activities, I was also the Missions to Seamen representative for Bangkok and on the committee of the Seafarers Club in the dock area. This entailed visiting ships in port and seafarers in hospital, which created an impossible workload. I therefore made representation to the general secretary of the Missions to Seamen for a full-time chaplain to be appointed. An immediate problem arose, which was the question of his accommodation. I had the now vacant old vicarage surveyed and found it to be structurally sound, although in need of renovation. I suggested that, if an appointment was made, the chaplain could also be a curate of the parish, in which case the parish would provide housing for him. This was agreed and John Croyle was duly appointed. Unfortunately he didn't fit in well and after two years his contract was terminated. I knew there was going to be trouble when on his first Sunday, he preached at the 8 am Holy Communion. I had explained to him that many of those who attended that service were the Sunday school teachers, working with the children at the next and main service of the day. After the first service ended we had a communal breakfast, which was always a rush as everyone concerned then had to get ready for the next service. I explained to John that the first sermon therefore had to be a maximum of ten minutes – his lasted thirty-five! Furthermore it was extremely charismatic in nature, which didn't go down at all well with the congregation. I had explained to him the background history of Christ Church, which meant that our services had to be somewhat middle of the road. I explained that we had coffee after the main service, and that many others had to get away immediately afterwards, which meant having sermons not lasting more than fifteen minutes. His sermon at the main service lasted forty, and once again its contents upset many!

This was a bitter disappointment to me, but as he was a Missions to Seamen appointment there was little I could do about it. There was more trouble when he became part of a charismatic prayer group consisting of people from other congregations, which apart from anything else practised exorcism! The first I knew about it was when an irate doctor rang me up to say that one of her patients, a subnormal child had been admitted to hospital after having been badly beaten. It appeared that the group were convinced that she was possessed with the devil, and their method of cure was to beat it out of her. After this episode I barred him from all activities to

380

do with the church, and reported the episode to his head office in London. Shortly afterwards his contract was terminated and David Whately was appointed in his stead. Before ordination he was a professional photographer, a talent from which we all benefited. (If I had only known at the time that I was one day going to write a book I would have kept a lot more of his photos!) Photography apart, he was an excellent priest, and made a considerable contribution to the work. In between appointments I tried to keep the seafaring work going and, just as in Dar es Salaam, I found it very challenging and enjoyable.

One incident particularly remains firmly rooted in my mind. I had a letter from the wife of a ship's Captain writing from the UK. She was very concerned about her husband because letters from him had almost dried up. She was aware that he was drinking heavily and was, in her words, 'letting himself go to the dogs'. His ship would be arriving in Bangkok shortly, so she would be most grateful if I could visit him, and 'sort him out'. I was aware of what inevitably happened when a new ship arrived offshore waiting for a berth ... the first boat alongside was one full of prostitutes complete with a 'madam' in charge of the girls. She went immediately to the Captain's cabin where some sort of deal was struck, including the first choice of companion should he so desire! I must stress that this did not happen on every ship that came into port, but the 'madam' seemed to know instinctively where and when they would be accepted. This is of course one of the reasons why the Mission was so important. It offered an alternative way of life, which was what the overwhelming majority of seamen desired and practised. Having said that, one can understand if men who have been cooped up at sea for a long period, deprived of female company, fell into temptations so blatantly offered.

The ship that I boarded was such a tramp, and seemed overrun with females. I made my way to the Captain's cabin and knocked on the door. After a few moments the door opened to reveal a sordid sight. The lady who opened the door was extremely dishevelled and scantily dressed. The room looked like a tip. There was a bottle of spirits and cans of beer on the table, most of them empty. The saddest thing of all, however, was to see the Captain lying half naked on his bed apparently in a drunken stupor. I left him a note saying I would return the next day at the request of his wife, who was very concerned about him. I did return the next day but really got nowhere, so was unable to write a very encouraging letter to his wife. Sadly the marriage broke up shortly afterwards.

Chapter 37

The Ministers Fraternal

When I returned the items that had been stolen by my server to the various churches in Bangkok, I was able to meet many of the clergy from the different denominations in the city. I was surprised just how many there were, and thought that some sort of fellowship should exist, so that we could meet and share ideas, as well as unite on special occasions in common worship and prayer. This suggestion was received enthusiastically, and, I suppose inevitably, resulted in me being elected as its first chairman, a position I held for most of my time in the city. Most of the ministers were American, which was an eye-opener to me (I had no idea how many different Christian denominations there were in the USA). It was actually at one of our earlier meetings that the ministers from two branches of the Baptist churches met each other for the first time! There were also US troops stationed in Thailand, and I was delighted when their chaplain also made an appearance. Not long afterwards he invited me to conduct a retreat for some of his troops who belonged to a religious fellowship at the base. I visited him at the vast complex that was the US base for troops in Thailand to discuss the programme and its contents; it was just like entering another world, or to be more exact, a typical American city. I was told that some of the men never even left the camp during their time in Thailand. Everything they could possibly need was on the campus: shops, cinemas, bowling alleys, and of course MacDonald's! It really was just like being in a small American town. Even the roads and the buildings were named in American fashion; 'Oh, it's just a block away,' I was told when enquiring where the Episcopal church was.

But an even bigger surprise to me was the different concept of what a retreat was between the chaplain and me. Retreats for me meant going off to a quiet and secluded place, so setting the right sort of atmosphere for a quiet, meditative period, including some form of fasting, and periods of silence. The first shock was to learn of the projected venue. It was to be in a hotel right in the middle of The Strip in Pattaya, the popular seaside resort close to Bangkok. It had recently become a popular centre for tourism, which inevitably meant sleaze, in the form of many bars, massage parlours and brothels. He had previously asked me not to make the retreat too religious, as it was also a time of rest and relaxation. As a consequence I had prepared a programme that in Africa would have been laughed out of court! To tell you the truth I felt ashamed that it qualified as a retreat at all. To my utter amazement he nearly had a fit when he saw it. 'That's far too heavy,' he exclaimed!

Two 'addresses' a day I therefore reduced to one. A daily Eucharist was reduced to one at the beginning of the retreat and another at the end. As for rules, such as silence, some token of fasting, and essential attendance at the programme, all had to be entirely voluntary. Understandably I began to have second thoughts about conducting the retreat at all, but the padre begged me to take it, so reluctantly I agreed. At the due date we all went down to Pattaya and signed into one of the top hotels. Although the atmosphere couldn't have been less monastic, we were given the use of a conference room, which I attempted to transform into something like a chapel. Once settled in, I realized that I too could benefit from the time set aside for the retreat, which indeed I did. It also allowed me to visit Father Ray Brennan, a Roman Catholic priest whom I first met in the clergy house at Rumi Rhudi in Bangkok, and who had now set up an orphanage at Pattaya. Today that orphanage is known the world over, and Father Ray is revered almost as a saint, but in those early days he struggled very hard to get the show on the road. I count it amongst my greatest privileges to have worked with him, not only by supporting him over the orphanage, but also in our combined work amongst the refugees. I particularly treasure the letter he sent me when I finally left Thailand.

Another priest I met at Rumi Rhudi was one Father Joe Maier. He too was a man after my own heart, with whom I also worked, especially amongst the refugees, as well as becoming involved with his work among the slum people in the port area of Bangkok (more of that later, for I need to return to the retreat).

As is usual on retreats I set aside time each day when anyone who wished could come and see me, either for counselling or confession, or just to have a chat. To ensure privacy one just had to put a tick against the time they were coming, so no one had any idea who had actually signed up. I was more than surprised therefore to find that the first 'customer' was none other than the chaplain himself. What is revealed at a confessional cannot of course be shared with anyone, but what I can say is that, if for no other reason than for my sessions with him, I found the retreat worthwhile.

There was a second blessing as a result of my involvement with the US Forces, and that concerned the furnishing of the new chapel under the vicarage. It was around this time that the US forces were destined to leave Thailand. The Chaplain General told me that he would be writing off many items of furniture, and other items to do with the chaplaincy, so would any of them be of any use to me? The size of the chapel on base was approximately the same size as ours. So it came to pass that the furnishings of the one found a perfect new home in the other. This included the altar, font and lectern, and all the chairs. I also received linen, books, Communion wafers and wine; in fact everything that was required to set up a new chapel. I'm not sure who was the more elated, the Chaplain General that a good home had been found for all their equipment or me that all I needed had been so miraculously provided. On top of all this I received some wonderful textbooks and Bible commentaries that I use to this day. Time and time without number I have found in my ministry (and the furnishing of the chapel was one such example), that one always receives more than one gives.

Probably because the Roman Catholic Church was the largest and most established of all the Christian denominations in Thailand, my first tentative outreach endeavours were in cooperation with them. Another huge factor was my admiration for Ray Brennan and Joe Maier, so within a very short time I found myself associated with them on various projects in and around Bangkok.

Chapter 38

The Immigration Detention Centre

One area that urgently needed attention was the Immigration Detention Centre which was situated about a quarter of a mile from Christ Church. It was notorious for all that went on there. In fact it was one of the few acts of outreach that was already in operation before I arrived. Once a fortnight ladies from our congregation took oranges and eggs to the inmates. On the whole they were not not hardened criminals, but persons who had fallen foul of the immigration laws. Some had been arrested because their visas had run out, and others were sent there whilst waiting to be deported. Sadly most of them were rather pathetic people. Some were drop-outs, others who had come to Thailand seeking fame and fortune, or who had come for a holiday, possibly met a Thai lady and moved in with her rather than returning to their own country. Others were tourists who had built up large bills in hotels, had run out of money, the police had been called and the culprits arrested. They were then detained in the immigration centre until they had paid their bills and fines, before being deported. As many of them were down-and-outs they couldn't raise the money, nor did they have anyone in their own country who might bail them out.

The immigration prison also held many illegal refugees, including those from Burma, who presented a special problem. Under the United Nations Charter for Refugees the Burmese did not qualify as refugees because their country was not in a state of civil war. Although the situation in Burma was deplorable, it didn't give its people refugee status. Helping those who had entered Thailand illegally therefore was extremely difficult. As with most young people throughout the world, university is a time of exploration and the forming of ideologies. It was while they were at university that many of the Burmese students came to see how corrupt their

Burmese illegal immigrants being assembled prior to being transported to the
Thai–Burmese border

Waiting to board the bus to take them to freedom

Thank you and goodbye

country was, and determined to do something about it. There was a compulsory time of national service, when every soldier was issued with a rifle. Many, complete with their rifles, absconded and went to the so-called 'golden triangle' to join the rebel forces there, alas only to discover that they were as corrupt as the government in power. They couldn't return home because they had stolen their rifles, which meant very severe punishment, so the only option was to move across the border into Thailand, which they did. Inevitably many were apprehended by the Thai authorities, and ended up in Bangkok's immigration centre. They couldn't be repatriated to Burma because of the punishment awaiting them, so the only answer was to take them up to the Thai-Burmese border, and there release them.

Some took a chance and sneaked back into their own country, whilst others retraced their footsteps back into Thailand, and were inevitably arrested again. I am not sure whether the correct word is famous or infamous, but the fact is my name became a byword amongst refugees (especially with the Burmese): if you can only get to Canon John at Christ Church you will be all right! Through our committee's efforts we were able to raise the funds to get the men released, and provide the transport to take them back to the border.

My appointment as honorary chaplain of the British embassy proved to be a great help as it gave me an official status in situations such as gaol visiting, which would have been far more difficult without it. On the other hand it greatly increased my workload, as any UK citizen in trouble immediately contacted the British embassy, who often passed the case on to me. It was when dealing with one such case that I first went to the immigration detention centre. An English lady had run up a bill at the hotel where she was staying, which she kept promising to pay the next day. The trouble with tomorrow is that it never comes! It should be explained that in Thai thinking most farangs (foreigners) were rich. Foreigners either held important positions in businesses, or else they were tourists who were always deemed to be 'loaded'. So it would come to pass that ladies such as the one I was visiting in the detention centre would be able to build up bills, which the indigenous would be denied. It must also be said that foreigners were treated kindly and with great respect, so if one was found to be wanting, it created a feeling of being let down. With the lady in question, as her bill increased the hotel's patience finally ran out and the police were

A donation to the Klong Toyee slum clinic, set up by father Joe Maier

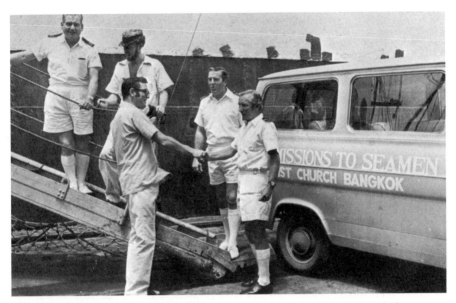

The Rev David Whately, Missions to Seamen chaplain at Bangkok,
collecting men from their ship in port

called. She was arrested and detained, but all her belongings were
left in her hotel room. When I visited, her first request was for
them, which she said she desperately needed, so would I please
collect them? I had found that to wear a cassock in such circumstances
helped a great deal. It marked me down as a religious person, so
equated with the monks, who were greatly revered. So I made my
way to the hotel and asked to see the manageress. She greeted me
kindly and respectfully, but as soon as I made my business clear,
the mood changed. She was vitriolic about the lady in question,
and at first refused to hand over the suitcase. Her intention, she
told me, was to sell the belongings to repay part of the bill. My
sympathies actually were very much with her, but as what she
intended doing was illegal, I had no option but to stick to my guns
and insist the belongings were handed over. I did promise, however,
that I would do my best to try and get the bill settled. In fact,
through the lady's relatives in the UK, I was able to clear her
hotel bill, and pay her fine, after which she was released.

Chapter 39

Buddhism and Other Thai Faiths

My increasing involvement with Thai people made me realize that before even considering a mission to the Thais I needed to better understand their faith and what it meant to them. I learnt that only half of one per cent of Thais were Christians. Hindus were small in number, but very important because they provided the traditional rites of state, and the classical sciences, such as astrology. Brahmin priests still annoint newly crowned kings, and appeased the deities like Siva and Vishnu. But the vast majority of Thais were Buddhist, inherited from classical India. Buddhism is basically a system of philosophy, but also provides an everyday code of ethics, which, whether observed or not, is respected as the ideal. Put very simply, Buddhism is a comfort, a source of safety and blessing. It provides images of the calm sage, which can be worshipped, and the means by which the individual may make merit to neutralize the evil he does, and ensure a better life in his next reincarnation. The onus for deeper commitment is vested in the monks, so it is easy to understand why Thais find it such a satisfactory faith to follow. The temple is the social centre, where the weddings, funerals and all major festivals take place, and of course where the layman can meet his monk. The lay person's chief religious acts consist of occasional ritual worship of Buddhist images, with flowers, candles and incense sticks, and in much more regular donations of food and other necessities to the monks.

Nearly every Thai male enters a monastery at some time in his life. The most usual time for ordinations is during the three-month rainy season (around July to August), which is a retreat period for monks. Actually the young Thais use the entire period of their monkhood in preparation for careers and marriage. The discipline and tranquillity of monastic life help them to prepare for adulthood.

Buddhism has four basic principles.

1. Existence is unsatisfactory (or why would one seek religion?)
2. That dissatisfaction is caused by desire
3. Release lies in the quieting of desire
4. Release is achieved through the practice of morality and meditation

This perfect release is called nirvana, which is what Buddhists strive to achieve.

The order of monks is open to all males over twenty years of age, but younger boys can join as novices. There is very rarely any intention of a young man becoming a lifelong monk; twelve to sixteen weeks being the usual norm. Leaving the order of monks is easier than joining it, and a monk becomes a layman once again when he sees fit, or when circumstances favour. Only a dedicated few make the monkhood their life. Nevertheless, the whole ceremony is a high point in the family's history, which incidentally gives great kudos to the mother of the boy. An early part of the ceremony is when the novice has all his hair shaved off.

During my time in the country, the crown prince entered a monastery, and for the period of time he was a monk he was treated exactly the same as any other novice, or rather that was the intention. Thousands witnessed the shaving of his hair with gold scissors, symbolically an important part of the ceremony. Actually the hair was very important in Thai culture and customs, especially for boys. Although the hair was sometimes shaved off when boys were young, there always remained a small amount of hair which was known as a topknot. This was often tied in a bow, which was considered a safeguard against sickness, especially between the ages of one to seven. It was usually cut off either on the eleventh or thirteenth year (even numbers were considered unlucky). When King Ramah IV had his cut off at thirteen years of age the ceremony took a week. Solid gold shears were used, after which, dressed in simple white clothes, he was given a candle, incense sticks and flowers and taken in joyous procession, accompanied by his proud parents, relatives and friends, to the monastery. The initiate begs the monks for entrance into their order, after which he is examined for his qualifications and possible impediments.

After being accepted by the chapter he is invested with the

yellow robe, and appears before the monks with all his accessories, including his food bowl, to hear his first admonition in monastic discipline. He is now a monk. Soon after dawn breaks the monks would leave their temple compound, and walk through the streets with their food bowls. People willingly give the monks food, as this earns merit. On the first few days the crown prince walked in procession with his brother monks, but was immediately mobbed as everyone wanted to feed him! Sadly, therefore, he had to forgo that part of the monk's routine.

The third religion practised in Thailand is Animism, based on the power and personality of nature, represented by spirits. Every plot of land had its spirit shrine wherein the spirit lives and is fed daily. Thus understood, humans only inhabited the plot as tenants. The spirit world is very real in Thailand!

Nirvana is a sort of mystical state, so in one sense could be compared to Heaven. This it seemed to me might be one way forward in mission endeavour, but only with tremendous back-up and support to converts. It became obvious to me that until a Thai-speaking priest could be appointed, development would have to be put on hold, and this is in fact what happened. This did not stop me, however, from sharing my vision with others, and in the meantime doing everything possible to hasten the day when such work could begin.

As part of my ministry I used to take school assemblies in three of the schools that tutored British students. One of them was quite a long way from Christ Church, so I had to leave very early to get there on time. The traffic in Bangkok was notoriously bad, so one never knew how long the journey would take. I found it helpful to wear my white cassock on such occasions, partly for effect, but also because it was cooler. If there were no hold-ups I would arrive too early. To kill time I would go to one of the innumerable local cafes for a cup of coffee. My Thai never was very good, but I did my best to make my wishes known. Sure enough in came the coffee but accompanied with an unordered meal. At first I thought I must have ordered badly, but became even more embarrassed when I went to pay. A deep wai and refusal to take my money. I mentioned this to the headmaster at school, who pointed out that because of my cassock they thought I was a monk!

Although not wearing my cassock I had similar experiences when I used to go out with a Thai member of the congregation who wanted to show me Bangkok as the indigenous saw it. Very few foreigners used public transport, preferring instead either their own cars or taxis. But not my Thai friend, who used them all the time, so I also did whenever I went with him. The problem arose when the conductor came to collect the fares; a long conversation ensued with much gesturing and finger pointing in my direction. Much to my embarrassment all eyes seemed to be turned on me. When I enquired what all the fuss was about he told me that, because I was a monk, I didn't have to pay a fare! What is more, very often there was standing room only, but not for long. My Thai friend spoke to the assembled passengers and as if by magic there were seats aplenty. Monks are not usually touched (and never by women), so I had plenty of space as well! Needless to say, as soon as I realized what was happening, I had to forgo the pleasure of his company on public transport, but it was fun while it lasted!

Chapter 40

The British Embassy

Being chaplain to the embassy soon taught me that many people had a totally wrong conception of why it exists at all! They genuinely believed that it is there to help out any Brit who falls on hard times, and, if necessary, to fly them home. Although embassy staff will do their best to help citizens in trouble, that is not their primary function; they are there to promote British interests and commerce. Being a priest meant that I could go the extra mile, and work not within certain limits but be extended to embrace the powers of discretion. Help was mostly required in contacting loved ones in the UK and as a result my phone bill grew alarmingly. Unfortunately, in so many cases those on the other end of the telephone had heard it all before. The person concerned had a history of disasters; they had helped out before, but no more!

Dropouts or not, these were real people, and what is more they were children of God. Jesus' way was one of compassion, forgiveness and a new beginning. As I explained to my PCC soon after I arrived, much as I enjoyed my ministry to my regular congregation, it needed to be expanded to cover the poor, the halt, the lame and the blind, as well as the prisoners in gaols. Furthermore this took money. They say that if the good Lord doesn't give, he sends, so it came to pass. Not only did a group of volunteers form a support group willing to engage in acts of mercy, but many also gave money to support the work, so I was able to create a discretionary fund. As it was not always possible to say exactly how the money was spent, it was necessary to build up total trust with the volunteers, which, thank God, I was able to achieve. The fund was to be used not only for Brits in trouble, but for poor Thais also. I soon found out that in certain circumstances a very small amount of money could change a person's life. There was no national health service or similar agencies in Thailand, so if a person was really destitute there was literally nowhere to obtain help.

So, for instance, a Thai mother would come to my office with two or three children, at least one of them obviously very sick indeed. Often their husbands had abandoned them, or were in prison. They had no money to buy even the simplest of medicines, nor to provide staple diets, which their children so badly needed. I had a strict policy of not giving money, but buying the medicine or food required. I well remember one lady returning some three weeks later with a smiling child, who had obviously benefited greatly from the medicines that had been given.

As mentioned, I also had a wonderful relationship with some of the doctors, who would in emergencies take on a suffering person as a patient without charge, at least to see them through their initial crisis. The situation for women was exacerbated by the fact that compared say, to the UK or any western country, women had very few rights. To give but one instance, the mother's name was not entered on a child's birth certificate, only the father's. Marriage break-ups were simple to effect, with little or no provision for the wife, which could result in acute poverty. The more involved I became, the more I realized the extent of the problem in Thailand and so was born the idea of forming a branch of the Samaritans in Bangkok. Where and how to start, however, seemed overwhelmingly difficult so I put the concept on the back burner for the time being.

It wasn't only dropouts who came upon hard times. Sometimes even the 'established members' of my congregation fell foul of the law. Included in the congregation was a very faithful Australian family. The wife sang in the choir, and the children were regular members of the Sunday school. Her husband was not a regular member of the congregation, but usually accompanied his family on social occasions and was a regular visitor at the British Club. Although generally regarded as a bit of a 'wild card', he was nevertheless accepted (mainly, it must be said, because of his wife and children). It was through his wife that I came to learn that things in the family were not good, neither in relationships nor with money. In fact things were so bad that she was taking her children back to Australia. He considered himself an entrepreneur, but sadly lacked the necessary talents to succeed. I also learnt that he had been borrowing sums of money from members of the community, was considerably in debt, and was failing to return the loans as and when promised. Not unsurprisingly the word got around so fresh sources of loans dried up.

Just when it seemed that things couldn't get worse, they did. I had a phone call from the local police station to say that a *farang* had been arrested, and was asking for me. I was also asked to take a large Bible with me, so complete with the precious book I went to the station. Looking very sorry for himself and with perspiration pouring off him, in the airless holding cell I found my Australian friend. He was 'banged up' with about twenty-five other people and being the only foreigner, stood out amongst the rest. I sought information from the officer in charge, and was told that he had been arrested on drug charges, although he wouldn't go into details. I asked for and was given permission to talk to him. He first of all thankfully received the Bible. That he had asked for one in the first place rather surprised me, but any hope for a conversion was squashed when I found out later why he wanted it, he used it as a pillow! Regarding his arrest I obviously can't go into details, but it was possible that he was on the fringe of a drug gang and, as can so easily happen, got sucked in deeper than intended. His wife was by now away in Australia, but his Thai servant, whom I contacted for him, was most supportive in taking him food and clothing, etc.

Came the day of his first hearing in court, and I went along to see if there was anything I could do. He was remanded in custody, which meant that he would not be returning to the police station but to one of the prisons with which I was very familiar. The courts sat all day so as time went on more and more prisoners who were put on remand were gathered together to wait for the prison vehicles that would transport them at the end of the session. I went round to see him, to find him in an awful panic. Apparently in court he had agreed to turn evidence against the members of the gang in return for monetary reward and discharge. The problem was that this had now become general knowledge. Until details were finalized, however, the judge had ruled that he should stay in gaol. Other prisoners gleefully told him that there was already a contract out on him and that by tomorrow morning he would be dead. I said he was in a panic – he was more, he was petrified and begged me to do something to save his life.

There was still about an hour to go before the prisoners would be transported to the gaol, so I ran back to the courtroom and saw one of the officials and enquired about bail. I was told that the system in Thailand was different from that in the UK. One did not have to put down a certain amount of money, but had to sign a surety, and if the prisoner failed to appear in court the surety would have to be met. When I enquired how much, my heart sank, as it would take every penny that we had; in fact we would have to go into debt ourselves to ensure the amount. It was not a decision that I could take on my own, as my family's security would also be on the line. So I rang Rose and explained the situation. Without any hesitation she said she would go along with my decision, whatever it was. I was overwhelmed by her courage and faith in my judgement, but had no time to dwell on it because by now another half hour had passed. I returned to where the prisoners were and outlined my conditions to him. First of all he had to sign all his accounts over to me. I told him I was aware of sums of money he owed to members of the British community, and other debts that he had accumulated. I said I wanted him to leave Thailand with his head held high, so he must agree that from the money he received for turning evidence, the first call on it would be to clear all his debts that the money he received was to be paid into my account, and that I had his permission to pay off all his debts, before anything else.

To this he agreed, so once again I rushed back to the courtroom and gave the necessary surety to the court officials. By the time I returned to the prisoners' compound the prison transport had actually arrived, and he was released into my care even as the other prisoners were boarding buses to take them to prison.

Needless to say, his gratitude knew no bounds, and from that moment on he was as good as his word. My relief matched his appreciation when he reported to the court and gave his evidence and my surety was released. He duly received a considerable sum of money for turning evidence, so I was able to clear all his debts before paying the balance over to him. Once back in Australia he was divorced, and sadly did not make a great success of his life thereafter. However he didn't get into any more trouble and wrote to me regularly for the next twenty-five years, before his death in 2000.

Troubles and problems seem to have no respect for any strata of society. I was amazed when the wife of a very high embassy official arrived at the vicarage one evening in an awful state, and asked me if I could put her up, without telling anyone where she was. She had obviously been in the wars and told me that her husband had beaten her up. The evidence of such abuse was obvious from her appearance. I knew the person concerned very well, which made the situation even more difficult. We immediately took her in, and after some tender loving care from Rose, she was sedated and put to bed. The next day she told me the full story, which, assuming it was all true, was very sad indeed. His violence was at its worst after drinking, she told me. Somehow he found out where she was and came round to the vicarage in a terrible rage. He was also very much the worse for drink. He demanded to see her and take her home. We stood eyeball to eyeball as I refused his request. At one time I thought he was going to attempt a forced entrance, but I stood firm in denying him access. After what seemed a very long time, he finally departed, threatening to return shortly. His wife was reluctant to report him to the ambassador, for fear

23   PERSONAL SERVICES

Troubled?
Discouraged?
Ring 235-4000 day or night

English service — from 2 each
Afternoon through the night to 7 a.m.
Thai service 6-10 each evening

THE BANGKOK SAMARITANS

A volunteer service reaching out to those in despair

**MARRIAGE GUIDANCE Ring   234-3634
for information on free and
confidential Counselling
ALCOHOLICS ANONYMOUS
Ring 252-5097 or 252-9148**

Free advert published daily in the *Bangkok Post*

that he might lose his job, but after convincing her that it was the only way forward, she agreed. The next day I took her to see the ambassador, who was the epitome of kindness and understanding. He assured me that he would deal with the situation, which he did.

The wife of one of the senior members of the embassy staff was a trained marriage guidance counsellor, and when she became aware of the situation was very sympathetic and offered to help. It seemed to me to be a golden opportunity to set up a marriage guidance organization; enquiries revealed that there were other people in the congregations with similar qualifications, who, likewise, offered their help. So from these small beginnings the organization began. In addition to the qualified counsellors, carefully selected individuals were trained, and within a year the organization was up and running. I know they performed wonderfully well, did an awful amount of good, as well as relieving me from a great deal of extra work, although I still became involved initially with members of the congregation who approached me with matrimonial problems.

It was not of course only matrimonial problems that existed throughout the community in Bangkok. Not everyone was suited to overseas postings, so became depressed and homesick, and in extreme cases even suicidal. Usually their companies repatriated them, but there were some situations when this was just not possible. Such people became isolated from the mainstream of society, led very lonely lives, and as a consequence had no one to whom they could turn for help. This convinced me even more of the need for an organization such as the Samaritans to be set up in Bangkok. In the main I have so far referred to the expatriate community, but I was aware of a similar need amongst the Thais. Knowing the need was one thing, how to get it going was another. It came by the grace of God. The gospel for the following Sunday was the parable of the Good Samaritan. Possibly because I felt so passionately about the need for such an organization, I was particularly fired up (so I was told after the service!) during my sermon. At coffee after the service three members of the congregation approached me and said they felt called to do something about it. So was formed a small committee to explore the possibility. All three had wonderful gifts and skills, which when put to common use, gave remarkable results. The problems, however, were immense; money to get the project off the ground; a building from which to operate; personnel to be recruited and trained, and official permission to start such an organization to be granted. There was another huge problem; none of the original group were competent Thai speakers. Reluctantly we accepted that the best way forward would be to start with an English speaking service, but once that was safely off the ground, then move on to a Thai-speaking organization.

The way we moved forward would merit a book in itself! Sufficient to say that by the grace of God, one milestone after another was passed, obstacles were overcome, funds raised, and volunteers trained. The icing on the cake came when we were offered three rooms in a business house, together with two telephones. Shortly afterwards we were up and running. Amongst my most treasured possessions is my Samaritan card with *John No. 1* on it (Samaritans, apart from a few officials such as those engaged in publicity or fund raising were not known by name, but by numbers). Through the kindness and support of Mike Gorman (Editor of the *Bangkok Post* and one time church warden of the congregation), we were given a free daily advert for The Marriage Guidance Counselling Service, Alcoholics Anonymous and The Samaritans, thus ensuring that all three organizations became well known and established.

We were thrilled when Chad Varah, the Church of England priest who started Samaritans in the UK, came out to Bangkok for the official opening. He was able to give us valuable advice on some matters, but not on all! Running Samaritans in Thailand was very different from doing so in the UK. Nevertheless, the basic method of operation was the same. At the first level were those operating the telephone. There was always a senior Sam (as they were affectionately called) on duty who could be contacted if the problem was beyond the capability of the operator, or if backup was required. To give but one example; I was on duty one evening in my capacity as a senior Sam, when I was contacted by the operator and told that there was a potential suicide on the phone. He said he was on the fourteenth floor of a certain hotel, and that after hanging up he was going to jump to his death. He gave the name and address of his mother in the UK and asked if we would forward his message to her. I told the operator to try and keep him talking, whilst I made my way to the hotel. Many of the cheaper hotels were in less salubrious areas of Bangkok, and this one was no exception. The hotel reception had been notified that I was coming, so they had the key to his room ready for me. I went immediately via the lift to the fourteenth floor, found his room, and opened the door. By now he had put down the phone and opened wide the window. So I found him sitting on the sill with his feet outside. He turned and looked at me as I entered and his first words were, 'Don't come near me or I will jump'. There was a chair just inside the door, so I immediately sat on it (where I actually remained for over an hour!). I told him I was from the Samaritans and then, in an effort to win his confidence, I asked him questions about how to contact his mother in the UK. Once I got him talking it all came out: a story, which, in one form or another, I had heard from others, and was exactly why the Samaritans in Thailand were formed.

After about half an hour of him sitting on the windowsill and me in my chair I sensed that I was making some progress, and he appeared to be more relaxed. It was a very hot time of the year, and because the window was open and the air conditioner off, it was stifling in the room. Perspiration was literally pouring off both of us, so after about another twenty minutes I said to him 'I'm absolutely parched and am dying for a drink. You must be dying for one too,' at this he nodded in agreement. 'I've got a suggestion,' I continued, 'why don't we go down to the bar, have a drink, after which we can return to the room and resume our present positions. I promise I will not interfere with you in any way.'

There was silence for a while before he said, 'Do you promise that when we come back you won't physically try and stop me?' To this I gave my solemn promise. After a seeming eternity he lifted his legs over the sill and turned back into the room. A few minutes later we were in the bar. Never has a beer tasted as pleasant to me, and I suspect him also! As we drank and continued talking, the spell had been broken, and after assurances of help and support, he finally agreed to come away with me, which he did. With help and contacts I was able to get him on a plane back to the UK. I never heard from him again.

Once we were up and running thoughts turned to moving into the Thai language. At first the difficulties in so doing seemed even more difficult than in English, but inspired by our initial success so far, we pressed on. The problems were monumental. In the first place most of the expatriates in Thailand, from wherever they came, knew of the work of Samaritans. In Thailand it was an entirely new concept. People in trouble or wanting advice went to visit the venerable monks. I say 'venerable' because in Thailand wisdom is equated with age. We would be introducing an entirely new culture, including confiding in women, who, as I have already indicated, would not be expected to do most of the things that men do in western culture. Once we did get the Thai operation going and the calls started pouring in, the first problem was that they wanted to speak to a male. Secondly came the question, 'How old are you?' Most of our volunteers were from the younger generation. Too young in the minds of the caller to have the wisdom to help solve the problem! This obstacle took a long time to overcome, but gradually progress was made.

It was truly a red-letter day when I was able to open the main English-speaking newspaper and see our daily advert – *Marriage Guidance, Alcoholics Anonymous and the Samaritans* – in Thai as well as in English. Actually a very useful side effect emerged from having these three organizations, and that was giving some of the many people in Bangkok who had a great deal of time on their hands, especially expatriate wives, something to do. By helping out in these organizations they developed a sense of purpose. One of the doctors confided in me that because of these organizations, fund-raising and other good works (like visiting the immigration prison, and then later our work amongst refugees), there were notably fewer appointments at the doctor's surgery!

The result of the 'good works' also had an important impact on the number of people attending services at Christ Church. There was a perceptible deepening of spirituality amongst the congregation, a deeper commitment towards all that we were doing. Furthermore, firms and families that had previously been nonstarters as far as Christ Church was concerned now became involved in our activities. To give just one example, a local garage offered to maintain the parish car free of charge.

Once the Samaritans started moving into the indigenous population I became even more aware of the fact that I was an expatriate priest, with the spiritual aspect of my work almost totally concentrated upon British people. It may have occurred to the reader that very little has been mentioned about my main duty as a priest in Thailand, which was the spiritual ministry to my congregations. Needless to say, it was at the core of all I did, but in that I was no different from any other Anglican priest serving in a parish anywhere in the world. The main purpose of this book, however, is to show the humane and practical ministry of the church. My ministry in Tanzania and Thailand offered a unique opportunity to be involved in this way, and it is these aspects of my ministry that I wish to record. The publication of *The Da Vinci Code* has led to many fanciful theories and much speculation about the church, but I am endeavouring to show the true church in action. The fulfilment of Christ's words, 'that whatever you do to the least of these my brethren, you do it unto me'. Nevertheless, it concerned me deeply that the third leg of my plan, missionary outreach into the Thai population, was still a non-starter.

Chapter 41

Moves Towards a Thai-Speaking Ministry

I knew that the first step was to win the support of the Bishop of Singapore, although I had a gut feeling that this was not going to be easy. Before my appointment to Bangkok I had corresponded with him, and outlined some of my hopes for the future. I was at this time still the archdeacon of Dar es Salaam but being a diocesan appointment I knew that I wouldn't be taking that rank with me. I was surprised therefore that, when replying to my letter, he specifically made it clear that he wouldn't be appointing me as archdeacon. Furthermore he was not sympathetic towards my hopes for expansion. In fact he specifically mentioned that Bangkok was no more than a chaplaincy, and that there were no plans at this time to expand Anglicanism into Thailand. Because everything was so new I didn't give it any further thought, although looking back on it later, the warning signs of what was to follow were already there.

It was only after attending my first diocesan synod in Singapore that the picture became crystal clear. Although strategically the diocese of Singapore was very important, geographically it was tiny – comprising, without Thailand, only the island of Singapore and some small parts of Malaysia. In theory one could also include Laos and Vietnam, as I visited them as embassy chaplain. Any step towards eventual diocesan 'independence' for Thailand, therefore would reduce the 'size' of Singapore drastically and presumably in importance too. The Bishop of Singapore was extremely and fundamentally charismatic, although not all his clergy were likewise oriented. Be that as it may, one would expect a charismatic Bishop to be very keen to evangelize in his diocese, so I was devastated therefore not to receive his support. This obviously did not make things easy for me, but the fact that I stood up to him, apparently won me respect at synod, with not a few sympathizers. In fact,

405

when I returned to Thailand I received letters from some discontented clergymen, asking me if I could do anything about some of the problems they were experiencing. One case was particularly distressing. Quite a few of his expatriate young clergy were from Australia, and some were newly married. The wife of one of them was pregnant, and the couple were over the moon at the prospect of becoming parents. One day the priest answered a knock on the door to find the Bishop standing on his doorstep, but was horrified when the Bishop explained why he was there.

'The Holy Spirit has just told me,' he said, 'that your unborn child is possessed by the devil, so I have come to exorcise them both.'

The priest refused him permission to see her, but was obviously terribly upset by the affair.

Evangelism apart I had other problems to cope with. Christ Church, like all Anglican churches, paid a 'quota' to the diocese. In addition we had to cover all expenses of the Bishop when he came to visit us, including his air fare. He was shortly due to come to us to take a confirmation, so I started to make the necessary arrangements. My candidates had never met a Bishop, so were somewhat apprehensive about meeting him. I assured them that there was nothing to be worried about, that he was a very kind and compassionate person and that they would all love him. There were quite a large number to be confirmed so there was great excitement in the parish, with everyone looking forward to his visit and the service.

My dealings with the business community ensured that I got to know friends in high places, including the airline industry. As a consequence I was able to obtain a complimentary ticket for him. Whereas before, the ticket had been purchased and posted off to him, this time all he had to do was to go to the relevant airline office in Singapore and pick up his ticket. He duly turned up to collect it but a problem arose when he discovered that they had got his name slightly wrong, so he refused to take it! On the night before he was due to arrive he rang me in a terrible rage. He said he wasn't coming to the confirmation tomorrow, because they had the wrong name on his ticket. I apologized profusely for the error, but said it was a mistake that could easily occur, and more easily be rectified. He seemed however to have 'lost it' completely, and reiterated that he wouldn't be coming, at which I became furious. I said there were candidates whom I had prepared very carefully, that they were all geared up for their confirmation, that their family and friends were excitedly looking forward to the service, and that a lot of people had worked very hard to prepare a reception party for him. I said, 'Bishop, you just have to come'.

Although I could hear him as clear as a bell throughout the conversation, he then said that the line was breaking up and he couldn't hear what I was saying.

'Bishop,' I told him, 'unless you turn up tomorrow I will create the biggest row imaginable. I will report you to the Archbishop of Canterbury, and go to every newspaper here, in Singapore and the UK.' I ended by saying that I would be at the airport to meet him, so please be there. He repeated that the line was breaking up, so he was putting the phone down, which he did. I spent a sleepless night, and then in great apprehension went to the airport and waited.

To my immense relief he appeared through the airport doors, and after a frosty reception I drove him back to the church. There was ironically a funny ending to this story. On a previous occasion the Bishop took Rose and me into the church to pray. He said he wanted us to be anointed with the Holy Spirit so he would lay his hands on us. This distinctly upset Rose, but I did my best to give her assurance that it would be all right, and that I would see that nothing untoward happened. The Bishop told us that God was working miracles through him, by healing and exorcism. Just before we went into the church he asked me to stretch my arms out before him, which I did. He said, 'Did you know that one of your arms is shorter than the other?'

'That's news to me,' I replied, but brushing that aside he held my arms and prayed that God would make them the same length!

After the prayer was over he exclaimed with great zeal, 'Praise the Lord they are now!' Without further ado he ushered us into the church, where he began praying in tongues. After this he laid his hands on our heads, calling for the Holy Spirit to descend upon us. What we both experienced – and confirmed with each other afterwards – was that when he laid his hands on us he shook them vigorously, as if to facilitate the process. We thought no more about it, but after the confirmation was over and I met with candidates, the following conversation took place:

The candidates: 'You told us when preparing us for confirmation not to be nervous when we met the Bishop.'

'Correct,' I replied.

'Well, you were right,' they replied, 'because the Bishop was more nervous than we were.'

'How do you mean,' I asked.

'Well, when he laid his hands on us he was so nervous that his hands were shaking violently.'

Although the Bishop never changed his opposition to opening up a Thai-speaking ministry, I never gave up hope. By now we had a chapel under the vicarage. Research uncovered the fact that there was a Thai-speaking Anglican priest who had worked in Bangkok a few years before, teaching foreign students to speak Thai. He returned to the UK and was ordained. I made contact with him and suggested that he might consider replacing me, when I moved on, or even possibly join me whilst I was still here to open up Thai work. There were two problems, it transpired. He was teaching in a public school and as a concession his children were students at the school. Until they had passed through the school he obviously didn't want to move. The other problem was I had no idea how much longer I would remain in Thailand, or when and if the Bishop would license him if he came, so it was impossible to plan ahead. When I was first appointed it was on a three-year contract, renewable with consent on both sides. After about two years, however, the PCC offered to change it into an open-ended contract, which I happily accepted. I felt sure that God would let me know when it was time to move on, and certainly did not feel that time had come yet. We agreed to keep in touch, which we did, although in the end nothing came of it.

Although the Bishop of Singapore was adamant that there should be no incursion into the Thai population, this feeling was not universal. One of the Anglican communion's leading evangelists, John Stott, headed a very high-powered conference in Bangkok, attended by many of the leading evangelicals of the day. Because of my various contacts I was able to be of some help in the organization of the conference, and as a consequence got to know John well. He had the opportunity to see some of the work that was going on under the umbrella of Christ Church. He was particularly impressed with our work amongst the refugees. I felt very humbled when the conference decided to send a message to every Anglican Bishop highlighting our involvement with the refugees and other work. As a consequence I was invited to visit the Archbishop of Canterbury when next on leave, which I did.

The Archbishop questioned me about various aspects of the work, after which he passed me on to Terry Waite, who at that time was the Archbishop's representative for overseas work. I remember sitting next to him on a settee and feeling utterly dwarfed by his physical presence. I had seen photos of him, but none of them conveyed his great size. He too was very interested in all that was going on and asked to be kept in touch. He then escorted me back to the Archbishop, who apart from the details of my work, expressed interest in my wife and family. Before I left we had a time of prayer, and I was most impressed in that the Archbishop included not only all the major points we had discussed, but also Rose and the children by name. Before I left he graciously took me on a mini tour of the palace, including the chapel and the library, before escorting me to the great doors of the palace to say goodbye. As we descended the wide and imposing staircase leading to the huge doors, the Archbishop said, 'What do you think of my carpet?'

I looked down and saw nothing too special about it so replied, 'Not much!'

'Oh,' came back the reply, 'that's a pity, because I've just had it cleaned as the Queen is coming to visit me!' Without more ado he opened the doors, escorted me down the steps and said, 'Goodbye'.

I replied, 'Goodbye, Archbishop, and God bless you.'

He looked at me rather quizzically and replied (I suspect with a twinkle in his eyes), 'God bless you too, Canon.'

Another Bishop who took a great interest in my work was Graham Leonard, then Bishop of Truro, later to become Bishop of London. He was convinced that, as a possible first step towards Thailand becoming a separate diocese, I should be appointed as archdeacon.

Chapter 42

Outreach to Pattaya and Chiang Mai

The future apart, there was always a great deal going on day by day. Following on from my retreat for the US forces in Pattaya, and seeing for myself the number of expatriates who lived or went down at the weekends from Bangkok, to say nothing of the tourists, I explored the possibility of setting up a monthly communion service there. Father Ray Brennan kindly offered me the use of his church, and indeed I did take one service in it. The trouble was that, because he had so many services going on, it was very difficult to fit mine in at a suitable time, so I decided to try and find an alternative venue. This I was able to do through the good offices of an American member of the congregation called Terry Clap, who was married into one of the richest Thai families in the land. How they met and got married is well worth recording.

Bangkok was a favourite place for US Troops for 'rest and relaxation' (R & R). Terry was an ordinary GI who duly arrived in Bangkok for this very purpose. By chance he met up with Kamala, the eldest daughter of this rich and extremely powerful Thai family, who owned many of the biggest stores and hotels throughout Thailand. It proved to be love at first sight, so naturally correspondence continued after he left. Some time later he was able to return for another R & R and the romance blossomed even further. Her parents were not pleased and did everything in their power to dissuade her from continuing the relationship. As in many of the eastern countries, it is not considered a good thing for a girl from a high-class family to marry anyone other than another suitable countryman. But true love is made of sterner stuff and, after the second visit, they became engaged. The parents were determined to break the relationship off, and such was his influence that her father was able to have every point of entry into Thailand notified of Terry's details, and for entry to be denied should he appear!

The American high command came to hear of this and didn't approve, so issued him a different name and army number, which enabled him to slip through the net! He and Kamala met up in Bangkok, eloped and were married. After a few weeks Kamala put a large advert into several of the leading Thai newspapers informing her parents that she was now married to Terry and wouldn't return unless her husband was fully accepted into the family. The parents had no option but to agree and so they returned to the family home. Shortly afterwards they set up their own beautiful house, quite near to Christ Church, and moved in. Terry's contribution (being a very keen golfer) was to set up a putting green in the garden!

Terry was given a managerial job in one of the large stores, but it was in name only, and he found it very frustrating not having a proper job to do. The family continued to expand its empire, with Kamala being more and more involved in the business. It was she who built a magnificent new hotel in Pattaya, and as a consequence I was offered accommodation whenever I wanted to take a service there. So began a monthly Holy Communion at her hotel. I never knew until I got there where the service would actually take place, but they always found me somewhere, whether that was in the conference hall big enough to hold 300 people, or in one of the numerous rooms that was commandeered for the service. I had posters printed, which I displayed in all the hotels in Pattaya, and although I never had huge congregations it was certainly worthwhile. The services continued all the time I was in Thailand.

Our friendship with Terry and Kamala grew over the years, so it was no real surprise that as our twenty-fifth wedding anniversary drew near, they offered to host the party for us in their lovely house and grounds. All they needed, they told us, were the numbers, everything else we could (and did) leave to them. The day itself was truly wonderful. It began with our children Michael and Elizabeth (who had flown out from England for the event) bringing us a champagne breakfast in bed. Throughout the day a constant stream of friends called by to offer their congratulations and bring presents. Came the evening and then, in fantastic surroundings in the presence of about a hundred friends, we enjoyed a wonderful reception and party. The food was out of this world, the drinks flowed, the live music was fantastic, and all we had to do was to enjoy it. We received so many silver presents that we had to have a special cabinet built to house them all. During the speeches many references were made to the next twenty-five years. There was no indication at that time that there was anything wrong with either of us. No one could have dreamt that within four years Rose would have lost a brave fight against cancer, and that she would be one of the first people to have her ashes interred in the new garden of remembrance in the grounds of Christ Church. Prophetically Rose said a few days later, 'Even if we were both to die next week, we would have enjoyed and experienced more in our short years than most achieve in a lifetime.'

The other part of Thailand that I knew would benefit from regular Anglican services was Chiang Mai. Apart from fast becoming a very popular tourist resort, there were a large number of resident expatriates. Chiang Mai had its own British consular officer who was able to provide some local services. At my request he sounded out members of the local community with positive results, so I decided to accept his invitation to go up to Chiang Mai and investigate further myself.

Thai festivals

Before I do, however, I must tell you that Thailand celebrates some wonderful festivals during the year, all of which are taken very seriously, because they concern nature, and in particular the rain which is so important in a rice-producing country. The monks play an important part, as they are basically Buddhist festivals also. By pure coincidence my visit to Chiang Mai in November coincided with the festival of Loy Krathong which celebrates a successful wet season with the 'short rice' season safely gathered in. There is a wonderful legend about its origin. Nang Noppanas (daughter of a learned Brahman priest at the court of the King) made a Lotus Krathong and presented it to his Majesty. It consisted of a little raft for floating on the water housing a candle, money and food for the spirits, as a reward for their kindness and protection. The King lit the candle, and put the Krathong in the river. As it floated away so it took with it all the sins and bad luck. (Christians will recognize the similarity to the Jewish custom of Old Testament times of anointing a goat or a sheep and sending it out into the wilderness, carrying the sins of the people with it.)

The river Ping flows through Chiang Mai and on the night I arrived I was taken to the spot where the ceremony was to take place. There must have been at least a thousand people gathered, all with their Krathongs, and, at a given signal and amid great excitement, the candles were lit and the Krathongs placed in the water. It was one of the most beautiful sights I have ever seen. No one moved until the current took the Krathongs round a bend in the river and out of sight. Everyone knew (but no one cared) that beyond the bend were scores of young Thai boys and girls who dived in and retrieved the money and goods on the Krathongs! Included in the crowd were many British and other foreigners, so it provided an excellent opportunity to meet them, and discuss the possibility of starting Anglican services. The response was most encouraging, indeed the word had got around that I was coming, so many people came up to me and expressed support for the venture, including an American Baptist minister who offered me the use of his church. So a Chiang Mai congregation came into being, and was a success from the word go. Between twenty-five and thirty souls became regular members at the monthly service.

Another very popular Thai custom, tied up with the lull between the first and second rice crop, was Songkran, which was celebrated on the thirteenth of April. The main rice harvest was finished, the new crops yet to be planted, so there was a brief time for relaxation and fun, hence Songkran. The beginning of the day was solemn, people going to the temple to sprinkle the hands of the monks with scented water. Older members of the family were likewise sprinkled. But as the day wore on everyone joined in the fun, and sprinkling turned into buckets of water (not always the cleanest) being thrown over all and sundry. I watched with a mixture of concern and amusement as tourists in Bangkok, unaware of the custom, would suddenly find themselves drenched to the skin in dirty water from a passer-by! It was one occasion when all is fair in love and war, and even our cook Et, plus her young assistant Dim (nicknamed Nit Noi, because she was so tiny) delighted in drenching any member of our family who came within range. Great fun, but deeply significant too for Thais, as water for the rice crop was the lifeblood for the majority of Thai people.

Chapter 43

Prison Visiting

Without any shadow of doubt, one of the most challenging of all priestly duties in Thailand was prison visiting. Prisons in any country are best described as godforsaken places, but to be in gaol in a foreign country is ten times worse. And this includes Thailand. The country's culture is very different from anywhere else. The main prison in Bangkok is ironically known as 'the Bangkok Hilton', but this title couldn't be further from the truth. During the course of my ministry I have visited gaols in six different countries. Without disrespect to the people of Thailand, for a foreigner to be in prison in Thailand is the worst punishment of all. Many would say, 'Serve them right'; most of the prisoners were there because of drug-related offences. True, but the 'drug barons' of the trade were rarely caught, rather the lowly couriers. One such person was Rodney Vickery. He came from a poor background but his life was transformed when he enlisted in the Royal Air Force as a regular airman. He was immensely proud of his uniform, which he wore with great pride. He was trained in radar and became very good at his job. He told me that one of the greatest moments of his life was when he had to swear allegiance to the Queen and secrecy regarding his work. For the first time in his life he told me he felt he was doing something worthwhile. He married and became a proud and contented father. Then disaster struck. There was a cutback in the numbers in the forces and he was made redundant.

He returned to civilian life but never settled down or found a rewarding job. He started drinking heavily, his relationship with his wife deteriorated, and she left him. He continued to drink, lost his job, and got hopelessly into debt. One evening when drinking in his local pub, a stranger approached him. 'I know all about you,' were his opening words, and what followed proved that he

414

did. After outlining his fall from grace he said, 'What you need is a new start and a holiday. I am prepared to give it to you.'

So it came to pass that within a short time Rodney found himself on an aircraft bound for Thailand with spending money in his pocket, and contacts to make his stay in Bangkok trouble-free and full of all that any man could desire. He had a wonderful time until his money ran out, but help was once again at hand. He was promised a large sum of money provided he delivered a parcel back home to his first benefactor. It must be said that he knew exactly what he was carrying, but the temptation was just too great. The first I knew about it was a photo in the *Bangkok Post* showing Rodney in police custody, literally with his pants down, with bags of heroin packed around his waist.

I met him in prison shortly afterwards, and so began a long relationship during which, in time, all the facts emerged. Prisons are full of people who are innocent, or so they protest. Rodney was not like that at all (indeed being caught literally with his pants down gave him no option!), but there was nevertheless an appealing side to his nature that became more apparent as I got to know him better. There was in Rodney a huge amount of hurt and bitterness at the way life had treated him, indeed it was through my association with him that I experienced just how tough and demanding prison visiting could be. Prisons are terrible places. They are not conducive to confidence sharing, or putting one's trust in another.

To give but one example. I met a Portuguese prisoner who had been incarcerated in the prison for many years. He had no friends, trusted no one and was a complete loner. I set about trying to break the barriers down. At first I had to seek him out, but eventually he came to meet me, and although at first communication was stinted, in time it did become more relaxed. One day I ventured to ask him if there was anything he wanted. I was rather surprised when he said what he really craved was a pair of trainers. Like most inmates, fitness was something they all strived for, but without trainers he was sadly disadvantaged. 'I have the money to buy them,' he told me, all I had to do was to buy and deliver. It was obviously important to him that he did use his own money so rather reluctantly I took it. Fifteen years in Lad Yao had left him hopelessly unaware of the current value of money and what he handed over would just about pay for the laces! I obviously said nothing and promised that I would bring them with me next time I came. I tried to make it a monthly visit to each prison so, duly armed with his precious trainers, some four weeks later I entered his compound. I was not surprised that he was the first person to meet me as I entered. Even as I approached he mouthed the words, 'Have you got them?' and I nodded in reply.

I handed them over and he grasped them rather like he was receiving the crown jewels! He admired them for a long time and then said, 'Where is my change?'

'I'm afraid there isn't any,' I replied in all innocence, obviously not adding that they had been bought mainly with my money. He went absolutely berserk and accused me of stealing his change! Nothing I could do would appease him, so what started out as an act of kindness turned into a nightmare. He ranted and raved, following me around the compound, so much so that one of the guards approached him in a menacing manner, but I managed to convey that the situation was well in hand (although to be honest I wasn't too sure!). On reflection I realized that all his emotions had been so pent up for so long, and as there was no one else to whom he could vent his anger I came into the firing line. I came to see that verbal abuse was one of the crosses that every Christian is called upon from time to time to bear. The same was true of Rodney Vickery. At first he just used me as a whipping post; venting his anger and frustration on the only person he could do so to without reprisal. Father Joe Maier agreed with me that it was the most stressful part of our ministry, and quite honestly without the support of each other, I do not believe that we could have continued. My patience with Rodney at last began to bear fruit. We always took communion into the prison when we went. On special occasions (such as Christmas) all prisoners attended the service, but at other times it was just those who wanted to receive their communion. One day Rodney asked if, although not confirmed, he could attend the service? To this I readily agreed.

After a few months Rodney confided with me that he would like to be confirmed. My monthly visit was extended by half an hour so that I could give him confirmation classes, and after about a year he was ready for confirmation. During the course of my visits I came to know the Inspector General of Prisons well, and he graciously received me when I requested an interview. I made my request, including the fact that the Bishop of Singapore would have to be present to conduct the confirmation. I also explained that it was a very special occasion not only for the candidate, but also for the whole church. I added that such a service was usually accompanied with hymns so could I please bring Christ Church choir into prison for the occasion. I added that at least half of the choir were women. As I had not seen a woman in the men's prison in all the years I had been visiting Lad Yao, I was not surprised when he said he would have to consult with others.

To my great joy the answer came in the affirmative, and so the great day was arranged. We hired a bus to convey us all to the prison. Once there I gave them a final briefing and told them what to expect. We, including the Bishop, changed into our clerical robes, and prepared to descend from the bus. Ladies being ladies, many had brought their handbags. Not to worry, I told them, bring them with you. The guards may well ask to examine them, but that is just normal practice. I was surprised at their reaction. 'We're not taking our handbags in there,' they exclaimed.' The men might steal them!' Nothing I said could convince them otherwise, so in the end they left them in the bus and we made our way to the prison entrance. There we were met with a reception committee including the Inspector General, who seemed thrilled to be introduced to the Bishop, resplendent in his robes.

Amid an air of great excitement we advanced through the prison until we came to the 'dang' where the foreign prisoners were housed. Led by the cross bearer and acolytes, and singing our opening hymn, we moved into our designated places. Every single inmate was present, including of course Rodney, supported by two (slightly apprehensive) friends. Came the wonderful moment when I brought Rodney before the Bishop: there in loud and resonant tones Rodney made his confirmation vows, and then knelt on the concrete as the Bishop laid his hands upon him in the rite of confirmation. Spontaneous clapping, which turned into cheering, erupted from the men as Rodney rose to his feet and rejoined the other prisoners. It was an experience that all present will never forget. Certainly for me one of the most memorable services I have ever attended. So Rodney took his first communion from the Bishop and became a full member of the body of Christ. The whole service went without a hitch, and I am sure that everyone present just didn't want it to end. But end it did, and once again to the accompaniment of renewed cheering from the prisoners we made our exit, and returned to the bus. Alas the drama was not yet over. We boarded only to find that whilst we were inside the prison thieves had broken into the bus and stolen the ladies' handbags! Luckily none of them had very much money with them, so it was pride that was hurt more than financial loss. I now understand the expression, 'there are more thieves outside a prison than in it!' Or, as said in seafaring circles, 'Seamen have more to fear from the sharks of the land than the sharks of the sea!'

On another occasion Father Joe Maier and myself, on a normal monthly visit, were stopped at the gate (despite that fact that the guards by now knew us well) and questioned about our business. Sometimes we took in a full communion set but on this occasion we were only giving communion in one kind, which Joe carried in a ciborium around his neck.

'What's that?' the guard wanted to know.

Not for the first time, we patiently explained that it contained the consecrated bread ready for distribution.

'I want to see it,' the guard insisted.

So rather reluctantly Joe took the ciborium from his neck and opened it up. The guard tried to take it, but Joe refused and in the struggle that followed all the wafers fell out of the ciborium onto the ground.

'Oh dear,' said Joe, 'Jesus is all over the sidewalk!' With great care and reverence we retrieved the wafers, gave them a good blow in an attempt to clean them up, and advanced into the prison. Neither of us said anything during the administration, but the look in our eyes was something else! Because of our different traditions we tended to have communion with the bread only when Joe was celebrating, but communion in both kinds when I was celebrating. Because of other duties we could not always go together, and it was on one such occasion that I ended up being arrested and frogmarched to the governor.

I was in the middle of a communion service in both kinds, when one of the guards approached me and asked, 'What's in that bottle?'

Here we go again, I thought to myself as I tried to explain about the bread and wine used in the service.

'Is that wine then?' he asked.

I replied in the affirmative, whereupon he confiscated the bottle, and arrested me for smuggling liquor into the prison! Despite my objections I was marched off to the governor's office, with an

escort of no less than three guards, one of whom proudly produced
the offending wine. The governor seemed non-plussed at first, but
then dismissed the guards, and invited me to sit down. Yet again
I repeated the story, after which there was a pregnant silence. The
governor eventually said, in a very kindly tone, 'Canon John, the
next time you come, could you not bring Ribena Juice instead?'

The next time I went was with Father Joe Maier, and it being
his turn to take the sacrament, there was no problem with the wine,
or with the ciborium. Roman Catholics are obliged to make their
confession before receiving their communion, and were reminded
of this as we approached that time in the service. About twenty
men responded to his invitation and formed a queue before him.
Joe took one look at the numbers and said, 'Right. The first ten
of you make your confession to Canon John!' Within seconds the
queue had divided into two, and I found myself hearing confessions!
Confession is practised in the Church of England but on slightly
different terms: 'All may, none must, but some should'. It is usually
heard on a one-to-one basis, which was very different from the
position I found myself in. To compound the situation the first in
the queue confessed to murder! As a consequence I was only a
third of the way through my candidates, by which time Joe had
finished with his.

'Right,' said Joe (with a slightly disparaging look in my direction)
'the rest of you lot, back to me!'

But without any doubt at all, the most uplifting occasion fell
upon a service at Christmas. I went once more to the Inspector
General of Prisons, who obviously knew about Christmas (the
decorated stores at this time of the year in Bangkok match those
anywhere in the world). He wasn't aware, however, of the religious
significance, so with a silent prayer that the Lord might bless the
meeting, I gave, in effect, a Christian message. He was not converted,
but he did agree to me holding a special service for everyone,
complete with Christ Church choir and all the trimmings in both
the men's and the women's prisons.

The choir enthusiastically embraced the opportunity to outreach
once again into the prisons, and practised hard on the Christmas
carols, plus anthems. Other members of the congregation pleaded
to be included, so much so that we were spoilt for cross-bearers
and acolytes. Came the long-awaited day, and it was a very proud
priest supported by many of his congregation who lined up outside

the gates. We were then solemnly admitted by no less a person than the Inspector General himself. We entered through the gates in procession with the choir in full voice singing 'Christians awake salute the happy morn'. Those words were, I am sure, heard all over the prison, bringing hope to those who, for one reason or another, couldn't be present at the service.

What I didn't know was that some of the foreign prisoners were 'in the hole' as it was called, for some infringement of the rules. My enthusiasm as a philatelist had taught me to look not so much at the stamps you have but at those spaces waiting for the stamps you haven't! So I immediately noticed that about ten of my 'regulars' were missing. I approached the senior warder present to enquire where they were, and was informed that for disciplinary reasons they were in 'the hole'. Then began an eyeball to eyeball confrontation with him. I reminded him that I had permission to take a service for every prisoner, so why weren't they there? He repeated his answer, but I came back with mine. I told him that I couldn't and wouldn't begin the service until everyone was present. The eyeball to eyeball continued for some time, but finally he ordered that the men in confinement be brought to the service. Another ten minutes passed and then, lo and behold, in they came, looking somewhat bemused and blinking in the daylight. A resounding cheer that would have taken the roof off if we had been in a building signalled the start of the service that moved everyone very deeply. The choir was magnificent, and the congregation joined in with great gusto and huge enjoyment.

I had briefed the choir (especially the ladies) that immediately after the service they were to move in amongst the prisoners and wish them 'a happy Christmas!' I watched with bated breath as they did just that. The warders at first looked very unsure, because this was not normally allowed, but the Lord carried the day, and move amongst them they did. Because we were moving on to the women's prison, and because of the delay in getting everyone together, we were already overdue, and I had no option therefore but to break up the party, wish them well, and then, departing as we had come in procession, and singing 'O come all you faithful', we made our exit.

A similar experience awaited us in the ladies' prison, and was actually recorded in a book written by Rita Nightingale, who was an inmate in the prison at that time (the only mistake she made was to call me Bishop John!). There is no doubt that the services in both prisons made a tremendous impact on the morale of the prison, both on the prisoners and the staff alike. I now understand the expression 'there was not a dry face to be seen' as I saw both men and women reduced to tears, with softness on some faces that I had not seen before or since.

The next time I visited Lad Yao everyone wanted to talk about the service, and to know when the next one would be. One of the men told me that when he saw the ladies assembled before them he couldn't believe it was real. 'It was just like watching a programme on television,' he said. 'And after the service when they came, mixed and talked to us, I felt sure I was dreaming!'

Rita Nightingale

It was around this time that Rita Nightingale's arrest on drug-carrying charges caused a great deal of interest both in Thailand and the UK, partly because of the historical significance of her name. Drugs were found in her luggage, which she claimed (as was common in so many similar cases) that she knew nothing about. Her English MP, Barbara Castle, supported her claim of innocence, and even went as far as suggesting that she be made a member of parliament, so that she couldn't be imprisoned in Thailand. Because of her influence many took up the cudgels on her behalf, especially when it was reported that Rita was at one time a nurse (in fact she was a ward cleaner). It was not widely known that before her arrest she worked for a time in a Hong Kong bar, which was similar to many others in that the barmaids were very scantily dressed. She was courted by a wealthy local businessman, and it was at his invitation that she found herself in Thailand, and then arrested for being in possession of drugs. Rita claimed that it was the first time she had ever been to Thailand, (although there was evidence to the contrary) and that she knew nothing about the drugs.

I got to know her well during my visits both before and after her trial. She was in fact found guilty and sentenced to twenty years in prison. Whilst serving her time she smuggled out letters to the press claiming very bad treatment. The prison Governor was incensed and not only stopped her mail but the other prisoners as well, which made her very unpopular all round. There was an American group of evangelical Christians who also used to visit the prisons, and she actually became converted during her time in prison. I remember making a special point of visiting her on her birthday, and couldn't but help notice the trouble she had taken to make herself look as attractive as possible, including wearing lipstick and make-up. Continuing efforts were made on her behalf, and it came as no great surprise when she was granted a pardon by the King and released from prison. She was taken to the British Embassy where a lunch was laid on for her, attended by about twelve of us who had visited her and helped during her time in prison. It was made abundantly clear however that she was still, in the eyes of the Thai courts, guilty, and that she was to be deported forthwith from the country, and barred from ever returning. Accompanied by a consular officer she was flown out the next day.

A few days later her photo accompanied by an article appeared in the *Daily Express*. It was headed:

RITA: I WANT TO BE GOD'S COURIER.

It continued:

Once she was an inadvertent courier for the Golden Triangle drug racketeers. But now 26-year-old Rita Nightingale, the Lancashire nurse freed from 20 years' jail by the King of Siam, is carrying a different message.

After her 34 month ordeal in a Thai jail she intends to become a missionary. Yesterday the carefree Blackburn girl declared 'In jail I was converted to believing in God. And now I want to carry his message wherever I can be useful. I cannot ever forget what has happened to me. And I shall never forget the friends who stayed by me. They have changed my life and made me see things through a wide angle.' At her side were the friends who consoled her throughout her ordeal in jail – Britain's consul in Bangkok, Mr Walter Coleshill, and John Taylor, the Church of England's Canon at the city's Christ Church.

She continued, 'The people who came to see me, like the lawyer and the missionaries, made me feel that I was not alone and that there might be a chance for me finally to live a worthwhile life.'

422

As she said farewell to Thailand she declared, 'I intend to devote the rest of my life to repaying that trust'.

I came into contact with her again when prison visiting in the UK Rita had become well known for prison visiting, discouraging others from taking up a life of crime. Sadly the story does not have a happy ending as many years later she was dismissed for abusing the privileges she enjoyed as a prison worker.

Possible repatriation and exchange of foreign prisoners?

Whilst in Thailand a group of us connected with prison work tried to introduce the possibility of British prisoners being repatriated to the UK to finish their sentences in a British gaol. There were many problems however. In the UK, for instance, a prison sentence was reduced for good behaviour – not so in Thailand, where fifty years meant fifty years! There was one exception. The King of Thailand could, and did, on occasions, give a pardon, or a reduction in the time of the sentence. This did not always apply to foreign prisoners though, especially if the crime was drug related. The question then of how long a prisoner should serve in his own country was a complicated matter. I was particularly concerned about Rodney Vickery, and in fact was delighted when some agreement was reached concerning him but only after I had left Thailand. My successor therefore was landed with the responsibility of housing him before he was sent back to the UK!

To return to the King's amnesties. There were certain state occasions, including the King's birthday, when these concessions were announced. The prisoners were aware of this, and as the day approached tension in the gaols reached fever pitch. An extra special occasion for the King (fifty years on the throne) was shortly to be celebrated so optimism ran even higher that huge concessions would be made. For those who benefited the joy was immense; for those who didn't the despair was devastating. Rumours abounded, including that the King was going to be especially merciful to drug-convicted prisoners. Knowing that there could be huge disappointment in some cases, I decided to be there on the day. I found the tension when I arrived overwhelming as I prepared myself either to share in their joy, or pick up the pieces. Whatever happened I felt it would be helpful to celebrate communion so I brought with me the communion set that I used on such occasions. There was a large grass compound in the dang with a cast iron table and chairs in the centre of it. It was here that I set up communion, and was joined by about half a dozen inmates. I was just about to recite the prayer of consecration when the King's amnesty was announced. It was given first of all in Thai, but as I was in the middle of reciting the prayer of consecration, I didn't take in all that was being said. It must also be admitted that my Thai wasn't that good to have understood it all anyway. I had just finished the prayer of consecration when the announcements were repeated in English. The King had been very gracious, we were told, and had made huge deductions for prisoners. He then went on to give the finer details, and the excitement reached boiling point as he outlined what they were. Then came the bombshell.

'This amnesty does not apply to foreign prisoners residing in Thai gaols, who have been convicted of drug-related crimes.' Just like a black storm cloud suddenly cutting out the sun, so the atmosphere immediately changed, becoming dark and ominous. Moments later screams of frustration, anger and hatred filled the air. Inmates started running all over the compound armed with stones, legs of chairs, anything they could lay their hands on. Old scores, pent-up emotions and frustrations poured out, resulting in absolute mayhem. Within seconds fighting, beatings, and loud screaming broke out everywhere. Bodies turned red with crimson blood flowing. Total chaos reigned, except for our little group gathered around the table in the centre of the compound, partaking in the Lord's Supper. True, some of the communicants cast anxious glances in my direction, looking to see what I would do. Without hesitation I decided to just carry on, ignoring all that was going on around us. It wasn't easy, as prisoners were fighting or being beaten only yards away from where we were gathered. Amazingly it was just as if a hole in the black cloud had opened up directly overhead, and the sun was casting its protective beams over us, which nothing or no one could penetrate. So we finished the service in peace, by which time guards had appeared and gradually some semblance of order was restored. Rodney Vickery was one of the communicants, and his thank you to me before I left amply compensated for all the venom I had received from him in recent years. It was only after I had left the prison and reached the sanctuary of my car that the full realization of what had happened came to me, and I shook uncontrollably for about ten minutes. As a result of that experience it has been my practice ever since, when visiting a hospital or prison, to pray for all those inside as I enter, and to give thanks to Almighty God for my health and freedom as I leave.

Visiting also continued at the immigration detention centre. Those detained were in the main not hardened criminals, but those who had fallen foul of Thailand's immigration regulations. The regime was not as draconian as in the prisons, but there were different problems to be endured. Those in prisons were incarcerated for a set period of time. Foreigners were visited by their country's consular staff, and every prisoner was known to someone somewhere. This was not always the case at the immigration detention centre, it was something like the old-time debtors' prison: you were there until your debt was paid, and the means of having you deported was in place. It was therefore a place where you could easily become incarcerated.

One such person was Mr Lai. He had been an inmate for many years. He arrived illegally from China, carrying a precious stone which he planned to sell to provide income. He was picked up somewhere along the line, imprisoned for infringement of the law, and after finishing his sentence was transferred to the immigration centre, where he was to all intents forgotten. On one of my visits I was told by another inmate of his plight. I was reminded of the cripple who had lain for thirty-six years by a pool in Jerusalem waiting for someone to pick him up and put him in the pool, when the spirit moved across the face of the waters. By the time he found someone to help him others had beaten him to the post, the ripples had ceased, so he had 'missed the boat'. Jesus told him to pick up his bed and walk.

Mr Lai had become institutionalized and had long ago given up any hope of ever being freed, but I promised to try and help him. I was by now a well-known figure at the centre, and as soon as I arrived someone would tell him I was present. A few moments later he would appear with a huge smile on his face, and clapping his hands. I discovered there was a fine to be paid, which wasn't all that much, considering the reward, and I was able to raise the necessary funds without too much trouble.

A bigger problem was to find somewhere for him to live. I

worked very closely with the Roman Catholics, who, being firmly established in the country, had many hospitals, nursing homes and orphanages. There was one such complex near to us, with a wonderful nun in charge. The Mother Superior was very sympathetic about Mr Lai, and agreed to house him if I could get him released. This I was eventually able to achieve, so came the great day when he was given into my care. With huge cheers from the other inmates we embraced, and then, armed with a few tiny possessions, departed to his new home.

I visited him often at first, and was thrilled to see how quickly he settled down. The only thing he asked for was a tiny plot of land, which he quickly turned into a beautiful little garden. He loved nothing more than to tend his little plot and then sit for hours admiring it. He eventually died there, perfectly contented and at peace. Someone else who benefited from the kindness and hospitality of this haven was Katrina, an elderly Russian lady, who became destitute, and was taken in by them. She was the exact opposite, though, from Mr Lai; she was very unhappy and kept saying all she wanted to do was to die! I used to take her Holy Communion, when all she did was to ask me to tell God to take her now to heaven. Not surprisingly she quickly deteriorated, and it was not long before she got her wish. The last time I visited her it was obvious that the end was near, and I offered to stay with her through the night. Mother Superior would have none of it, however, and assured me that she would stay with her during her last hours. I went back the next day, and was actually there when she died. As she breathed her last Mother Superior leaned over her and shouted in a very loud voice, 'Jesus'. 'That would be the last word she heard on earth,' she told me, 'and the first person she would see on the other side.'

Chapter 44

Illegal Burmese in Thailand

My admiration for the Roman Catholic nuns knows no bounds, and I never once went to them for help without receiving it. One instance that stands out from all the rest concerned a young Burmese girl who was illegally in Thailand, having arrived with her Burmese boyfriend. One day she came to my office asking for help. She actually came from a high-ranking family, her father being an important official in the Burmese government. She told her father of her intentions, and despite all his efforts he was unable to dissuade her. He then said that he would not report her missing (which meant that should things not work out well she may be able to sneak back in again). He gave her a considerable sum of money, telling her to tell no one she had it (not even her boyfriend), as it was only to be used to help her return to Burma.

Although the United Nations for Refugees could officially do nothing for the Burmese, they were nevertheless very sympathetic, and fully supported anything we could do for them. The boy got picked up by the police and ended up in the immigration prison. The Thai authorities wanted to get rid of them, so agreed that, provided we could supply the transport, they would be taken up and dropped off at the border. This came to pass on several occasions, and as a consequence the boy friend was one of those taken up to the border and released. His girlfriend then was only about seventeen years of age and was left behind in Bangkok, but through ours and other efforts was able to survive. He returned to Bangkok and they met up again. To add to their problems she became pregnant, and she rang me one day in complete desperation. He had discovered the money she had kept to facilitate her return to Burma, beaten her up, taken the money and left her. (Some time later he ended up for the second time in the immigration prison, but this time I didn't help him at all.)

I immediately went to visit her to see what I could do. I had worked with another group of Catholic Nuns, who I knew took in Thai prostitutes whilst they were having their babies. I said I would ask them if they would take her in whilst she had hers, and I left her with a little money, asking her to ring me in two days' time. The nuns turned up trumps and agreed to take her in, so I arranged to pick her up and take her to the convent. The monsoon season was in full swing, which meant lots of rain and flooding. I arranged to meet her at about 5.30 pm at which time it was pouring with rain. There she was standing by the side of the road with a carrier bag that contained all her earthly possessions. She was soaked to the skin, and looked a terribly pathetic sight, as I drew up. On the way to the convent I did my best to assure her that all would be well. She made me promise I would visit her regularly, which of course I did. Just before we arrived at the convent she said there was something she wanted to ask me.

'Go ahead,' I replied.

'Please, Canon John,' she said, 'can I call my baby son John Taylor after you?'

I said I was extremely honoured by her request, but apart from anything else it might be a girl! She was insistent, however, that it would be a boy and she repeated she wanted to name him after me.

By now we had arrived at the convent. The ground was covered by about 18 inches of water, so the level was some way up the steps leading to the house. I drove my car as close as I possibly could and opened my car door to let her out. Simultaneously the large double doors to the convent swung open and there, framed in the doorway, was Mother Superior. She was a very large lady but with a beautiful face. The rain was teeming down as the Burmese girl advanced up the steps towards her. It was a sight I will never forget. Mother Superior broke into a wonderful smile; she opened her arms wide and embraced the soaking wet girl in her arms, before leading her in. A quick wave to me and the doors closed behind them.

The nuns were as good as their word and there she stayed until after the baby was born. I visited her regularly, including immediately after receiving a call to say the baby was safely delivered. She greeted me with her baby, and I couldn't help but contrast the scene as it was now with the day I took her to the convent. The baby was beautiful, and despite all her assurances that it would be

428

a boy, it turned out to be a girl! She nevertheless begged me to let her call her daughter after me! It wouldn't have been too difficult except for the fact that she wanted the baby to be christened, and me to officiate at the baptism.

So it came to pass that on a Sunday morning not long after the baby was born she brought her to Christ Church for her baptism. I had found three of our congregation willing to be to be godparents for her, and by coincidence all of them were women. This seemed to highlight the fact that she had no man standing by her side, making her look vulnerable and alone. Possibly it was for this reason that she moved as close as possible to me when we arrived at the font. There was a very large congregation present, but only a handful knew anything about her background. Came the moment in the baptism service when I said, 'Name this child,' in a loud clear voice she replied, 'John Taylor'! An audible gasp came from the congregation, followed by an embarrassing silence! 'Hang on everybody,' I called out, 'I can explain everything!' But of course I couldn't!

Baby John Taylor

429

But, unlike so many sad stories regarding refugees, this one had almost a fairy-tale ending. Once the excitement of the baptism had died down, serious thought was given as to the future for mother and daughter. One thing was certain, and that was that it was not in Thailand. The only alternative seemed to be that she should return home to her parents in Burma. This was difficult enough for a single person but for a young mother with a child, the problems increased enormously. There were two main problems. The first was to get them across the border, and the second was to get them back across the country to her home in Rangoon without the authorities finding out that she had left in the first place. Through the work with the Burmese refugees we had acquired many contacts, so it became possible to organize a series of cars to take her and her baby from the border back to her home. But how to get them across the border without being detected was something else. They say 'The Lord works in mysterious ways his wonders to perform' and so it proved.

There were refugee camps on the Burmese side of the border, and the nuns from the Thai side were allowed to cross daily to administer to them. After a while (as this was a daily occurrence) the border guards tended to take less and less notice of them, and usually just waved them through. But unknown to them on this day something was very different. One of the nuns dressed in her habit looked somewhat plumper than was normal, because it wasn't a nun but a Burmese girl clutching her baby. So they set off towards the border with everyone praying that the baby wouldn't cry. She didn't, so with mother and baby surrounded by a circle of nuns, they crossed over the border without incident. The rest, as they say, is history. The convoy of cars across the country also worked well and in due time she was reunited with her parents, and the rest of her family. We waited anxiously to hear that they had arrived back safely, anxiety which changed into joy when we received the good news that all was well. Inevitably, after a while contact ceased, but as far as I know, everyone lived happily ever after.

Sadly not every story had such a happy ending. A member of my congregation called Alan Davies had married a Vietnamese girl and brought her to Bangkok. She was a tiny slip of a girl, who adored him, and they seemed very happy. I was awoken late one night by the telephone, to be told by his distraught wife that there had been an accident and that she thought Alan was dead. Would I please come over at once? On arrival she took me to their bedroom and there, lying in a pool of blood, was Alan. He had a gun in his hand and had obviously shot himself. Although seriously wounded he was still alive so an ambulance was called and he was rushed off to hospital. He survived for about ten days, but never recovered consciousness. She spent hours and hours by his bedside, and seemed completely lost without him. I did what I could, including burning the blood-stained mattress, as well as contacting his relatives in the UK and hers in Vietnam. Without her husband she was in a similar position to a refugee, except for the fact that, through the church members, she was supported and helped in many ways. Through our help she was also repatriated to her own country. Her mother came to Thailand for a short while and insisted on cooking me a wonderful Vietnamese meal, which she cooked on an open fire with us squatting on the paving stones to enjoy. Yet again, after a while I lost contact, but before she left she gave me a little silver ornament, which I treasure to this day. I sometimes think back to my theological college days and the pastoral training received. All I can say is, it didn't cater for what happens to a priest working in Thailand!

Nor did it train you to cope with some of the ethical situations that arose! When I first arrived the fact that I held a British driving licence was sufficient for me to receive a similar one in Thai. Then came a change in the law, when it was decreed that everyone holding a Thai licence had to sit a 'Highway Code' test before being allowed to continue driving in Thailand. The main problem was that the test was in Thai, which meant that for me it was a non-starter!

'No problem,' said a highly respected Thai member of my congregation, 'I have a contact with someone from that section of the police force and will arrange for you to meet him.'

And so it came to pass that I duly arrived at the centre where the tests were held, where I met his friend who just happened to be the officer in charge. He immediately whisked me off to his office where I was offered refreshments. A bell was rung and a sergeant appeared who spoke excellent English, produced a standard form requiring general information and filled it in for me. By now lunchtime was approaching and, to my surprise, the superintendent then said, 'Well now, we're off to lunch and we will deal with the rest upon our return!' So off we went to a marvellous Thai restaurant, where I was wined and dined magnificently. The only problem was I felt even less like taking a test in Thai that I knew awaited me on our return, but I needn't have worried. My friendly sergeant appeared as if by magic, led me to a large hall where about forty people were also taking the test. It was one of those papers with three questions, and one had to tick the right answer. The sergeant sat beside me and pointed out the right box for me to tick, until all the questions were answered. Within ten minutes I was back in the superintendent's office, where he asked me to kindly wait a few minutes while my licence was being prepared.

Sure enough some five minutes later my new Thai licence was in my hand and with lots of wais and thank you's I was on my way. Did I have a guilty conscience? Well, even if I did, I consoled myself with the thought that for most of the time it was my driver, and not me, who would be doing the driving!

This event coincided with a visit from our son, Michael, during one of his school holidays. We always looked forward with tremendous anticipation to our children being with us, and were always amazed to see how much they had both 'sprung up' since we saw them last! It also made us aware that they were indeed growing up in every sense of the word, and prompted me to ask them both what they wanted to do when they left school. Because Michael was three years older than Elizabeth, he was more forthcoming with his views, and expressed the normal jobs that young boys seemed to aspire too. Train driver, pilot, policeman were but three, but being Michael he had to be different also! The first time I asked the question was when he was about nine years old.

'Dad, I want to be a postman,' he enthusiastically exclaimed.

'Why?' I asked.

Back like a rocket came the reply, 'Well, I can read and write, and I can walk. Which means I could be a postman now. So can I stay at home and not go back to school?'

In my heart of hearts I always hoped that he would follow me into the ministry. I never tried to persuade him, although every time I asked the same question, I offered up a silent prayer that I might get the answer I craved. I didn't, until one day he replied, 'When I grow up, Dad, I want to be a Bishop.'

Scarcely able to believe what I was hearing, I asked him, 'Why, son?'

Quick as light came back the answer, 'Because then I can tell you what to do!'

These were the days before women priests so I didn't have the same aspirations for Elizabeth.

Chapter 45

The Garden of Remembrance and Other Developments

On one occasion I called on an expatriate called Tommy Madar. It transpired in conversation that he still had the cremated remains of his deceased wife, actually in a cupboard under the sink! When I asked him why, he said because there was nowhere suitable or appropriate to place them. So was born the idea of building a garden of remembrance in the grounds of Christ Church. There appeared to be some legal problems with interring ashes in the ground, so I investigated the possibility of building a cavity wall with niches in it to contain the ashes. This actually came to pass, although I never in my wildest dreams thought that I would make use of it myself. We developed the garden within the walls and with the addition of some seats it became a little haven within the compound.

The restoration of the old vicarage, improvements to the church, normal maintenance, plus our outreach work, required a lot of fund-raising. Apart from this the British community held a yearly fair in the grounds of the British Embassy to raise funds for Thai charities, including a leper colony. 'The Plunchet Fair' as it was called, grew year by year, to a large extent because of the efforts of Rose, who became the secretary of the organizing committee, and worked tirelessly for the cause.

The great advantage of holding such an event in the grounds of the embassy was that Thai laws could not be enforced within the grounds. Normally, for example, raffles were not allowed. Also a limited amount of duty-free items became available through the kindness of the embassy staff. Impressed with the success of the Plunchet Fair, I asked the ambassador if I could please hold a fête for the church in the grounds? Lady Cole, the ambassador's wife, was a devout member of our congregation, and through her influence my request was granted. The fête proved a great success, but because I was calling on, in the main, the same people and firms as helped in the Plunchet Fair, it did not go down too well with lots of people. The thought then occurred to me – why not try another embassy with different helpers? As the American ambassador at the time had previously been in Laos, and on my church organizing committee, he became the natural target for my request. The US Embassy had never opened its doors before to such a venture, and no one thought I stood a chance of my request being granted. It probably wouldn't have been except for the fact that through my ministry I had become involved with the ambassador in a different context. As they say, 'he owed me one'!

Chapter 46

An Extra Special Case!

As described earlier, it became essential for there to be a general office as well as my private sanctuary because of the amount of confidential counselling that necessitated privacy. It also allowed for some discretion in determining if I needed to cope with any given situation, or if it could be dealt with by someone else. Rose, with the aid of volunteers, efficiently ran the outer office, which relieved me of a huge amount of hassle and saving of time. Inevitably, however, there were many situations when I had to become involved. On this particular morning Rose came into my office and told me, 'There's a man here who wants to see you urgently. I think he's a drunken seaman.'

It became obvious to me that he wasn't drunk but under the influence of drugs. His story was confused and bizarre. He said that he had taken an overdose in an attempt to kill himself, but he came round instead, and as he was living just over the road, he had come to see me. Because of the effect of the drugs it was very difficult to make head or tail of his rambling, but in any case I knew he needed medical assistance immediately. A call to one of my friendly doctors ensured that he was admitted at once to the British Nursing Home next door, where he remained for about ten days.

I visited him regularly and after a few false starts he came out with his story. He was, he said, one of the Americans who were sent into the villages in Vietnam to seek out the communists who lived there and kill them. He said that in the course of his work he had committed many atrocities, and was so ashamed that he had tried to kill himself. He also confessed to being wanted in the States for murder. It was very difficult to determine how much of what he said was true, but what did become very evident was his intense anger for US authority. He then told me that once he was out he was going to assassinate the present ambassador. It put me in a very difficult position of trying to determine whether what he was telling me was 'confessional' or not. As it happened, an American security officer, who also happened to be one of the churchwardens, was actually staying with us before returning to the US at the end of his contract, so I was able to issue a warning through him to the ambassador, and also, to pass on the knowledge that the man in question was (according to him) wanted in the States for murder.

Events then took a strange turn. I received a telephone call from the Matron to say that he had suddenly discharged himself, and left the country. But that was not all, one of the Thai nurses who had been looking after him had gone with him! I immediately informed the embassy of this latest development. They seemed quite relieved that he was no longer with us!

I thought that was the end of the story, until about two weeks later I received a letter from the Thai nurse who said that they were shortly returning to Thailand, and gave the time of arrival of the plane. She said she was terrified of him and wanted to escape, and could I please help her? I informed the embassy of this latest development. They asked me if I would meet him off the plane and take him to the airport cafeteria to a pre-arranged table with a hidden microphone installed. I duly met the couple off the plane and he accepted my suggestion to have a drink before moving on. It was a strange experience to see, as we moved through the various booths, such as passport control, etc, officials watching our every move. From the conversation at the bugged table I, and those listening, learned that they were booked in to a low-class hotel (not one used by the normal tourist trade). He accepted my offer to drop them off at the hotel. Luckily he asked to be excused as he needed the toilet, so this gave me an opportunity to talk to his Thai girlfriend. I told her to ring me at the right moment from her hotel room, and I would come to the hotel and knock on her door. I told her to answer it but to walk straight out whilst I would engage him in conversation so allowing her to get away. He duly returned and we set off in my car for the hotel. Once there I dropped them off and returned to Christ Church compound. In talking to the US officials beforehand, the possibility of him coming to my office had been discussed and as I swung into the compound a powerful light was switched on. As I stopped the car, officials appeared all around me. I confirmed where I had dropped them, and immediately some went to the hotel to question him. When they arrived the receptionist told them that they had indeed called there, but that they had not confirmed their booking and the rooms had been let to someone else. So despite all the planning the trail went cold.

A few days later his girlfriend rang me in total panic. She told me that she was ringing from a hotel room, not far from where they had originally intended to stay; that he had assembled his gun, and was threatening to go off and assassinate the ambassador. She said she was also afraid for her own safety, and could I please help? I told her I would get there as soon as possible, and repeated the drill. I would knock on the door, she was to open it, then keep walking. I was still in a dilemma about how much of what I knew was safeguarded by the confessional, so hesitated to tell my American friend, Bill, of this latest development. As it happened my son Michael was out on holiday at this time, so I told him that if I didn't contact him within the hour he was to tell Bill where I had gone.

I arrived at the hotel shortly afterwards, knocked on the door and nervously waited. A few moments later it opened and there she was with him standing right behind her. He was completely taken by surprise when she stepped past me and ran into the night. He moved to chase but I blocked his path. I then saw he was holding a gun, which he immediately pushed into my stomach. Strangely enough, even as he motioned me inside, closed the front door and pointed for me to precede him up the stairs I felt somehow in control of the situation, so not afraid. He was, I had already surmised, a strange creature lost between fact and fiction. I had been told that enquiries in the States had failed to connect him with any murder or similar crime, but the fact that he had a gun pointing at me left me in no doubt that he was a dangerous character. Nevertheless, I felt that, providing I kept my cool, I could turn the situation round in my favour.

We reached the top of the stairs and entered the bedroom. I sat on the unmade bed, and he sat next to me, still with the gun in his hand, pointing at me.

I said, 'What you are doing is very rude and upsetting. Please put the gun down, although you can always pick it up again if you want to.'

There followed a pregnant pause, after which to my immense relief, he did.

I asked him, 'How come you were able to bring a gun through immigration without detection?'

'That's easy,' he said, 'because this gun can be dismantled into several small pieces.'

'Show me,' was my reply, and after some hesitation he proceeded to do so. The gun chamber had about six bullets and as he turned the drum around, one by one they fell onto the bed.

'Have you any more bullets?' I asked him, and by means of reply he went to a drawer and produced a cardboard box containing about twenty more.

'Well, we won't need them any more today will we?' I said, 'So why not put them all safely away?'

Again, to my immense relief, he did. Then he started telling me about what he had to do when he was in Vietnam, and produced the tools to show how he did it. The first was like two police truncheons, joined together at the top by a leather thong. Its use was simple but effective. One came up behind the victim slipped the thong around his neck, and then with the aid of the two truncheons strangled him. He next produced a cane that, with the flick of a small switch, revealed a knife at the base, which he told me he had often used to kill. He also explained various holds that caused death. Luckily for me he didn't offer to give a demonstration!

He was still very agitated but more rational than when I first saw him at the foot of the stairs. I reasoned with him, saying that the embassy was aware of his presence, and any attempt at assassination would only get him into greater trouble. His Thai girlfriend had fled, so really there was nothing left for him here, so the best thing he could do was to leave the country as soon as possible. I said that through my connections I could probably get him a flight out first thing in the morning, and this is what I strongly advised him to accept. I also said that he might be the subject of a close search by security officers at the airport, so I strongly advised him to get rid of his weapons before going to the airport in the morning. He agreed to go providing I could get him a ticket. I told him that I would confirm the booking for him as soon as possible, and would take him to the airport in the morning.

The US officials just wanted to see the back of him, and the price of a one-way ticket was therefore no problem! Once it was confirmed, I let him know and told him what time I would pick him up in the morning. After which I returned with a sense of great relief to the vicarage.

I was up bright and early the next morning and arrived in plenty of time to take him to the airport. I should add that all this was taking place during the rainy season; that the road to the airport was notorious for flooding, and as a consequence my rather aged car succumbed to the challenge of the water. I sat for a few moments in disbelief and dismay at this unfortunate turn of events, but quickly resolved what to do. I left my car, and vigorously waved down an approaching vehicle. Putting on a brave face I told the driver I was a security official; that I had someone in my car who had to be taken to the airport immediately, and that he had to take him. What were his thoughts I will never know, but what I do know is that he agreed. My passenger changed cars and departed for the airport, and that's the last I ever saw of him. I do know that he was declared 'persona non grata' and to the best of my knowledge never returned to Bangkok.

The US Embassy

As a result of this episode, the US ambassador was extremely grateful, and asked if there was anything he could do for me, which explains why we were able to hold a fête in the grounds of the US embassy later on that year. There was a funny postscript to this drama, which occurred when I visited the US ambassador to confirm details.

Security at all embassies was extremely tight. There were actually steel bars that segregated the consular staff from the main entrance of the embassy. Apart from them there were also US Marines on duty, who screened all callers at the reception area. The ambassador had told me that if ever I was passing and wanted to see him, just pop in and ask for him. Consular staff were always immaculately dressed, as indeed were the marines on duty. On the day in question I happened to be in shorts and an open-necked shirt as I drove past the embassy. On the spur of the moment I decided to pop in so told Joe, my driver, to take me in. There were also guards on duty who normally opened the door for visiting VIPs but when they saw me in shorts and an open-necked shirt, no one even came near! Unperturbed, I ascended the steps leading to the embassy's most impressive entrance. As I entered all eyes seemed to focus on me. They were obviously not used to seeing men in shorts coming through the doors!

I advanced to the reception area, where a huge, immaculate marine sergeant looked at me in a most threatening manner and in a voice full of suspicion asked me what I wanted. The only words I felt were left out were, 'What the hell?' When I said, 'I would like to see the ambassador please,' I thought he was going to have a fit! I don't know whether or not he pressed some sort of alarm button but I do know that suddenly even more eyes appeared to be on me.

He picked up a phone, pressed a button, and then said in a most apologetic tone, 'I'm sorry to bother you, but some (I didn't hear the next few words but think they were something like a nut case) is asking to see the ambassador.' A few seconds passed before he asked me, 'What is your name?'

'Canon John,' I replied.

This information he grudgingly passed along the line. There was a short pause before he said to me, 'Wait'. A few moments later, an efficient-looking lady descended the stairs behind the barrier, pressed a button, which opened a door through it and advanced towards me with a charming smile. 'Hello, Canon John,' she said, 'please come with me.'

I cast a superior glance at the hapless marine before I swept past him and ascended the staircase. The ambassador greeted me warmly, and indeed I was with him for about an hour, as there were many things he also wanted to discuss. When the time came for me to leave, he insisted on escorting me down the stairs, through the barrier, and out to my car. What is more he opened my car door for me, all this before the rather incredulous eyes of the marine who had greeted me so differently! I couldn't help giving him a triumphant glance as I sped away.

Because of my friendship with the ambassador I found myself on the invitation list to several functions hosted by him. One I remember vividly was to lunch at the embassy on the occasion of an American VIP visiting Bangkok: Mr Kissinger, if I remember correctly. This was obviously not a shorts and open-necked shirt occasion, so properly attired, I drove into the grounds of the embassy, squeezed between two huge limousines and came to a halt. This time with no hesitation a marine opened my door for me, and there was the ambassador with a friendly hand outstretched to greet me. Greetings over I was immediately handed a glass of ice-cold champagne before mixing with the other guests. The lunch was delicious, as were the wines, so the next hour and a half passed extremely pleasantly. The luncheon ended and I returned to my house, but as I did a shameful realization almost took my breath away. I recalled that it was Ash Wednesday, and that before even the first morning had passed I had broken my vow of abstaining from alcohol during Lent.

Chapter 47

Indo-China Refugees

Christ Church had been given a grant to help us in our efforts for refugees on behalf of the UN, and had opened up 'The Relief and Welfare Committee Account' with a Bangkok bank. I should explain that the UN High Commissioner for Refugees tended to work through existing charities. Our small committee, consisting of Fathers Brennan, Maier and myself, was the only charity registered at that time, so we became the official organization through which relief and help were given to thousands of refugees from Vietnam, Cambodia and Laos. The members of my congregation responded magnificently to my request for volunteers to turn Christ Church into a reception area The old vicarage became the obvious centre for the work, and was immediately opened from 8.30 in the morning till 5.30 in the evening. But long before 8.30 am there were queues of hapless people milling in the grounds waiting to be helped.

Our task was, first of all to register them, deal with any emergencies, such as chronic sickness, find accommodation either at hospitals, hostels and (later) camps that were set up. We gave them some cash and clothes so that they could buy something to eat; tried to answer questions, and then sent them on their way. Our account was originally set up requiring two signatures before we could draw money, but after a short while necessity dictated that this safeguard was abandoned, and I was given permission to draw whatever I needed on my signature only. A special teller was allocated to deal with my requests, and I was thrilled when, about three months later, when some sort of normality was resumed, and after thousands of baht had passed through our hands, an audit found that there was only about 100 baht that had seemed to have gone astray. When one considers that I withdrew thousands of baht in any one day, that it was administered by members of my congregation, most of whom were housewives without any book-

443

keeping experience, I think that was a miraculous result.

We learnt as we went along. The first thing I organized was refreshments for my helpers, who worked ceaselessly for hours on end, until they themselves stopped it.

'We can't sit here drinking tea,' they told me, 'when these poor souls before us haven't drunk anything at all.' The next step, then, was to set up some sort of refreshment for the refugees themselves. But when one realizes that we were no more than volunteers without any previous experience in such matters, I consider it amazing that we were able to do what we did. Between June and September 1975, three and a half thousand people were referred to our committee from the United Nations Representative for Refugees.

Not unsurprisingly my name became synonymous with refugee help, and as I walked and worked among them I was immediately recognized and, unfortunately, revered. I became acutely embarrassed by this, so much so that after about two months I felt it imperative to get away from it all by going on retreat. I announced to my congregation that after Evensong the next Sunday I would spend the next four days and nights in Christ Church fasting (my good

Christ Church becomes a reception area

444

The hand of fellowship

'Suffer the little children'

A MAN WITH A MISSION

NATIONS UNIES

HAUT COMMISSARIAT
POUR LES RÉFUGIÉS

Délégation pour l'Asie du Sud-Est

Télégrammes: HICOMREF Bangkok
Téléphone 51 15 52-2

UNITED NATIONS

HIGH COMMISSIONER
FOR REFUGEES

Office of the Regional Representative
for South-East Asia

B.P. 618 - BANGKOK, Thaïlande

12 September 1975

Dear Canon Taylor,

    I should like to take the opportunity presented by my visit to Thailand to thank your Committee for their kindness in undertaking on behalf of my Office the administration of a care and maintenance project for displaced persons from Indochina in the Bangkok area.

    As you know, in the last few months my Office in Thailand has been facing an emergency situation of unprecedented proportions. It has been a source of great comfort to my staff and to me that we were able to use the Committee as an operational partner in channelling humanitarian assistance to the large number of displaced persons residing in the Bangkok area who have approached my Regional Office for temporary relief pending solutions to their problems.

    I understand that in the period between June and September 1975 more than 3,500 persons have been referred to your Committee by my Representative. Despite the limited administrative and other personnel resources at the disposal of the Committee it has risen to the challenge in a splendid manner, providing material support and advice to the needy, humanely and effectively. In this connection, I should like to place on record my deep appreciation of the devoted efforts of the large number of volunteers whom your Committee has been able to mobilize in the service of these unfortunate persons.

    Yours sincerely,

Sadruddin Aga Khan

The Rev. Canon John R. Taylor, OBE., OCF.,
Chairman, Relief and Welfare Committee,
Christ Church,
The Parsonage,
11 Convent Road,
BANGKOK.

friend Dr Colin Britton insisted that there was a bare minimum which I needed to eat and drink, and to which I grudgingly agreed). So, after Sunday evensong, the church was locked for the night with me safely inside. I have always enjoyed writing but due to the recent pressure of work I had been unable to do so. This meant there was a lot of work (parish magazine, bulletins, reports, sermons and addresses, to say nothing of unanswered correspondence) to catch up on. I entered the church well equipped with everything necessary to carry out these tasks. I also wanted to make my confession, so asked Father Joe if he would kindly come in on Monday morning (9.30 was the time agreed) to hear it.

No sooner had the doors shut than I began writing. I had brought with me a new pad of foolscap paper, and before long the first page was full and I moved on to the second. I became so absorbed with my writing that the whole night passed with me hardly ever putting down my pen. It was only when dawn broke and the windows let in the early morning light that I realized my first night had gone. By the time I had a wash and said my morning offices more time had passed, and I realized with a start that before long Father Joe would be with me to hear my confession. Because he was a Roman Catholic priest and would, I presumed, expect a 'proper confessional' including a chair for him and a kneeler for me, I hastily set one up. I also realized that I hadn't made any notes to help me in my confession. So I picked up my foolscap pad, drew a line under what I had been writing all night (some fourteen pages of it) and made the necessary notes for my confession. I then renewed my place on the communion rail and waited for him to arrive.

Actually I didn't hear him come in and the first I knew of his presence was when he knelt down beside me, put his arms around my shoulders and said, 'How's my old friend John?' As he was coming to hear my confession I had anticipated a more formal approach, so tried to rectify it by telling him I had set up the confessional, and called him Father.

'There's nothing wrong with where we are,' he replied, 'so let's get on with it.'

I picked up my foolscap pad and started turning the pages to reach to my confessional notes.

Joe watched me with a look of fascination on his face. 'What – all that lot?' he exploded. 'I haven't got time to hear all that!'

Mustering all the dignity I could find I told him that my confession was just the few lines I had written at the end of the pages of foolscap.

'Thank goodness,' was his only comment.

I have made my confession on a few occasions before, and in more formal conditions, but none of them helped me more than this one. When we were finished he put his arm around me, gave me a special blessing, was up and gone. All that was left for me to do was to dismantle the temporary confessional that I had needlessly set up. There was, of course, plenty left to consider during the rest of my retreat. On top of the agenda was how best we could continue to help the refugees.

The rest of the retreat passed extremely quickly and before I knew it Thursday morning had come. After a celebration of Holy Communion which many parishioners attended, I left the church, had a shower and my favourite meal of shepherd's pie and went to bed. My lasting memory of that time in church was the awesome realization that I was utterly alone in the presence of Almighty God, stripped bare of any pretence, unable to be anything other than what you are, your soul laid bare in the presence of one's creator. Without having made my confession at the beginning of the retreat, I do not believe I could have finished it.

Chapter 48

The Plight of the Cambodian Orphans

The influx of refugees in 1975 from Cambodia, Vietnam and Laos meant suffering of unprecedented proportions to all concerned. Not only were they in a distressed state when they arrived, but the horror of what they had gone through before they fled to the sanctuary which Thailand offered had affected them deeply. The killing fields of Cambodia left scars especially amongst the young who had witnessed the slaughter of their own parents and families. This haunted their minds during the day, and in nightmares, as darkness fell. As well as the help our little group at Christ Church was able to give, we also became aware of the plight of refugees in the camps hastily set up by the goodness and compassion of the Thai people. In the early days, there was a lot to be desired in the organization and running of them. Not least that amongst the refugees were members of the Potpol, who had committed the atrocities. As a result there was some intimidation in the camps.

I particularly remember one Friday morning, which was already committed to many tasks, that Rose informed me that there was a Mr Robert Ashe asking to see me. Robert turned out to be a very likeable young man, who had come out to Thailand on behalf of a charity started by his father called 'Project Vietnam Orphans'. Patrick Ashe, an Anglican priest, had been very moved by a television programme showing the suffering of Vietnamese children, and determined to do something about it. The project later extended its charter to help all Asian orphans, so on hearing that there were twelve Cambodian refugees in one of the refugee camps in Thailand, Robert was sent out to see if there was anything they could do to ease their suffering.

Others in the UK had also heard of their plight, and had travelled to Thailand with the same objective in mind. One such lady was Mrs Eileen Gough. She ran 'The Cambodian Children's Welfare

Association'. She arrived before Robert Ashe, and made considerable progress regarding the care and future of the twelve. The lady in question went to the British Embassy in Bangkok, and was given a letter requesting she be given all help necessary in her endeavours to help lndo China orphans. Such a letter on official paper at that particular time proved extremely useful, and she was given total access to the children concerned. She had already obtained the names of good folk who were willing to adopt the children back in the UK. Furthermore, some had paid her certain sums of money to ensure that the child would be given to them. One such couple were the Elders, who gave her £300 to cover her air fares to Thailand, and were promised that Phala (one of the twelve) would shortly come to them. Mr and Mrs B Shaw gave Mrs Gough £300 to fly two of the children back to the UK. Indeed, within a very short time she had allocated all the children to different homes, and had sent photos of them back to the UK. She had arrived armed with photos of the prospective parents and had already shown photos to the children of their new mummies and daddies.

All this Robert conveyed to me in my office, as he considered there were many irregularities in all that was going on. He was depressed, and said because of the progress already made there was nothing he could do to stop the process; as far as he was concerned it was 'mission impossible', so he was flying back to the UK in three days' time. I tackled him about this. If he was so convinced that what she was doing was not in the best interest of the children, shouldn't he stay on to fight? I suggested that he went away and thought about it, then, if he changed his mind, to come back to me on Monday morning, in which case I would do my best to help him.

Robert did return on the Monday morning, and with my help he had decided to stay and fight the cause. Investigations seemed to support Robert's claims, and we were able to halt the progress, which involved painful meetings, and difficult letters to prospective families back in the UK. But nothing compared to the day when I assembled the twelve children together to tell them that the arrangements so far made had now fallen through, and the photos they had of their new mothers and fathers were no longer correct. Leakhena, who was the eldest of the twelve, and had a brother and a sister in the group, became their natural leader. On entering Thailand she had lowered her age by two years, so that she could remain with the others. She exerted a maturity long beyond her years, and the other children trusted and obeyed her. She spoke excellent English, and I was confident that she would pass on any information that I gave her correctly to the others. In the meantime, Mrs Gough had moved them to a tiny apartment in Bangkok which was totally unsuitable for their needs.

On 24th October 1975 I wrote a letter to my parishioners outlining my plans and naming needs. It included the renting of a large apartment or house; volunteers who would be prepared to visit the children regularly, so establishing a worthwhile relationship; to set up a school, including English classes; activities to keep them occupied, such as sewing, cooking, model-making and exercises; history and hygiene; a gradual introduction to English food and eating habits; clothing, including shoes for those who had none, and all of them needed suitcases. There were also more basic requirements, such as using western-style toilets, and general hygiene. The response was instantaneous and generous. As a consequence, and after meeting with my church council, it was agreed that we would rent a house in Bangkok, under the umbrella of Christ Church and 'Project Vietnam Orphans'. We would set up a school and employ a suitable housekeeper to look after them. In a surprisingly short time all the arrangements and formalities were completed, and amid great excitement and joy they moved in. The congregation at Christ Church produced some excellent teachers, so the school flourished. Apart from running a school, friendly doctors were marvellous and gave their services free.

On top of this, many of our families took the children home for the weekend, or out on treats. It was heartening to see the change in the children as life returned to something nearer normal. Nevertheless, this could only be a temporary solution to the rest of their lives, and so, with the aid of Robert Ashe, the lot fell on me to try and find a permanent home for them all. In the UK, before adoption can be completed there are many complicated procedures to go through including suitability tests, medical examinations and many interviews. There was no such system in operation for refugees in Thailand, and I found the responsibility of making sure the right family got the right child (or children) onerous in the extreme. Particularly difficult was to find someone prepared to take on Leakhena, and her brother and sister, but in the end families were found for them all. By the time the last left

Baptism of the 12 Cambodian orphan children at Christ Church

I felt a great personal loss as I had grown extremely fond of them. I was particularly pleased that I was able to place two of them with a family who had originally applied through Mrs Gough to adopt a child. We were particularly blessed in that Tim and Fran Lewis (a Canadian expatriate family in Bangkok) adopted Leakhena and her brother and sister, so we were able to keep all three together.

I have two outstanding memories of them. The first was preparing them all for, and then baptizing them, at a wonderful service at Christ Church.

The second was on Christmas Day. We always looked out for any who would be alone at Christmas and invited them to lunch. My children were also with us for Christmas so in all about twenty-four of us sat down for a magnificent meal prepared by Et, our

Robert Ashe and Chris Hall with the children after their baptism

cook. As with many families, one of the highlights on Christmas Day was toasting 'absent friends', and as a consequence there were wine glasses laid out for all the adults. I wanted the children to share in this ceremony, but because of their age, only put tiny sherry glasses before them, fondly believing that such a tiny drop wouldn't affect them! At the appropriate moment, after explaining to the children the reason for it, we all drank to 'absent friends'. This was in fact the first time in their lives that any of them had even tasted alcohol, and within a very short time we had twelve little children decidedly the worse for drink! One by one they slipped off their chairs – lay on the floor and fell asleep! They all looked so peaceful that we decided to leave them there. After about twenty minutes, one by one they awoke, climbed back on their chairs and carried on as if nothing had happened. I had nightmares because I was at this time interviewing parents to see that they were suitable for adopting. I had visions of them arriving and seeing the children in this state whilst under my care.

Such was the chaotic state of things in those early days that some who came into the camp as orphans were later found to have parents still alive. In almost every case, however, the child stayed on in the new home, where security and education were ensured. This was also the case with Leakhena, her brother and sister. The last word on the children I leave with her. She graduated from school and college and then returned to work for the same refugees from which she was taken.

I value to this day a poem she wrote, addressed to me. Considering her age (15 or 16, I think) and previous experiences, the depth of spirituality is awesome. There were some who questioned whether it was right to baptize the children at this stage of their lives and so quickly. I can only reply that in my entire ministry I have never found a deeper level of spirituality in those so young, and after reading this, who could doubt that she and indeed all of them were more than ready for baptism?

To Uncle John,

I praise you Lord when I was lost and you found me,
I praise you Lord when I feel your everlasting love,
I praise you Lord when I am in love and feel being on top
   of the highest Mountain,
I praise you Lord when I lost everything, my home-country,
   my beloved ones,
I praise you Lord when I am deep in the valley of life!
I praise you Lord when I am in time of trials
I praise you Lord when I am with strangers,
I praise you Lord when I am among your lambs,
I praise you Lord to be our shepherd,
I praise you Lord when I wake up, light-hearted and so thankful
   for your glorious and amazing creations,
I praise you Lord when I see the blue sky touching the remote
   sea, when I hear
The birds singing happily, when the sunlight warms me up,
   when the cool breeze
Gently blows my hair,

I praise you Lord whenever I can talk about you and call for
your mercy,

I praise you Lord when you bring light to those broken hearts
and love to lonely ones,

I praise you Lord when you take everything away from me
so I need more of You.

O Father, here I am, please take me home, guide me, use me,

O Lord I want to love you more and more each passing day,

O Father how wonderful to praise you!

O Lord I need more of you!

Thank you father for teaching me to love and to give away,

I praise you Lord for your wonderful love and everlasting
words

I praise you Lord because you are the truth, the way and the
life!

With much love Leakhena xx.

Leakhena (the self-appointed 'mother' of the orphans)

455

Sadly, one of the twelve had been so badly traumatized by what he had gone through, that he became insane, and died shortly afterwards. What a terrible waste of a young life. Bho Pa, on the other hand, another of the orphans, was adopted by a wonderful family in the UK, so we were able to keep contact with her when we returned home on leave.

Prayers for peace in Cambodia

Apart from our work with the children and other refugees who still made their way to Bangkok, I also became involved in the wider issue, working to restore peace in the countries affected. So

MISSIONARIES OF CHARITY

54A LOWER CIRCULAR ROAD, CALCUTTA-700016

"As long as you did it to one of these My least brethren. You did it to Me"

30th May, 1980

The Rev Canon J.R. Taylor OBE
Khmer Council of Religion For Peace
Christ Church,
11 Convent Road,
Bangkok 5, Thailand

Dear Rev Taylor,

Thank you for your letter of 15th May,80 inviting Mother Teresa to the World Day of Prayer For Peace in Kampuchea on the weekend of 7/8th June.

Mother Teresa has gone abroad and will be in Germany on the 7th and 8th of June. We are sending her your letter and are sure she will be with you in spirit and prayer.

You will be happy to know that we are opening a house in Korea in the near future to bring God's love and compassion to the refugees.

We assure you of our prayers and those of our poor for peace in Kampuchea - true peace - that comes from love and caring and from respecting the rights of every human being.

Yours sincerely in Christ,

Sr M. Frederick M.C.

456

was formed the concept of holding a day of prayers for peace in the two main refugee camps, Sa-Kaeo and Khao-I-Dang refugee centres, which held twenty-eight and fifty thousand souls respectively. It took place on 7th/8th June 1980, and arose out of a previous visit to the camps in April 1980. At the request of the Umer refugees, a small group of us including Phra Maha Ghosananda, the senior Kampuchean monk who was deeply revered by his people, and Roman Catholic Archbishop Michai Kitboonchu visited the camps, and agreed to hold a day of prayer for peace involving as many worldwide religious leaders as possible. I was appointed convenor and, apart from organizing events for the day, wrote to as many world religious leaders as I could. In the end about a hundred and twenty people from the Buddhist, Muslim and Christian faiths made the journey. Because of the shortage of time very few leaders from other countries were able to attend, but we did receive messages of encouragement and support (which were read out to

MESSAGE FROM HIS HOLINESS POPE JOHN PAUL II TO
KAMPUCHEAN PRAYERS FOR PEACE AT SA-KAEO AND KHAO-I-DANG

During his weekly noon address on Sunday, 8th June, 1980 to the crowds in St. Peter's Square, Rome, His Holiness Pope John Paul II made special mention of the plight of the Kampuchean Refugees - expressed his concern and called for United Prayers on their behalf and for Peace in Kampuchea.

He said:

"I AM INFORMED THAT TODAY THE KAMPUCHEAN REFUGEES ARE HOLDING A DAY OF PRAYER FOR PEACE.

I UNITE MYSELF WILLINGLY WITH THEM AND INVITE ALL OF YOU TO DO THE SAME, IN ORDER TO UNITE IN COMMON PRAYER TO GOD WE EXPRESS OUR BROTHERHOOD AND OUR CONCERN FOR THOSE WHO ARE IN NEED.

I WISH TO ASSURE ALL THE KAMPUCHEAN REFUGEES AS WELL AS THOSE FROM OTHER COUNTRIES THAT I AM VERY NEAR TO THEM WITH MY LOVE AND THAT I CONSTANTLY REMEMBER THEM TO THE LORD TOGETHER WITH ALL THOSE WHO ARE AFFLICTED. PARTICULARLY I THINK OF THE CHILDREN AND OF THEIR INNOCENT SUFFERING.

LET US PRAY THAT THE ASPIRATIONS OF ALL THOSE PEOPLE FOR PEACE MAY BE REALISED, AND THAT THE WORLD MAY BECOME MORE HUMAN AND MORE CHRISTIAN.

THE DALAI LAMA

THEKCHEN CHOLING
DHARMSALA CANTT
KANGRA DISTRICT
HIMACHAL PRADESH

MESSAGE

I am glad to learn that a special 'All Faith
Prayer Gathering' will be held for the suffering
refugees of Kampuchea and I highly appreciate your
kind invitation to me. I earnestly pray for the
success of this special prayer congregation. I
would also like to take this opportunity to convey
a brief message.

It is indeed unbearable to see the Kampuchean
refugees undergoing tremendous sufferings. Let
me, at this critical juncture, express some important
Buddhist views. We believe that past actions influence
one's present circumstances and that one's present
acts will determine one's future: that man determines
his own fate. One should not be discouraged by
cruel circumstances. As Buddhists we believe in the
law of cause-and-effects or Karma, that is, virtuous
deeds will overcome evil deeds. Therefore, sufferings
and harsh circumstances can be overcome if one has
the will, the correct mental attitude and follows
the right path. Feeling discouraged or dejected
over difficult circumstances will not help to free
yourself from the onslaught of sufferings. It is,

2/-

458

THE PLIGHT OF THE CAMBODIAN ORPHANS

therefore, of paramount importance to counter the
assault of sufferings with a bold and enlightened
mind.

We Tibetans also face a similar difficult period
and this is exactly what the Tibetan people are trying
to do today.

Lord Buddha, for the welfare of others, faced
untold sufferings over an interminably long time, and
ultimately attained Enlightenment. We should face
sufferings with the same indomitable will. Then and
only then will we be able to exterminate the root
cause of all sufferings. We must, therefore, seek
refuge in the Triple Precious Gems and strive hard
to develop a strong will, brotherhood and altruism.
It is my firm belief that this will bring lasting peace
and happiness for the entire human race.

I earnestly pray that the suffering refugees of
Kampuchea will soon be free from your present sufferings
and ultimately will reach the realm of eternal peace
and happiness.

June 3, 1980

the refugees on the day) from His Holiness Pope John Paul II,
Mother Teresa, The Archbishop of Canterbury and the Dalai Lama.

On behalf of the committee I also wrote to other church leaders,
and received verbal support from many. Someone whom I didn't
get a reply from, however, was the Roman Catholic Archbishop
Sin of the Philippines. I did receive a news flash however to say
that he had just been exalted as a cardinal. We joked that it was
a cardinal sin that he didn't reply!

The schedule for the day was very challenging:

Sa-Kaeo: 9.30 Buddhist meditations
               10.00 United Christian Act of Witness.
Khao–I–Dang: 12.30 Muslim Prayers for Peace
               1.00 Buddhist Meditation
               2.00 United Christian Act of Witness,
               2.30 Meeting religious leaders and Khmer
                     Council

To me was accorded the honour and the responsibility of addressing more than fifty thousand Khmer refugees at the largest camp at Khao-I-Dang. A noticeable feature at the service was traditional Thai music played by Roman Catholic nuns. After the service, Phra Maha Ghosananda introduced a period of silence which was followed by Umer dancing. Monks are not normally touched (and never by women), so I was utterly amazed that when the dancing was finished Ghosandanda (who was not much more than skin and bones) suddenly lifted me up in front of the vast congregation. A spontaneous loud roaring, cheering and clapping erupted all around. He then signalled to the other leaders to join us and we circulated through the vast crowds, with great veneration being shown to all.

Preaching to a congregation of 50,000

460

The banners tell it all

The women also out in force

The meeting held after the service reiterated a request for the world leaders to visit them, and called for an end to violence in Kampuchea through disarmament supervised by the UN. It thanked the Thai government for its open-door policy, and asked for better conditions in the camps.

As I have mentioned elsewhere, the Rev Chad Varah, who was in Thailand to officially open the Samaritans of Bangkok, came with us to the camps. He was deeply moved by the experience and began his sermon at Christ Church the following morning by saying, 'Yesterday I saw the face of Jesus Christ fifty thousand times on the faces of Khmer refugees.'

Chapter 49

Some Unusual Confessions

'Confession' is conceived by most in a 'catholic' sense. Usually held within the confines of a confessional box in a church, priest and penitent separated by a partition with a grille at face level, all taking place in semi-darkness, and with anonymity strictly observed, so that the priest is not necessarily even aware of who it is making the confession. It was with this concept in mind that I would prepare for Father Joe. These days, 'confessional' has been extended to include doctors, solicitors and social workers. The work of the Samaritans has extended this concept even further, but hearing a confession in a Bangkok bar stretches the concept further still. Let me explain.

One evening at about 8.30 pm (a time when usually the phone became a little quieter), the silence was shattered by what seemed to me were particularly strident rings. I picked it up to hear background music playing; not of the usual type heard on such occasions but rather of a seedy and sexual nature. Then, over the noise of the background music came an educated English voice, which I immediately recognized as belonging to one of the well-known expatriates who had been in the news recently by marrying into a high-class Thai family. He was a bachelor of rather mature age, had been in Bangkok for many years, and had enjoyed all the perks that went with that situation. It came as no little surprise when he decided to put that all behind him and get married. I recognized his voice immediately, even if it were a little blurred by drink!

'Can I speak to the vicar?' were his opening words, and once he established that it was me, he burst into tears.

I offered some soothing and compassionate words, after which the tears abated and then he said, 'Vicar, I need to make my confession before I go home'. He didn't say why, but the sleazy music in the background gave me a good clue.

Rose, who had been busily engaged in preparing our supper, then appeared on the scene, wagged her finger at me and said, 'You're not doing anything or going anywhere until you've had your supper!' The look on her face brooked no argument so I told him to come to the church at 9 pm, when I would hear his confession.

This brought on a fresh wave of tears, followed by, 'Father, I'm too ashamed to come to the church, so would you please come to me?'

'Where are you?' I asked, after which he named one of the popular bars in Patpong.

Patpong was the centre of the red light district, only about 400 yards from the church, and very much part of my parish. Reluctantly I agreed that I would come and find him and to expect me in just over half an hour. A rather hasty but delicious supper was quickly consumed, and then, after Rose had read me the riot act about being careful, I set off to Patpong. The bar in question was rather like one of the American bars of the good old cowboy days, complete with swing doors. I entered and was immediately aware of the difference between the bright lights outside and the acute dimness within. So much so that, for a few moments, I couldn't see a thing. Then torchlight was shone onto my face, and a lady's voice said, 'Welcome darling'! As my eyes adjusted to the light, I could see that it wasn't only light that was in short supply. My hostess was carrying a torch and very little else! At best she could be described as wearing a very skimpy bikini.

I realized that this was time for strong and forcible action, so I explained that I had only come to look for a friend whom I believed was in the bar.

'I'll be your friend,' she immediately replied in sultry tones, but I declined her invitation for the second time in as many seconds in terms that broached no argument. At this her attitude changed, and with an air of resignation she led me inside. The seating in the bar resembled that of the train carriages of my youth. Seats for two or three either side with a table in the middle. As we moved down the bar she shone her torch into the various compartments to see if my friend was there. Just as well he wasn't, because as a married man he definitely shouldn't have been involved in what I witnessed as we progressed down the bar. At the far end of the room there was a small stage, and it wasn't until we reached the last compartment next to it that we found him.

464

He was alone as far as human company was concerned, which was just as well, because with all the empty beer bottles that surrounded him there wasn't a lot of space left! I should explain that expatriates who frequented such bars often had their own little wooden blocks with their names printed on, which was produced on arrival. The empty bottles were counted up at the end so they only had to pay once. His printed name plus the number of empty bottles was proof positive that I had found my man. I sat opposite him and declined a drink, but listened to his tale of woe. Being a confession I cannot disclose what it was, but I suspect that would not be necessary anyway. What was certain, and is necessary before an absolution can be given, was his sincerity in being sorry for what he had done. I pointed out that this was neither the right time nor the place for such ministry, but after receiving his assurance that he would come and see me in the morning at church, I agreed to listen to what he had to say.

All went well for a few minutes, but then I sensed that somehow I had lost him. To help my concentration I had closed my eyes, which I now opened and focused on him. I immediately knew my suspicions were correct. His eyes were glued to what was happening on the stage only a few feet away. It was of an intimate sexual nature. Again I cannot describe all that was going on, so you must rely on your imagination to complete the picture. What I can say is that it was not conducive to making a confession.

'Stop!' I cried, and he did. I did some quick thinking, and came up with an obvious solution. 'Swap seats with me,' I commanded, and he did. The trouble was that now in front of my very eyes was going on what, only seconds before, his eyes had been avidly devouring. I decided therefore that I would keep my eyes firmly on the floor. But as I did I saw what I can only describe as two saucers glaring up at me. As any Bangkok resident will confirm, many places are infested with rats, and looking up at me was one of them, surely the largest I have ever seen. I couldn't look up, I couldn't look down, and I was too scared to shut my eyes. I tried lifting my feet up into the lotus position, but that didn't work either, so with a great sense of relief (I suspect to both of us), the whole exercise was aborted, until the following morning.

Another harrowing event arose out of an entirely different situation. The Christians from Goa are very religious, faithful in church attendance and Christian commitment. We had about five such

465

families worshipping at Christ Church, most of whom worked for the United Nations. At about 6 pm one evening one of them rang me in a very agitated state.

'Can I please come and see you immediately?' he pleaded.

'Where are you?' I asked, thinking that it might be better if I went to him.

'I'm at the airport,' he replied. 'I've just come off a plane from the Philippines, and I can't go home to my family until I've been to see you.'

He arrived about half an hour later in a very distressed state. Whilst in Manila, he told me he went to visit one of those 'doctors' who claimed to be able to operate without any instruments, curing patients of their ills. He said it was fascinating to see the woman at work, and that he couldn't believe what he was seeing with his own eyes. She appeared to put her hand into the chest of the patient and bring out a cancerous growth. But even as he witnessed what appeared to be a miracle, he was overwhelmed with a sense of evil and shame that he had come to witness her at work. He felt he had been completely possessed by evil, so begged me to exorcise him there and then.

Going home as he was, he believed, would contaminate all his family too, and they would also become affected. He made his confession, after which I carried out exorcism, followed by more prayers and counselling. I had never been involved in such a situation before, nor was I aware of the complete ritual to follow, but it must have been along the right lines as he departed in peace, leaving me, however, feeling like a nervous wreck!

On another occasion I was working in my office at about 8.30 in the evening, when I noticed from its headlights that a car had entered the church compound. I vaguely wondered who it might be, but was surprised when I saw who it actually was. He was a very well-known member of the congregation, hard-working, but very aggressive, and if the truth be known, not a very happy person. Within a few minutes I realized that, although not drunk, he had certainly been drinking. Probably had just come from one of the numerous cocktail parties that were part and parcel of Bangkok life. This loosened his tongue, gave him Dutch courage, which was just as well as he obviously wanted to talk. It transpired that he wanted to make his confession. Confessions cannot be revealed, but I can say that what he was confessing went back to the war years, and had worried him ever since. Again it wasn't the most perfect of confessions, but it was totally sincere, and I had no hesitation in giving him absolution. I can also say without hesitation that he was a totally different person afterwards, and I had an inward chuckle and praised the Lord when I heard more than one person say, 'What's come over ... lately? He seems to be an entirely different sort of person now.'

Chapter 50

Some Very Special Parishioners

Herbert and Alma Link

One of the challenges of ministering to a largely expatriate community is the extraordinary turnover of one's congregation. Most ex-pats are on contract, often for three years, but that does not mean that they always see it out. Takeover bids, company reorganization, resignations, can result in a sudden departure. At one time it got so difficult that one had to be certain (or as certain as possible) that residence in Thailand would be at least for another year before accepting any church office, such as serving on the PCC.

Others had made Thailand their home, and one such family were the Links; Herbert was German, Alma was English. He had built up a very successful business in Bangkok, whilst she had the great distinction of being the only expatriate to be made a Kun Ying (the equivalent of a Dame in the British honours list). She had been so honoured for her efforts in supporting charitable works with Buddhist monks, and especially for a revered and famous Abbot, whom she had singled out for her charitable work. In recognition of her work for him, the abbot had presented his food bowl to Alma. Made of empty tins welded together, it had been painted with gold motifs and Alma treasured it. Talking of treasures, their house was crammed with those that they had accumulated during their many years in Thailand. The firm had been extremely successful and their house, grounds, furniture and artefacts reflected this fact. For many reasons we became very good friends of the Links, and Rose and I were often guests at their house for fabulous meals, always with extremely exalted and interesting people.

Although well into their eighties, they decided to return to Germany, and many parties and receptions were held in their honour, some of which we attended. One day we received a call from Alma saying that they wanted us alone to have a meal with them at their house. Their parties usually consisted of about twelve people so we were surprised to learn that there would only be the four of us on this occasion. After the meal was over we found out why. 'We are, as you know, returning to spend our remaining days in Germany. Our house there is already furnished so we are going to dispose of most of our bits and pieces. Herbert and I have decided to give you first choice of anything you like, whether that is furniture, an antique, in fact anything at all!' We were understandably flabbergasted by this incredibly generous offer, in fact speechless.

Having been a guest in their house on many previous occasions we were aware of many of their treasures, had long admired them, but never in our wildest dreams had we ever envisaged that one day we might become the proud owner of one of them. 'We realize that this might be a bit of a shock,' said Alma, 'so take your time in choosing and then just let us know.' Still in somewhat of a daze we stuttered our thanks and took our leave. Once we arrived home we realized the enormity of their kind offer, being aware that some of the items were extremely valuable. As so often happened in such circumstance Rose passed the choice over to me. One piece of furniture that I had always admired was a Chinese antique solid jade cabinet, the value of which I couldn't even begin to contemplate. I told Rose of my choice, to which she agreed. But when it came to telling the Links of our choice, courage failed me, even though their last word on the subject was, 'We really want you to have exactly what you want.' So the next time we saw her came the moment of truth.

'Alma, we have decided that we want whatever you think we would treasure most, so can we please leave the choice to you.'

'I'll think about it, and let you know,' was her reply. A few days later her car swung into the church compound and out came a servant clutching an object wrapped beautifully as only the Thais can wrap them. The first thing I realized was that because of its size it wasn't the jade cabinet. Also because of its lightness it wasn't one of the antiques. So with undue haste I tore off the paper wrapping to reveal the Abbot's bowl! Beautifully decorated it was, but only tin cans welded together nevertheless! The only consolation; it's proved a good talking point over the years when someone asks me what it was!

469

Connie Mangskau

Another well-known character was Connie Mangskau. Her mother married a ship's Captain and for some reason they set up home in Bangkok. Connie lived all her life in Bangkok and, by coincidence, also married a ship's Captain. Neither husband figures in the story, as they both died very young. Connie became interested and involved in Thai antiques, set up shops in three of the major hotels and elsewhere, and as a consequence became exceedingly rich. We often used to go to her house for meals, and were fascinated by the antiques there. Although not a regular churchgoer, she supported us whenever asked, and seemed very fond of both of us. Rose was one of the most undemanding persons I have ever met, so when she expressed a desire to have an antique wooden Buddhist monk carving, I determined if possible to buy one for her. I spoke to Connie, asking her which was the best shop to visit, to which she replied, 'That's not necessary, John, I'll send some round for you to look at'. About half a dozen arrived, and Rose had much deliberation before deciding which one she wanted. There was no price tag on any of them which worried me no end, but even more so when (to my admittedly inexperienced eye) she selected what seemed to be the best and therefore most expensive! With heart in my mouth I visited Connie in one of her fabulous shops. I told her which one Rose had chosen, to which she replied 'She obviously has good taste, because that's the most expensive!' Taking out my cheque book I asked, 'How much please?' and nearly had a fit when she told me! Trying not to allow my hand to shake I wrote out the cheque and gave it to her. She looked up, gave me a charming smile, and then proceeded to rip up the cheque. 'A little present to you both from me,' she said.

My Mother

Presents of a different sort also came from my mother. She had always religiously followed and supported my ministry throughout the whole of my time in Holy Orders. What my father lacked in that regard she compensated for by her interest and support. She was incredibly gifted in needlecraft, leatherwork, sewing and even woodwork. Altar frontals and church linen bear testimony to this

470

in Africa, Thailand and the Netherlands (where I subsequently served). She enjoyed her visit so much to us in Tanzania that we determined to have her out in Thailand as well. She duly arrived and had the time of her life; so much so that she asked if she could stay on for an extra month. The only problem was that her visa only covered the time of her original proposed stay. A Thai princess worked in the British embassy, her principal task being to help with immigration laws, etc, and when I asked her if she would help me to get my mother's visa extended she willingly agreed. This entailed taking Mother to the British embassy, and when I told her that she would be meeting with a Thai princess her excitement knew no bounds. All went well and the extension to the visa was granted. It was a toss-up which meant the most to her, the extended visa, or the fact that she had met the princess! When the time finally came for her to leave, we put on a farewell dinner, letting her choose the guests. Whilst she was with us she was invited to most of the functions that Rose and I attended, so had met up with many of the VIPs. Her desired guest list read like a 'who's who' but to my amazement all but one of them accepted. Et, our cook, rustled up a lot of her friends to help, and I must say the food and its presentation impressed all. Mother had never before or since been so feted and continued to talk about it until her death some twenty years later.

Most of the guests that Mother had invited to her farewell dinner were members of my congregation. Being an expatriate in Bangkok usually meant that you were in your own right a gifted or talented person, and I personally never ceased to wonder just how gifted they were. Christ Church was blessed in that the congregation willingly gave of their time, talents and money in the service of the church. Rather surprisingly, although managing directors, or holders of high positions in government or commerce, many were also very clever with DIY, and others could turn their hands to almost anything.

One example of this concerned an outdoor Christmas pageant which we held in the grounds of Christ Church. Rather than the normal nativity play acted by the children, we put on a Christmas play complete with adult players, a full-sized inn and stable, live animals, plus the Bethlehem star moving across the sky!

News of what we were attempting created a great deal of interest, so much so that other church congregations offered to, and did help and participate. At the back of my mind was the hope that by re-enacting the nativity in the grounds of the church, many people might come to watch, including Thais. This is what happened. The production proved to be outstanding; the full-size stable was maintained all over the Christmas festivities, and became a means of Christian witness in a Buddhist country. An event that happened on the evening was a personal high for me, especially as I witnessed it myself. All but the most chronic cases of sickness in the nursing home next door had been sent home for Christmas. Adrienne Roberts, a member of our congregation, was one of those who unfortunately had to stay. She knew about the pageant, and was desperately sad that she would miss it. Bangkok, however, is one of those places where providing there's the will there is a way. A word with the matron was all that was needed, so shortly before it was all to begin a hospital bed, accompanied by two nurses was wheeled into the compound, with Adrienne in it. The bedlinen was immaculate and shining white, and not unsurprisingly caused quite a stir, especially as she was wheeled to the front row of the audience area. Just as I popped by to see she was all right, about ten excited children congregated around her bedside. One of them, eyes bright with excitement, asked her, 'Are you the Virgin Mary?'

Chapter 51

The Overseas Mission Fellowship

A most tragic accident occurred around the same time. It involved a group of devoted Christians working for the Overseas Missionary Fellowship who were running a mission hospital upcountry. Living as we did in Bangkok at a very high standard of living I was aware that theirs was considerably less, as were their salaries. We became particularly friendly with Dr John Townsend and his wife, and always put our house at their disposal when they came down to Bangkok.

A small group of us decided to visit them just before Christmas taking up Christmas goodies and presents. It was about a four-hour journey, and we had to get there and back in one day because of other commitments. One of our parties arranged for a company car complete with driver to take us. Including the driver we were five, which meant that Rose and I had to share the back seat with another one of our group, who was quite heavily built. As a consequence it was very crowded, so we were relieved as we neared the end of our outward journey. Our driver was travelling at a fast speed when there was a tyre blow-out, and the car, completely out of control, left the road, overturning about four times before coming to a shuddering halt, and upside-down. I realized that, apart from being thoroughly shaken, I was all right, and managed to get the door open and clamber out. I discovered that we had landed on top of a viaduct, and that there was a distinct possibility of the car falling further still. Rose was badly hurt with severe chest pains, but miraculously no one else was seriously injured. Because the car was precariously perched on the viaduct we had to move Rose out of the car as quickly as possible. We were in fact almost at the hospital, so instead of entering the grounds complete with goodies, many of which (especially the Christmas puddings I recall) were lying all around the car as the

473

boot had opened up in the crash, we arrived in an ambulance to be attended to by the very doctors we had come to visit. Apart from Rose we were all released after minor treatment. Rose was taken back to Bangkok by ambulance and admitted to the British nursing home. Although she did recover and was duly released, I don't think she was ever quite the same again. Sadly she died of lung cancer within eighteen months of the accident, but to this day I wonder whether the accident had anything to do with the onset of it.

Our accident was, however, completely overshadowed by one that followed shortly afterwards concerning the same members of the OMF working at the hospital. A happy group of the wives and children, plus one or two fathers who were off duty, loaded up into a minibus, and went off for a picnic. Sadly they were involved in a horrendous crash resulting in the death of seven of them. They were brought down to Bangkok and buried in the original graveyard given by King Mongkut in 1861 on the bend of the river.

It was the most harrowing funeral I have ever taken, seven coffins lying side by side by an open mass grave. It was obvious by their size which of those contained children. They were a very close-knit group of people, all possessed with incredibly strong faith, so much so that there was in the air a sense of joy that the deceased were now with the Lord in heaven. There was nevertheless an abundance of grief shared by those who were not members of that inner circle. As for the chief mourners, such was their closeness that they seemed to keep their grief to themselves. Possibly this was just as well as I needed to remain totally professional, both during and after the service. The mass grave seemed thereafter to dominate the cemetery, despite the fact that it contained many famous names, including Anna Leonowens of *The King and I* fame.

Apart from the special cases, some of which I have recalled, and the normal activities of a parish priest, there was, as a result of all that was going on, a constant need for money. We were always thinking of new ways to raise funds, so when someone came up with the idea of running auctions, the committee embraced the idea wholeheartedly. We were extremely fortunate in that Mike Perry, MD of Lever Brothers in Thailand (now Sir Michael), agreed to chair the event, which proved to be a great success, and raised a lot of money. It always amazes me how, starting from scratch, a concept can take shape and come to fruition. Such was the success that auctions became a regular feature at Christ Church, and apart from being very successful fund-raising events, became highly popular social events also. Bangkok was the ideal place to hold such auctions because Thai antiques were in great demand, especially amongst the expatriate community. That is not to say that we didn't make mistakes!

For our first auction a well-wisher presented an ancient-looking Christmas scene housed in an equally ancient picture frame. It created a lot of interest, and bidding for it was brisk. It was actually obtained by one of the organizing committee, which proved just as well. When he got it home and took the print from the frame to examine it more closely he discovered it was the front of a normal Christmas card! Thereafter, we arranged for an expert to examine objects before the auction, to ensure the same mistakes were not repeated in future.

Chapter 52

The Bridge Over the River Kwai, and the Infamous Burmese Railway

How many times do we hear, read, or say after a tragedy that possibly could have been avoided, 'we must make sure that this will never happen again?' One thing for certain that my ministry has taught me, is that so many of the world's tragedies need never have happened, indeed, once the heat of the moment has passed, they are seen as totally unnecessary, with no lasting good effect or value. Nowhere is this more apparent than in the war grave cemeteries around the world. Their immaculate condition and uniformity just seems to highlight the waste of life that lies beneath, 'forever in a foreign land'. Nowhere is this more apparent then where graves of the heroes killed in the Second World War lie next to that section of the cemetery that houses those who died in the First. In such circumstances, 'They gave their tomorrow that we might have our today' can seem like empty words.

I have seen and indeed taken services at war grave cemeteries in the UK, Hong Kong, East Africa, the Netherlands and Thailand, but nowhere have I been more affected than in Thailand. This is partly because of their sites. The main cemetery lies in sight of the famous bridge over the River Kwai. The second is situated on the original prisoner of war camp that witnessed such horrors and suffering. During my eight years in Thailand never a year went by without a party of ex-prisoners of war arriving to visit their fallen comrades. As embassy chaplain it was my privilege to take services for them at the cemeteries in Kanchanaburi. Many of them came on yearly pilgrimages so I got to know them very well, especially ex-marine Peter Dunstan, whose friendship I value to this day. I well remember him telling me why he came and the importance of the pilgrimage. 'Most of us,' he said, 'were aged

Ex-prisoners of war posing by one of the original trains used on the so-called
'Burmese death railway'

The British Ambassador, Sir David Cole, ex-prisoner-of-war Peter Dunstain
and the Mayor of Kanchanaburi at the famous bridge

477

Service of Remembrance at Kanchanaburi War Cemetery

'We remember' those who died at Chunkai War Cemetery

478

between twenty and twenty-five, normally the best years of one's life, and we sometimes wondered whether the experience had been real, or was it just a bad dream? We needed to see for ourselves where we had suffered and toiled, and somehow survived those hellish years. We also wanted to pay tribute to those of our comrades who did not make the journey home. Also to have the opportunity to make contact with and thank the Thai people, who, although under the boot of the Japanese, had helped us in many ways.'

He also remarked that Thai philosophies, even in the horror of their situation, were helpful and gave encouragement. Namely, every smile adds a minute to their lives thus they are forever smiling in hope of long life; that a gift must be reciprocated by one of a similar value. Paradoxically, however, this caused problems because the gifts we brought for them were by their standards very expensive!

There was a Roman Catholic Mission not far from the camps, run by Father John Ulliana, SDB, who did all he could to help alleviate the men's suffering. He was still running his church when the first group of ex-prisoners of war returned, and amid great emotion there was a wonderful reunion. I must add that in the post-war years Christ Church became the centre for the returning ex-POWs and I felt it a great honour when my church was named the official overseas church for ex-prisoners of war; St Paul's Cathedral holds the honour in the UK. In my study to this day hangs a presentation they gave to me after sharing with Father John in a memorial service on 22nd January 1976. He actually took the service at the Ban Pong camp (on the site of the original camp) whilst I conducted the ceremony at the Chunkai war cemetery (near the bridge).

Because of the personality and efficiency of Peter Dunstan, the organization of such trips and services inevitably fell to him, and I never ceased to be moved by his sincerity and passion to honour and remember his fallen comrades. Depending on which cemetery the service was held at, so I sensed different emotions. At the cemetery on the campsite I was reminded of a wonderful Christian major who was imprisoned there. He wrote that although there was no chapel, nor prayer books, nor a chaplain in the camp, Christians saw the camp as a cathedral. It had no roof, but the heavens above; no sides but the edge of the jungle; no nave or sanctuary, and no organized services. The Christians, however, would simply congregate together, and worship God. Despite the passing of the years it still

479

held for me an aura of cathedral-like holiness. The words 'Be still and know that I am God' inevitably found their way into any services that I conducted there. I was also reminded of Christopher Robin's prayer 'Hush, hush, whispers who dares,' a remarkable testimony when one considers all the horrors and atrocities that took place within the prison compound.

Services in the main and largest cemetery served to keep my feet firmly rooted to the ground. There were many reasons for this. The first concerned the number of graves, each containing the names of those whose remains lie forever in a foreign land. But possibly above all the young ages of so many whose lives were cruelly sacrificed in the construction of the 'death railway', as the prisoners named it. I never ever got used to being overwhelmed by the unnecessary and fruitless waste of lives, and never succeeded in conducting a service without tears in my eyes. The second reason, however, was like the silver lining in the cloud. It concerned the cemetery keeper, who maintained the sites in immaculate condition. During the war he lived in a village near the camps and used to regularly risk his life by smuggling in eggs and fruit to the prisoners. As a consequence they never forgot him, so when the war graves were erected after the war, his name came up again and again as a possible keeper. Enquiries in the area happily unearthed him, and he was duly appointed. On more than one occasion I witnessed an emotional reunion between an ex-prisoner and Kiion Boon Pong. There was another family that also helped the prisoners, and they set up a restaurant by the side of the bridge, which was understandably popular with all.

Apart from taking services for the ex-prisoners of war on pilgrimage, yearly services were also held to honour special remembrance days, and not only for the British but other nationals as well. Anzac day, for example, was always honoured by the Australian and the New Zealand ambassadors and their defence attachés.

It was whilst preparing for a service for a group of ex-POWs who had come out to remember their fallen comrades, that I was visited by a group of Japanese nationals. They explained that they were also in Thailand to honour their comrades who had died during the construction of the infamous railway. There was in fact a small Japanese war graves cemetery very near to the bridge, which I had visited myself. I was struck at the time by how badly it was maintained in comparison to the British cemeteries, and wondered who in fact looked after it. The group leader explained that they were aware that British ex-prisoners of war also visited their dead, and that they would very much like to meet up with them and express their sorrow at all that had happened. They were aware that there was, at present, a party of them in the country and wondered if I would arrange a meeting?

I agreed to pass on their request and let them know. In fact Peter Dunstan and his group were most distressed by the suggestion, and dismissed it outright. They said that the wounds and scars and memories were still too open and painful; maybe their children or even their children's children might be able to meet up, but not them. Even I, although not personally possessed of memories of the camps, was reduced to tears when taking the services, and witnessing the distress of the men as they relived their experiences and the loss of fallen comrades. I was not surprised, therefore, by their decision and duly conveyed it to the Japanese, who were upset by the outcome. I often wonder what the response would be if the same situation arose today.

Chapter 53

My Family

Something that never ceased to amaze us was the speed with which the years rolled by. During the time we were in Bangkok we saw our children grow from schoolchildren to young adults. Never was this more evident than in their correspondence; from the weekly enforced letter by their house master, to real letters that told us something of what was going on. Like any healthy children they came to that age when the opposite sex became more important in their lives, and it became obvious that names which meant nothing to us, meant a great deal to them! For Michael, the eldest, romance blossomed into engagement, and on to marriage. Plans for our annual leave in 1979 were timed to coincide with Michael's wedding in August, so it was in great excitement that we boarded the plane that was to take us back to the UK. Both Rose and I worked extremely hard in the weeks before leave to make sure that all would go well and be covered during our absence. It was with a great sense of relief, therefore, that we finally boarded the plane and were able to relax. I was slightly perturbed that Rose seemed to have lost some of her sparkle, but put it down to natural tiredness, believing that after a few days normality would be resumed. Although it didn't worry me unduly I was conscious that throughout the leave she just wasn't her normal self, but thought no more of it until almost at the end, when my niece, who was a nurse at Kettering Hospital, seemed concerned about the extent of her coughing, and took her in to see a doctor.

Rose

Rose smoked up to forty cigarettes a day (her grandmother started her off when she was only about fifteen, by giving her a cigarette as a treat!) and as a result her voice had become rough, and she coughed a great deal. I had got used to it, but my niece, hearing it for the first time, was alarmed. The doctor was fairly non-committal but said that as soon as we got back to Thailand she should go and see her own GP. As we boarded the plane to take us back home I was aware that despite the excitement of the wedding, the leave had not been as successful as others. We always discussed matters concerning us very openly, and I was guilty of saying that I thought she had been uncharacteristically grumpy during our UK stay. She replied that she just hadn't felt well, and was tired all the time. Home leaves always were hectic times so I was not too worried, but determined that she should take it easier once we got back into the Bangkok routine. Nevertheless, I asked my best friend and doctor, Colin Britton, to have a look at her. He said that she was probably just exhausted after a hectic leave and made her stay in bed for a couple of days.

As the nursing home was next door, Colin would often come in and see us after doing his early morning rounds, staying on for breakfast. One morning Rose mentioned that she was having trouble swallowing and for the first time I saw concern on his face. 'You'd better come into the nursing home for a couple of days,' he said, 'and I will give you a good check-out.' The media had recently been giving a great deal of attention to the fact that smoking could cause cancer. I hadn't associated Rose's poor health with cancer but with hindsight I think she had been worrying in case this was the problem. She had lots of tests and X-rays and on his Friday visit Colin told her he would have the results by Monday. She then asked him that, whatever the result, he must promise to give her the results first because she wanted to tell me herself. On the following day (i.e. the Saturday), Colin appeared and said he wanted to talk to me. He repeated what Rose had made him promise, but said that she was going to need all the help she could get, especially from me. He felt that I ought to be aware of the situation before she told me so that I could be prepared and able to offer the support she needed. He then told me that she had lung cancer at an advanced stage, that it was inoperable and that there was no cure. I asked him how long and he replied about six months. It was impossible to explain the depth of my anguish. Furthermore, when I visited Rose shortly, I would have to conceal the devastating news I had just been given.

That weekend was a nightmare, so much so that Monday morning came almost as a relief. I waited outside her door when Colin went in. His visit lasted about five minutes; he came out and signalled for me to go in. I mouthed a silent prayer and entered to see her sitting up in bed seemingly remarkably composed. So she told me her news and we embraced and held each other for a long time. She then added that during the course of the various tests and questions she thought it more and more likely that she did indeed have cancer, so there was almost a sense of relief when she was told that she had. Colin had not of course told her how serious it was, or that it was inoperable, but that everyone was agreed that radiotherapy was the best way to treat it. Nor had she any idea how long the prognosis was for the illness to take its course.

Needless to say, everyone was devastated, and I know that she was prayed for by Christian groups all over the world. I was amazed at the offers that came in for help. One parishioner told me that he would cover the cost of treatment no matter for how long or wherever it might take. He mentioned that there were many cancer clinics in the USA, all claiming remarkable cures. There was also the option of returning to the UK, but Rose was adamant that she wanted to stay just where she was. She had the utmost faith in God and Colin Britton. The nursing home was right next door to our house and church; we were in the midst of a loving community, and she was convinced that the treatment she would receive in Bangkok would match any in the world.

The parish was absolutely marvellous. They paid for both children to come out and visit. Michael was by now in the police force, and was given compassionate leave. Elizabeth at that time was not doing anything too special so stayed on until after Rose died, and individual parishioners set up a rota to cover Rose's work in the general office. Being the only priest I had to continue taking the services, but that apart, was able to accompany Rose wherever she went, including daily trips to the clinic where she received her treatment. Ours had always been a good marriage, but in the six months or so before she died we became so close that, despite the cancer, it became an extremely blessed time. She was perfectly at peace with God. Confession was even more alien to her than it was to me, but at my suggestion she agreed that Father Joe Maier would come and visit her, which he did. From then on she became what I can only describe as perfectly serene. So much so that many people used to go and visit her just to see her and experience the aura of peace that embraced her in the room. She spent her time between the nursing home and our house, but gradually the time in the nursing home became more than in her bedroom. Michael was kept fully aware of her deteriorating condition, applied for and received further compassionate leave, so was able to fly out and join us, as her health deteriorated even more.

I have mentioned elsewhere the festival of Loy Krathong, which came around just as Rose's illness showed a marked deterioration, but she insisted on celebrating it as usual. Et our cook made her a truly remarkable krathong, which seemed almost too exquisite to float away. Et told us that all we needed to do was to load all our problems on it, put food and money on it for the spirits to enjoy, light the candle, and watch it float away. There was a tiny klong (stream) that separated the grounds of the church from those of the nursing home, and it was to this spot that we slowly made our way. It was a particularly poignant moment for me, for I crossed

Rose launching her krathong

485

this little bridge nearly every day of my life to visit patients and knew that shortly Rose would walk over it for the last time. Nevertheless, the magic of the moment pushed away such thoughts, as Rose launched her krathong and it started to float away.

It was around this time, in fact on my fifty-second birthday, when Rose was back yet again in the nursing home, that I wrote the following:

> Today is my fifty-second birthday, which I have celebrated by taking services at Christ Church and bringing Rose the Blessed Sacrament. She is very low indeed. Her body is so sick but her spirits are so high – I would say reaching up to heaven itself. I sit by her bed – my face three feet from hers. There is a frown on her face and her eyes are closed, but there is also an aura of peace which is very difficult to describe, I only know that it is there. If it weren't I couldn't be writing as I am now. I have long accepted that Rose is going to die despite the prayers of us all; the best medical care and attention; the most loving of nursing: this cancer is shortly going to claim her earthly body – but I rejoice with the communion of saints that Christ has overcome death and that the beautiful love and attention that has surrounded her in these last months is as nothing compared with the crescendo of love that will greet her as (with her earthly race completed) she is greeted at the gates of heaven itself with a victory salute.
>
> 'Well done thou good and faithful servant, enter into the joy of the lord.'
>
> I pray that my son Michael whom I expect to fly out this coming week may arrive in time to join with Elizabeth and me in kissing her goodbye, to share in our grief, but more important even than that, that her suffering will not be prolonged.
>
> As a husband and priest I wish to assure you that my faith has never been stronger and my trust in Christ more complete. So I can say with complete confidence, honesty and in peace 'Into thy hands O Lord I commend her spirit' and 'Into thy hands O lord I commend my spirit too'.

One of the highlights of every week, as far as I was concerned, was every Wednesday afternoon. It was given over to children's

Children's groups at Christ Church display their banners

Listen to me!

Nativity play with full-size stable

Children's Church at Christ Church

Children waving after singing farewell to Rose

activities including cubs and brownies, etc. Because of the variation in the age group of the children we had other groups such as chinchooks and bluebirds as well. In all between fifty and sixty children attended, plus at least twenty adult helpers. The afternoon always began with a service in church, so in my talk I mentioned that one of our congregation was sick at the nursing home so we would pray for her. One of the children piped up, 'Yes we know, Canon John, it's Mrs Taylor'. We always used to pick someone's favourite hymn to sing at the service, and another child suggested, 'Why don't we go over to the nursing home and sing Mrs Taylor's favourite hymn to her?' Some of this I had planned anyway, but it proved all the more memorable because in the end the suggestions came from the children, without prompting from me.

Rose's room had a balcony, which actually looked out onto the church compound, although the church itself was partly hidden by trees. There was the little klong with a bridge over it, which gave access from the church to the nursing home. Michael and Elizabeth preceded us to Rose's room to persuade her to come out onto the balcony, so that she would be able to see us all below. I said to the children that we wanted it to be a surprise for Mrs Taylor, so please no talking and to creep over the bridge so that she wouldn't hear anything. The silence was deafening. Every one of them actually crept from the church to where we were to assemble; it was without any shadow of doubt one of the most moving occasions of my life as we assembled in the grounds below her balcony, and waited in complete silence for Rose to appear. She of course had no idea of what was to follow, and in fact it required a huge effort on her behalf to leave her bed and make it to the balcony, and she only succeeded because of Michael's and Elizabeth's help. As the minutes ticked by I was beginning to wonder whether she was going to make it at all. Some seventy pairs of eyes were strained upwards, and then wonderfully we could see a small group making their way to the front of the balcony. Spontaneous clapping and cheering broke out from the children, which prompted Rose to look down to where we were. My children told me that her eyes lit up, and she had a little weep, but from where we were all we could see was her waving to us. We sang her favourite hymn, said some prayers, waved our goodbyes, and returned back to the church. That was actually the last time Rose walked, but I cannot think of a more precious journey that will, I am sure, live on in the memories of all those who witnessed it. Unbeknown to me a visitor to the nursing home saw what was going on and took a photo, so putting on record a very special event.

The deterioration in her health continued, and to such an extent that I now prayed that her suffering would cease as soon as possible. So came the day when my prayer was answered. We all sensed it would be her last. Colin Britton, her doctor and my best friend, and the matron, who was also a good friend, said that they would stay with us during the evening. I remember querying this with the matron, Edith Stuart, because I knew she had been on duty all day. 'I will come back without my uniform,' was her reply. Rose's favourite meal was duck, which we decided that we would all eat in her honour in her room in the nursing home – and that's exactly what happened. Rose was by now unconscious, but because we all wanted to see an end to her suffering we found this comforting. Supper was finished and cleared away, after which I sat on the chair by her bed and held her hand, the others also sitting quietly in the room. I had cried, as indeed had we all, till there were no more tears left. I had prayed without ceasing until there was nothing else to pray. All there was left was silence broken only by the laboured breathing of Rose. Then suddenly that too was broken

by a voice that said to me, 'Why are you here? He is no longer
here, he has risen.' These were almost exactly the same words as
were spoken to Mary when she went to the grave of Jesus on that
first Easter morning. I glanced around the room but apparently no
one else had heard them. I turned to Colin and asked him how
long we had got, explaining I felt an overwhelming desire to go
the chapel and pray. 'No problem,' he replied 'nothing will happen
for some time yet.' I disentangled my hand from Rose and went
to leave. Michael jumped to his feet and asked where I was going.
'To the chapel to pray,' I replied, 'so don't worry.' I made my
way to the little chapel under the vicarage, picked up a hymn book
and started to sing at random the hymns on the pages I opened. I
then sat down and comforted myself with the beautiful words of
the poem by AL Frank that someone had given me.

Near shady wall a rose once grew
Budded and blossomed
In God's free light
Watered and fed by morning dew,
Shedding its sweetness day and night

As it grew and blossomed
Fair and tall,
Slowly rising to loftier height,
It came to a crevice in the wall
Through which there shone
A beam of light

Onward it crept with added strength
With never a thought of fear or pride,
It followed the light
Through the crevice's length
And unfolded itself on the other side.

The light, the dew, the broadening view
Were found the same
As they were before,
And lost itself in beauties new,
Breathing its fragrance
More and more.

Shall claim of death
Cause us to grieve
And make our courage faint and fall?
Nay! Let us faith and hope receive –
The rose still grows beyond the wall,
Scattering fragrance far and wide
Just as did in days of yore
Just as it did on the other side
Just as it will forevermore.

Did I see his hands?

Then I knelt down to pray. As I did I experienced an emptying of
self and a deep sense of moving into somewhere, or something
that I had never experienced before. An incredible peace and calm
seemed to enter my soul and I became lost in time and space, and
as it were entered a void. I should add that we had just laid a
brand new gold-coloured carpet in the main church. It covered the
length of the building right from the main doors up to and into
the sanctuary, under the altar and on to the wall beyond. The next
thing I knew was that I was no longer in the chapel under the
vicarage but in the main church, which was as usual locked up
for the night. Strangely enough I wasn't in my usual vicar's stall
but kneeling in the back of the church in the very seat where Rose
always sat. She (unlike most vicars' wives) always sat at the back
of the church so that she could see if anyone was in trouble or
needed help.

Then an even more miraculous thing happened. Rose appeared
through the curtains that covered the locked main doors, and started
to walk serenely, head held high, down the aisle towards the
sanctuary. Her feet made no sound on the luscious new carpet, and
I couldn't help comparing how easily she walked now compared
to her last tortuous journey from bed to balcony only a few days
earlier. So graciously and effortlessly she advanced down the aisle
towards the sanctuary. As she reached it she arose from the ground
and started ascending towards the highest point of the church
immediately above the high altar. I then saw what I can only
describe as a tunnel of light, and it was to this that Rose ascended
and then entered. The only point in the whole experience that I

492

cannot swear to is that it seemed to me that as she entered the tunnel a pair of hands was outstretched to greet her. Then she was gone.

I have never in my life, before or since, been in such a state of serenity, peacefulness and holy awe. The one thing I knew for certain was that I never wanted the experience to end. But that was not to be. The quietness was shattered by the sound of running feet, followed by someone calling my name. This brought me out of the trance or whatever it was that I was in, and as I came to I found myself back in the chapel. Seconds later Michael came bursting into the chapel, crying, 'Come quickly, Mummy's going'.

'No, Michael,' I corrected him, 'Mummy's gone. I have just seen her go to heaven.' She had indeed died during my absence, but it was as if she had taken my grief and pain with her. As a consequence I was the calmest person present and was able to offer comfort and help to all around.

At that time very few places had a direct telephone line to the UK. One had to go to the main post office on appointment, and even this did not guarantee that you would get through, or that the line would be all that good if you did. The nursing home was one of the few establishments that did have a direct line, which the matron immediately put at my disposal. Almost miraculously (and if you think that is far-fetched then ask anyone who was in Bangkok during those days!) I managed to get through immediately and contact all the nearest and dearest in the UK and the States. During these calls I again was the calmest involved and tried to wipe away their tears even though they were thousands of miles away.

There were two remarkable events that I would like to share with you over this period. The first concerned Michael. Although we had always got on very well together, it was a relationship between father and son. When I returned to Rose's room and embraced my children, that relationship with Michael changed, no longer father to son, but friend to friend.

The second concerned another patient in the nursing home. Daily visiting ensured that I got to know everyone very well, including the patients, staff and visitors. In a room not far from Rose's there was a Thai male also suffering from cancer. But unlike Rose, who was so peaceful and serene, he was exactly the opposite. He gave hell to everyone involved, complained about everyone and everything, and was so disliked that the staff dreaded going in to his room. He had a very charming wife, whom I used to bump into when visiting Rose. Inevitably when leaving his room she was in tears over the way he behaved. She confessed that she was beginning to dread going in to see him, but there was no one else who would put up with his behaviour, so if she didn't go it meant he would have no visitor. I had visited him as I did all the patients, so felt very sympathetic towards her. I offered to 'babysit' so that she could have a break from time to time, an offer which she gratefully accepted. Whilst with him I often used to say my offices, which actually prompted him to ask me questions about the faith.

On the night that Rose died I met her leaving his room in floods of tears. I have always been a 'hands-on' person, especially in hospital visiting, or when counselling someone in distress. I immediately put my arms around her and told her not to worry. (These were the days before clergy were told no touching, in case it was misunderstood, especially with children.) I shared with her my recent experience, and said it is the same God of love who will look after him, just as he had with Rose. Something of my calm seemed to be passed on to her; she stopped crying, and indeed remained calmer until he also died, not long after Rose. I was overwhelmed when she came to see me with a request: would I please give him a Christian burial? Unbeknown to me he had been tremendously moved by my visits, especially the reciting of my offices, so was actually converted on his deathbed. She also said that she, like so many others, couldn't help comparing the serenity of Rose with the rantings and ravings of her husband. But above all, she had felt such strength and a sense of peace after our meeting on the night that Rose died, that she wanted more of it, hence her request for a funeral.

Rose died just before Easter, which could have been an awful ordeal for me, having to take such important services so soon after her death, but my recent experience decreed otherwise. Instead of preaching about the resurrection I just told it as it was. Many, I was told, were deeply moved by what I said. What I do know is that Rose did as much good and helped as many souls during the eight months of her illness as I did during my eight years in Thailand. Indeed I believe that throughout the twenty-eight years of our life together Rose played an equal role in our joint ministry.

On the same night that Rose died, the Army chose to stage yet another coup. Coups at this time in Thailand were a very regular occurrence. The deciding factor in almost every case was whether or not the King approved. If he did, the coup succeeded, if he didn't, then it failed. They were usually accomplished without any loss of blood, so that the majority of people were unaffected. There were minor irritations, however, such as no newspapers, and as a consequence Rose's death went unannounced. Indeed, there were many who didn't know she had died until after the funeral. Nevertheless the grapevine was, as always, very active, and a large number of people attended the service. The Reverend Bill Smith conducted the funeral service in church, but it fell to me to take the cremation service at the Wat where such services were held. At the best of times this was an unpleasant experience as the priest conducting the service had to help place the coffin into the kiln, and then start the fire with an oily cloth on the end of a pole. The fire started with a loud explosion that even with prior experience made one jump. My children and our closest friends were there of course to support, but nothing could take away, despite my vision, the devastation of her passing.

What I was aware of, however, was being upheld by what I can only describe 'as a blanket of love' which would not let me go. This enabled me to cope with the Sundays following her death. What I found unbearable though, for at least a year was when a favourite hymn was sung, which made me burst into tears. This especially seemed to occur during the singing of the last hymn, which meant that the blessing was often delayed whilst I struggled to recover my composure. Never once did anyone mention this or complain.

Never in my wildest dreams had I ever thought when we built the garden of remembrance, that one day Rose would be interred within its cavity walls. As it happened she was one of the first to be interred, and her ashes lie there still. Various members of the family have returned since to visit the garden. A dear friend from the congregation has laid flowers every year without fail on the anniversary of her death. As for me, I left a part of me within the grounds of Christ Church when I left Thailand, so in one way whenever I have returned it has been like going home.

Apart from the plaque in the garden of remembrance Rose's name lives on in other ways. A fund was started to honour her memory to provide a permanent memorial to her in Bangkok. Such was the response that in October 1981 I officially opened a new respiratory unit at the children's hospital in Bangkok. Because of the sensitivity of the equipment it could only operate in air-conditioning. The equipment had been donated from America but couldn't be used because there was no air-conditioning available. A plaque in the hospital records that through Rose's fund it was now in use. The children of the parish presented a lectern in her memory, and I gave a chalice for use in the chapel. But above all she will be remembered because of what she was, and always will be.

Chapter 54

My Future?

The months immediately following Rose's death were extremely difficult for me. Because we had done everything as a team, no matter what I did it brought painful memories of us doing things together. My initial reaction was to move on as quickly as possible, but the advice I was given (I would have said exactly the same thing to another in a similar position myself) was to make no decision for at least a year. In any case I had to return to the UK to sort personal business out, and meet members of both our families. These arrangements took some time to complete, including finding cover for Christ Church whilst I was away, so it was actually some time before I returned to the UK. In the meantime I tried to decide what the future held for me. I was left in no doubt that the congregation wanted me to continue, but equally I came to realize that Bangkok on a permanent basis without Rose was a non-starter, or, more accurately, a non-finisher.

But that was not all. I had long been a sympathizer towards the lay membership order of St Francis. Members promised to live as simple a life as possible. As embassy chaplain and a parish priest in Bangkok it would have been impossible to keep that vow, so I had put such thoughts on the back burner. But as I struggled to find God's will for me in the future, not only did lay membership of St Francis return to the forefront of my thinking, but the concept of actually becoming a monk became increasingly vivid, despite the fact that to take the vows of poverty, chastity and obedience would necessitate a way of life totally different from my life to date. I also had to make up my mind regarding my position in Thailand. If I were to leave, what was I going to do?

The Missions to Seamen asked me to rejoin the society as Secretary for the Netherlands and senior chaplain at the port of Rotterdam, which was then the largest port in the world. I made

497

contact with Canon Hardaker, whose task it was to try and find jobs for those on the move, but especially for returning missionaries, but he was not very encouraging. Because I had been abroad on and off since 1953, he thought I would find it extremely difficult to find a suitable position in the UK. He was aware of the Missions to Seamen offer and urged me to accept it. Other offers did come in, but after eight years of travelling between three countries over which I had oversight I felt almost claustrophobic about being confined to one parish! Such comments as, 'I know this will be the right parish for you because we have a refugee family who have settled here,' seemed particularly unchallenging after dealing with thousands of such families in Bangkok. In Bangkok I was involved with hospitals, prisons, marriage guidance, alcoholics anonymous, Samaritans, drug addicts, refugees, seamen's work and my work among the Thais. In most of the parishes I was offered I would be lucky if there was more than one of these aspects of ministry that had been my lot for the last eight years.

But there was still a nagging desire to enter a monastery and take the vows. Included, then, in my UK itinerary was a week's retreat in a monastery. The only thing I could say for certain was that I could not continue in Bangkok without Rose, and this fact I duly conveyed to the churchwardens and the PCC. The senior warden was Charles Edmonds, whose reference I treasure as it aptly illustrated the extent of the work of the vicar of Christ Church. It was agreed that I should return to the UK, taking as long as needed to sort out my personal affairs and confirm what the future held for me. After which I would return to Bangkok to finish off any loose ends and pack up all our belongings (which were considerable after living there for eight years) before leaving for good. I was thrilled and most grateful when a UK shipping line offered me a passage home as well as providing me with a free container. The weeks before I left were hectic in the extreme, both regarding the work and social activities as so many people and organizations kindly gave me farewell parties and presentations.

One event above all others I will never forget. On my last but one visit to the foreigners in prison I told them that my next visit would be my last as I was returning to the UK. Prisons are tough places and to survive in them people have to be tough too. I was amazed therefore at the reaction given to my news. There was genuine sorrow, indeed grief that I was leaving. I have said elsewhere that prison visiting in Thailand was the hardest part of my ministry, but until that day I had no idea how much my visits were appreciated. A month later I returned for the last time, and the congregation at the service was the largest ever. After the service was over it was me who was reduced to tears. Even in prison and amongst the prisoners there is always a leader. The person in question was one of the hardest men I have ever met, yet it was he who came to the front and thanked me for my visits and the help I had given over the years. He then said that all the prisoners had clubbed together to buy me a farewell present. He presented me with a parcel which, with their urging, I opened and examined. It was a silver mug inscribed with the words

TO CANON JOHN TAYLOR
WITH MUCH APPRECIATION FROM THE RESIDENTS
OF LARD YAO BANGKOK. BON VOYAGE OCT 1981.

Even as I received it I was aware of the effort that went into the giving of that gift. Apart from organizing the collection, from a group of people for whom money was so important and could make so much difference to their harsh regime, I knew that guards would have to have been bribed, favours sought and regulations overcome. Without any doubt it was the most meaningful present I have ever received, either before or since. My face streaming with tears, I turned and left the compound to the sound of clapping and cheers. As I left I turned and waved to them for the last time. To a man no one had moved, some were still clapping, and without exception every one of them enthusiastically returned their waves to me.

The mug was only one of the items and letters that meant so much to me, and which I took back to the UK. My house today is still full of those mementoes, and I still read much of the correspondence that covered my time in Thailand.

Chapter 55

The Final Chapter

It was with very mixed feelings that I contemplated all that lay ahead. Whatever the outcome of my trip to the UK, I knew it was the beginning of the end of my time in Thailand. I knew it would be a very painful experience as I relived with all my loved ones in the UK the last months of Rose's life, her death and funeral. I knew that it was to be decision-time regarding my future, and at a time when I was struggling with my own grief and sense of loss. I realized anew the wisdom of my churchwardens at Christ Church in begging me to make no changes, or make any decisions for at least a year. But I had already passed the point of no return. I was positive in my own mind that I had to move on. I had already received half a dozen invitations (through the kind offices of Canon Hardaker) to consider various appointments in the UK, and knew the least I could do would be to visit and meet with those concerned.

Just as with Tanzania, so too with Thailand; I left not only with some moving and incredible memories, but also with some precious letters from people, which I value deeply. I include some of them at the end of the book, as a lasting memorial to my involvement with people and causes in Thailand.

Above all, of course, were my memories of twenty-nine wonderful years with Rose. Together we had sailed and flown to Hong Kong, Africa, Thailand and Europe. It had always been with a sense of great relief as we boarded a plane at the beginning of a holiday, or at the end of a tour, knowing we had done everything possible to ensure a smooth transition during our absence. We always held hands as the plane taxied onto the runway and lifted majestically into the air. There was a feeling of closeness and well-being, as our holiday began with a carefree attitude to what lay ahead. We felt totally relaxed, without a care in the world. My flight back to

500

the UK couldn't have been more different. I was on my own, a stranger in the seat next to me. There was no sense of excitement or satisfaction at a chapter in my life safely concluded, but only grief and, if I dare to admit it, a sense of despair. The warmth of the reception when loved ones met me at the airport forced me into a more positive mood, except when darkness found me alone, and the grief returned.

Unlike some who have been through similar experiences, the one thing that remained constant was my total trust and faith in God. Indeed it was this blessing that enabled me to get my act together, and make the necessary plans to visit the various parishes and other situations I had been offered. The first thing I had to obtain was a car, and through the help of a colleague I soon became the proud owner of an 'old banger' that took me safely to various parts of the country, including Cornwall, the Midlands and up north to Durham. It was very difficult for me to assess these work possibilities objectively, because the concept of monastic life was continually on my mind. Towards the end of my leave I had signed myself in to a monastery for a week's retreat, which was to be conducted in fasting and total silence. Its one objective – to seek God's will for my future and especially as to whether or not I should become a monk. Wherever I travelled I shared with those present my dilemma, which was greeted in the main either with amusement or embarrassed silence, especially by those who knew me best! I had timed my retreat to take place at the end of my holiday, after staying for a few days with my old friends the Metcalfes in Shap Wells. They kindly agreed to run me over to the Franciscan retreat house at Alnmouth which was on the east coast. They also agreed to pick me up on the following Saturday at about 12.30 pm. The luxury of the hotel and the excellence of the food – and drink – were in complete contrast to the starkness of my cell and fasting. So also, after being in the midst of loved ones with their friendly chatter, was the silence, which strangely I can best describe as deafening.

In a surprisingly short time, however, I adapted to the new routine, and found the retreat to be the haven that I desperately (although I had not been aware of it) needed. Ever since the death of Rose one event had followed immediately upon another, as had my moods, ranging from ecstasy as I recalled my 'vision' on the night Rose died, to the utter desolation that from time to time engulfed me as I tried in vain to adjust to life without her. So for the first few days I just waited upon the Lord, neither seeking nor receiving any guidance on whether or not I was to change a vicarage for a monastery, my old way of life to a new rule of life, or my cassock for a monk's habit.

So passed peacefully and contentedly the first few days. But came the Thursday, with the realization that I still was no nearer to an answer, and a sort of panic set in. I prayed as I have never prayed before that God would show me which way I was to follow 'the way, the truth and the life'. He didn't. I was reminded of my early school days when my Latin master would ask me, 'Taylor, what is the Latin word for...?' Then followed an embarrassed silence because I didn't have a clue. 'No answer,' was the stern reply, 'come out here, Taylor, and hold out your hand.'

Thursday rolled on into Friday and Friday into Saturday morning, and still not a word. The simple chapel was set slightly apart from the monastery and was situated on top of the cliffs overlooking the sea. During the many hours I had spent within its walls I had situated myself in different positions for prayer and meditation, but on this last morning I moved as close as I could to the large plain window that overlooked the sea. I prayed, I meditated and I contemplated. Nothing. I tried plain speaking, I pleaded, I begged for an answer. The result? Nothing. A glance at my watch showed it to be 11.30 am, which meant that my friends were coming to pick me up in one hour. I tried to pull myself together to decide what I should do. I rose to my feet and as I did my eyes noticed something moving high across the window.

My first reaction was to think that it was a bird, but as it flew even higher then started dropping I realized that it was a golf ball. I took up golf aged fifty, so not surprisingly I watched its descent with interest. Looking down I noticed, for the first time, that there was a links golf course at the foot of the cliffs which explained the presence of the ball. Its height and distance marked it down as a good shot, so not unnaturally I looked in the direction from whence it had come to see who had driven it. Although the two players were some distance away I could see by their clothes that they were both ladies. My admiration for the excellence of the shot increased with the knowledge that she had hit the ball further than I could. The green was about a hundred and fifty yards further on, so I impatiently waited to see whether her next shot would be as good as the last. As she came up to her ball and addressed it I couldn't help but notice that she was attractively dressed in a matching skirt and blouse. She teed up the ball and then went into a perfect back swing before making solid contact with her ball, which flew majestically towards the pin. Did it end on the green? Alas, I cannot tell you. Why? Because my eyes remained firmly on she who had just hit the ball. As she swung so did her skirt and for a second (rather like on the centre court at Wimbledon) a little more than usual was revealed! At that split second I knew for certain that I didn't want to be a monk, God had answered my question. They say that if God doesn't come he sends. He sent a sign and left me in no doubt where my future lay!

I greeted my friends with the news that I wasn't going to be a monk, and the relieved look on their faces told its own story. I left the monastery in high spirits, because although not yet knowing in what direction my ongoing pilgrimage in life would take me, I knew it would not be on entirely uncharted waters. I also knew that provided the grace of God continued to bless my ministry, I would be helping to bring ever nearer that great and wonderful day when the Kingdom of God would cover the earth, as the waters cover the sea.

Postscript

Because of the untimely death of Rose, resulting in me leaving Thailand before I otherwise would have done, I never actually witnessed the advent of a Thai-speaking priest, and the formation of a Thai congregation, which was my third and ultimate aim for Christ Church. Nevertheless, it was something I worked for, and sowed as many seeds as possible in the hope that this richest of harvests would be gathered in. We are often told that some sow that others may reap. The harvest did come, a Thai-speaking priest was appointed, and there is now a Thai-speaking congregation worshipping at Christ Church. As a consequence I can close this biography with a joyful heart and safe in the knowledge that the earth is the Lord's, that we are all God's children, and in his good time all will be safely gathered in.

POSTSCRIPT

The Ambassador of New Zealand
Bangkok, Thailand

10 July 1979

Dear John,

Your numerous visits to my hospital room gave me comfort in the early stages when I needed it and later, intellectual stimulus when I enjoyed discussing matters of substance.

I know that hospital visiting is only one aspect of your many sided ministry and that sometimes you see a need for financial assistance to those to whom you are ministering. Please accept the enclosed for use in any way you see fit. I do not need a receipt.

With warm personal regards,

Yours sincerely,

Richard

Richard B. Taylor

Encl.

The Rev. Canon J.R. Taylor, OBE, OCF,
Vicar of Christ Church,
Convent Road,
BANGKOK. *Good travelling and a happy holiday to you & Rose.*

505

A MAN WITH A MISSION

DR. J. PATRICK DICKSON
DR. PETER COMER · DR. COLIN BRITTON

BRITISH DISPENSARY, 109 SUKUMVIT ROAD, BANGKOK, THAILAND. TEL. 2528056, 2529179

4th August 1981

TO WHOM IT MAY CONCERN

I would whole-heartedly recommend Canon John Taylor for the post of hospital chaplain at any hospital. I am a General Practitioner in practice for 12 years in Bangkok and have known John for 8 years both as a friend and a colleague. The Anglican church, Christ Church, in Bangkok where he has long ministered to the expatriate, foreign, and local communities, is situated next door to the Bangkok Nursing Home Hospital which is a private hospital mostly used by the foreign community and also where most psychiatrically disturbed foreigners are admitted.

My recommendation of John Taylor rests on these 8 years of working with him, and seeing him in action on a wide variety of patient, medical social, psychiatric, and community care. Specifically I may say that he has good working relationships with doctors and has had to deal with doctors of several nationalities. He is excellent with patients and has not only empathy and unprejudiced sympathy with all personalities but a practical pragmatic outlook to helping with their problems. He has been deeply invomved not only in visiting patients in hospital and ministering to them but also at their homes; councilling them in their grief, or affliction, helping relatives of the sick and bereaved, and enjoying with them their triumphs. I personally have often referred patients to him where his expertise and spiritual outlook have benefited many. We have worked together on many 'crisis' cases. He started a marriage guidance course, and was instrumental in setting up in Bangkok a branch of the Samaritans among both the foreign and Thai communities. He has been involved in a very practical way in prison visiting and improving the lot of prisoners of all nationalities. He works closely and successfully with priests and people of other religious denominations enjoying their friendship and cooperation. He has done outstanding work with refugees problems of which Thailand has a full quota.

In the psychiatric field he has many times above what reasonably could be asked responded to crisis calls day and night for those in severe distress over drug problems, psychoses, or life crisises. I would say that he has great experience in all the problems that beset people, material, spiritual, and emotional. Perhaps his greatest attribute ability to cheer people up and make them feel they have worth and that he cares. He is easy to talk to and children enjoy his company.

He emplifies the truth of Christian pastoral care. He also has had extensive experience of Missions to Seamen work so there is little in the way of human problems he has not seen; whatever the situation he

.../..

506

copes with common sense and wisdom. On top of all this he has a thriving
and active Church parish with all its attendant duties.

In his own personal life his wife has recently died after a prolonged
illness with Cancer and this has served, whatever his personal tragedy
to add a dimension of personal suffering to his empathy with others.

He would be a marvellous person to have as chaplain at your hospital
and we are sorry to see him leave.

Yours sincerely,

Dr. Collin M. Britton

DR COLIN M. BRITTON
MA., MB., B. Chir. (Cantab)
LRCP. MRCS (London)
D. Obst. RCOG (London)
D.T.M. & H (L. pool)

(Overseaslist)

HOLY REDEEMER CHURC

26 Oct., 1981

Dear John,

The purpose of this letter is a bit of nostalgia and to wish you Blessings.

It's been great working together with you in so many ways in the priesthood.

You started going with me to the Maximum Security Prison, and then you took the initiative and organized visiting the other long term prison, and through your efforts, were able to have all the foreign prisoners in one area. I admit that prison visiting is the most difficult task I have, and going with you each month lightens the burden. Thanks for being a friend. And it's so obvious that through the years, God has been so good to us. Also thanks for the help and encouragement in working with the sailors in the Port; for your help in organizing the joint conference a couple of years back here in Bangkok for the Port Chaplains. You were a life-saver that time!

And the visiting of the Immigration jail. It was one of your flock who started that one, so neither you or I can take the credit, but we did carry it on and you now have it well under control. And the assistance you and Christ Church have given to me in my work in the Klong Toey Slums, and for all the involvement you've had. And how much fun and head-aches we had setting up the Welfare and Refugee Relief Committee to help the Burmese, and how the U.N. used our committee of 3 of us, and we were able to help thousands of people during those early days of the Refugee movement, and how you used Christ Church's facilities, and organised the ladies and we could work in 9 languages.....

And all the other things, priestly things we have done together, like praying office for guidance so often....

In short, John, thank-you for being you, and keep up your work for the Church. You've faults, John Taylor, like us all, but your greatest virtue is your love for the Church.

Blessings. Prayers.

Jos. Maier. CSSR

508

สถานสงเคราะห์เด็กกำพร้าพัทยา
ตู้ ป.ณ. ๑๕ พัทยา. ชลบุรี
บ้านเลขที่ ๑๑๑ หมู่ที่ ๖ ต.นาเกลือ อ.บางละมุง จ.ชลบุรี
โทร. ๔๑๘๐๒๒๓

August 10, 1981

Canon Taylor
Christ Church
Bangkok

Dear John,

It is hard for me to believe that you will be leaving Thailand, and although I know its already decided and you have resigned, I wish you would stay. No doubt many, many, people have told you the same.

The amount of work you have done since your arrival in Thailand has been stupendous. I began hearing about shortly after you arrival, years ago. People of Burmese, Pakistan, Bangladesh etc nationality began talking to me about a " Father Taylor ", who had helped them. Since I knew about every priest in Thailand, I was puzzled as to who this Father Taylor was.

When I found out it was a priest at Christ Church, I then knew it was not a Roman Catholic Father Taylor. When I first met you, I watched to see if you were going to be " stand-offish " or " Uppity ". I also wondered if you were going to be anti-Catholic. I know it sounds crazy now,....but that is how I wondered then.

It did not take long to find out my wonderings were baseless. At that first meeting (at Holy Redeemer Church) you charmed me off my feet. We didn't say much to each other, since I was listening as you spoke to others. But I knew immediately, " I like this man " .

When a Burmese showed up at my door one day with the news Father Taylor sent him,.... I had to laugh. Who does this crazy priest think he is, sending me one more Burmese!! But then a letter was produced from you, explaining the whole thing and promising to help. No one had ever done that before. All kinds of people send me Burmese,..but no one ever gave me help to care for them. When I went to visit you later, it was like we had been friends for years. We did not have to tell each other that we both felt the same way about the poor. We simply knew it. That was the first long talk we ever had, and when I was sitting in a taxi going to Holy Redeemer after leaving you, I said most definitely,.... " I do like that man !! ".

And that is the way it has been ever since.

The work you have started here in Thailand is greater than any building

---

สถานสงเคราะห์เด็กกำพร้าพัทยา

ตู้ ป. ณ. ๑๕   พัทยา. ชลบุรี

บ้านเลขที่ ๓๘ หมู่ที่ ๑ ต.นากลือ อ.บางละมุง จ.ชลบุรี

โทร. ๔๑๘๗๑๗

in Bangkok. The Seaman work, the Samaritans, the "dek pikan " school
at your church, the immigration work, your tremendous amount of consu-
ling (even to R.C. priests !!) etc etc etc have had an influence
on thousands of people.   That little corner on Sathorn & Convent will
never be the same when you leave!

I say this honestly and sincerely,...I have never met a man like you
before. I value the friendship we have shared all these years. I hate
like hell to see you go.

You have always been extremely helpful to me.... and you have always told
me to come to you if I need help. I hate to ask for help in this letter,
for fear you will think I was buttering you up before the final kill. But
I will anyway, since I am sure you believe my love for you is sincere.

Here at the orphanage we wish to begin a new program. It is a program for
deaf children. I have been investigating all the facts concerned, and we
are now about ready to give the final O.K. if we can get the funds. And
the funds are the thing that is holding us back. In Thiland there is a
deaf school, but in all of Thailand there is no " annuban " (pre-school)
for deaf children. The Thai government has told us they would cooperate
with us 100% on this project, but cannot give funds. They have told us
that a 'pre-school' for the deaf is what they have wanted for years, and
is sorely needed. Just yesterday the Assistant to the Director of the
government deaf program came to me. She is urging us to open this school.

The school would accept, without charge, children from four to seven years
old. The program would last two years for each child. The children would
be taught sign language and the reading of lips. Besides that, the children
would begin education to learn how to speak, even though they cannot hear.
It is a very wonderful program for children, and each child's life will be
changed because of the help we can give them. After they leave our school,
the government has guaranteed that our seven year old graduates would be
accepted into the government deaf school for further speech training. All
in all, its wonderful,....except for the money.

That is where I need your help. I don't know how you do it,..but you have
always managed to stick a gun to somebody's head and somehow come up with
the help needed.

The materials needed for this deaf school are staggering, but essential
for a school of this type. All types of machinery, special teachers ,
and extra rooms for the deaf children are absolutely necessary if the
children are to be helped.

In this letter you will find photo copies of the machines we need. Their
cost will raise the hair off your head!

สถานสงเคราะห์เด็กกำพร้าพัทยา

ตู้ ป. ณ. ๑๕ พัทยา. ชลบุรี

บ้านเลขที่ ๑๔๘ หมู่ที่ ๒ ต. นาเกลือ อ. บางละมุง จ. ชลบุรี

โทร ๔๑๘๗๑๗

I don't know what you can do John, but we can't start this school without
those funds. You are about the only person who can help.

If you want to scream after reading this letter,...call the Samaritans
and ask for help! I understand there is a Father Taylor who,......

God bless &
thanks.....

Fr. Raymond A. Brennan
Director:

PATTAYA ORPHANAGE, BOX 15, BANGLAMUNG, CHOLBURI, THAILAND
TELEPHONE : 418717 - CABLE ADDRESS ORPHAN PATTAYA

511

A MAN WITH A MISSION

Vicar :

The Rev. Canon J.R. Taylor, OBE., OCF.

CHRIST CHURCH

11 Convent Road

Bangkok, Thailand

Tel. 31634

THE REV. CANON J.R. TAYLOR O.B.E.

POSITION: Vicar of Christ Church, Bangkok

FROM: September 1973 - October 1981

        Christ Church is somewhat unusual, in that it is a completely self-supporting Church. In 1973, Christ Church was at a low ebb, particularly financially, but to-day it is a thriving Church, not only fully supporting itself, but taking its full part in Stewardship in Thailand. The driving force behind this has been John Taylor. John is:-

- One who strives to fulfill GOD'S WILL.

- DETERMINED. He is determined to communicate God's message to all.

- FULL OF ENTHUSIASM. His days are long and be pushes himself to the limit.

- a person, full of new ideas.

- A DRIVING FORCE. His unboundless energy has meant that not only has Christ Church been able to "make ends meet", but Christ Church has expanded - new Offices, Church Hall, etc. Christ Church has become better known for its Stewardship throughout the community - and especially amongst refugees where John led the effort personally.

- CARING. He cares for people, particularly those in distress, in prison, sick. There are a great number of people who have to thank John for his counselling.

.../...

512

POSTSCRIPT

- *DEDICATED.* Nothing is too much trouble. One has never heard him complain of overwork.

- *A LEADER.* He can get the best out of people. This is a transient congregation, but John has always been able to ensure a hard-working band of helpers.

- *A FRIEND.* His home is an open house. One is impressed by his circle of friends world-wide. He makes friends wherever he goes.

CONCLUSION

After John had completed his first contract, the P.C.C. realised what a "find" they had, and offered him a "permanent" contract. We are delighted to have been able to keep him 8 years, and we are more than sorry to see him depart.

C.H.P. EDMONDS
Vicar's Warden
(Christ Church P.C.C. 1975-81)

CHPE:NA   Bangkok/10 August, 1981